Mayan Visions

Mayan Visions

THE QUEST FOR AUTONOMY
IN AN AGE OF GLOBALIZATION

JUNE C. NASH

ROUTLEDGE
NEW YORK AND LONDON

Published in 2001 by
Routledge
29 West 35th Street
New York, NY 10001

Published in Great Britain by
Routledge
11 New Fetter Lane
London EC4P 4EE

Routledge is an imprint of the Taylor & Francis Group.

Printed in the United States of America on acid-free paper.

10   9   8   7   6   5   4   3   2   1

Library of Congress Cataloging-in-Publication Data

Nash, June C., 1927–
   Mayan visions : the quest for autonomy in an age of globalization / June C. Nash.
p. cm.
Includes bibliographical references and index.
ISBN 0-415-92861-3 0-415-92862-1
   1. Mayas—Mexico—Chiapas—Politics and government. 2. Mayas—Mexico—
Chiapas—Government relations. 3. Mayas—Wars—Mexico—Chiapas. 4. Ejército
Zapatista de Liberación Nacional (Mexico)—History. 5. Chiapas (Mexico)—History—Peasant
Uprising, 1994– 6. Chiapas (Mexico)—Social conditions. 7. Chiapas (Mexico)—Economic
conditions. I. Title.

F1435.3.P7 N37 2001
972'.750836 dc21   00-04578

In the *Popol Vuh*, the Mayan book of the World, it is said that "the vision of the motherfathers, ancestors to the Mayas, came all at once, so that they saw perfectly, they knew everything under the sky whenever they sighted the four sides, the four corners in the sky on the earth." Their limits then were those of the world itself. But, fearing their vision, "the Gods blinded their creations, as the face of a mirror is breathed upon. Their vision flickered. Now it was only when they looked nearby that things were clear." Commenting on this myth, Dennis Tedlock in *Breath on the Mirror: Mythic Voices and Visions of the Living Maya* notes that then began the quest of the motherfathers of the Mayas to find their destiny.

CONTENTS

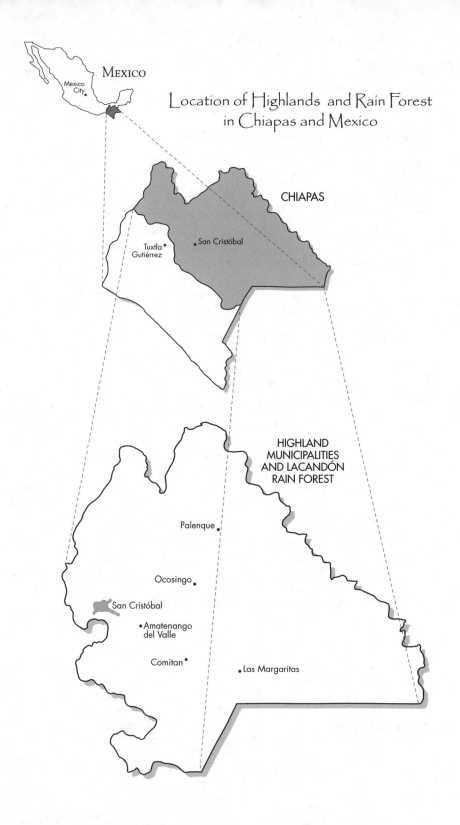

MEXICO

Mexico
City

Location of Highlands and Rain Forest
in Chiapas and Mexico

CHIAPAS

Tuxtla
Gutiérrez

San Cristóbal

HIGHLAND
MUNICIPALITIES
AND LACANDÓN
RAIN FOREST

Palenque

Ocosingo

San Cristóbal

Amatenango
del Valle

Comitan

Las Margaritas

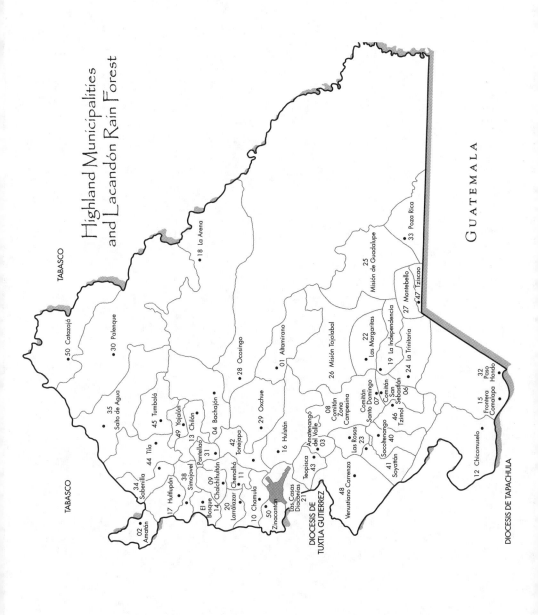

Highland Municipalities
and Lacandón Rain Forest

TABASCO

TABASCO

GUATEMALA

50 Catazajá

30 Palenque

18 La Arena

35 Salto de Agua

45 Tumbalá

44 Tila

34 Sabanilla

02 Amatán

17 Huitiupán

38 Simojovel

49 Yajalón

13 Chilón

09 Pantelhó

31

14 Chalchihuitán

El Bosque

20 Larráinzar

11 Chenalhó

42 Tonejapa

04 Bachajón

29 Oxchuc

28 Ocosingo

16 Huistán

01 Altamirano

26 Misión Tojolabal

25 Misión de Guadalupe

33 Poza Rica

10 Chamula

50 Zinacantán

Las Casas Diaconías

21

DIOCESIS DE
TUXTLA GUTIERREZ

Teopisca

43

Amatenango del Valle

03

08 Comitán Zona Campesina

23 Las Rosas

07 Comitán Santo Domingo

46 San Tzimol Sebastián

40 Socoltenango

41 Soyatitán

48 Venustiano Carranza

22 Las Margaritas

19 La Independencia

06 Comitán

24 La Trinitaria

27 Tzsicao

Montebello

15 Frontera Comalapa

12 Chicomuselo

32 Paso Hondo

DIOCESIS DE TAPACHULA

GUATEMALA

PREFACE

EACH YEAR AS I return to old field sites I experience the reality of radical change in the worlds. Transformations in the way local populations relate to their nation and their world are shaking up the ways of life in Chiapas, in the mining centers of Bolivia, and in Pittsfield, Massachusetts, where I have done ethnographic studies. The most radical changes are those that have occurred in the settings that were in the past the most marginal to the centers of power.

Marginality was characteristic of highland Chiapas when I began fieldwork in the Mayan community of Amatenango del Valle in the late 1950s. Small-plot cultivators—whom I shall designate with their own term as *campesinos*—and artisans could conceive of their town center as the umbilicus of the world and that whatever happened there defined their destiny and that of the cosmos. Although men worked in coastal plantations to supplement their needs for cash and women sold artisan products in regional markets, their sense of security and order was defined in relation to the ancestors who watched over them from the hill in the eastern perimeter of the township.

In the 1970s, the tin miners in the Bolivian highland mining center were aware of how their fate was affected by the prices of tin in world markets. At the same time these *cholos*—a term relating to the partial integration of indigenous peoples generations removed from the rural Quechua- and Aymara-speaking communities of the highlands from which they were recruited to work in the mines—maintained a sense of historical agency in collective actions mediated through the Federation of Bolivian Mine Workers Unions (FSTMB) and the nation-state.

General Electric workers in Pittsfield lived in fear of the layoffs that decimated the workforce in power transformer production throughout the 1980s, when I did most of my research. The search for cheap labor production sites overseas had already eliminated the assembly workforce in electrical appliances when I first began my investigation in 1982. High-tech production for the Defense Department during the cold war absorbed a few hundred of the seven thousand employees, but by the end of the decade fewer than a thousand were left. In contrast to the tin miners, whose protests against decapitalization of the mines were inspired by a Marxist vision of the historic agency of the proletariat, Pittsfield's aging workforce lamented the past and accepted the "golden handshake" of early retirement.

Returning to these field sites throughout the decades, I have tried to understand the impact of changes in the lives of people who are differentially situated in global circuits. As an anthropologist trained in the empirical tradition of the 1950s, I was well aware of the need to take into account a variety of sources of information, not only what is said in interviews, but what is seen and the context in which it is enacted. In the traumatic changes of the 1960s that were shaking up societies in which I chose to work, I realized that I had to go beyond the immediate frame of reference in time and space to consider world political and market trends.

Small-plot cultivators of Amatenango experienced the agrarian crisis of the 1960s, when their communal lands could no longer sustain a growing population, as an internal problem. The limited *ejido* allotments once allowed two hectares for each household, but as the population doubled from 1960 to 1980, the share dropped to half a hectare (about 1.67 acres to each hectare), and not every household held even that. In the decades of the 1970s and 1980s the average holding declined to a low of one-half hectare per family that no longer sufficed for the basic staples of corn and beans. Conflicts once settled in terms of witchcraft and the exorcism of those who opposed collective "traditions" became an exercise of power by an elite of *caciques*. These were indigenous officials, often co-opted by the state through programs for *pueblos indios,* or Indian towns, after the National Indigenist Institute (Instituto Nacional Indígena, INI) opened a branch in Chiapas in 1952. After a decade of extraordinary ferment, the program gradually eliminated the visionaries who sought a solution in collective ways of life. In some towns, such as Amatenango, the rising incidence of homicide revealed the clash of traditional authorities and young literate leaders, some of whom maximized their own interests over that of the *pueblo*. Two of the collaborators from my early field study were killed, along with a much-respected teacher who tried to counter the growing corruption in the town hall and a woman who organized the first pottery cooperative. Expulsions of *comuneros*, or residents who had access to common lands, became frequent in highland municipalities of Chamula, Chenalhó, Zinacantán, and Amatenango, exceeding 40,000 by 1990.

It was to escape this involuted revolution that I went to Bolivia to do research in the mining community of Oruro. There I learned what nineteenth-century mobilizations around class identity could mean in the context of twentieth-century industrial mining. I arrived shortly after the massacre committed by General René Barrientos in Siglo XX-Catavi mines in 1967 to find miners struggling to regain the power they had exercised after helping to overthrow the tin oligarchy in 1952. Workers saw themselves as the vanguard of a class that knew who their enemies were, and against whom they defended their interests, in the class struggle. The first protest I witnessed in Oruro in 1969 was a hunger strike of pensioners protesting the failure of the Bolivian Mining Company (COMIBOL) to increase—or in some cases deliver—their pensions, earned during the days when Simón Patiño was the owner. They staged their protest in front of Patiño's town house in Oruro. It was a place that still contained symbolic force from the days of their active working lives, even though the mines had been nationalized after the Revolution of 1952, and Patiño had long since died in one of the many mansions he had built throughout the world.

My ethnographic view of the world system is shaped by field experiences in these three sites that I have continually visited over the past forty years. This was particularly true of Bolivia, where I joined discussion groups with miners in the University of Oruro on Marx, Trotsky, and dependency theory. Trotsky was more important in the theory and practice of mine union leaders than Lenin because of his greater attention to the international framework of the class struggle. Guillermo Lora, an historian and theoretician of the Bolivian labor movement, gave a series of lectures that drew upon Trotsky's work on the international labor movement to elaborate a theory of dependency that preceded that of the Economic Commission for Latin America. He was one of the authors of the "Thesis of Pulacayo" that was first presented during the annual meeting of the Federation of Mine Workers' Unions of Bolivia in 1947. He demonstrated how the struggles of indigenous workers against an alien capitalist bourgeoisie in extractive industries figured in the vanguard of worldwide revolutionary change.

In the decade of the 1980s, Bolivia became one of the first experiments in neoliberal restructuring of Latin America's debt-ridden economies. In the summer of 1985 I witnessed the election campaign that brought Victor Paz Estenssoro, the president who ushered in the 1952 Revolution, back to power. Within a year he had reversed the historic changes he had introduced in 1953, privatizing the mines he had nationalized and imposing taxes on peasant cultivators who had been the beneficiaries of the first land reform.

These were the International Monetary Fund (IMF) conditions for Bolivia regaining creditability in the world economy. In reaction to the "New Economic Plan" that Paz Estenssoro drew up on the basis of these conditions, miners, teachers, merchants, and Catholic activists of Oruro and other mining communities organized the March for Peace and Life in July 1986. Their intention was to bring their demands for saving the mining economy to President Paz Estenssoro. The march was joined by *campesinos* in communities along the route who rejected Paz Estenssoro's plan because of the proposed taxes on the sale of their crops. I joined the thousands of marchers as they approached La Paz on the last day of their hundred-mile trek. On the following day, I rejoined them in Calamarca, where I found them encircled by almost as many heavily armed soldiers. After a day of confrontation, the women and men of the mining community withdrew, to carry out a hunger strike in La Paz and in the mine shafts and union halls of the mining communities. I saw the men during the tenth day of their hunger strike, lying huddled in blankets in the mine shafts that were beginning to fill with venomous air. For them, closing the mines symbolized the demise of an era that they embodied in their hunger strike.

My view of the New World Order as threatening the subsistence base of indigenous cultivators and Bolivian tin miners was also shaped by fieldwork in my own backyard. Challenged by the miners' questions about giant U.S. corporations they had heard about, but of which I knew little, I tried doing ethnography in my native land. Pittsfield, Massachusetts, was not far from the town where I had grown up and where I had worked briefly in the last year of World War II as a V (for victory) worker on the afternoon shift after high school let out. In returning to my home state, I was also trying out the role of native ethnographer, one that I would not recommend because of the hard work in overcoming self-doubt and suppressing the assumptions I made on the basis of partial knowledge. The "greening of America" that came to children of the urban middle class in the late 1960s barely touched Pittsfield's working population until a decade later. In what was still called a "blue-collar" town, whose industrial prosperity was stimulated by World

War I and II, the children of workers who organized the unions in the 1930s and 1940s enlisted in the army to go fight in Vietnam.

The tragic consequences of that war were just beginning to be addressed when I began my work in Pittsfeld in 1981. The Vietnam veterans were emerging from the shame of that conflict to demand the benefits that veterans of past wars had assumed were their due. They marched in the Memorial Day parade for the first time, taking their place in combat gear along with, but separated from, Veterans of Foreign Wars in full dress uniform. Some took jobs in General Electric's ordnance department that produced Nikon and Polaris missiles for the Pentagon's cold war armaments buildup. But there were dissidents even within the plant who called for conversion to peace production and who maintained vigils on the anniversaries of the bombing of Hiroshima and Nagasaki to protest the use of weapons of mass destruction.

In the deindustrialization going on in the 1970s and 1980s, the General Electric payroll had declined from a workforce of 12,000 during World War II to 7,000. Many of the hourly workforce laid off in power transformer production were assigned to defense production during the cold war years of the Reagan administration. After the shutdown of the main plant producing power transformers and the decline in defense contracts in 1986, only a few dozen blue-collar workers remained in maintenance work. Faced by the threat of lawsuits related to the high incidence of cancer among former workers, General Electric reduced the scope of the plastics Research and Development headquarters. John F. Welch, the executive officer of General Electric who had once been manager of the Pittsfield plant, proceeded to invest the vast capital resources of the corporation in buying finance and communications companies. The General Credit Corporation, which was instituted to make it possible for workers to buy major appliances on credit, became a core part of G.E.'s growing transnational operations.

When I return on my many trips to the Berkshires now, I find retired workers eking out their social security and pensions with jobs as baggers in the supermarkets or security guards in the resort areas of the Berkshires. Young workers left town or went to lower-paid small industries as the population declined from 50,000 to 40,000. The community is now devastated by polychlorinated biphenyls, or PCBs, dumped by General Electric in the rivers and lakes of the region for over a quarter of a century. Values of real estate, which is the only form of investment most working-class families have, were in decline, and people were afraid of the consequences of their city being declared a "superfund cleanup site," even though that could bring in federal funds for cleaning up the river and removing the contaminated production facilities. On July 22, 2000, *The Berkshire Eagle* declared that Pittsfield was a modern industrial ghost town.

In 1986 I chose Chiapas as a site for the National Science Foundation Research Experience for Undergraduates fieldwork. Bolivia was in chaos after the closing of the mines and the turmoil in the wake of the first neoliberal restructuring in the hemisphere. Pittsfield was becoming a pastiche of fast-food chains and shopping malls, as tourism and retail selling took precedence over industrial production in the economy. Its citizens were up in arms because of the discovery of the carcinogenic properties of PCBs. In Chiapas, highland communities still expressed in their ritual life the coherence of a plurality of cultures that had drawn anthropologists to the area from the early decades of the twentieth century. Artisan products, now produced for an international market as well as domestic use, manifested the local traditions that were enhanced by the cash income they generated. It seemed an idyllic setting in which to train students in fieldwork.

In the following years, from 1988 to 1993, Mayan farmers were entering the center stage of popular uprising that had been occupied by Bolivian tin miners a decade earlier. As I traveled to the indigenous highland Chiapas communities with students from City College and the Graduate School,[1] we became aware of the mobilization of *campesino* organizations that were breaking away from corporatist national structures. The transformation in indigenous community relations with the state from a paternalistic but nonetheless exploitative relationship of dependency to a hostile standoff was ever more palpable each year. Returning with students from a meeting of the Venustiano Carranza artisan cooperative in 1989, we changed *combis*—converted Volkswagon vans—in Pujiltic, the location of a large sugar refinery. We were told of an army attack on sugarcane growers just the day before, when over two hundred *campesinos* protested the excessive charges for fertilizer and other inputs once supplied by the government when the sugar refinery was publicly owned. They were met by an armed force of over five hundred soldiers who fired on the crowd, killing one and wounding four others, who were jailed along with dozens of the other *campesinos*.   *tensions in community*

Within the indigenous communities, discord that was once expressed in witchcraft accusations was more frequently demonstrated in partisan politics and religious conversions. The competition for power was destroying the veneer of harmony that communities presented to the outside world when they were organized by an age-ordered and patriarchal hierarchy. As women's income from pottery and weaving, which they had traditionally produced in indigenous communities, equaled and even surpassed that of men's income from subsistence and cash crops, the gender balance that sustained a household economy was threatened. Domestic violence was on the increase, and male officials who still dominated political life subjected women in the artisan cooperatives to threats and even physical violence (Nash 1993).   *domestic violence?*

Salinas's neoliberal plans for development were becoming ever more visible throughout the state of Chiapas. The Federal Army's headquarters were completed in Rancho Nuevo on the outskirts of San Cristóbal, and the 23rd Batallion was expanding its control over the national park that had been created around the tourist attraction of the caves. *Campesinos* were intensifying their demands on the government to deliver land titles. They rejected the so-called "reform" of Article 27 of the 1927 Constitution passed in 1991 that effectively nullified the Land Reform Act. Their protests met with armed repression. The Center for Human Rights "Fray Bartolomé de Las Casas" became one of our study sites, along with the Center for Research and Higher Studies in Social Anthropology (CIESAS). The libraries of the Chiapas Autonomous University (UNACH) and of EcoSur were important sites for research and meeting places for anthropological colleagues whose advice and discussions benefited us all.

Each of the students in the National Science Foundation program developed a project related to our field trips to the many sites where we learned of the social ferment in the state. One of the undergraduate students in 1990, Pedro Farias Nardi, joined members of the Union of Unions, Union of Agropastoral and Industrial Credit of the States of Chiapas and Oaxaca "Pajal Yakaltic" in their visits with local groups of coffee growers. The agents of the Union were not receiving their wages from the government, and the coffee growers felt abandoned by the government agencies that had encouraged them to shift to a cash crop not many years before. Robert Martinez stayed in the Casa del Pueblo in Venustiano Caranza when the Emiliano Zapata Campesino Organization (OCEZ) was planning its campaigns to regain land seized during the colonial and independence periods but never delivered after the Revolution of 1910. The Center for Human Rights "Fray Bartolomé de Las Casas" provided the documentation for the repression of the rising protest movement of *campesinos*. One of the most striking protests we viewed was one that involved men and women from Marqués de Comillas in the Lacandón rain forest in 1991. The large participation of women in the march to Tuxtla Gutierrez to express their grievances was a growing feature of the new social movements that were sweeping through the state. The women were jailed along with their children in Palenque, deprived of food and even water for several days. The men were taken to the more secure prison of Cerro Hueco in Tuxtla Gutierrez. The Center for Human Rights "Fray Bartolomé de Las Casas" became an important base for Christine Kovic's research on indigenous perceptions of human rights, which later became her thesis research (Kovic 1997).

Chamulas were still pouring in from the neighboring indigenous town of San Juan Chamula in an exodus that had begun in the decades of the 1980s and 1990s. Expelled for religious and political heterodoxies that were not tolerated by the traditionalists of their community, the women and children sold artisan products in the plaza and adjacent streets of San Cristóbal where tourists thronged. Kathleen Sullivan began work with Chamula street vendors in 1991 when she came as an undergraduate student, and later returned to carry out research for her dissertation on religious conversion (Sullivan 1998). Other students worked with government-sponsored programs in San Cristóbal: Gina Peña-Campodonico and Ramón Vargas worked in the Albarrada, a technical training school for indigenous youths; Emilce Ortiz worked with potters in Amatenango, and Michelle McKenzie made a documentary of their pottery production and marketing. We were able to show it at the town hall to an enthusiastic crowd of revellers celebrating the fiesta of Santiago. Richard "Jeff" Angeley, a City College student who supported himself as a carpenter while going to school, set up a shop in Chamula for a woodworking cooperative. He designed a child's coffin which became the most popular item sold in the rural hamlet. Two of the students, Donald Craig and César Naupari, wrote about tourism and the proposed Ruta Maya that was projected to be the fastest growing enterprise for the 1990s. Miriam Greenberg studied teachers in the Bilingual Education Program, which was beginning to introduce indigenous teachers into professions from which they had been excluded. The airport in San Cristóbal that was to be the centerpiece of the project is now used primarily by military planes that are stationed in a huge military encampment next to the Mayan classic site of Toniná. The army now intrudes on this site where César interviewed indigenous guides, and where future excavation to discover the relations between this major site and Palenque were planned.

The *campesino* organizations that had broken away from the National Confederation of Campesinos (CNC), particularly after the National Congress of Indigenous Peoples in 1974, formed the bases for the growing protests. These crystallized in the indigenous movement commemorating the quincentennial anniversary of the Spanish conquest. I was not in Chiapas to witness the October 12, 1992, march when thousands of indigenous people, many from the Lacandón rain forest, took over the city of San Cristóbal de Las Casas that was the principal site of colonial domination. But video and photographic images, of men and women carrying bows and arrows to symbolize their indigenous origins, capture the determination of the marchers to take back their history. Striding through the streets where they were despised as aliens, over 10,000 men and women arrive at the plaza of Santo Domingo church. There, one of the marchers knocks the hollow metal statue of the Spanish conqueror, Diego Mazariegos, off its pedestal, and boys rush in to smash its dismembered parts.

It was in this setting that we became aware of the global integration bringing together the destinies of people separated by centuries of domination. Indigenous peoples of Chiapas no longer denied the intrusion of the world beyond their control as they had in the 1960s. In 1992 I summarized the findings of the three years of summer research sponsored by the National Science Foundation grants, with the help of one of the undergraduate students who accompanied the last group in 1991. We tried to show how the conditions in Chiapas paralleled those of the Porfiriato in 1910, when Mexicans emerged from the earlier liberal period ready to fight to the death to recuperate their lands (Nash and Sullivan 1992). It did not surprise us to hear of the New Year's uprising in January 1994.

My experiences in all of the field sites in which I have worked give me a chilling sense of what will happen worldwide as subsistence enterprises become a diminishing part of world production. At the same time they provide some basis for optimism in the social movements they are generating. I was living with a mining family in Oruro, Bolivia in June 1985 when the currency went from 350,000 *bolivianos* to a dollar to a million. I know the trauma this causes to a pensioner trying to make ends meet with dependent children still at home. When I met miners on their long March for Life and Bread in 1986 protesting the closing of the mines, I realized the resentment of a revolution betrayed. They voted Paz Estenssoro back into office in 1985 only to have him undo all he had done while in office from 1952 to 1956, as he carried out the New Economic Plan dictated by the IMF. The small sums that miners were given when they were dismissed were not enough for them to relocate.

Marginalization and the deprivation of work sites is also happening in core industrial countries as investment priorities seek higher returns in global markets. I remember the anger with which an IUE steward, confronted with the news that GE was combining with Westinghouse to open a new plant in Canada in 1986, expressed his dismay at what he considered a betrayal of the competitive capitalist system. "GE is climbing into bed with the competition and leaving us bare-assed out in the cold!" he exploded to the delegates in the union hall.

Yet the resignation of workers as they watched the last power transformer leave the gates six months later was tempered by the fact that unemployment compensation would

Connects U.S. & Mexican workers

be available. The city of Pittsfield lost over 10,000 of its residents—predominantly mid-life wage earners and their children—who were forced to leave their communities and seek jobs elsewhere. The colonizers of the Lacandón rain forest communities in Chiapas had none of these social security fallbacks when they were faced with the possibility that some would never gain title to the lands they had colonized with the "reform" of the agrarian reform law and the loss of markets for their cash crops with the North American Free Trade Agreement (NAFTA). Their cry of *Basta!* ("Enough!") when they rose up in arms on January 1, 1994, resonated throughout a world that has also had enough of the assault on human survival implicit in the crises of global capitalism.

As do U.S. workers

The social movements that have emerged in the cities and rural pueblos of Latin America have a great deal to teach their North American neighbors. Mayans retain a sense of their communal identity and the values that sustain an alternative vision to that offered by capitalist development. This is also true of Bolivian tin miners, whose collective actions draw upon primordial identification with hill spirits and the Pachamama (Nash 1979). Given the vulnerability of the country to foreign intervention and the miners' consciousness of their strategic position in the international exchange system, they staged a class struggle fought in terms of the Third International defined by Trotsky. Yet this was still tied to solutions that presumed national control over the means of economic production and provisions for social reproduction. Confronted with IMF conditions that subverted nationalistic solutions, the miners mobilized the March for Life to oppose the closing of the mines in 1986. When the nationalized mining economy was destroyed, laid-off miners migrated to the Chapare, where they are now organizing to defend their right to grow coca, a basic ingredient in the production of cocaine.

Yet the resilience of cultivators faced with losing the lands to which they were promised title, and of miners laid off when the mines were closed, is a counterpoint to the alienation that is rampant in many of the cities and towns of the North. Although General Electric workers have experienced in their own lives the movement of capital overseas and the destruction of the industrial base, I found a lower level of consciousness of their interdependence in the global system than in Bolivia. In interviews of a few laid-off workers in 1991 the majority justified the reduction in employment and layoffs of thousands in terms of the decline in profit. The repression of a critical political consciousness in the McCarthy era of communist witch-hunts has borne its fruits in narrowing the sphere of union organization and fostering the pursuit of individual ends. Caught in the hegemonic ideology forged by corporations in their heyday, only the marginalized workers in Pittsfield's competitive firms and nurses were able to mobilize collective action in the 1980s when I was doing fieldwork. These predominantly female workers, many of whom were single heads of families, felt the pinch of a rising cost of living and low-wage segregated jobs more keenly than the preferred labor force hired in the corporation. Pittsfield residents organized only a decade after the main plant producing power transformers was closed, when they became alarmed over the contamination of the waterways by General Electric dumping PCBs.

Clearly, people's awareness of the global dimensions of their conditions is not isomorphic with the social relations in production. Countering one of the main precepts of

when protest happens

Marxism, it is not only when exploitation in the workplace is most severe, but rather when subsistence and survival strategies are threatened, that people move into protest actions. Mayans are more aware of this threat than the other populations I have studied, perhaps because, as Kay Warren has taught us (Warren 1985), they are still integrated into an indigenous cosmology and a syncretic religious paradigm that provides them with a framework for resistance to colonialism and domination.

This book draws on past experience in the many sites where I have viewed the advance of globalization processes over time. I dedicate it to the people in Oruro, Pittsfield, and Chiapas, who have demonstrated their resilience and resourcefulness in the face of the enormous changes that have transformed their lives.

ACKNOWLEDGMENTS

MY RESEARCH IN the summers of 1988 to 1993 was funded by the National Science Foundation's innovative Research Experience for Undergraduates and the Graduate Field-work Training Programs introduced by Stuart Plattner. In the spring of 1995, the City College of the City University of New York enabled me to teach two courses to students of the college and of the UNACH, which then allowed my students to take two or three courses free. The John D. and Catherine F. MacArthur Foundation provided partial funding for my writing and research in the fall of 1995. I am very grateful for funding that allowed me to teach while carrying out research, which I consider the most rewarding way of arriving at collective knowledge. Ann Zulawski invited me to teach one semester at Smith College as the Neilson Professor in 1996, which allowed me the free time and excellent library facilities to polish chapters four and five. Ann and my colleagues, especially Susan Bourque and Christine Shelton, were a responsive critical audience to my preparation of the lectures which were the first tryout of the ideas I present here. Their care and assistance, and that of my inspiring students, especially Elizabeth Bolton, enabled me to fulfill my responsibilities at the college after a devestating fall.

During the years that I have been working in Chiapas I have benefited from many anthropological colleagues who chose Chiapas as their field site, often to return after many years of absence, as I did. Sol Tax provided me with the training and knowledge as a graduate student at the University of Chicago that enabled me to do fieldwork in Chiapas. Alfonso Villa Rojas introduced me to my field site in Amatenango del Valle, where I carried out my first fieldwork. George Collier, who was the first to set the 1994 uprising in the anthropological context, has provided us many insights into the connection of the local with the global setting. Victoria Bricker, Frank Cancian, Jane Collier, Gary Gossen, Robert Laughlin, Ronald Nigh, Stuart Plattner and Phyllis Plattner, and Jan Rus and Diane Rus, all of whom have devoted years since they arrived as undergraduates of the research team led by Evon Z. Vogt provide part of the framework in which we now envision the new indigenous movements that are transforming the countryside. Robert Laughlin and Miriam Laughlin have amplified their own studies of Mayan traditions by providing the guidance and resources that enable indigenous men and women to expand their creative talents in the organizations of Sna Tzi'bajon and Fomento de la Mujer Maya that they helped form. Lynn Stephen has brought her experience with Zapotec and Salvadoran societies to bear on her study of the Zapatista movement in Chiapas. She was generous with her time and knowledge in reading and critiquing an earlier version of the manuscript.

A new generation of our students provide case studies of the transformations occurring daily. Christine Kovic, who joined the classes I taught at the Universidád Nacional de Chiapas in 1993, brought the human rights issues that animated the exile community of catechists in San Cristóbal to light in her thesis. Kathleen Sullivan has shown the other side of conversion in the exile community of Protestant converts in San Cristóbal. Maria Ramona Hart chose to study problems of refugees in the conflict zone. Patti Kelley's study of prostitution in the "galactic city" of Tuxtla Gutierrez gives us an extraordinary view of the underworld of development. Molly Doane's brief research experience as another recipient of the National Science Foundation research training grant, along with Patti, Maria Hart, Liliana Fasanella, and Kathleen Sullivan, inspired her to go on to Oaxaca to study ecological problems. Rosalva Aida Hernandez Castillo returned to Chiapas, after earning her degree at Stanford with George and Jane Collier, to continue her focus on the women's part in the Zapatista movement. I have enjoyed collaborating with Gary Gossen's students, Brenda Rosenbaum and Christine Eber, on artisan production, with whom I have gained an appreciation of the common problems of indigenous women through their portrayals of women in San Juan Chamula and San Pedro Chenalhó. Jeanne Simonelli and Kate O'Donnell came to San Cristóbal in 1997 and, like so many of us, returned. Peter Brown pursued some of the themes developed in Frank Cancian's long career in the area.

Colleagues in the study centers, Centro de Investigaciones y Estudios Superiores en Antropología Social (CIESAS), especially Lourdes de León, Rosalva Aida Hernandez Castillo, Gabrielle Vargas-Cetina, and Stefan Igor Ayora Diaz, welcomed collaboration with investigators from the United States. Along with investigators at EcoSur, INAREMAC, and the Instituto de Estudios Indígenas, they contribute to the stimulating environment of San Cristóbal de Las Casas. Our anthropological colleagues in the city opened their doors to communication about what we were all experiencing in ways that enhanced our own perceptions: María Eugenia Santana, with whom I taught a class at the Universidád Autónoma de Chiapas, and the colleagues I came into contact with while there, especially Jan de Vos, Mario Ruz Luihller, Silvia Marcos, and Jacinto Arias, gave lectures in our program funded by the National Science Foundation Research Experience for Undergraduates program. Marielena Fernandez kept us briefed on the latest research as librarian for UNACH. Our colleagues who work with Guatemalan Mayans, especially Susanne Jonas, Kay Warren, and John Watanabe, have provided us with the ethnographic basis for future comparative studies. Kay Warren has done the kind of insightful critical reading of an earlier version of this manuscript that enabled me to carry the project to an end. At Routledge, Ilene Kalish, Kimberly Guinta, and Nicole Ellis have been of great help in bringing the project to publication. The inspiring work of the Human Rights Center "Fray Bartolomé de Las Casas," especially that of the founder, Bishop Samuel Ruiz, and director, Padre Pablo Romo, provide us with the knowledge of indigenous people's struggles to attain their rights. Socorro Velásquez, a dedicated sponsor of cultural pursuits for mestizo and indigenous children, is an inspiration for us all. My children Eric Nash and Laura Nash, who accompanied me in what must have been for them the many tiresome field stays when they were little and after they grew up, validated the enterprise just by being there. I owe a special debt to my husband, Frank Reynolds, who helped me envision the last revision. His patience and consideration of the text and the context in which he became involved made me realize why his students consider him to be the great teacher he is.

ACRONYMS AND ABBREVIATIONS

AC	Alianza Civica
AEDPCH	Asamblea Estatal Democratica del Pueblo Chiapaneco
ANIPA	Asamblea Nacional de Indígenas Plurinacional para Autonomía
ANCIEZ	Alianza Nacional de Campesinos Independiente Emiliano Zapata
ARIC	Asociación Rural de Interes Colectivo
CAP	Congreso Agraria Permanente
CCI	Central Campesina Independiente
CCLCA	Confederación de Campesinos y Ligas de Comunidades Agrarias
CCRI	Coordinadora de Campesinos Revolucionarios Independiente
CELAM	Conferencia Eclesiastica Latinoamericana
CEM	Conferencia Eclesiastica de México
CEOIC	Consejo Estatal de Organizaciones Indígenas y Campesinos
CIESAS	Centro de Investigaciones y Estudios Superiores de Antropología Social
CIOAC	Central Independiente de Obreros Agrícolas y Campesinos
CNC	Confederacíon Nacional de Campesinos
CND	Convención Nacional Democratica
CNDH	Comisión Nacional de Derechos Humano
CNI	Congreso Nacional Indígena
CNPA	Coordinadora Nacional Plan de Ayala
CNPI	Consejo Nacional de Pueblos Indígenas
CNPP	Confederacíon Nacional de Pequeño Propiedad
COCECH	Coordinadora Organizaciones de Ciudadanos del Estado de Chiapas
COCOPA	Comisión de Concordia y Pacificación
CODIMUJ	Coordinadora Diocesana de Mujeres
CONAI	Comisión Nacional de Intermediación
CONAMIM	Coordinadora Nacional de Mujeres Indígenas
CONASUPO	Campaña Nacional de Subsistencias Populares
CONAFRUT	Cooperativo Nacional Fruitería
CONAI	Comisión Nacional de Intermediación
COA	Coordinadora Organizaciones Autónomas
CONPAZ	Coordinación de Organizaciones No-gubernamental para Paz
COPLADE	Comité de Planificación de Desarrollo
CRIACH	Consejo de Representantes Indígenas de los Altos de Chiapas
CTM	Confederación de Trabajadores Mexicanos

DIF   Desarrollo Integral de la Familia
EZLN   Ejercito Zapatista de Liberación Nacional
FLZN   Frente Zapatista de Liberación Nacional
GDP   Gross Domestic Product
GRO   Grassroots Organizations
IMF   International Monetary Fund
INMECAFE   Instituto Mexicana de Café
INEGI   Instituto Nacional Estadistica del Gobierno
INI   Instituto Nacional Indígena
NAFTA   North American Free Trade Agreement
NGO   Nongovernmental Organizations
OCEZ   Organización Campesina Emiliano Zapata
OIMI   Organización Independiente de Mujeres Indígenas
OPECH   Organización del Pueblo Evangelico en Chiapas
ORIACH   Organización Regional de los Indígenas de los Altos de Chiapas
PAN   Partido Acción Nacional
PEMEX   Petroleos Mexicanos
PRD   Partido de la Revolución Democratica
PRI   Partido Revolucionario Institucional
PRODESCH   Programa de Desarrollo Económica y Social de Chiapas
PRONASOL   Programa Nacional de Solidaridad
PST   Partido Socialista de Trabajadores
PT   Partido de Trabajadores
RAP   Regiones Autónomas Pluricultural
SAM   Sistema Alimentaria Mexicano
SARH   Secretaría de Agricultura y Recursos Hidráulicos
SEP   Secretaría de Educación Pública
SOCAMO   Solidaridad Campesina Magisterial
TABAMEX   Tabaco Mexicano
TLC   Tratado de Libre Comercio (equivalent of U.S. NAFTA)
UCD   Unidad Campesina Democratica
UCP   Unidad Campesina Popular
UGOCP   Unión General de Obreros y Campesinos Popular
UNAL   Unión Nacional de Lombardistas
UNCAFESUR   Uniones Cafetales del Sur
UNPA   Unión Nacional Plan de Ayala
UNORCA   Unión Nacional de Organizaciones Regionales de Campesinos Autónomos
UU   Unión de Uniones Ejidales y Grupos Campesinos Solidarios de Chiapas
XI'NICH   Coordinadora de Organizaciones Sociales Indígenas (Coalition of three
                 organizations: Comité de Defensa de la Libertad Indígena, Tsobel Yu'un
                 jWocoltic, —Reunión para resolver nuestros problemas), and Unión de
                 comunidades de la Selva de Chiapas.

CHAPTER 1

INDIGENOUS COUNTERPLOTS TO GLOBALIZATION PROCESSES

ANTHROPOLOGISTS ARE PRIVILEGED in their study of cultures with distinct worldviews since it allows us to explore alternatives to mainstream thought and action, and through this lens to examine critically the assumptions that prevail in the centers of power. Whether we remain at home to study people whose class or cultural identity situates them outside the mainstream, or whether we travel to other lands, we can find ourselves awakened to possible alternatives to centrist ideas and ideologies. That privilege no longer goes unchallenged. The internal critique in anthropology, combined with the critique by subjects of anthropological investigation who are also writing their own ethnographies, requires an engaged partnership that takes on political responsibility for the impact of their publications.

In this book I return to my first field site in a place called Chiapas, Mexico, that has only recently become known worldwide because of the uprising of Zapatistas on New Year's Eve of January 1, 1994. Faced with the possible loss of their collective resource base as marginalized cultivators in the global society, they said, "*Basta!*" ("Enough!"). In the years since the armed uprising, which lasted only a fortnight, the Zapatistas and their supporters have been framing an alternative path to that of being subsumed in global capitalist circuits as "people without faces and without voices." *Th*

Alternative ways of life such as that of Chiapas Mayans are diminishing in a world in *globali.* which globalization processes are encompassing most societies. Those processes are set *driving* in motion by the penetration of unregulated market exchanges in all aspects of life *force* throughout the globe and by the imposition of regimens of work and rewards without *def* representation by those affected. Globalization studies often take as a given the very conditions that are the premises for the resistance and rebellion of those who are most marginalized by the new capital flows. These conditions are the growing "deterritorialization" of peoples, products, and the production process itself, the "fragmentation" or atomization of personal relations and political units, the "homogenization" or "hybridization" of culture, and the "alienation" of people from community, kin groups, and even self.

In the current phase of enterprise capitalism there is no intention of absorbing the disrupted populations as proletarians or consumers. Hunter-gatherers and cultivators in the few remaining tropical forests as well as semi-subsistence small-plot farmers are of interest to global capital enterprises only because of the resources in their territories

enterprise capitalism

properties of the plants, animals, and even their own bodies in the biosch they are the custodians. Populations already dependent on global enters, markets, or handouts become ever more vulnerable to the cyclical crises of capitalism bringing about changes in employment levels. The fallback once provided by subsistence economies is often no longer available to cushion the impact. These recurrent cycles are further compounded by an environmental crisis caused by intensive agricultural practices, widespread exploitation of forests, fossil fuels, and mineral resources, and contamination of water, earth, and air. The invasion of territories and communities that existed on the margins of earlier capital expansion of the global economy puts semi-subsistence cultivators and hunter-gatherers in the center of the storm over territorial control and the debates over development and environment. At the same time, the withdrawal of capital from old industrial areas leaves communities devastated in its wake, forced to resort to subsistence strategies that are no longer adequate.

Because they are not complicit in the universalizing notions of capitalist expansion, indigenous societies often retain unique worldviews that place them in the center of a collective enterprise to maintain the world in balance. These distinct visions, predicated as they are on substantive economies responding to the needs of people in a particular society regardless of their power as consumers in a market, provide a positive coexisting alternative to a world predicated on universal self-regulating markets.[1] By substantive economies, I refer to those which have as their goal the provisioning and servicing of a social group. These may include contemporary as well as past societies in which the economic behavior is governed by kinship or communalistic considerations rather than formal economic claims (Polanyi 1957). I am also supposing that we can characterize some aspects of all societies as falling into substantive economy, even when they occur in highly rational market settings. I do not restrict the term to economies that are exclusively engaged in self-production for a bounded social group, since few, if any, such societies persist. What I should like to emphasize is the ends of production, whether it involves commercial transactions in open market or not.[2]

Anthropologists have demonstrated the remarkable ability of indigenous peoples throughout the world to carry out commercial transactions with Europeans in their midst while retaining a distinctive logic and practice.[3] In their resistance to the latest advance of capitalism, indigenous peoples are formulating innovative ways of rethinking citizenship in pluricultural settings that deny the hierarchical basis for citizenship defined in colonial and postindependence settings. Their attempts to expand the range of collective and individual autonomy offer the most innovative response to the loss of self-determination, often posed as an inevitable consequence of globalization.

The social movements that arise in such settings are now being played out in ways that have been neither predicted nor analyzed in mainstream economic analysis. As the crisis moves from the workplace to the streets and fields, to collective kitchens of the Andes or the soup kitchens of U.S. charities, the protest is phrased in moral terms and the right to survive rather than the end of exploitation. Impoverishment is more often the crucible in which the contradictions of capitalism on a global scale are confronted than is exploitation of the labor force. The unemployed or landless multitudes have problems distinct from those of the working poor, and these provide the motivation for new forms of struggle. Social movements generated by people deprived of their subsistence resources or of gainful employment, and those marginalized or excluded from commodity markets in which to sell their products, appeal to morality more often than the rational calculus of surplus value extortion. These movements become linked with global nongovernmental organizations (NGOs) concerned with issues of environmental damage and human rights deprivation, including the right to live. It is in these transnational spaces that new forms of governance are emerging which may enable the human species to survive in a globally integrated world that permits alternative ways of survival and coexistence.

In reenvisioning Mayans as they emerge as major combatants in changing the relationship between ethnic groups and the nation-state, I am also reenvisioning anthropological models as we include the global processes in the local settings that we study. As we expand the parameters of our studies, we become critics of existing paradigms of the global system and of our own contributions to those paradigms. I will briefly review some of the paradigmatic shifts in our view of the world and our strategies for correlating local ethnographies with our knowledge of globalization processes.

RETHINKING CAPITALIST CRISES IN GLOBALIZATION

Globalization is the process of integrating the world economy in key production and investment sites. The ideological premise is a self-regulated market ensuring the free movement of goods and resources that escapes national and international controls over production processes and labor conditions. For economies of the South it entails a shift from domestic to export production, commitment of an ever larger percentage of gross domestic product (GDP) to debt payment, decline in public responsibility for welfare, privatization of enterprises, and breaking up of communally based resources. Recurrent crises caused by indebtedness in countries often ruled by corrupt governments incur "restructuring" conditions that shift the burden of debt repayment to workers and peasants.

The diverse ways in which people of areas considered peripheral to advanced capitalism confront the problems of survival in a global economy force us to rethink theories of the crisis, taking into account subsistence systems and the question of survival. Economists of the neoclassical school have always left subsistence production out of their equations, limited as they are to market exchanges. Karl Marx was among the first to recognize the global reach of capitalism, as manufacturers and shippers competed with their counterparts in other nations for overseas markets and trade. Nations were the product of, not the impulse for, this dynamic expansion of commercial interests that needed the protection for their goods through tariffs, and for their property through armies (Marx 1964:133–135, manuscripts written in 1857–1858). Marx and his collaborator, Frederick Engels (1959), predicted the inevitability of capitalist advance throughout the world yet cast a nostalgic glance at the subsistence economies that were devastated in its wake. The dynamic for them lay in the contradiction between expansive production systems and restrictive distribution, leaving real needs unsatisfied as the failure in market demand lead to periodic crises. Only Rosa Luxemburg (1971) foresaw the ultimate crisis in capitalism in the subsumption of all substantive economies when they could no longer provide the resources necessary for their expansion (see below).

Neo-Marxists have extended the analysis of nationally based capitalist enterprises to show how mature economies trying to overcome cycles of recession in their own country tie peripheral economies into an unequal exchange that subverts the development of the latter. Both dependency theorists, who maintained that the underdevelopment of peripheral economies resulted from surplus capital accumulation at the center (Amin 1970; Frank 1967, 1980), and world systems theorists, who asserted the dynamism of core industrial centers determining the levels of production in a worldwide division of labor between core and center, and periphery (Arrighi 1985; Wallerstein 1983), sought solutions within existing trade networks and mediated by nation-states to overcome inequalities. Those who envisioned a "postindustrial" world (Bell 1973; Touraine 1971) chose the new technocrats as the vanguard of social change. Yet the continued growth of industry, particularly in the Asian periphery, required a more global perspective to relate the rise of the newly industrializing countries to the decline of industry in metropolitan centers as they became caught up in the expansion of finance capitalism.

Analyses of the expansion of investments in low-wage areas throughout the world demonstrated the intensified competition among labor markets that depressed wages and reduced the basis for organization in the work site (Fröbel, Heinrichs, and Kreye 1980; MacEwan and Tabb 1989; Nash and Fernandez-Kelly 1983; Rothstein and Blim 1992; Safa 1981). This critique showed that development that focused strictly on industrialization was inadequate, leaving the subsistence sector in countries that hosted export-oriented industrialization impoverished and the substantive needs of wage workers in an ever more precarious condition. It was no coincidence that women were the primary losers, since they were dedicated to the subsistence sector as mothers, wives, and superexploited workers when they entered the wage sector.

The question of why impoverishment persisted with industrial development was left unanswered by most of the macro-theorists who sought the answers within the "wastelands" created by "the capitalist core" and extended to "the periphery" through development programs (Conde et al. 1984; Bowles, Gordon, and Weisskopf 1990). The rise of East Asian industrializing countries in the 1980s and the subsequent shift to finance capitalization by the 1990s provoked speculation about multiple tracks in the expansion of the modern world system that build on chaos theory rather than fixed hegemonic control (Arrighi and Silver 1999:21–22). The greater dynamism in the emergent models of globalization allows for an expansion of the "collective power of the system's dominant groups" that can fulfill supply-and-demand conditions needed for stability (Arrighi and Silver 1999:28). Yet the fixation on hegemonic cores overlooks alternative sites of governance that promote stability. These are the sites of social reproduction in households, communities, and religious sodalities that confront the new forces let loose by globalization in alternative ways.

Rethinking the problematic of capitalist expansion in terms of the relations between capitalist production and the domestic reproductive and subsistence sector has a long

genealogy

history/Nineteenth- and early twentieth-century feminists had embraced the interrelationship of production and reproduction in a holistic analysis that included the personal and community dimension of crises. Before Marx and Engels wrote *The Communist Manifesto*, Flora Tristan (1983, translated and republished from the 1837 publication in France) published her book, *L'Union Ouvrier*, calling for an organization of the employed with the unemployed and (in Marx's terms) unemployable lumpen proletariat of the world—the pimps and prostitutes, the thieves and jailed populations of the London and Paris underworld—along with wage slaves and self-employed peasants. This was anathema to a theory of capitalist accumulation that saw the expropriation of profit as exclusively related to exploitation in the workplace. So, too, were Tristan's attempts to organize a world union focusing on bread-and-butter issues that preoccupied all workers and the unemployed. Marxists who were her contemporaries considered consumption concerns counterproductive to the struggle to seize the means of production.

The problematic posed by groups marginal to capitalist growth centers was central to Rosa Luxemburg's (1971 [1913]) thesis concerning the necessary coexistence of a noncapitalist subsistence sector with the advance of capitalism. She recognized the importance of what she called the "natural economy," or the petty commodity producers and cultivators, as a vital element in the process of accumulation.

> The historic process of the development of capitalism on the world stage in all of its colorful and moving variety takes place first in the exchange relation of capital with its non-capitalist environment as it confronts the difficulties of a barter economy, secure social relations and the limited demand of patriarchal peasant economy and artisan production. Capital uses heroic means to conquer the feudal barter economy at home and the subjugation and destruction of traditional communities overseas, laying open the doors to commodity exchange and production. (Luxemburg 1971 [1913]:92)

Marx also recognized the importance of natural economies in the primitive state of accumulation, but what Luxemburg added was the continuing importance of the non-capitalist systems for advanced industrialized countries as well. Comparing simple reproduction with expanded reproduction, she states:

> It is quite different with the realization of surplus value. Here outside consumers *qua* other than capitalist are really essential. Thus the immediate and vital conditions for capital and its accumulation is the existence of non-capitalist buyers of the surplus value, which is decisive to this extent for the problem of capitalist accumulation.
>
> Whatever the theoretical aspects, the accumulation of capital as an historic process depends in every respect upon non-capitalist social strata and the forms of social organization. (Luxemburg 1951 [1913]:365)

She adds to this argument the particular reasons for their essential importance:

> The existence and development of capitalism requires an environment of non-capi-
> talist forms of production, but not every one of these forms will serve its ends. Cap-
> italism needs non-capitalist social strata as a market for its surplus value, as a source
> of supply for its means of production, and as a reservoir of labour power for its wage
> system. (Luxemburg [1913]1951:368)

To state as its primary need "a market for its surplus value," not simply as a market for its
commodities, reveals the essence of her argument. In the recurrent crises of capitalism,
she argues that capitalists have to go beyond selling to other capitalists, which does not
enhance the reproductive base for the process of accumulation. It is for this reason that
she asserts that:

> Their [the natural economies'] mode of production and their labour power, no less
> than their demand for surplus products, is necessary to capitalism. Yet the latter is
> fully determined to undermine their independence as social units in order to gain
> possession of their means of production and labour power and to convert them into
> commodity buyers. This method is the most expedient for capital. In fact, it is invari-
> ably accompanied by a growing military, whose importance will be demonstrated
> below. (Luxemburg 1971:[1913] 92)

She encountered opposition from Marxists of her day who objected to her thesis that
the "third market" of subsistence producers competed in importance with, or even over-
shadowed, the surplus value rendered in the workplace as a major and continuing component of the process of capital accumulation.

Rosa Luxemburg's emphasis on the importance of subsistence-based societies as a
condition for enlarged reproduction takes on added significance as global expansion
threatens to subsume all non-capitalist sectors. Her premonition that this requires militarization of the society in this predatory expansion was almost a blueprint for what is
happening as the jungle retreats of the hemisphere are being overtaken:

> Since primitive associations of the natives are the strongest protection for their social
> organization and for their material bases of existence capital must begin by planning
> the systematic destruction and annihilation of all non-capitalist social units which
> obstruct their development. (Luxemborg 1951:370)

militarization of societies

We can begin to comprehend in these terms how globalization often leads to the militarization of societies that resist being drawn into capitalist markets. We have reached a
point when the predatory expansion of capitalism threatens with extinction not only the
marginalized domestic or subsistence economies but also the capitalist sector itself as it
eliminates nonrenewable resources and the basis for biodiversity alternatives. Anthropologists, particularly those with a gendered perspective of social reproduction, have
taken a lead in expanding our awareness of alternative paths of growth.

speculation?

DIMENSIONS OF THE WORLD CRISIS

Global integration heightens the cyclical crises of capitalism by reducing the funds devoted to wages while increasing the activity of financial networks. This reduces the self-correcting mechanisms of free market flows by promoting speculation while reducing human claims on surpluses. Concomitant with this is an increase in unemployment, with redundant selling and trafficking in drugs that undercut the production of less *drugs* lucrative subsistence crops and reduce the redistributive function of the state. The terms of trade, that is, that which developing countries receive for their goods and services, have fallen across the board from 1985 to 1994, but the drop in developing economies (from an index of 108 to 96) is greater than that for developed economies of the North (106 to 101) (United Nations 1996, Table 5).

The crisis that was tipped off by sharp rises in oil prices in the middle of the 1970s and *crisis* culminated in the financial crisis of Asian and Latin American countries in the 1980s differs from that of the 1930s because of three major changes: 1) the growing integration *①* of the world economy, 2) the shift from industrial production to financial capital as the *②* principle basis for accumulation, and 3) the diminishing resources, including labor *③* power, devoted to subsistence production throughout the world. Neoliberal governments are now dismantling the regulations put into place in the decades following the Depression and World War II. Some of the effects of these policies are addressed below.

Integration of the World Economy and Widening Discrepancies

Measures of global integration ① foriegn investment

One of the most significant measures of global integration is direct foreign investment. The high point of $178,589 million of investments from OECD countries in 1992–1993 more than doubled in the next five years, with a year-end projection of $382,022 million (Direct Investment Yearbook 1998:8, 23). Financial transactions in the periphery were formerly invested in production or extraction, but in the volatile stock markets of countries vying for entry into global financial sectors there is an increase in credit transactions, stock speculation, and debt. The higher returns in peripheral economies are offset by the necessity of paying off debt in foreign currency that is hard to come by. Debt itself has entered into speculative transactions, as the debt of peripheral economies is traded in international exchange markets.

The most striking trend in the global economic integration during the 1980s was the reversal of the net transfer of funds between developing and developed countries, as payments of profits and interest to foreign capital by indebted nations rose by 32 percent (Inter-American Development Bank 1987). The deterioration of the terms of trade between debtor nations and the developed world, which the Inter-American Development Bank (1987) estimated as 11 percent below the 1979–1980 averages, fell another 16 percent between 1980 and 1988 (Magdoff 1992:31). The fall in the exchange rates of national currencies relative to the dollar contributes to the widening gap between poor countries and rich, making it ever more difficult to overcome the indebtedness incurred in preceding decades. The net effect is that wages in the developing world fell more than per capita net product, aggravating an already large disparity between rich and poor nations and threatening the balance between production potential and consumption (United Nations 1991). The impact can be measured in rising crime rates, breakup of families, deteriorating quality of life, and the increasing gap between wealthy and impoverished sectors worldwide.

Although capital flows reverted to earlier trends, that is, from developed to the developing economies, the gap between rich and poor continues to grow in the 1990s. The World Bank insists that the interdependence of the global economy has favored economic growth, and the editors of the annual report demonstrate this with world GNP figures showing an annual 2.5 percent per capita rate of growth in the period from 1965 to 1989. Yet statistical summaries in the Annual Reports (World Bank 1987, 1989, 1990a and b, 1994) document the devastation of selected areas even while global figures indicate growth after 1990. The debt crisis of the 1980s resulted in severe stagnation and even decline in most Latin American countries, occurring precisely in those areas where "reforms" (read liberalization of trade and privatization of industry) have been instituted (Lustig 1995). The percentage below the poverty level increased in Latin America from 33 percent in 1980 to 39 percent in 1985, with an absolute increase in the number of the poor from 120 to 160 million (Lustig 1995:62).

The compliance of indebted governments throughout Latin America to conditions set by international financial agencies for gaining credit during the 1980s continues to facilitate the penetration of modernizing trends into the farthest reaches of former subsistence systems. These conditions include the shift from domestic to export production and commitment of shrinking governmental revenues to debt payment, implying a decline in social welfare programs and freezing wages. Throughout the 1980s, when the debt burden of peripheral economies peaked and whole countries were threatened with bankruptcy, the flow of capital was reversed as indebted economies paid more than half of their export earnings to core economies in payment for the interest and principle on debts contracted in the preceding decade. Mexico averaged a minus 0.5 gross domestic product in the period from 1983 to 1986 and suffered a drop in the real wage to 66 percent of the 1978 wage index at the lowest point of the country's decline in 1988 (Lara Resende 1995). The earthquake of 1985 and the decline in petroleum prices expected to fuel recovery delayed the kind of stabilization that would encourage venture capitalism to invest further resources for another five years. Unemployment increased and the minimum wage level in 1995 is lower than in 1980. The new private enterprises that replaced subsidized national enterprises were often export-processing assembly plants lured by government subsidies and promises of tax abatements that undercut the redistributive role of national governments. In the period between 1979–1981 to 1986–1988, Mexico's share of social expenditures in relation to GDP fell 30 percent, exceeding that of Bolivia (25 percent) and Argentina (14 percent). Even after the recovery in capital accounts began in 1990, wages in 1995 had not yet reached the 1978 levels (Lara Resende 1995:63). The 1994 World Bank Annual Report claimed that the signing of NAFTA bolstered the long-term outlook (World Bank Annual Report 1994:28) at the very moment when sectors of the Mexican population most affected by the agreement, that is, the subsistence producers in rural and particularly indigenous areas, were rejecting it in armed uprisings and massive demonstrations.

Simultaneous cuts in social spending further deepened the crisis for those below the poverty line. In the period from 1981 to 1983, the ratio of social to public spending in Mexico declined from 31.2 percent of GDP to 23 percent (Lustig 1992:79). Even with recovery in the early 1990s, the sectoral imbalances in Latin America remained, with the 33 percent below the poverty line in 1980 rising to 39 percent in 1985 and hovering at the same proportion in the early 1990s (Lustig 1995). The postrecovery trends show: 1) a rise in unemployment, 2) a decline in social welfare (including education, health, and the infrastructure of pure water and waste disposal), 3) persistence of unemployment, 4) the worldwide drop in real wages (see World Bank 1994, World Tables).

The reduction in subsidies for basic foodstuffs in the face of a drop in real average incomes and rising poverty (Lustig 1995:61) indicates that most Latin American governments are not committed to changing these trends. In response to the question posed of the Inter-American Development Bank (June 1997:8): "Does globalization hurt wage earners?" the answer was no, but a growing portion of the labor force without the necessary skills is permanently left out of the job markets. The position of Mexico's indigenous population is steadily declining in relation to other sectors and even to recent past conditions (Inter-American Development Bank, 1997:150). The failure to address this growing gap between the rich and the poor during the recent recovery suggests that the long-term trends toward a declining standard of living (Beneria 1992; United Nations Development Program 1991) will persist for the one-third of the population that fell into impoverishment during the crisis.

The Shift from Industrial to Finance Capital

This brings us to our second proposition concerning the distinctiveness of this crisis in the predominance of finance capital over industrial capital. The vulnerability of the world economy is compounded by instability in financial institutions throughout the world. Regulations that had existed since the Bretton Woods agreement were canceled during the Nixon presidency. Clearly a change was needed to bridge the gap between real currency evaluation and financial flows, but without any substitutes, most governments were unable or unwilling to control the banks operating within their boundaries in the succeeding decades. International financial analysts of the 1980s (Wachtel 1986:3; Pecchioli 1983:13) pointed out the danger of more flexible procedures in the supervision of international risks than those applying to domestic transactions, but with new banking procedures developed in the 1980s, rapid transfers of money throughout the world added further vulnerability to local economies. On the basis of precipitous fluctuations in the stock market during the 1990s, financial expert George Soros (1998) predicted a world collapse unless international regulations were put into place to fortify the existing structure of financial institutions. He called for an international bank and political institutions to legitimize the movement of capital and credit that now bypass national controls.

The volatility of finance markets threatens state economies and disrupts the political order. If governments fail to address protests of the magnitude that we have seen in Latin America and Asia, it can mean a toppling of the government. The growing risk in this highly competitive global financial setting has resulted in policies that stress concentration of resources, unprecedented imbalances, high speculation in currency exchange, and rapid inflation at a time when sluggish economic activity depletes the bases for future growth (Magdoff 1992; Soros 1998). The volatility in currency exchange rates negates long-range planning, particularly of the debt-burdened countries. Even those societies which are most removed from the play of the market economy have experienced the inflationary effects resulting from abrupt changes in the exchange rate of the national currencies. The massive movement of financial transactions unconnected to trade (Drucker 1986) contributes to a phantasmagoric economy that escapes regulation by national governments, leading to the corruption at high levels that has been particularly marked in Mexico's growing international economy.[4]

With the threat of entire nations going into default in the 1980s, the International Monetary Fund (IMF) assumed enormous power in directing the economic policies of these countries. Stabilization policies required privatization of state enterprises, even closing down entire operations employing thousands of workers, as was done in Bolivia in 1986. Along with its demands for the privatization of nationalized economies, the IMF forced governments to give priority to export production rather than internal consumption in order to ensure payment of the debt. Redistributive politics of populist governments in Latin America were left with a shrinking economic base with which to generate payments for social welfare. Although larger debtor nations such as Brazil and Mexico had negotiated some reduction in the financing costs in the last round, not a single penny of debt has been repudiated by debtor countries. Those countries that respond positively to the IMF demands by making draconian cuts in government spending and privatizing formerly nationalized enterprises, such as Argentina and Bolivia, are rewarded with investment capital, while those that resist the terms of payment, as in Peru during the presidency of Alan Garcia, become pariahs in international financial circles. President Fujimori was desperately trying to convince international financiers that Peru was not another Mexico in 1997, but with his own election in 2000 under attack, when Mexico reversed the PRI monopoly he was in an even more vulnerable position. By 1997 the economist Jeffrey Sachs, who had mediated the first IMF package in Bolivia in 1995 (Nash 1992a), was deploring the package as it was being deployed in the Asian crisis (*The New York Times* November 3, 1997 op. ed. A23).

Devaluation of national currencies, which was a central condition of IMF restructuring, imposed the greatest cutbacks on wage earners, since the reduced spending power of income was not as quick to adjust as consumer prices. Taken together with the reduction in the "social wage" (government expenditures on education, health, and rural program assistance), the total disposable wages of workers were considerably reduced (Lustig 1992:62). In Mexico, the share of public expenditures dedicated to debt servicing in the interest of regaining financial stability rose to 40 percent during the debt crisis of 1983 to 1985 while social welfare expenditures dropped by 26 percent. This is one indication of the greater burden borne by the middle- and lower-income population, many of whom were forced to migrate to the United States.

Shrinking Subsistence Margins

The third point that distinguishes this crisis from the recurrent crises of capitalism, the loss of subsistence reserves, has three dimensions: 1) the encroachment of capitalist enterprises in the territories of agropastoral and hunter-gatherer-cultivators, 2) the reduction of subsistence crop production and the growing food dependency, and 3) the reduction of resources in national as well as household budgets, with debt financing resorted to as a regular stratagem.   *decline in income*

Along with the loss of food self-sufficiency in the developing economies, personal income has declined at most levels except for the very top income earners. Because of high inflation—consumer prices have risen from a 1980 index of 100 for Latin America to 1,157.6 in 1989—real average wages in urban areas have dropped to less than 50 percent of their 1980 levels in Peru and Venezuela, while in Mexico and Argentina they have been less than 75 percent (ECLAS 1991; Lustig 1990). In Argentina, for example, the lowest 40 percent of income earners went from 16 to 14 percent of GNP, while the richest 10 percent increased its share (World Bank 1988).

These world trends, showing the integration of economies, the dependence on finance capital combined with the decline in productive enterprises, and the erosion of subsistence security, have profound consequences for the societies we study, whether they are located in core industrial countries or in developing areas. Their implications can be read even in the most remote areas of Mexico, in the rain forest and mountain ranges. For those people who are most threatened by the crisis in the world system, it is no wonder that they are attempting to reverse the trends that affect them daily.

Yet, paradoxically, the process of integration in world markets gives power to those ☆ marginalized by the global economy. News of the Chiapas uprising on January 1, 1994, shook the global financial system. The instantaneous transmission of the news made possible by the worldwide integration of communication (Sassen 1996a) set off a downturn in financial markets. Shortly after the Zapatista uprising, Mexican stocks lost over three points in the Dow Jones on January 3 (*U.S. News and World Report* January 24, 1994:72). The shock waves further widened in the climate of uncertainty raised by events in Mexico but aggravated by breakoff in the U.S.-Japan trade talks in February, resulting in an overall fall of 10 percent in U.S. investment markets from February to July 1994. The stock market responds to electoral results and charges of fraud with volatility, as events in Mexico in the years following the uprising demonstrated. The good news for investors following the August 1994 elections, which political observers interpreted as a vote against change, led to an immediate recuperation in stock markets in November 1994, but the victory at the polls turned to ashes by the end of the year when citizens in the states of Chiapas and Tabasco claimed fraud in the election of the Institutional Revolutionary Party (PRI) candidates for governor. Protest grew as the newly elected president, Ernesto Zedillo Ponce de León, discovered huge deficits in the economy and instituted an austerity program. As the dimensions of the crisis, measured in the flight of capital and the lack of reserves, came to light, the new president publicly announced the need to devalue the peso.[5]

ANTHROPOLOGISTS
IN THE GLOBAL ECUMENE

The global framework is an undeniable part of the ethnographic task. As people throughout the world experienced the restructuring of an increasingly integrated global economy, the differences that once marked First and Third World seemed to be erased, along with the terms of our "cross-cultural" comparisons. Ethnographic strategies and theories based on the premise of holistically integrated "habitats" of hunter-gatherers and subsistence cultivators were incompatible with the changing global ecumene. "Peasants" became the stepchildren adopted by ethnographers in the aftermath of World War II as they tried to overcome the timeless and bounded horizons of "tribal" societies.[6] Yet the permeability of cultural boundaries and the fragmentation of "modes of production" in a variety of survival techniques defied analyses premised on the historical categories of feudalism.

In the past two decades, anthropologists have been making the process of globalization the subject of ethnology. The strategies for encompassing both the local and the global responses to these transformations are the subject of intense debate in anthropology. From their earliest entry into the global domain, anthropologists have criticized unitary paradigms, whether originating within their own discipline, as in the debate over "unilineal evolution," or from outside, as in the debates over world systems paradigms. In order to encompass global dimensions of change, anthropologists have had to break the mold of static cultural wholes as they expanded the temporal and spatial horizons of the discipline. In order to set the current debates into perspective, I shall review the paradigm shifts in the self-critique of a discipline that began as an adjunct of colonial expansion and that led to the present state of the art in global anthropology.

The Critique of Unilineal Evolution
and its Resolution in Functionalism

Unilineal evolutionists of the nineteenth century imposed an ordering of cultures throughout the world that was premised on the superiority of Western civilization. The ghost of Sir Francis Galton still haunts those who dismiss alternative paths to modernity with global integration. Galton objected to Tylor's (1889) paper on the development of institutions, raising questions as to how one could assume linear evolution when societies in contact may have adopted the customs of the dominant group rather than having evolved in the same direction (cf. Zucher 1977). Functionalist explanations promoted in the first half of the nineteenth century were a counter to speculative history predicated on unilineal evolutionary models that saw the non-Western societies as primitive pro-genitors of what became modernizing states. Later attacked as reactionary attempts to justify the status quo defined by colonial powers, functionalism originated as a radical attempt to judge cultural traits in the particular context in which they appeared rather than from Eurocentric perspectives.

As colonized subjects became their own ethnographers, Cartesian dichotomies came under criticism. The opposition of "civilized and primitive" had nearly been laid to rest in the 1950s, and even the euphemisms of "simple and complex" or "developed" and "underdeveloped" and, later, "developing," were anathema to anthropologists in a post-colonial world. Third World anthropologists—I include here the colonizers who had migrated from their "home" countries—also exposed the inadequacies of some of the most cherished assumptions of colonialism. Max Gluckman (1947) launched one of the first attacks on functionalism when he criticized Malinowski for his ahistoricism and fail-ure to see conflict as part of an integrated colonial picture. Talal Asad (1973) showed that "holistic" studies that presumably encompassed all aspects of "tribal" life yet left out imperialist institutions "obscured the systematic character of colonial domination and masked the fundamental contradictions of interest." Criticism of our colonial past has been central to the anthropological discipline for over thirty years, yet contemporary critics often overlook this earlier critique and the sympathetic view of liberation move-ments held by most anthropologists prior to independence of the colonized states of Africa and Latin America (Maquet 1964).

Relativism also came under attack as a correlative of functionalist explanations, set-ting a double standard of morality—one for informants and another for ethnographers. The critique of functionalist studies for their tendency to reify the status quo under colo-nial and neocolonial regimes opened up the field to historically situated and empirically grounded ethnographies that facilitated studies of globalization. The contributors to Dell Hymes's anthology, *Reinventing Anthropology* (Hymes 1972), questioned the tradi-tional/modern dichotomy in a critique that expanded a theory of process, situating stud-ies of colonized cultures within a worldwide framework of capitalist advance.[7]

Mexican anthropologists coming of age in the same period launched a critique of functionalists in their origins. Bonfil Batalla, Warman, and others (Warman et al. 1970) showed that *indigenismo*, or the indophile perspective that was the dominant paradigm for both theoretical and applied work in the institutionalizing of the 1910 Revolution, culti-vated a respect for indigenous roots at the same time that it negated self-determination for the Indian population. The paradigm of *indigenismo*, like that of functionalism, con-tains a history that began with a radical proposition and became the ideological core for preserving a status quo. Just as functionalists challenged a Eurocentric notion of unilin-eal evolution, calling for a relativistic criteria in assessing the value of cultural traits and ending with conservative propositions validating the status quo, so did *indigenismo* in the early decades of the twentieth century begin with a critique of racism, pointing to the value of preconquest cultures, and ended with unilineal assumptions equating progress with acculturation to European ways.

Living with the contradictions of a national policy that embraces integration of the Indians in an ideology of *indigenismo*, espousing a pro-Indian policy that is ultimately bent on eradicating cultural differences in their nation, Mexican anthropologists are more aware than their colleagues from the United States of the persistence of unilineal thinking in their field. The civilizing project was defined from the colonial period as becoming a homogeneous nation. Although the language has changed from what Miguel Alberto Bartolomé calls an indianist policy of integration to one of participation, the contemporary policies of directed cultural change still hold a unilineal evolutionary model, with acculturation considered as synonymous with evolution (Bartolomé 1994:6). Since Mexican anthropology is closer to applied problems related to ethnic minorities, issues of power have been central to their reassessment of *indigenismo*. This critique is coming to fruition in the assessment of the current wave of ethnic reassertion in reaction to globalization, as indigenous people are beginning to make clear a strong sense of what coexistence in a global ecumene might mean.

The Critique of World Systems Theory

The subject matter of anthropology is inherently global, but the paradigm of cultures as integrated wholes inhibited research on the dynamics of globalism. Wallerstein's (1974) unified theory of world systems stimulated a countercritique by anthropologists, joined by world historians. This addressed the issues of local difference and global trends in novel ways that recaptured the vitality of ethnographic research within a historical world frame. The coexistence of distinct modes of expropriating value within a dominant mode of accumulation had to be resolved in order to comprehend the apparent contradictions of nascent capitalist enterprises in peripheral areas. Anthropological studies were crucial in demonstrating that regional economies within peripheral nations provided independent growth centers that were not dominated by trends in core industrial areas. Ethnohistorical studies of peasant export crop production in Middle and South America showed the changing relations of production on a world stage.[8] Studies of export processing zones and military bases that proliferated throughout the world in the1970s and 1980s fostered an awareness of the emergent world order. The focus on gender roles in these new sites enhanced our perceptions of the generative basis for new cultural patterns in male-female and worker-manager relations.[9] Transnational circuits cultivated by migrants enhanced our awareness of the deepening of ethnic identity rather than its elimination with globalization.[10]

The frameworks of dependency (Cardoso and Faletto 1971; Frank 1967) and of world systems (Wallerstein 1974) were the kind of totalizing schemes that provoked scholars concerned with local settings to reconceptualize the global pressures experienced by indigenous peoples in a local setting. Among the critics in anthropology were Carol Smith (1984), Jane Schneider (1977), and others included in my review of ethnographic aspects of the world systems paradigm (Nash 1981). I have tried to show in my studies of Bolivian tin miners and Mayan semi-subsistence cultivators how resistance and rebellion deter and sometimes destabilize the thrust of world economic forces. The value of the world systems

Cf.
Wallers.

paradigm was to focus our attention on the power issues that affected populations throughout the world. Resistance and rebellion are a continuous counterpoint to global advance.

The Feminist Critique

Contemporary Marxist feminists (Dalla Costa 1972; Bennholdt-Thomsen 1981) have
picked up Rosa Luxemburg's focus on expanded reproduction as they underscore the
importance of housework to the process of capital accumulation. Feminist studies of
Latin America (Beneria 1992; León de Leal and Deere 1980; Collins and Gimenez 1990)
demonstrate the contribution to gross domestic product of women's work in semi-subsistence cultivation, artisan production, and housework. The multiplicity of household
activities women perform in subsistence as well as artisan production ensures the reproduction of *campesino* society (Cook 1984; Deere 1990; Nash 1982, 1993; Stephen 1991).
Since women's contributions have not been valorized in market calculations, development programs ignore women's unpaid work, further undermining the subsistence
structures within which they operate. *feminist →substantive*
Feminist scholarship reinforces the importance of substantive economic theory since it
focuses on meeting the needs of social reproduction rather than measuring growth by
market indicators alone. Studies of the gendered division of labor in the household demonstrate not only the viability, but also the importance, of the semi-subsistence sector. This
position, which has parallels in that of Luxemburg, was taken by proponents of small-plot
cultivation, or "*campesinistas*" (Stavenhagen 1978; Warman 1980). They argued against those
who predicted the inevitable retreat of *campesinos* into proletarian status, a position identified as "*descampesinistas*" (Bartra 1982). Feminist analyses go beyond the assumptions of
complementary and equal shares in the redistribution of household production implicit in
the *campesinista* debate to show the systematic inequalities that prevail in patriarchal peasant households (Deere 1990; Eber 1995; Nash 1993; Rosenbaum 1993). Gender analyses
on women drawn into global export processing plants demystifies the *Myth of the Male
Breadwinner*, to use Helen Safa's (1996) memorable title for her book on assembly workers
in Puerto Rico, Cuba, and the Dominican Republic. Women's low-wage labor is the driving force for direct foreign investment in the countries of the South, though the workers do
not enjoy even the minimum protections of the state available to male workers in unionized
enterprises (Fernandez-Kelly 1983; Nash and Fernandez-Kelly 1984; Safa 1996).

The gendered perspective in social science advanced the understanding of women's
substantive contribution to the economic, political, and social life of society (Boserup
1970). In the following two decades, the feminist critique contributed major advances in
the social sciences with the development of multivocalic, reflexive, and dialectical
approaches. As Margery Wolf (1992) demonstrates in *A Thrice-Told Tale*, these insights
resurfaced over two decades later in a cultural critique that ignored its precursors.

The Development Critique

The anthropological critique of development followed close on the heels of direct foreign investment in the post–World War II era. Sol Tax (1952) taught us to appreciate the

complex interworkings of small-plot cultivators who rejected the ox and plow and other colonial technology based on a rational calculus of the greater returns from intensive cultivation of cash crops in favor of fodder for draft animals. McKim Marriott (1952) pointed to the paradox of overdevelopment as the basis for resistance to modernizing development programs in India. There he found that the very overdetermination in highly interrelated customary practices made it questionable, if not impossible, for Indian peasants to adopt changes considered more rational by developers. These studies, now labeled "functionalist" (and by implication conservative) were, in the 1950s, a radical rejection of propositions that dominated the development field. Programs that were favored in the 1950s called for capital-intensive agroindustrial techniques that ignored indigenous peoples' culturally transmitted knowledge of how to maximize production with self-sustaining agricultural practices. This is only now being rescued with the movement of sustainable development that recognizes the superiority of traditional techniques that were nearly obliterated.

Anthropological studies are replete with documentation of the ingenuity and adaptability of subsistence-based economies, defined as those in which the producers consume a majority of production and sell only to meet basic needs of food, housing, and health.[11] Anthropologists—and those economists who take microsystems into account—have also documented the devastation of these systems by development and export-oriented growth.[12] Societies like these, in which a major part of the economic activities is oriented to subsistence, are becoming extremely rare after a half-century of concerted attempts to draw their resources into international markets. The most advantageous conditions for growth in subsistence economies are precisely those considered negative for development: remoteness from areas with large populations of landless people, lack of commercially attractive resources, and absence of competing capital ventures.[13] Yet development agencies have paid little attention to investments in subsistence crops or artisan activities other than those directed toward international commerce. As a result, countries with a predominantly agrarian base like Mexico have become increasingly dependent on grain imports since the 1950s and 1960s (Barkin 1987, 1990), and this dependency has increased with the liberalization of trade in the 1990s.

The power of ethnology in disclosing insights of indigenous people remains an important framework for thinking about the embeddedness of social practices in a wider field of social relations. This is the essence of Karl Polanyi's discussion of "The Economy as Instituted Process" (1957). Calling for a shift in perspective from "a type of rational action to the configuration of goods and person movements, which actually make up the economy," Polanyi's message is even more significant in the era of globalization than it was nearly half a century ago.

Substantive economics have begun to influence policies in the World Bank Poverty Programs and other nongovernmental organizations that work with grassroots development programs. One measure of this is that social indicators are beginning to take into account the problem of distribution of the world's resources that was ignored in earlier development paradigms.[14] This concession toward substantive economic analysis reveals a growing awareness of the need to focus on the real needs of people rather than the market demand for goods that is the bottom line of a self-regulating market. Robert Cox (1996) has recently elaborated the contrast between substantist and formalist positions drawn from Polanyi, Arensberg, and Pearson (1957:239) to show the variety of capitalism in the globalization processes. He delineates a hyperliberal Anglo-American form, a social-market central and northern European form, and an East Asian form. He does not stretch this variation to include a fourth noncapitalist form of semi-subsistence cultivation posited by the *campesinistas*. Yet this is on the agenda of some of the South East Asian countries, following the 1997 crisis currency in global financial circuits.[15]

The custodianship by indigenous peoples of their habitats, which contain the remaining unexploited reserves of resources, has only recently been recognized by international agencies (IUCN Inter-Commission Task Force on Indigenous Peoples 1997). Environmentalists now consider efforts to oppose destruction of natural environment must take into account not only the cultural traditions of the indigenous populations that have ensured their survival, but also the full social organization and ritual responses that maintain conservation practices. The threat of the extinction of subsistence producers is thus a threat to the global economy. In consideration of the importance of indigenous peoples' "harmonious relationship with Nature," representatives of the international community have named them "as distinct and vital sources of knowledge" (IUCN Inter-Commission Task Force of Indigenous Peoples 1997). At the 1992 Rio de Janeiro summit meeting on environment, the United Nations drew up a covenant calling for the full incorporation of indigenous women and men in the planning of development in order to change the course of world capital to flow in more equitable channels. Yet some postmodernists dismiss the claim of harmonious adjustment of Indians to their environment as essentializing romanticism.[16] It is a paradox that the delayed autocritique within the field of anthropology should position many practitioners against what is conceived of as essentializing romanticism at a moment when indigenous people are finding a universalizing discourse in which to express their concerns about the predatory advance of capitalist ventures in their territories.

The Anticritique of Poststructuralism and Postmodernism

Anthropological studies of globalization in the 1970s and 1980s emphasized political economic conditions in a decade marked by reverse flows of capital from poor indebted nations to developed nations, with widening gaps between rich and poor within nations. A decade later, attention shifted to global "ethnoscapes" and "ecumenes"[17] as ways of conceptualizing hybrid forms of consumerism in the "mirror of production." Simultaneously, there was a change in focus from structural propositions to cultural interpretations, with the individual rather than the collectivity the subject for investigation (Escobar and Alvarez 1992). Ethnographic studies were enriched by the broader humanistic and psychic representation of subjects, but this was often achieved by jettisoning the ballast of structural representation.

Poststructuralism staked out its domain in a minefield of posthumous "wasims" (past ideologies related to cultures in contrast to current "isms," e.g., functionalism, structuralism, etc. [*cf.* Nash 1997d]), as critics jumped blithely from postindustrialism to postmodernism, sometimes building on the very same propositions cast in a new language. What differentiates the poststructuralists from past post hoc posturing is the skepticism fostered in the disengagement from what are called "modernist" projects. Anthropologists who situate themselves in the landscape rather than the ideology of postmodernism continue to relate to structuralist propositions contained in postindustrial and post-Fordist analyses of Touraine (1971), Lipietz (1987), and Mahane (1987). Insightful comments on the global reach by dominant economic and political interests advanced by Frederic Jameson (1982) and David Harvey (1989) should not be overlooked when we draw upon their exposition of multiple new subject positions in the conditions of postmodernity. The identity that we call class related to position in an occupational hierarchy is as much a cultural construct as those of ethnicity and gender. As Ida Susser (1997) shows in her review of current research on poverty in the United States and in the world economy, it is in the intersection of class, race/ethnicity, and gender that we gain insights into the dynamics of impoverishment and marginalization in global restructuring.

Postmodern approaches sharpen our strategies of representation with discourse analysis, identity formation, and the exploration of new time-space coordinates. But these explorations have meaning in the context of power and the material resources that maintain structures of power. As Warman and colleagues (1970) revealed in their critique of *indigenismo*, a proindigenous rhetoric regarding development projects for indigenous communities had the goal of deculturing indigenous societies. But when multiculturalism became the preferred position in the 1980s after the passage of the International Labor Office convention on the cultural rights of indigenous peoples, the change in rhetoric did little to change the objectives of government policy, which still maintained acculturation to Eurocentric goals (Bartolomé 1994). Without changing the structure of dominance and subordination, the injection of new language masquerades as progress without ensuring the substance of change.

The current challenge in ethnography is to relate the fragmentary lifestyles and identity issues of gender and ethnicity in the global economy to declining capital earnings, the destruction of social welfare provisions, or the flight of capital to Third World countries without class-based union movements. Postmodern emphasis on the cultural parameters of identity formation enhances our understanding of social movements, but we cannot ignore the empirical indices of gross national product and the demographics of work roles when we attempt to tie impoverishment, racism, and sexism to structural positions related to power.[18] Growing disparities in wealth in those nations that gain entry into the global economy by virtue of low-wage and antidemocratic policies are generating cultural strategies of rebellion to confront rising militarization and repression.

An ongoing critique of our practice of anthropology is essential to the enterprise. Historical materialism of the 1970s indicated the limitation of community and tribal studies viewed as timeless wholes, homogeneous and largely unchanging. The critiques of functionalist studies that reified the status quo under colonialism led to an efflorescence of

historically situated and empirically grounded writing. The questioning of the tradi-
tional/modern dichotomies made it possible to expand a theory of process situating
studies of colonized cultures within a worldwide framework of capitalist advance.

The cultural critique (Clifford and Marcus 1986) opens the door to ethnographic
analyses cast in a broader humanistic perspective. At the same time, it often cultivates the
involution of the discipline of anthropology in a critique not just of the ways of representing the other but of the very process of representation. In order to rescue ourselves from
what Jean Comaroff and John Comaroff (1992:37) call the "vapid theoreticism" derived
from "our current conceptual obsession with agency, subjectivity, and consciousness," a
key to reconnect with the field might be found within postmodernist strategies for developing the "reflexivity," "polyphony," and "dialogue" that Steven Sangren (1988) poses as
their core values. Recalling an earlier crisis of representation in the eighteenth century
that Giambattista Vico bridged with his interpretations of "pagan" myths in his *Scienza
Nuova* (1725, revised 1744), we are turning again to mythopoetic imagery to find insights.
Gary Gossen (1999), Nathaniel Tarn (1997), and Dennis Tedlock (1984) are among those
interpreters who succeed in imaginatively recreating the Mayan world while drawing on
sound ethnographic research of their imagery and metaphors.[19]

Kay Warren provides a sophisticated response to the debate raised by postmodernist
concerns with "essentializing" ethnic identity, that is, the reference to a set of essences in
order to define a cultural group, in her analysis of Mayan intellectuals in Guatemala
(1992). Her engagement with Mayan intellectuals as they renegotiate a new relationship
with the state enables her to raise the critique of essentialism to a new level. The dilemma
she raises is faced by most anthropologists concerned with the problem of appropriating
knowledge and cultural properties without adequately crediting indigenous authors. Les
Field (1999) distinguishes the "essentialist" determination of identity as more a part of
common parlance from the "constructivist" approach that asserts the social construction
of identities involving a collaboration between subjects and anthropologists. The dilemma
for anthropologists lies in the fact that essentialism can be used to establish rights to a territory, thus making it an extremely useful term of self-representation yet, as Field points
out, one that threatens identification if the assigned essences are lost or abandoned.

Scholars outside of academia are now more often engaged in promoting the reconstitution of culture. Archeologists are often funded by state agencies to rescue cultural evidence
of territorial possession from antiquities that were buried or fragmented. A veritable industry of ethnic identity is cultivated in NGOs that draw on narrative discourses of the elders
or reexamination of texts and artifacts that survived the destruction of conquests. Recovery of crafts and the cultural repertoires they symbolize is a multibillion-dollar industry fur-
thered by alternative trade organizations, museums, and religious organizations (Grimes
n.d.; Nash 1993). Even more impressive is the recognition by international representatives
of the superiority of indigenous knowledge systems in development projects that embody
the principle of sustainability. At the 1992 Summit Conference on Environment and Development in Rio de Janeiro, 160 heads of state called for strengthening the rights of indigenous people in recognition of their superior stewardship of the world's cultural and

biological diversity (IUCN Inter-Commission Task Force on Indigenous Peoples 1997:21).
We can anticipate a growth industry in the near future for establishing such claims.

This augurs the need for ever sharper analytical observation in ethnographic studies
of the rapidly changing worlds of the localities we pretend to analyze, including those in
our own backyard. We are particularly obligated because we often find ourselves in field
settings where the last frontiers of populations, marginalized in the earlier world expansion, have maintained a distinctive worldview. Populations that have retained a foothold,
or those that have recently colonized settlements in these regions, are the chosen field
sites for more adventurous anthropologists.

This book is an affirmation of the important role of anthropological investigations as
we respond to the changing needs and interests of the people in the worlds we explore.
I have tried to strike a balance in writing an ethnography that is situated in the context of
economic trends as measured in financial and investment figures and power blocks that
operate at great distances from the field, but at the same time is grounded in observations and participation in ongoing events in local settings that are still the essence of the
anthropological task. The indigenous strategies for survival as a distinct cultural group
provide an alternative vision to that of neoliberalism in the global setting.

INDIGENOUS COUNTERPLOTS
TO THE NEW WORLD ORDER

Global integration has disrupted old bases for collective action while creating new
modes of organization. With the loss of stable production sites, the basis for collective
action by an organized working class becomes fragmented, yet new sites for dissent emerge
to contest the consolidation of power in global settings. These movements are more prevalent in the margins of technologically advanced economies or in remote highland or jungle
environments where the threat to subsistence and survival activities has become a central
arena for the development of consciousness and action. The media combined with electronic communication can provide a global arena for protests that might never have been
broadcast a few decades ago. The form of struggle cannot be predicted from existing
models since there is no preexisting class formation or special arena in which it takes place.
During the past decade, the terms of conflict in sub-Saharan Africa (Conable 1990), the *barriadas* of Lima (Barrig 1990; Blondet 1992), Amazonia (Ramos de Castro 1992), Bolivia
(Nash 1992a), the Caribbean (Bolles 1986), and Chiapas (Collier and Quaratiello 1994) are
not so much the struggle against exploitation defined in the workplace as they are the assertion of the right to live in a world with a diminishing subsistence base.

Yet the emergence of new social actors cannot be subsumed in "identity struggles"
without addressing the institutional and economic systems which both define and are
reconstituted by their presence. The emergence of "women" and "ethnic groups" as protagonists of change is due not so much to what were once considered to be "ascribed"
characteristics as to the special responsibilities these groups bear in the new structural
conditions they encounter. Women are central to these conflicts because of their commitment to social reproduction. The difficulty women face in performing "mother work"

clearly affects the political work they do. Nicaraguan women began to oppose Somosa when they could not minimally carry out their responsibilities in the household, and similarly they turned against the Sandinistas when the *contra* war in which they were embroiled exacted too high a toll in the death and maiming of their sons. In El Salvador, the added burden for women, whose family lives were disrupted by the civil war and remain highly problematic in the reconstruction of the 1990s, has promoted political consciousness and activism.[20] Stephen (1997a) shows in her comparative study of women and social movements throughout Latin America the merging of gender and class-based issues in the creation of new forms of political culture.

In the three decades in which the task of contextualizing women as actors has come about, feminist theoreticians have expanded a dialectical approach that encompasses the multiple roles of women in the domains of social and biological reproduction. This promotes our awareness of the socially constituted terms of class and ethnicity, peasant and Indian (N. Harvey 1998:211–212; Kearney 1996). Ethnic revindication movements may be triggered by the invasion of a group's territories and destruction of subsistence resources, but they are also premised on the everyday denial of an ethnic group's sense of dignity (Joseph and Nugent 1994). Policies formulated at a distance, such as the North American Free Trade Agreement (NAFTA), ratified by the Mexican congress as the Tratado de Libre Comercio (TLC) in 1993, or the currency devaluation in Ecuador in January 2000, are now compelling motivations for the rebellion of semi-subsistence cultivators. The entry of *campesinos*, both men and women, Indian and *mestizo*, into political arenas signals the contradictions between a national economy dependent on external stimuli and the needs of the productive workers in fulfilling their life pursuits.

The loci of resistance and protest by those who are threatened by the disordering of their lives in the "New World Order" lies beyond the conventional sites where the relations of production once defined the major conflict. Protests occur in the multiple sites of distress where people experience the crisis or symbolically identify its source. In these sites the rioters have demonstrated their power to threaten or even destabilize governments. When over 10,000 miners, *campesinos*, teachers, and housewives undertook the March for Life in 1986 on the highway between the mining centers and La Paz in Bolivia, it took 8,000 soldiers, three armed tanks, and two airplanes to deter them from bringing their protest to the president (Nash 1992a). In Mexico, *campesinos* protested in front of government offices that had abandoned their support of subsistence producers, such as the National Commission for Popular Consumption (CONASUPO) in the debt crisis of 1988 (Nugent and Alonso 1994), or the National Indian Institute (INI) in Chiapas. The *zocalo*, or central plaza of Mexico City, drew huge demonstrations throughout the debt crisis of the 1980s and the subsequent currency devaluation and flight of capital in 1994. In the spring of 1995, the *zocalo* hosted an almost permanent encampment of civil society protestors against the invasion of the Lacandón rain forest, urging a peaceful negotiation. Massive marches of Ecuadoran Indians threatened to take over the government buildings of the capital city of Quito in January 2000 when the "dolarization" of the economy left them unable to pay for seed and fertilizers with the low return for their products.

These protests have the power to topple governments, as students in Jakarta demonstrated in 1998 with Suharto's government, or derail global trade conferences, as protestors in Seattle did when the World Trade Organization met in November and December 1999. They pose a challenge for analysts to relate the issues raised in "identity politics" to the context in which the new social actors frame their action in the new regime of capital accumulation. The protagonists for change are exerting pressure for governance that exceeds national boundaries in the global arenas they create. Although the incentive for mobilization may arise in global sites of power, it is important to recall, as Kpell Enge and Scott Whiteford (1989:8) insist, that: "It is at the level of individuals, households, and communities that . . . traditions are kept, local organizations forged, class or ethnic consciousness developed, and quiescence or rebellion chosen." Even while communities are being fragmented and identities transformed, it is still the task of anthropology to relate these generative bases to global transformations.

The Chiapas Conflict on the World Stage

In 1988 I returned to Chiapas after two decades of research in other sites that were experiencing global changes, to find a transformed countryside. For the past five decades, indigenous communities of Chiapas had relied on a form of national paternalism directing the flow of limited resources and legitimization of land claims through the *ejido*, or land reform program. Land reform came late or not at all to many highland villages, but the impoverished *ejido* lands that were incorporated in the highland enabled the government to control the Chiapas *campesinos*. They had endured a decade of belt-tightening during which the PRI maintained monolithic control that required increasing use of armed force. It required a definitive break with the co-optive claims exerted through half a century to launch the uprising. This happened during Salinas's term of office, when government outreach programs abandoned the Mayan colonizers who had left their villages to settle in the Lacandón rain forest. As they became active in the opposition organizations that broke away from official confederations, *campesinos* began to identify and oppose the threat of neoliberal reforms. The Zapatista Army for National Liberation (EZLN) was ten years in formation when these base communities in the Lacandón rain forest staged what seemed to be a suicidal uprisings, taking over the town halls of four gateway cities to the rain forest.[21]

Many of the Zapatistas and thousands of their supporters are illiterate. Those who can *deletrar*—read haltingly, letter by letter—are cut off from most media communication (though their supreme command had access to e-mail[22]). They live in villages that lack electricity even while power lines pass over their heads carrying electricity to northern cities and to Central America. Perhaps because of this they are able to experience the injustices of their society more clearly than workers tuned in to CNN channels that promote the illusion of being *au courant* in world affairs. Local class distinctions reflect trends in the growing disparities occurring in national society in the course of Mexico's integration in global markets, as the leadership of the PRI is abandoning the corporatist strategies for maintaining the loyalties of indigenous communities that characterized the revolutionary government for the past seven decades. The break from redistribution programs for development that began during the debt crisis of the 1980s became ever more marked in the 1990s during the Salinas-Zedillo regimes. This break was sealed by NAFTA, which went into effect in 1994.

It is, therefore, not paradoxical that colonizers of the Lacandón rain forest in Chiapas, Mexico, particularly those who arrived after 1970, are setting the pace for forging a new social contract with the state. Their rebellion recasts the nationalist formulation of the rights of liberty, equality, and justice of the Constitution of 1917 in collective goals of those marginalized in the earlier revolution. A Zapatista communiqué sent in the early months of the uprising, attributed to El Viejo Antonio, redefines these words in terms that accord with indigenous reality: justice: "not to punish, but to give back to each what s/he deserves"; liberty: "not that each one does what s/he wants, but to choose whatever road that the mirror[23] wants in order to arrive at the true word"; democracy: "not that all think the same, but that all thoughts or the majority of the thoughts seek and arrive at a good agreement" (cited in Nash 1997b). They want title to the lands they cleared in the Lacandón rain forest, access to education, health programs, and markets for the commercial crops and artisan products that are taken for granted by most Mexican *campesinos*; they also want the right to define their own cultural conditions. The desire for autonomy in both political and cultural terms has grown in importance in the years since the uprising has stalemated negotiations and cut them off from dialogue with the government. Because of conflicting views of what the balance between autonomy and collective aims should be, the tensions are the bases for divisions within the Zapatista movement.

Not all Mayans share this desire for autonomy cast in regional administrative units, nor is it an irreducible norm for political behavior. In some highland Chiapas communities where elite PRI leaders still monopolize traditions, regional autonomy would threaten their control. They continue to exile members of the community who have joined opposition parties or converted to a religion other than the folk Catholicism practiced by the civil-religious after the uprising. The Indians of the Lacandón are themselves divided among those who have lived in the rain forest since the conquest and who are beneficiaries of the bioreserve allocated by the government, those of the Marqués de Comillas where colonization was directed by the official government National Campesino Confederation (CNC), and the settlers of the *cañadas* (canyons) of Ocosingo and Margaritas, all of whom have distinct relations with the central government. Exclusion from the benefits of government funds and programs that were allotted to the bioreserve and the Marqués de Comillas made the colonizers of the *cañadas* feel even more deprived (Leyva Solano and Franco 1996). Even as the indigenous populations of Chiapas are becoming more integrated in the larger economic and political processes of their nation and the world, they experience this entry in ways that threaten the fabric of their lives. Religious and political differences within indigenous towns reflect wealth differences and differential access to power by villagers once united in a common opposition to the *ladino* world from which they were excluded.

The success of the EZLN in drawing support from other indigenous people within the nation and attracting a worldwide support network is now threatened. Internal divisions grow daily as a military force of 70,000 heavily armed soldiers, a third of the Mexican armed forces and numbering one to every family in the Lacandón rain forest, dedicate themselves to disrupting the daily routines of survival. Assassinations of indigenous people by paramilitary forces, some hired by ranchers and large landowners and others organized by PRI opponents of the Zapatistas, have taken the lives of over 1,500 people since the armed uprising of January 1, 1994 (Hernández C. 1998:7). Internecine fights among indigenous groups, some of them armed by the PRI government and trained by federal troops, have terrorized communities of the northeastern region ever since they declared their autonomy on October 12, 1994. These paramilitary groups provoked the massacre of 45 indigenous women, children, and men in Acteal in December 1997, the culmination of months of harassment and which led to the exile of over 16,000 indigenous people from villages in the region. Whether this extraordinary movement will survive internal fissions and government and military attempts to fragment the rebellion is a question in the minds of the many civil and religious NGOs and communities that sustain the EZLN. It is the legacy that they will leave, regardless of their ultimate fate, that is central to this book.

Reflecting on how people in such diverse settings are responding to what many call the global crisis of capitalism raises questions: Why is it that people living in the Lacandón rain forest are more willing to take the risk of promoting fundamental political and economic changes? How are people accommodating to the breakdown in their subsistence security and the ever-lessening return for their production in international exchange circuits? Why are women among the most vociferous in asserting their rights to reproduce their ways of life? What alternatives are available to those who are losing productive roles in the societies in which they are socialized? How are people responding to their conditions of life in collective action? How do the media affect their own perceptions of these conditions, and in what ways do they try to influence the media? What are the forms that society will take in order to accommodate a plurality of distinct cultural visions?

I shall address these questions in terms used by the people who taught me how to phrase them. This requires a rethinking of the paradigms for analyzing class conflict and social movements. Mayan rebels are asserting the viability of collectivist, noncapitalist alternatives in semi-subsistence cultivation coexisting with capitalist exchange. This challenges assumptions about lineal evolution and the single dominant mode of production that were central to both Marxist and liberal economic theory.

The Premises of Indigenous Rebellion

My guiding assumption in assessing indigenous social movements is that the reference points for action in indigenous societies stem from a logic distinct from that governing international capitalism. The central premise is the right of self-determination and moral validation of power. Even as the economic relations integrating core and periphery are merging, the moral premises for political action remain central. James Scott (1976) summed up the ethnographic evidence for this over two decades ago, and ethnographies written before and since affirm the significance of morality in the assessment of their conditions of life by semi-subsistence cultivators with distinct cultural premises. This morality differs from that of a capitalist Protestant ethic in stressing collective, rather than individual, goods.

The moral premises animating the Zapatista uprising are based on Mayan people's reactions to what are taken to be inherent characterizations of globalization. These characteristics, prominent in the literature on globalization, are 1) "deterritorialization," or the pressure to migrate because of land seizure, pollution, or the search for wage work required because of the loss of subsistence resources; 2) fragmentation of social relations, often promoted by divisive state policies or the commoditization of social exchange; and 3) "deculturation," or the loss of the symbolic and material reference points to cultural identity. When politicized sectors of indigenous societies engage in economic struggles such as those of the landless against large landowners and ranchers, or the poor against the rich, or even those with access to water and those who are cut off from this basic resource (Gelles 1998), they often phrase them in terms of the rights to dignity and respect. In the competition between the moral logic of indigenous people and rational logic of free market globalization, indigenous people are the protagonists for change who offer the greatest challenge to the New World Order defined by superpowers. In the process of the struggle, those who are least integrated in the communication and exchange networks of the emerging global market are gaining skills that enable them to pose an alternative to global hierarchies.

My second point, based on my observations of the new generations that have come of age in my field sites in the 1980s and 1990s, is a corollary of the emphasis on human dignity and moral values. This is the appeal to human rights as civil society seeks to clarify those rights and to mobilize in defense of them. As a result, indigenous peoples move into action in ways that are not predictable in a unified political economic theory.[24]

My third point is a corollary of the above considerations: women, as caretakers for the young and old, are central actors in the emergent social movements of indigenous peoples in the hemisphere precisely because of their connectedness to the issues of the survival of past traditions and future generations in their own lives. The concurrent rise of women's stature in global settings with their subordination in patriarchal families and communities has intensified gender conflict. The call for action expressed in the United Nations Convention in Geneva in 1993 and the resolution in 1995 to give further protection and promote the dignity and human rights of women and girls provide the direction for changing gender relations. So long as women lack a voice in public arenas, their particular concerns in survival and care for dependents will be ignored or marginalized. Insofar as violence against women is tolerated and even promoted by the military and judicial arms of the state, human dignity can not be conceived of and transmitted in the socialization of the young. The rhetoric of the organizations of indigenous peoples in international forums was picked up in the Beijing Declaration on the occasion of the 1995 Women's Tribunal.[25]

The Earth is our Mother: From her we get our life, and our ability to live. It is our
responsibility to care for our Mother and in caring for our Mother, we care for ourselves. Women, all females, are manifestations of Mother Earth in human form.

Some postmodern feminists reject such appeals to maternity as a basis for political identity,[26] yet the assembled representatives of indigenous peoples throughout the world
found common cause in such language, justified in terms of the burden women have carried in the family and their self-perception as guardians of the land.

My final consideration on globalization and its impact on social movements is that
indigenous peoples will become the chief protagonists of change in the coming millennium. Not only have their five hundred years of resistance and outright rebellion prepared them to reject the excesses of the dominant world order, but they have the unique
bases for alternative social formations to the New World Order that emerged in the
aftermath of the Cold War. This is linked to their own guardianship of resources in the
regions that they still populate and which are now being invaded. The Inter-Commission
Task Force on Indigenous Peoples makes the case that, since indigenous peoples are
responsible for most of the world's cultural and biological diversity, and since their
knowledge systems embody the principle of sustainability, we must ensure their empowerment (IUCN Inter-Commission Task Force on Indigenous Peoples 1997:21). Participants at the Conference on Environment and Development at Rio de Janeiro in 1992
adopted a comprehensive program for sustainable development with more space for
indigenous management and policy influence. The charter of the Indigenous Tribal Peoples of the Tropical Forests drafted at the conference proclaim that:

> Indigenous communities, peoples, and nations are those which, having a historical
> continuity with pre-invasion and pre-colonial societies that have developed on their
> territories, consider themselves distinct from other sectors of the societies now pre-
> vailing in those territories or parts of them. (IUCN 1997:27)

The executive committee of the IUCN goes on to assert (IUCN 1997:31):

> Indigenous societies possess what can be described as an environmental ethic, not
> abstractly stated in biological terms, but built on specific experiences by a specific
> group of people living in a particular locale with sacred ties with the land.

The question of identity and how this is constructed is at the heart of efforts to
reclaim territories and power over resources. The difference in contemporary indigenous
social movements for reassertion of their land and culture from the resistance and rebellions of the past is that an international community of ecologists and activists support the
efforts in the interest of global survival. The Charter of the Indigenous Tribal Peoples of
the Tropical Forest drawn up at the conference on Environment and Diversity adopted a
comprehensive program for sustainable development with the involvement of indigenous peoples and their communities, and the convention on biological diversity signed

appropriation implies two distinct cultures → not true

by more than 160 heads of states calls for strengthening the rights of indigenous peoples (IUCN 1997:21).

OVERVIEW OF THE BOOK

The field site of Amatenango del Valle in Chiapas, Mexico, where I first began my studies in anthropology provides the umbilicus to my exploration of the world, as it does to Amatenangueros wherever they migrate. The distinct consciousness of Mayans about the cosmos and how they might relate to it provides the touchstone on which I test the premise that indigenous cultures provide alternative approaches to development that may ensure the survival of the human species. Their logic of cooperative effort among members of the same community, and between humans and the cosmological and natural forces, mediated through civil and religious *cargos*, promotes reciprocal exchanges that run counter to private individualistic exploitation of the environment.

This book is about indigenous social movements and their challenge to the course of globalization. My focus on how the Mayans of Chiapas are charting a new course for the coexistence of multiple cultures as they enter into and invigorate civil society is an anthropological view of the process from simultaneously local and transnational perspectives. It is also a book about anthropological representation and how this has changed in my own views over the decades that I have remained in contact with Mayans and in the discipline. In chapter 2, I consider the anthropological study of communities in Chiapas over the past thirty years and try to show how they have absorbed, resisted, and transformed the cultural impositions and loans from the dominant Latino society while retaining their own center. The chapter portrays my impressions of the community when I first began field work in Amatenango del Valle in Chiapas in 1957, seen in the dominant paradigm of the community study viewed almost as a self-reproducing totality. My willingness—indeed eagerness—to become complicit in the Amatenangueros' representation of the harmonious balance in the cosmos equated with a gendered balance in human society was counterpointed with cumulative evidence of conflict and violence that I was recording in my field notes. I contrast the functionalist explanations for this in earlier decades with reflections on the economic, social, and political forces exerted on these communities.

approp.

These forces are highlighted in chapter 3. In the forty years between my first extended stay in the Chiapas community of Amatenango del Valle and my most recent visits, Mayans have increasingly promoted social movements that go beyond municipal boundaries, many of them motivated by the desire to maintain the beliefs and way of life of their ancestors. These include the multifaceted organizations that bring together *comuneros*, residents that hold communal lands, *campesinos,* or rural agricultural smallholders, laborers, and artisans, as well as the specifically indigenous groups that draw special attention to their custodianship of the land and their relations to state institutions. In chapter 3, I draw upon national macroeconomic and social changes to contextualize the changes transforming family and community processes in the 1970s and 1980 that triggered the protest actions and celebrations convoked during the past decade, during which I have traveled to Chiapas each year, residing there from two to three months. These transformations, along with the changing conceptual schema I have used (and sometimes abandoned) for recording them, are discussed.

The development of democracy responding to Mayan traditions that grew out of the uprising and the subsequent formation of autonomous communities in the Chiapas highlands and Lacandón rain forest is analyzed in chapter 4. During the years following the January 1, 1994 uprising, when Zapatistas eagerly responded to the government's promise of a negotiated conclusion, Mayans joined with other indigenous peoples and with foreign delegations in a series of conventions and dialogues. Their deliberations opened up space for women and oppressed ethnic groups throughout the continent as they redefined eighteenth-century ideals of liberty and equality to address collective aspirations for these goals. Zapatistas moved from the symbolic warfare staged in the January 1994 uprising in a series of negotiations that culminated in the February 1996 agreements signed by the high command of the Zapatistas and the government at San Andrés. The failure on the part of Zedillo's government to implement the agreement led to a protracted withdrawal from negotiations, followed by government-instigated massacres in the Zapatista villages that attempted to put into practice the accord on autonomy.

Militarism and the movement for peace in Chiapas will be discussed in chapter 5. The government withdrawal from its agreements of February 1996 and its reinforcement of the military forces in the rain forest have changed the terms of the peace negotiations. Despite the growing awareness of the high costs and low returns of military action in the neighboring country of Guatemala, Mexico's recourse to low-intensity warfare now finds a new justification in the 1990s post–Cold War climate with the expansion of narcotraffic police squads and "antiterrorist" attacks on all forms of popular protest. Counterinsurgency warfare waged against the entire indigenous population obliterates the boundary between civilian and military and unmasks the violence of armed men against women and children. The gender dynamic stressed throughout the book will be of special importance in this chapter viewing women as protagonists of change. As women join the Zapatista ranks, their presence challenges the military construction of masculine identity. The presence of transnational NGOs concerned with violations of human rights by both military and paramilitary forces will be juxtaposed with the struggle for land and the reassertion of economic and political autonomy that bring Zapatistas back into the center of Mexican politics. This redemptionist movement, calling for many of the same rights embodied in the 1917 Constitution, has a strangely archaic ring as neo-Zapatistas, now wearing ski masks, challenge the legitimacy of the PRI government that denied them their rights in the name of the institutionalized revolution.

The convergence of indigenous advocates with international human rights advocates throughout the Americas is gaining momentum as the protagonists open the space for dialogue on alternative development in the "new world disorder." This will be the focus of the final chapter 6, where I address the Mayans' struggle for autonomy in a pluricultural political environment. I engage postmodernist strategies for analyzing global society, including discourse analysis, identity formation, and the spatial geography of globalization. I then attempt to develop an approach that grounds these approaches in space and anchors them in structural conditions in a reconceptualization of holistic inquiry. The internationalization of indigenous political movements combined with the convergence of indigenous women's political participation is revolutionizing the way global trends are being defined and resisted. Mayans of Chiapas have not yet reached the stage of pan-Mayan programs across the border in Guatemala (Warren 1998), but they are beginning to forge links with NGOs that will be central to my argument about their place in a transnational civil society that they are helping to create.

This book is both a case study of the response of a distinctive ethnic group to the processes of globalization, and a view en route of the anthropological approaches for appraising those processes. Since I was involved in many phases of that process both as ethnographer and participant observer, it is an apology as well as a critique. It has put me in awe of the remarkable survival value of the Mayans I have met en route and caused me to despair of ever capturing in words their remarkable culture.

CHAPTER 2

INDIGENOUS COMMUNITIES:
Uneasy Alliances with Empire and Nation

THE MAYAN VISION of their universe once embraced the world. The Spanish conquest shrank that world vision to the boundaries of communities. The Mayans are now engaged in a quest to ensure their own terms for engagement in the global nexus. We can think of that nexus as the habitus of Mayan culture. This has been reconfigured over time in geopolitical units that have reflected the changing relations of power from the zenith of Mesoamerican civilization to its submergence in the Spanish Empire, and currently within the Mexican nation. During the five hundred years of conquest, colonization, and independence, the survival of distinctive Mayan characteristics seemed to require the defensive boundaries of "closed corporate communities." Now that the exaggerated sense of isolation, homogeneity, and egalitarianism that seemed to ensure the cultural integrity and autonomy of indigenous communities is fractured, Mayans are undertaking another quest to realize their destiny. Will the utopian harmony that perpetuated their cultural distinction be abandoned? Now that indigenous people compete with global enterprises for the forest, oil and hydraulic energy sources, and the biodiversity once in their custodianship, in what new geopolitical spaces will indigenous peoples revitalize their culture? Will they be able to promote a resource base that can respond to a grow-ing population? In a global world, where disjunctures in financial, technological, ethnic, and media flows exacerbate the burdens involved in cultural reproduction, the answer seems to be negative. Yet in these disjunctures cultural forms that lay dormant in colonial and dependent societies are regenerating. *Bourdieu's habitus*

In this chapter I shall consider the community as a habitus in which Mayans cultivate practices and beliefs that reproduce their cultures. I will then consider the critique of community studies for their lack of historical depth and political-economic context.

Rethinking communities as an ongoing process of adaptation and resistance to colo-nial and national policies permits us to reevaluate some of the contributions of these studies. Comparing the continuities and disjunctures of what were treated as distinct social formations in the widening circuits in which all social relations are located then allows us to assess the transformations within and beyond Chiapas Mayan communities. This is of strategic importance in assessing the potential for autonomy that has become the central demand of indigenous peoples.

habitus — cornerstone of analysis

HARMONY AND CONFLICT
IN THE INDIGENOUS HABITUS

habitus

Habitus is the closest approximation in contemporary anthropology to what was called holistic inquiry. In his extended dialogue with Loïc Wacquant, Pierre Bourdieu (1992:126–127) opened up the concept of habitus to examine the systems of preception resulting from the institution of the social in the body. He posed this as "the space through which we learn who or what we are in society" (1977:163). David Harvey expanded its meaning as the site for relating "generative principles of regulated improvisations" to practices that "reproduce the objective conditions which produced the generative principles of habitus in the first place" (Harvey 1989:219–221). The meanings attributed to habitus are sufficiently flexible to allow me to appropriate the concept to examine cultural reproduction among Mayans in Chiapas.

cult. reproduction

When I was beginning to undertake my field study in Amatenango del Valle, the habitus in which indigenous peoples of Chiapas learn to be who they are and to reproduce their culture and society was concentrated within the territorially based community and projected into a cosmo-vision that includes the moon and the sun in their diurnal cycle through the underworld and the overworld. It was not always that way, as preconquest archeological records attest and the historical record affirm. But what the early ethnographies reveal is a conscious containment of the habitus within community boundaries. Reinforced by endogamy and culturally distinguishing marks in dress and dialect, this habitus provided coherence over time to the culturally distinctive ways of incorporating Spanish colonial beliefs and practices, along with *mestizo* interventions during the Porfiriato (1871–1910), in indigenous society. Production and reproduction are unified in a cosmic whole that relies on a balance between forces of the upper and lower worlds, of gender and their cosmic counterparts. Within this habitus, the ideal of harmony, which Laura Nader (1990) proposed as an ideological defense of the separate existence of indigenous people, exists as a never completely realized ideal. It coexists with conflictive relations, some of which are channeled in prestige hierarchies, while others find expression in envy and witchcraft.

cosmic aspect

warren

Indigenous communities constructed the ideology of harmony within their borders both as a shield to defend themselves against a hostile world and as a mask for internal dissension that was not channeled in the institutions developed during the colonial and independence period.[1] Conflict itself was contained in the logic of witchcraft and envy. The degree to which behavior conformed to the ideal differed among Mayan communities of highland Chiapas in ways that were not consistently correlated with Tzeltal compared with Tzotzil speakers, and that varied in the degree to which Spanish traditions figured. These distinctions among communities allow us to put together the changing kaleidoscope of cultural practices as they reflect larger processes.

Being There

Community studies were our main entry into the interior lives of the people we studied. The sheer accident of being there when the people had tired of acting out a role led to major insights in the course of fieldwork. It is this emic, or insider's, sense of community that we learn from participating in the daily life of the people. It is the "there" expressed in the existential state of "being there" that gave authority to our work. The mere fact of our trying to survive living in their midst seemed to overcome some of their worst fears of us as aliens. Of course, we were being observed by dozens of children who gathered nightly to watch us in the glass-front bathhouse where I lived with my family while we waited for our wattle-and-daub thatched house to be finished. The householders also became accustomed to our presence as we walked around town, greeting people with our limited Tzeltal phrases. Even the dogs stopped barking when we arrived at the patios of our friends.

Our greatest asset, as we learned later, was that we were not offering them anything to improve their lives or even asking any questions other than the most mundane issues related to our survival: Who has some eggs to sell? Who butchered a pig or calf this week? After a month of our living in the town, the mayor arrived with the local *síndico*, or constable, and two auxiliaries, offering a drink of the homemade cane liquor. After the first two rounds of drinks, we asked what had occasioned their visit, and the president replied, "We voted to allow you to stay in town." After another round we ventured further, asking, "Why?" and they said, "You never claimed you were going to civilize us." We learned that two previous anthropologists who worked with the National Indian Institute (INI) had been expelled only a year before. Shortly afterward, I was quite flattered when a neighbor offered to sell me a small parcel of his land that bordered the Pan American highway. I learned later that people shunned such land because they believed only evil spirits walked on the highway and they were afraid to live or work near it after some who had dared walk on it had been killed by trucks.

Living in any of these communities prior to the mid-1960s, it was easy to fall into the indigenous people's sense that it was a bounded universe and that the town center was the center of the world. In most highland Chiapas Mayan communities, the metaphor of umbilicus applied to the town center embodies the connection of the people to the world. For indigenous people, the town is the site where their placenta is buried when they are born, and the place to which they hope to return when they are sick or die. This centering was tangible when I lived in Amatenango in 1957 and 1958. There were no telephones, buses, or newspapers to distract people with an imagined nation or world beyond that. Except for the church clock, which was not always kept wound, my watch was the only timepiece; the church caretaker would consult with me on high fiestas so that he could strike the bells precisely at twelve o'clock. Since the argument people advanced if questioned why they believed that Amatenango was the center of the world was that the sun was directly overhead, I felt a special responsibility to maintain my watch in good running order.

Indigenous local traffic by foot and horseback was continuous among communities and to the departmental center of San Cristóbal de Las Casas, but the abysmal road conditions discouraged wheeled transportation. Although the muddy track that skirted the town was part of the Pan American highway, only those vehicles with four-wheel traction attempted to get through in the rainy season, and only the priest and a few government agents came even during the dry months from November to April. The forestry agent was the most persistent. Because of the hundreds of rules concerning the cutting of trees, he would hang out in the empty plaza that marked the town center, waiting for a violator to show up using one of the prohibited wheeled carts that youths in pottery-making households used to bring wood from the hills. Called "El Señor Milagro," because, the town officials explained to me, he always asked for his "*mil pesos*" (thousand pesos), he was a target of verbal abuse and jokes in Tzeltal.

The moral community also seemed to end at the exits of the town center. These were marked by large crosses which were decorated with palm fronds and garlands of flowers during the May 3rd Day of the Cross ceremony. Marriages were endogamous, and the "true people" (*batz'il winiketik*) were those who spoke Tzeltal and who undertook offices in the traditional civil religious hierarchy. Even homicide seemed to be internecine; during an extended witch-hunt that I lived through during the 1960s, I asked my research assistant, a man who served as president at the time of my arrival in 1957, why he always assumed that the killer was a member of the community, and he replied, "Who else would bother to kill us?"

I was impressed in my first six-month stay in Amatenango del Valle with the sense people conveyed that the meaningful world was indeed contained within the village boundaries. The *cabecera*—literally, "head" site, or town center—served much like the county seat in New England as the locus of administrative offices, the church, school, and jail. Families that lived in the town center tended to dominate the civil-religious cargo system and important municipal posts such as the Land Grant Commission (Comisión Ejidal) that determined the distribution of communally controlled land. Residents of the town center treated those who lived in scattered hamlets as "*kurik,*" or "country hicks."

The town center was constituted of two moieties, with each half divided by the central plaza. Marriages were endogamous within moieties[2] and outlying hamlets. Transgressions led to threats of death and an occasional killing by youths who objected to the competition of interlopers from the other side.[3] Social control was still exerted by the curing-divining hierarchy on each side of the moiety. The *bankil u'ul*, or elder seer, in each curing-divining hierarchy used his power over illness both as a sanction against wrongdoing and as promotion for well-being and harmony. When I first arrived in the town in 1997, the elder curer of each side was a representative in the *ejido* commission.

I think what we managed to do well, in simply "being there," trying to survive in the ethnographic present without reflexive snares or disquieting histories, was to capture the informants' sense of who they were and what they were about. This was the culture core that our immediate predecessors, Ruth Benedict, Robert Redfield, and Clyde Kluckhohn defined as worldview, or ethos. In Amatenango, the core of the harmony construct consisted in the customs and practices that maintained intact "the traditions of our ancestors," *hme'tik-tatik,* or our mothers-fathers in Tzeltal. These are invoked in the prayers, called *pat'otan,* or behind the heart,[4] at fiestas in honor of the saints, inauguration of the civil religious official, and during curing ceremonies. In these prayers, the curer-diviners, called *u'uletik,* or seers, and those who learn the prayers in order to serve in the civil religious hierarchy for a year at a time, invoke the dimensions of their habitus. I will cite an oration of the oldest and most honored of the curers in Amatenango in 1964:

Sacred earth, sacred world
Thirteen holy worlds, holy flowers
In the center of another holy world
See the mother, its clay
I am a child of its clay
Holy heaven Jesus Christ
Holy herbs give the spirit
The companions of the patient are gathered here with his father
In the center of this other holy earth
Holy earth, take out the fever.

The reference to clay relates to the creation myth in which the ancestors created "the true people" (*batz'il winiketik*) from clay.[5] Following this prayer to the world, the curer invoked the major saints of the pueblo, then those of the neighboring towns and villages.

The invocation of the spiritual world extends far beyond what is assumed to be the limits of the closed corporate community. Amatenangueros considered themselves to be in the center of this thirteen-tiered world that has a heavenly as well as a subterranean dimension. This was the world that was protected by the seer's command of the prayers that they taught to the officials as they were inaugurated into the civil-religious hierarchy. The curer, whose prayer to the earth I have cited, admitted that he did not know how to speak to the earth as well as the curers in Chamula, but he clearly felt that he was in communication with the spirits invoked. People were in awe of him and of his counterpart on the other side of the moiety division, the man who later became my landlord. Both curers died in the 1980s of liver disease caused, undoubtedly, by the enormous quantities of locally brewed liquor that they were forced to drink in their professional careers. Liquor, referred to as "*sakil ha,*" cold water, or as "the washings of the arms and legs of our holy lord Jesus Christ," was believed to have a powerful sacred quality that enabled those who drank it to communicate with the earth.[6]

All members of the community were committed to maintaining the spiritual dimensions of the community through an active ceremonial life that was the measure of time and space. The annual cycle of fiestas set the calendar for all other activities, including cultivation, planting, and harvesting of the land. Sickness was a sign of the breakdown in this spiritual unity, and discord, even without physical signs of illness, was treated as sickness with a curing ceremony to heal the rupture. Preserving the harmony of the community internally and in its relations with the world was everybody's responsibility. Drought, heavy rains, hail or wind, the physical distress of the sun and the moon as revealed in eclipses, human illness—all indicated a breakdown in the cosmic balance that had to be repaired with communal festivities. Extended droughts were a sign that Our Father Sun—*Htatik K'ak'al*—was angered by human misdeeds. I learned this when a man who was a youth during revolutionary times cited as the reason for the extended drought the fact that soldiers seized women and raped them in the milpa in the daylight. The Sun, like the Moon, expressed emotions of jealousy and anger, like human beings. They could be mollified by festivals, and it was the duty of all members to keep them happy.

The stories of the brothers referred to as the Shuntonetik, or members of the local lineage of Shuntón, were the parables illustrating appropriate or unacceptable behavior in learning how we can live in the world. As emissaries of Our Mothers and Fathers in periodic visits to the distant city of Antigua, the capital of the Province of Guatemala to which Chiapas belonged prior to independence, the Shuntonetik endured many tests of their valor and wit. Jailed by the denizens of this threatening world, they outwitted their captors only to return and find the officials of the welcoming committee sleeping at their outpost near Comitán. The brothers turned the waiting officials into stone, which can still be see in a hamlet of Comitán. I learned years later when I read the *Popol Vuh* that the tales paralleled the adventures of the twin brothers.

This harmonious world was actively invoked in the festivals for the saints and for the world when I lived in Amatenango in the late 1950s and 1960s. May 3rd, the Day of the Cross in the Catholic calendar, was the day when the chief curers led the procession, accompanied by the four *alféreces*, or captains of the fiestas, to the hill overlooking the town center. Circling the four major entries to the town center where crosses were implanted, the *alféreces* added palm leaves and flowers while speaking to the world. They rose in a procession with hundreds of the villagers up the narrow path to the promontory capped with an arch of leaves and flowers over a huge cross. There the curers invoked the world spirits, then descended into the nearby cave to speak with the ancestors. Similarly,

Alféreces light candles at the entry to the Cave of the Me'tiktatik in Amatenango, 1991.

[handwritten marginalia: can we be there & pay attention to state/local power relations? →]

the curers and assembled members of the family of a patient invoked the spirit curing ceremonies orchestrated to keep evil and discord at bay. A path made of pine needles led from the hole at the center of the house where offerings were made to the house spirit before an arch of flowers and leaves of curative plants, where four candles were lit to guide the spirit of the patient back into the body.

I was happy totally preoccupying myself with decoding this core of beliefs and behaviors from the repetitions and paralleling of imagery that pervaded these rituals. I was impressed by the ability of the Amatenangueros not only to transmit and implant the behaviors and beliefs expected of the true people, but also to overcome the alienation one might have expected in such an impoverished environment. Drinking the home-brewed *aguardiente*, or liquor distilled from cane sugar, which was incumbent upon all participants in ceremonies, enabled them to communicate with the ancestors and us (the anthropologists) to communicate with them. *[handwritten: Being there blinded her]*

The overpowering experience of being there, relatively cut off from my world as their world appeared to be, made it difficult to assess the power relations between indigenous entities and the state. Yet, as soon as I tried fixing the community in time and place, the apparent integrity of the world the Amatenangueros constructed in their prayers and celebrations collapsed. Their life as impoverished cultivators and artisans, superexploited in the markets where they sold their goods and labor, emerged. So long as I stayed in the community, feeling relatively safe in the wattle-and-daub house in the compound of the powerful curer who was my landlord, I could appreciate the power of their curer diviners, fear those who defied this power, and revel in their celebrations of life.

I shall review some of these earlier preoccupations with the need for historical depth and class analysis. I shall then return to the problem of habitus and field in the regeneration of indigenous Mayan culture, applying what we have learned about the need for historical depth and the wider economic and political context.

THE COMMUNITY AS SUBJECT AND OBJECT OF ANTHROPOLOGY

It seemed reasonable for those of us who were students of Sol Tax's "Man in Nature" National Science Foundation project to contain our efforts to a community. Each of us was located at a different altitudinal level in the Tzeltal-speaking region to consider specific ecological adaptations. We had been trained in the ecological approach of Chicago University community studies with Louis Wirth and Robert Redfield as mentors. Communities as an object of study in Mesoamerica began with Robert Redfield's study of Tepoztlán, carried out in the late 1920s (Redfield 1930) and later developed with the folk-urban continuum in the Yucatan (Redfield 1941). Community studies were further validated by Sol Tax, who defined them as the ethnographic unit corresponding to Mesoamerican identity as subjects. The Spanish *municipio*, equivalent to a New England county, which I will refer to as municipality, included within its boundaries one or more hamlets called in Kaqchikel *chinamit* (Tax 1937) and in Tzeltal *teklum*. The town center, called *cabecera*, designated the territorially based center of community life where public buildings were concentrated, and of the surrounding hamlets, some of which had chapels. Until Tax undertook the first community study in Panajachel, in the Department of Sololá in Guatemala, ethnographers studied "tribal" units based on language dialects. As Tax pointed out, these linguistic units were no longer identified with political or administrative entities at the time of his field surveys in the 1930s.

Eric Wolf's ethnohistorical analysis (1957) of the origins of corporate communities added another dimension to the redefinition of such groups within Spanish colonial society. He demonstrated that the corporate community was a construct of the Spanish crown in its attempt to wrest control of the colony from the hands of the conquerors who, as *encomenderos,* held tribute rights to the labor of Indians. It was also a means of intervening in the power of the Church over communities. Communal lands granted by the crown to each municipality provided a minimal subsistence basis that substantiated the fictions of economic and political autonomy.

George Foster (1965) called the perspective based on the bounded horizons of peasants "the notion of the limited good." The limited corporate landholdings were one of these bonds that both held members of the community together yet inspired envy of anyone who exceeded communal norms in their harvests or any other pursuit. Foster proposed that this "zero-sum game," in which any player's gain was at the expense of other players, provoked breaches in the communal ideal of harmony. His analysis threatened the notion of internal harmony inspired by images of Robert Redfield's (1941) folk community in which conflict was treated as extraneous, and critics still fault him for what they consider his negative caricature of peasants. His depiction of the peasants was not at fault so much as his failure to attribute the narrowing of their vision to the structural limitations in the rural economy. Locked in the diminishing returns to the peasant economy, small-plot cultivators and agricultural laborers turned against neighbors and kin who had marginal success, blaming them for their impoverishment. The PRI hegemony was predicated on the ability of its leaders to turn the logic of this involuted rebellion against fellow sufferers.

The Closed Community and Its Critics

From the very beginning of their publication, community studies were criticized, at first for the ideal type models that flowed from them (Lewis 1963; Tax 1941) and then for functionalist assumptions promoting the status quo (*cf.* bibliography on *indigenismo* in Hewitt de Alcántara 1984). In the debate over the primordial basis for cultural continuity within communities (Vogt 1976b; Gossen 1986) and that stressing domination from above (González Casanova 1970; Harris 1964), structuralists attacked the functionalism of those emphasizing the rational basis for distinctive indigenous characteristics (Stavenhagen 1965; Wasserstrom 1983a), while their opponents challenged economic determinists for failing to recognize the preconquest ideological constructs manifested across wide regions (Gossen 1986; Vogt 1976a, 1976b). Critics maintained that the "closed corporate community" was not closed (Wasserstrom 1983a), that it was not homogeneous (Lewis 1963), and that it never even functioned as a self-sustaining small society (Hewitt de Alcántara 1984). A close reading of Eric Wolf (1957) shows that he was very much aware of the fact that the "closed" community was, in fact, constructed by dominant c interests to respond to their needs. Even a cursory reading of Redfield (1941) sho awareness of the movement from ethnic cohesiveness in the newly incorporated town of Chan Kom to the class relations prevalent in Dzitas and Mérida in the Yucatan peninsular. Given the paucity of historical data in his day, it was no wonder that he took the *cofradias,* or religious brotherhoods, of Tusik in Quintano Roo to be what they purported to be, not a rebellion against the state.

But the tendency on the part of critics of community studies to see them as organized uniquely in the interest of domination from the outside, or as a form of the class struggle, is also reductionist. With his focus on external domination in markets and plantations controlled by *ladinos,* Wasserstrom (1983a) failed to take into account the structures of inequality and the subordination of women in patriarchal indigenous communities that were certainly influenced, if not institutionalized, by the Spanish conquerors. It also overlooks or trivializes the insider's view of community which enabled us to find evidence for the deep-rooted continuity of preconquest Mayan culture in communities dominated by empire and state (Carlsen 1997; Gossen 1974; Nash 1970; Warren 1989; Watanabe 1992).[7]

Current debates on ethnicity criticize the community study approach for its failure to take into account the combined force of antagonistic but interpenetrating relationships between *indígenas* and *ladinos* in a wider field of social relations that generate and sustain ethnic diversity. While this conjuncture of forces has provided a basis for subordinate groups to mobilize claims on the state for resources (Ehrenreich 1989; Hill 1989; Selverston 1992), and to resist exploitation and repression (Nagengast and Kearney 1990; C. Smith 1984), it has also reinforced relations of subordination and domination (Díaz-Polanco 1992). By evoking the dialogue between ancient and present traditions (Gossen and Leventhal 1989), and at the same time addressing the economic opportunities that condition their survival (Cancian 1992; Collier 1990; Nash 1993, 1994b), we can assess both the motivation and the potential for maintaining distinct cultures. For those indigenous populations that are facing ethnocidal threats in the current advance of capitalist enterprises, ethnicity becomes an instrumental factor in achieving political solidarity. Instead of viewing ethnic mobilization as an obstacle to progress, left-wing intellectuals and organizations are beginning to accept indigenous organizers as allies against the state monopoly of power (Bartolomé 1995:370). The willingness of indigenous people to sacrifice life and fortune to remain culturally distinct, as revealed in their "narrative strategies for resisting terror" (Warren 1993), is a testimony to their commitment to overcoming the structures of subordination without losing their identity. Our theoretical premises must recognize both the structural imperatives of colonial and postcolonial systems in which indigenous peoples were encapsulated and the indigenous search for a cultural base from which to defend themselves and generate collective action. That dynamic persists even now, when the old structures are waning.[8]

The critique of community studies is justified in pointing to the failure of those ethnologists who did not look beyond the community boundaries to analyze the source of many problems that were seen as local aberrations. It also discloses the functionalist formulations supportive of the status quo that were implicit in analyses framed in terms of community studies. But the critique often failed to assess how community studies captured the informants' construction of harmony that served as armor against external power, and how this defense affected their behavior. Critics even blamed the anthropologists for creating community as though they were in partnership with the powers that would limit and fragment indigenous rebellion.

In Defense of Community Studies

A blanket condemnation of these studies as "functionalist" and serving the status quo meant that macrotheorists often ignored the ethnographic diversity that underlay what was glossed as "indigenous pueblos." This left the critics free to derive their propositions from deductive universal principles about the class struggle or the world system. Others chose to take one community study as exemplary of the region, as they generalized beyond community boundaries in ways that ignored the mosaic of distinct cultural, ecological, and historical conditions that had a differential impact on each of the community settings. Having denied the significance of the community as a locus of identity, some anthropologists deny even the fiction of community autonomy that inspired indigenous communities to confront a hostile *ladino* world with a front of unity, homogeneity, and common interests. This harmonious front enabled indigenous peoples to retain a fount of local customs and traditions in their own language with which to defend themselves from the dominant society and other competing indigenous communities (*cf.* Nader 1990). Yet it is precisely this harmonious front, the product of laborious self-sacrifice on the part of impoverished indigenous communities who expend their surpluses to create a sense of plentitude in sumptuous banquets and flowing liquor on fiesta days, that is now being attacked in the current critique.[9]

The richness of those ethnographies remained almost unmined until recent reevaluations.[10] Contemporary ethnologists are going back to these studies in order to explore the origins of distinct symbols that are reenacted in contemporary rituals (Bricker 1981; Hunt 1977), to trace continuity in cultural patterns from the preconquest (Gossen 1986), and to assess the local impact of regional and national processes (Collier and Quaratiello 1994; Nash 1994c, 1994d, 1995a; J. Rus 1994). We can also surmise from contemporary ethnographic studies the cost of this unequal engagement between indigenous and *ladino* societies within and outside of their communities. Once ethnologists penetrated the fiction of harmony that indigenous people presented to the outside world, they could assess the penalties of internecine witch-hunts (Nash 1967), abusive familial relations (Rosenbaum 1993), alcoholism (Eber 1995; Sivert 1973), and wealth differences (Collier 1990) that were often addressed with expulsions of compatriots charged with violating custom (Gomez Cruz and Kovic 1995; Kovic 1997; Sullivan 1995; Tickell 1991).

As indigenous people attempt to define the ethnic basis for autonomy at a regional level, they are establishing the authenticity of their claims by reference to the collective basis in communities with a majority of people speaking an indigenous language and sharing collective traditions. Community studies will attain a new significance as evidential support for their claims to distinctive ethnic identity. With cumulative knowledge of the broader landscape in which the communities are located, anthropologists can take advantage of the ethnographies to situate the separate histories of each locality in the global context of change that is engulfing the region. Just as historians have learned to treat community studies with the respect that they accord to slave narratives, prison memoirs, and other texts of the same genre (*cf.* Stern 1995; Mallon 1994), so too can anthropologists learn to draw understandings from community studies, rather than treating them as competing models of the reality they try to confront.[11]

"Being there" is no longer validation in itself for producing ethnographic descriptions. In the following section I shall explore what we have learned about Mayan culture and community over time with a historically situated, place-centered focus. I shall conclude the chapter with an analysis of what we can learn from these community studies that may contribute to the new challenges Mayans face as they attempt to gain cultural autonomy.

TRANSFORMATIONS IN MAYAN CULTURE AND COMMUNITY

The indigenous community is a construct of historically grounded processes that has served to define the national Mexican identity. The major changes are: 1) from preconquest empires and subject indigenous states to Indian Republics (*Repúblicas de Indios*) in the early decades of colonization; 2) from Indian Republics to Indian pueblos (*pueblos indios*), subject to and dependent on initiatives stemming from colonial and postindependence centralized power within the three centuries of colonial rule; and 3) from Indian pueblos to what Jan Rus (1994) calls institutional revolutionary communities (*comunidades revolucionarias institucional*), after the 1910–1917 Revolution. The current period of transition is from institutional revolutionary communities to autonomous pueblos and regions (*pueblos y regiones autónomas*).

These transitions, briefly sketched below, indicate the progressive fractionating of regional indigenous society with the conquest and the eventual dismembering of the Indian structures in the postindependence liberal regime. The 1910 Revolution rescued the Indian pueblos from near annihilation, reconstituting them as institutional revolutionary communities. These historical transformations are reflected in changing anthropological models discussed in this chapter. Autonomous pueblos and regions will be discussed in chapter 5.

From Preconquest Empires to Indian Republics

The archeological record shows that Chiapas is a mosaic of linguistic, cultural and ethnic groups that began migration into the area thousands of years ago (Lee-Whiting 1994). In the Late Archaic period (4650–2150 B.C.), a sedentary agricultural group of Mixe-Xoque that John Clark and Michael Blake (1993:39) call Mokayo, or "People of Corn," developed a ranked society with nucleated centers of 400 to 1200 inhabitants led by *caciques*, or native leaders who competed for leadership over surrounding hamlets.

Even before the Olmecs entered the area around 1650 B.C., coastal communities were integrated in wide regional political and economic relations, as shown in the ritual exchange of obsidian and pottery (Clark and Blake 1993:30–33). Clark and Blake hypothesize that the Olmecs, who had their roots in Maya, Oto-Mangue, and Mixe-Zoque linguistic groups, were not so much the great mother culture but the first great *mestiza* culture of Middle America, whose genius consisted in incorporating the various traditions of its multiple roots around 1300 B.C. In the process of "Olmecization," Mokayo villages were integrated in larger political circuits, linked by a political-religious ideology (Clark and Blake 1993:43), fragments of which are still discernible in contemporary villages (Gossen 1986).

Archeologists and ethnohistorians amply demonstrate this art of incorporating new populations and cultural traits in an expanding network of ceremonial centers, with peripheral settlements organically linked through the exchange of special products, during the 3,000 years of Olmec and then Mayan expansion in the Chiapas area. Successive waves of Teotihuanecos, Chiapanecos, and Toltecas exchanged their Gods and products in territories where Mayan hegemonic control operated until the Late Classic period (Lee-Whiting 1994).[12] The integrative reformulation of these pluricultural societies is a process distinct from that of empires in the Old World, where dominance and suppression of local cultures marked the advanced state of formation.

The regional links through state and religious institutions persisted until the Late Classic period in Mesoamerica, around A.D. 800. Civil and commercial contacts became more important as political control was limited to smaller areas during the post-Classic period. In highland Chiapas and Guatemala, it was a period of warfare and social upheaval, with most cities located in defensible positions on hills overlooking arable lands (Adams 1961:347). At the time of conquest, Chiapas was divided into warring principalities (Calnek 1962). Although Chiapas was remote from the powerful core states of Mesoamerica, the population was part of what Blanton and Feinman (1984:678) call a Mesoamerican world system arena that influenced production strategies and incorporated local groups.[13]

The Toltec arrival in the eleventh century brought Nahuatl place names and changing symbols observed in ceremonial sites. People of Amatenango del Valle still refer to their town as Tzo'ontahal, although the Nahuatl suffix, "tenango," meaning "place of," indicates its Toltec origins. The area in which the municipality is located was occupied for at least a thousand years, with preconquest towns occupying the headlands, possibly as a defensive position in an area marginal to the classic Mayan settlements to the north and west (Adams 1961:341). Tzeltal speakers occupy a band of land juxtaposed with Tzotzil speakers to the West, Tojolabal speakers to the East, and Chol speakers to the North.

The integrative process of preconquest states was broken by the Spanish invasion into southern New Spain in 1528. In the transition to colonization under Spanish rule, the conquerors allied themselves with preconquest states that they referred to as Indian Republics. These republics often encompassed large territories made up of many communities sharing the same language, traditions, and governance. The nobility provided continuity in facilitating the transfer of power to the Spanish Crown and Church over tribute-paying Indian Republics. The Spanish conquerors as *encomenderos*, conquerors who received the right to exact labor tribute for which they were charged with maintaining the spiritual welfare of the Indians, used the same tribute lists as their predecessors, often engaging members of the indigenous nobility to rule indirectly Gibson (1964:27).

The significance of the Indian Republics varied regionally: whereas segregation of the republics of Indians from the *hacienda*, or landed estate, as the seat of Spanish presence, facilitated a castelike relation between the conquerors and Indians in Morelos (Lomnitz-Adler 1992:20), it was instrumental in Fray Bartolomé de Las Casas's efforts to preserve the Indians from the encroachment by Spaniards in the San Cristóbal diocese (Wasserstrom 1983a:12). His missionary priests defended the communities of the Indian Republics with the New Laws that Fray Bartolomé had drafted, even taking away the tribute rights of *encomenderos* accused of enslaving Indians. When a new bishop replaced Las Casas, the settlers set out to destroy Indian culture. They attempted this by interfering with indigenous marriage patterns, which were the principal means of establishing alliances in the region (Wasserstrom 1983a:19).

By the third quarter of the sixteenth century, the Spanish Crown, intent on regaining control over its colonies, abolished tribute rights and limited regional ties of indigenous populations beyond the level of pueblos (Cabrera Vargas 1995:35). The term "pueblo" still conveyed an entity equated with people that went beyond the boundaries of a restricted community. In the bipolar construction of the colonial state that emerged at the end of the sixteenth century, a dominant class of colonizers and deculturated Indians and *mestizos*, or *ladinos,* succeeded in fragmenting preconquest pluriethnic regions that had maintained extensive religious, commercial, and political interrelationships among Mayans and their predecessors for over two millennia.

From Indian Republics to Indian Pueblos

These changes in the regional relationships among pluriethnic groups occurred along with the decline of Indian Republics and the containment of Indian pueblos. Even those territories in the central plateau that had made alliances with the Spaniards in their conquest of the Aztecs were relegated to tribute-paying *barrios,* town districts that were sometimes called by the Aztec term, *tlaxilacalli.* The indigenous populations often fled to refuge zones when their *caciques* were treated as slaves (Cabrera Vargas, quoting Diego Ramirez, letter of November 1535:14, 1995:34). Those that remained within Spanish dominion were brought together through the *concentración*, or drawing together of distinct populations into pueblos that included diverse Indian cultures. The distinct groups often retained their separateness in *barrios*, each with their own church and community representatives.[14]

Within a generation, Indian Republics, with sovereignty over their resources and populations, were converted into Indian pueblos, with limited power to control water, woods, and lands within their boundaries. The corporate landholding communities served in this transition. These were created sometimes on the basis of existing populations and sometimes in the concentration of diverse populations through the *reducción*, or reduction, of populations into a concentrated area. Eric Wolf (1957) recognized the dual significance of the corporate community: as a creation of the Spanish Crown, it allowed the Crown to wrest control from the hands of the *encomenderos*, but by allocating communal lands to provide a subsistence basis for Indians, the corporate community enabled indigenous peoples to survive but not to escape extreme exploitation in forced labor for the colonizers. By putting local authorities in charge of the distribution of the land, the Crown effectively concentrated power within communities and dissociated them from regional alliances. While the fictive cultural autonomy within Indian pueblos masked an exploitative relationship that tapped the communities for labor power and products in an unequal exchange that benefited the state and *ladino*-dominated towns, it nonetheless allowed Indians to exercise distinctive cultural practices within their communities (MacLeod 1973; E.Wolf 1957). This dual dynamic of capitulation and resistance was played out in work sites and in religious congregations.

Internal divisions within communities often provided the fissures along which the dialectic of aggression was played out. This was the case in the Tzeltal-speaking municipality of Amatenango, where the moiety division divided the town center into *calpules*, the Nahuatl term for a kinship-based territorial unit. Unlike many of the indigenous towns, Indians predominated in the head town, with *mestizos* in the *barrios* or *parajes*. It was also true of the neighboring town of Aguacatenango, which did not have independent status as a municipality but remained a dependent *agencia* of Venustiano Carranza (Hunt and Nash 1967:264). Despite its proximity to San Cristóbal, Chamula was able to retain an exclusively indigenous population in the center, in part because of the fear instilled in *ladinos* during the War of the Castes in 1867–1869 that was kept alive in their festivals. This pattern contrasts with many of the highland communities, where the centers, until recently, were dominated by *ladinos*. The pattern of dispersed hamlets seems more amenable to the retention of lineage kinship organization, as in Zinacantán and Oxchuc. The separation of women from their kin group limits the kind of daily interaction that breaks down exclusive membership by lineage (Nash 1970).

The organization of work. Following the abolition of *encomienda* rights to labor tribute in the mid-sixteenth century, various forms of debt labor were resorted to in the haciendas, mines, and plantations operated by *mestizos* and *creoles*. In marginalized areas such as Chiapas, where *encomenderos* had almost unlimited power to exploit indigenous labor and their resources, populations were decimated: in the period from 1570 to a century later, the population of the state declined from 224,400 to 74,990 (Wasserstrom 1983a:93). Wage work provided Indians with a supplement to subsistence as they tried to survive on the marginal lands allotted to their communities, but it never allowed surpluses to accumulate, nor did it even cover the costs of social reproduction.

The extreme subordination of the indigenous population in Chiapas promoted a conservative outlook in agricultural practices and artisan production that fostered retention of preconquest technologies and techniques. Only the simplest plows and looms of Spanish fifteenth-century technology found their way into the Chiapas highlands, and these were usually found in towns rather than rural areas. Indians adopted domesticated animals abandoned by Spaniards and developed herbal remedies to protect the sheep, horses, mules, and fowl from local pests. With the help of pack animals, Indian peddlers followed old trade routes in intervillage exchanges that insulated them from the more rapacious practices permitted in the cities.

When Indians ventured into towns dominated by *ladinos* they were subject to extreme abuse and exploitation. Wholesalers positioned on the outskirts of town seized the goods of Indians coming to sell in markets, throwing the money they arbitrarily set at the Indians, who had no recourse to law (Favre 1983:101). Wasserstrom (1983a:98 *et seq.*) recounts the myriad attempts of mayors (*alcalde mayores*) to take advantage of Indian vendors in the marketplace and even to force them to raise cash crops such as cocoa on their milpa lands. Spanish officials and ecclesiastics constantly encroached on lands allocated to indigenous communities, eroding their subsistence base.

Resistance and rebellion. Indigenous resistance and rebelliousness during the colonial and independence period drew upon the spiritual world made up of Christian saints, who represented the compassionate side of Christianity, even as they often masked preconquest powers. When the native nobles were either assassinated or disinherited, indigenous varieties of Christianity "provided the idiom in which these people organized their world and simultaneously expressed their radical disaffection with the colonial order" (Wasserstrom 1983a:106). Catholic saints represent not just a fusion of preconquest and Spanish beliefs but, as Watanabe (1990) demonstrates, "a highly differentiated recombination of conventional forms that serves primarily to articulate the moral and physical—and thus ethnic—boundaries of the community."

It is through this "recombination of conventional forms" that the local saints worshipped in communities inspired revolts against the very rulers that introduced them. García de León (1984:185 *et seq.*) recounts in his history of the Chiapas rebellions that the miraculous appearance of the Virgin Santa Marta in 1711 before an indigenous couple was rejected by ecclesiastics and civil officials, who tried the couple as idolaters. But when the Virgin again appeared the next year before a young girl, calling upon her to found a new church for Indians in the hills, this provided what García de León called "The spark [that] kindled a vast movement that would encompass, at its height, thirty-two Tzeltal, Tzotzil, and Chol communities, who would create their own political and religious hierarchy, independent of the established order."

The logic of the rebellion revealed both the depths of Catholic spiritual penetration and the retention of native resistance to the oppression that it carried. Wasserstrom (1983b:107) quotes the *alcalde mayor* of Tabasco, to which the rebellion had spread, who said the rebels carried the message that "It was God's will that [the Virgin] should come only for His native children to free them from the Spaniards and the ministers of the Church, and that the Angels would plant and tend their milpas, and that the sun and the moon had given signs that the King of Spain was dead, and that they must choose another."

The *alcalde mayor*'s reference to the signs of the sun and moon relates to the cosmological balance that Mayans continue to cultivate even as they accept conversion.[15] Clearly the impoverishment of the Indians and the devastation of their subsistence base in the early eighteenth century raised their worst fears of the disastrous imbalance in the cosmos.

Before the rebellion was quelled, the Indians had attacked the corrupt church officials, assassinated monks, priests, plantation owners, tax collectors, merchants, "and those natives who rejected their new order," killing thousands. The Indians then ordained their own priests, until they were routed by armed reinforcements. The repression of Indians in the highlands of Chiapas became even more oppressive after the rebellion was overcome.

The Church presented contradictions in its parish role as well as in its spiritual role. Although priests were the only ones concerned with preserving the history of the indigenous society, they were also the strongest forces in acculturation. The Church ordered the *reducciones,* or drawing together, of diverse indigenous communities to concentrate populations "within the sound of the church bells." This broke up the commitment to territorial integrity of the Indian Republics that Cortés promised to his allies in the conquest (Cabrera Vargas 1995:35). While clerics were the only colonizers to learn and promote the preservation of native languages, they also cultivated literacy in Spanish and acculturation to the Catholic doctrine.

The clerics were virtually the only ones to concern themselves with the education of the new subjects of the Crown in New Spain. In the early years of colonization, the priests reopened the *calmecacs,* or schools of the Aztecs, and taught children of *principales* and *caciques* to read and write, and to speak in Spanish. They were designated to disseminate Christianity, and during the first twenty-five years after the conquest, the sons of indigenous women and Spanish men became ordained priests (García García 1995:56). *Encomenderos* intervened where they could to prevent indigenous children from attending schools, since they wanted them only for their labor in the tribute system (Cabrera Vargas 1995:56–62).

By the latter part of the seventeenth century, when Carlos II set the boundaries of Indian pueblos (*pueblos indios*), he also specified the criteria for mayors (*alcaldes*): they must be residents of the town and speak Spanish in order to encourage Spanish fluency for this much-coveted role. Church officials also established their priorities, which were to segregate indigenous people from Spanish populations, since the priests opposed Indians learning the "vices of the Spaniards" (García García 1995). Ethnic regions were no longer recognized as corporate entities, and their identity was limited to common languages or dialects. In the current attempt to designate autonomous indigenous regions, this transition has become crucial.

From Indian Pueblos to Institutional Revolutionary Communities

From the War of Independence to the Revolution of 1910, major changes came about in the relationship between indigenous peoples and the state. The *creoles,* which in Mexico refers to the offspring of Spanish descent who were born in the Americas, established hegemony in the ideology of liberalism derived from European revolutionary currents of the late eighteenth and early nineteenth centuries. It was during the century following the declaration of independence that Indian pueblos experienced the greatest assault from the nation-state. Those who benefited from the Independence War were the elite creoles, not the Indians and *mestizos* who often fought in the ranks of the revolutionary leaders. Moved by the ideology of liberalism that claimed freedom from the constraints of Church and state, the new leaders seized the corporate lands of the Indian pueblos as well as those of the Catholic Church. Those who were disinherited by the Independence War then entered the ranks of the new resistance movements that culminated in the Revolution of 1910. The protracted wars fought from 1910 to 1913 marked the ascendance of *mestizos* as the core of the new institutional revolutionary state. The new power elite established its hegemony through the ideology of *indigenismo*, a purportedly pro-Indian stance that masked the premises of unilineal evolutionary progress through conformity to the dominant culture.

These two decisive moments in establishing relations between indigenous pueblos and the nation-state—the War of Independence and the Revolution of 1910—are explored in the following sections.

Independence and the formation of the liberal nation-state. Although the Spanish courts decreed the social and civil equality of Indians and *mestizos* and abolished the forced labor as well as all personal services in the last days of their empire, indigenous experience in three hundred years of colonization caused them to mistrust these belated reforms. Miguel Hidalgo was able to mobilize 80,000 to 100,000 indigenes and *mestizos* in the central states to fight in an independence movement that benefited the creoles. Huastecas of Tamaulipas also fought on the side of the independence movement, but Yaquis and Opatas fought on the royalist side (Gomezcésar Hernandez 1995:75). Chiapas remained outside the contending forces until the large landowners formally broke from their alliance with Guatemala, and Chiapas became the last state of Mexico in 1824.

Once independence was declared, the latent class contradictions held in check during Spanish colonial hegemony were let loose, as freedom of commerce and business opened up the floodgates of unrestricted investments and expropriation by creole elites and foreigners. United States migrants settled in Texas in the 1830s, leading to annexation by the U.S. government in 1845. By 1848, Mexico had ceded all land north of the Rio Grande and the Gila River. The governing creole elite attacked Church and communal corporations and, backed by the credo of liberalism, appropriated these forms of property, making them available for sale (Gomezcésar Hernandez 1995:720).

The newly independent government went beyond the Spanish Crown in its attack on the economy, religious practices, and education, as well as the property of the indigenous communities. Responding to liberal European ideas that a mass of middle *campesinos* holding small properties would assure the prosperity of the state, the Constitution of 1857 destroyed the legal basis for communal lands (Durand Alcántara 1994:165).[16] Many haciendas appropriated communal lands as *tierras baldías*, or fallow lands held in reserve, and communities were dispossessed of most of the fertile lands. The Mexican government realized few revenues from the expropriation of land. Burdened with debts, President Benito Juárez canceled the foreign debt, which engendered a new invasion from the alliance of the debt-holding countries of Great Britain, Spain, and France. Only Napoleon III of France remained committed to the invasion, finally succeeding in setting up Maximilian of Hapsburg as emperor in 1864. Unable to control the unruly republic-turned-empire, Maximilian yielded to insurgent forces and was executed in 1867. Reinstated as president, Juárez again served in office until his death in 1871. He faced opposition from Indians and *campesinos* in the central states of the republic who rallied under the leadership of Julio López Chavez; he issued a manifesto to all the oppressed in 1868 denouncing the seizure of lands. Over 184,000 Indians died in the Yucatán, and thousands of Indians died in Guanajuato and the Sierra Gorda, as well as in the North in the wars of resistance against the growing encroachment of the new state on indigenous communities (Gomezcésar Hernandez 1995:82). After Juárez' death in 1871, his successor, President Lerdo, lost the presidency in 1874 to Porfirio Díaz, whose indigenous ancestry did not dissuade him from supporting the liberal concessions to powerful landed interests that marked over three decades of authoritarian rule that disappropriated Indians.

In Chiapas, the rebellion of the indigenous population against the encroachment on their patrimony again took on a religious bent similar to the Cancuc rebellion a century and a half before. Chamula Indians, inspired by a talking saint who urged them to attack and destroy the *ladinos,* carried out a series of skirmishes called the War of the Castes, lasting from 1867 to 1869 (Bricker 1981; Gossen 1974; Meggid 1996). They held the inhabitants of San Cristóbal de Las Casas in fear of an invasion for weeks before the rebellion was overcome. The reenactment of the rebellion each year during Carnival is a focal point of community solidarity. As they perform the "monkey dance," Chamula religious officials wear their version of a French grenadier's uniform in recognition of the leadership of the troops by a *ladino,* Galindo, who had served in Emperor Maximilian's army before leading the rebellion. The dance itself recalls the second creation of human beings in the form of monkeys by their origin deities.

The indigenous rebellions in the second half of the nineteenth century were not just over land but over the defense of the cultural and political rights of indigenous people that proved their ability to act as a collective entity. Although they fought on losing ground, they reinforced a spirit of resistance and forged alliances with impoverished *mestizo* small landholders, ranchers, and herders that became the basis for the Revolution of 1910.

The Revolution of 1910–1917 and "Institutional Revolutionary Communities." Indigenous peoples of Chiapas were not voluntary participants in the wars that swept through the countryside during the 1910–1917 Revolution, and its gains came late or, in some regions of Chiapas, never. There were few indigenous volunteers in either army, though men would sometimes be forced by either side to carry loads for, and even to join, the army. Indians fled before both the federal army, the Carrancistas, and bands of local counterrevolutionary landlords (J. Rus 1994:265). They recall that period with disdain for the soldiers, whom they called "*carranza cho*" or "carrancista rat" (Gossen 1996), who appeared simultaneously with Carrancista troop movements, spreading a deadly influenza (J. Rus personal communication). Juan Pérez Jolote, a Chamulan Indian whose autobiography was recorded by Ricardo Pozas (1952), was released from jail along with other prisoners by federal troops and forced to enlist. When he returned to his natal village of Chamula, his father told him that he heard the neighbors say, "See, there goes

→ Tools people w/ basis for claims

Juan. They say he goes around killing people. He is very *ladinoized"* (acculturated to non-Indian ways).

Through a series of constitutional changes introduced especially during Lázaro Cárdenas's term as president (1934–1940), the Indian pueblos became incorporated as "institutional revolutionary communities" (J. Rus 1994). Among the measures to incorporate indigenous people in the nation were cultural autonomy, land reform, political reforms, and education, based on Articles 4, 27, and 123 of the 1917 Constitution.

1. Cultural autonomy. Article 4 of the 1917 Constitution affirms the autonomy of Indian pueblos, which was in jeopardy throughout the independence period, by guaranteeing municipal autonomy and ridding towns of the rule by *ladinos* or *mestizos*. This was a major indigenous demand in the Revolution. Article 4 states that the cultural distinctions of each community should be respected, but since it is so general, the government itself negated the law with almost every development program it introduced into highland Chiapas. It further states that "The Mexican nation has a pluricultural basis sustained originally in its indigenous pueblos" *(pueblos indígenas)* and promises that "The law will protect and promote the growth of their languages, cultures, uses, customs, resources and specific forms of social organization, and will guarantee to its members effective access to the jurisdiction of the states" (Rabasa and Caballero 1996:94). The pluricultural status of indigenous communities is also premised on the International Labor Organization (ILO) convention No. 169, committing nations like Mexico that signed it to protect and promote the pluricultural basis in language, culture, uses, customs, resources, and forms of social organization. The convention influenced the reform of Article 4, which asserts the self-determination of communities, but distinguishes pueblos "of a first category" *(de primera)*, which have full rights of self determination, from pueblos "of a second category" *(de segunda)*, which lack this quality. The problem is that the basis for determining the categories rests on primordial characteristics that are not clearly stated (Díaz-Polanco 1997:214). We are again confronted with the problem of defining ethnicity for legislative and administrative purposes that Warren (1992) and Field (1999) have raised (see chapter 1).

2. Land reform. Article 27 of the 1917 Constitution provides for the "restitution," or return of lands unlawfully taken during the Porfiriato, and the "donation," or assignment of national lands *(territorias nacionales)* by the central government. This provision was first articulated in Article 6 of Emiliano Zapata's and Otelio Montaño's Plan de Ayala in 1911, which states that "the lands, mountains, and waters that the plantation owners *(hacendados)*, scientists *(cientificos)*,[17] and *caciques* seized in the time of tyranny and injustice, will enter into the possession of the pueblos or citizens who hold titles to lands taken from them. . . " Land grants according to Article 27 rested on two premises: the first premise was the *"dotación,"* or giving land taken from neighboring haciendas, and the second was restitution of communal lands taken by private owners, usually during the Porfiriato (Durand Alcántra 1994:176). The former premise confirmed the hegemonic power of the state by presenting land as a gift by the ruling party to the petitioner, and served to bind the communities to the state (Nugent and Alonso 1994:229). This construction of the article committed those states where Indians and *mestizos* had been heavily involved in fighting to allegiance to the new government.[18]

Constitutional reforms strengthened and legitimated the power of the national government. President Cárdenas (1934–1940) instituted many changes that were designed to integrate members of indigenous communities as citizens with rights to vote, own land, receive an education, and receive social services. The government distributed about 17,000,000 hectares of land in *ejidos*,[19] and armed the *campesinos* to defend their rights to it. Cárdenas did not, however, supply the basis for the cultural practices of collective cultivation nor did he promote the languages of indigenous peoples. Since juridical practices related to conflicts over land distribution remained in the hands of government bureaucrats, land reform sometimes reinforced the power and practices of large landowners, especially in Chiapas, as we shall see below. Only 15 percent of *ejido* lands are in the name of women, and many of these were acquired by widows who had sons 14 years of age or older at the time of the father's death (Nash 1970; Stephen 1994:27–28).

3. Political reforms. The Constitution of 1917 guarantees the vote to all men; women did not gain the right to vote until 1953. In indigenous villages, women rarely exercised this right until the Zapatista uprising and the challenge to PRI power by opposition parties. The political process was highly centralized, with the federal district controlling a great deal of power, although Chiapas remained beyond the direct control of the central government for decades. It was only after the PRI government channeled resources to the pueblos through the INI that communities began to recognize allegiance to the state. In Chamula, an elite of indigenous *caciques* who benefited directly from the cash flow ensured centralized control by the party (J. Rus 1994). Although this model is often generalized for the relationship between indigenous communities and the state, it varied from one municipality to another, and from one moment in time to another. As I shall illustrate below, Amatenango conformed to this pattern for a decade in the 1970s but, through an internal reform movement, ousted an extended family that monopolized municipal office to benefit family members. The institutional framework constructed by the PRI also defined male hegemonic control of political offices and the land grant commissions.

4. Education. Article 3 of the Constitution guarantees that everyone has the right to receive an education, and that all education would be provided free by the government. This article was put into effect in indigenous communities of Chiapas during Cárdenas's presidency with the creation of the Autonomous Department of Indian Affairs in 1936, and was later implemented with the INI. School authorities overcame resistance to education by setting up boarding schools outside of the communities of origin of the inmates. In these settings the pupils were submitted to what Bonfil Batalla (1996:118) called "a brainwashing, as a result of which they would recognize the inferiority of their own culture and the superiority of national culture." Even while education was promoted in the name of *indigenismo,* the children were prohibited from using indigenous languages.

Like most European constitutions on which it was patterned, the Mexican Constitution of 1917 is presented in universalistic terms applying to all citizens of the nation. However, there were profound variations in the way it became institutionalized. Chiapas was one of the last states to gain some of the basic provisions, and there were many variations from one community to another in the institutionalization of the reforms in the decades following the drafting of the Constitution. Despite the universalizing claims of the Constitution, the benefits were distributed in such a way as to enhance distinctions between the central and northern states and those in the south, and between indigenous and *mestizo* regions and communities. The Constitution failed to redress the inequities between genders, promoting patriarchy in ways that may have even enhanced the subordination of women. These variations are discussed in relation to the involution of indigenous communities of the Chiapas Highlands in the decades shortly after the Revolution. This is followed by a discussion of the more aggressive policies of development pursued by the central government following the mid-1960s.

THE INVOLUTION OF *COMUNIDADES REVOLUCIONARIAS INSTITUCIONAL*

The changes introduced by the PRI government reinforced the semi-subsistence, small-plot adaptation of the highland Chiapas communities in the early postrevolutionary nation. The involution of the revolution took several forms, in the process of which the indigenous communities of the highlands entrenched themselves in the political and economic life of the nation while reinforcing their cultural prescriptions for living. They were able to reinforce community boundaries because of several key provisions of the new government. In the first place, the economic base of small-plot corn and bean cultivation was reinforced with the Land Reform Act and with small-scale development projects fostered by the National Indian Institute (INI) with programs that complemented traditional agricultural and artisan production. Secondly, the political autonomy of indigenous communities was reinforced by the state government turning over the paid posts of mayor and secretary to indigenous officers in 1958. Finally, in cultural terms, indigenous customs were not directly challenged until serious attempts were made to introduce secondary-level education, which came to communities after the 1960s and, in many cases, never came. Since these propositions go against common perceptions, I shall turn to the ethnographic record to support my claims.

Agricultural Involution

Compared with northern states, land reform came late, and, in some communities in Chiapas, never. The "Chiapas family" of large landowners fought in the revolution with an "army" of peons, who became the troop of *Mapaches* (raccoons) who maintained the old order in power. The governors who followed were all members of the Chiapas family. The impact of the Land Reform Act was delayed longer and land was never donated in the form of a gift. The large landowners instituted conditions for carrying out the reform that preserved the agrarian structure (Reyes Ramos 1991:96; Villafuerte Solis et al. 1999:18). Each community fought separately for the communal lands that had been expropriated during the Liberal era.

The first postrevolutionary governor, Tiburcio Fernández Ruiz, decreed that the agrarian law of the state signed in 1921 allowed a maximum property holding of 8,000 hectares for each individual within a family. This interpretation of the constitutional requirement for distribution of land effectively preserved the *latifundia*, or large land-holdings, by enabling large landholders to claim up to 50,000 and more hectares per family unit (Gonzalez Esponda 1989, cited in Villafuerte Solis et al. 1999:19; N. Harvey 1991:55). The coincident problem of finding a labor supply, due to the passage in 1914 of the Law of Workers limiting involuntary servitude and putting an end to the company store, provoked coffee plantation owners of Soconusco to introduce new modes of ensuring a labor supply. Large landowners instigated the *ejido* grants in order to ensure an available labor supply where labor was scarce: twelve of the nineteen townships in which lands were first distributed in the period from 1920 to 1929 were in Soconusco, where coffee plantation owners were most in need of a reliable workforce (Reyes Ramos 1991:110). Erasto Urbina, one of the outstanding promoters of Lázaro Cárdenas's pro-gram to realize the land reform, objected strenuously to the state policy that allowed many Guatemalans to become citizens, even distributing *ejido* lands to them in the mar-gins of the plantations where they worked (Villafuerte Solis et al. 1999:21).

In highland communities, the implementation of the Land Reform Act differed in each of the distinct ecological zones and from one municipality to another. In some towns land reform provided an opening for incorporating Indians in the national society. In other areas it confirmed the autonomy of the township, diminishing, though never eliminating, the need for wage work in the plantations. It was rarely, if ever, conceived of as a "gift of the state" in the way that occurred in the central plateau. The richer lands of towns such as San Andrés Larrainzar remained in the hands of the large landowners until the 1970s, and some are still being contested.

This is also the case in Venustiano Carranza, once called San Bartolomé, before the anticlerical movement of the revolutionary period. The land struggle has a long history in the township, where the first communal lands were seized during the revolution by the *"Mapaches,"* a movement made up of ex-soldiers from the old federal army who opposed the revolutionary changes (Moncada 1983:67). Indians call for the return of land that had been seized in 1767, still referring to these land titles when they make their demands (Jan de Vos 1991, lecture to the National Science Foundation Research Experi-ence for Undergraduates). When *campesinos* again attempted to regain the land in 1923, indigenous leaders were imprisoned. Successive attempts were made by leaders of the *ejido* commission in 1929 and 1945, but they received no official document until 1967. Cattlemen invaded the lands that the Indians were repossessing, and seven years later the Office of Agrarian Affairs and Colonization ordered the cattlemen to leave.

The basis for local power changed as the local agrarian commissions, charged with dis-tributing lands during Lázaro Cárdenas's presidency from 1934 to 1940, assumed control in each municipality. With the exception of Zinacantán, where young men in the town hall who were knowledgeable about the land reform guaranteed in Article 27 of the 1917 Con-stitution started legal action to regain communal lands in 1920, most indigenous commu-nities in Chiapas did not begin to make claims until the 1930s. Since most highland Chiapas

Indians were monolingual and nonliterate in the 1930s, it was frequently the *colonos*, or wage workers on plantations, who learned of the revolutionary gains and initiated the land restitution guaranteed in Article 27. This was the case in Amatenango del Valle, where farm laborers who had worked in the plantation of San Nicolás within its boundaries seized the rich flat lands in 1929. They in turn were expelled by Amatenangueros when they tried to move into the town center and occupy public offices (Nash 1970).

Pottery production had always supplemented agriculture as a product sold or bartered for corn, especially in the spring when the corn and bean stores were running low. It was also a means for gaining cash income for fiestas, and women in all the households increased the production of pottery in the weeks preceding the major saints' festivals. The price of pottery would drop to half the normal price during these weeks as women glutted the nearby shops in Teopisca and San Cristóbal with their wares. With the increase of land gained after the implementation of the Land Reform Act, the substantive economy was strengthened. The growing commodification of pottery production reinforced the household organization of labor revolving around corn production.[20] Young men were obliged to seek wage work in the coffee plantations on the Pacific coast or in nearby cash-crop farms in order to raise money for betrothal ceremonies or to begin their ritual obligations in the fiesta cycle. But, because Amatenango had more and better *ejido* lands than neighboring towns, with an average of two hectares of *ejido* land held by each household, they were not forced to migrate for six months of the year, as Chamulan and other indigenes were forced to do.

For highland communities, the decades immediately following the implementation of land reform were a period of retrenchment that forestalled adjustment to the rising population and diminishing fertility of soils. With increased funding flowing into the communities, their boundaries were further eroded through state programs extending communication, transportation, and development projects to the countryside. The revolutionary potential of the villages was turned inward as the members used the gains of a limited land reform and development program to reinforce priorities of household production in a semi-self-sufficient economy.

Political Involution

Given the monopoly of power by the PRI, electoral politics had little immediate impact on the relations between the highly centralized government and the indigenous communities. When I arrived in Amatenango, political authority, embodied by responsibilities in ritual ceremonies and spiritual power, was derived from possession of *nahwales,* or animal spirits, that guided and informed their possessors. Indian authorities still acted on consensual principles, a cultural predisposition that fit with the monopoly of the political process by the PRI. In some towns, notably Chamula, this collective responsibility promoted electoral abuses in which the *caciques* filled out the voting ballots for the entire municipality. But even in towns where voters filled out the ballot, the sense was that unanimity must prevail: to vote for any other than PRI candidates was taken to be defiance of indigenous tradition. Until the mid-1950s, Chiapas towns were still run by *ladino* mayors and secretaries, with unpaid posts occupied by indigenous men. When these local offices were made available for literate indigenous men in 1956, graduates of the boarding school were given priority. In fact, this innovation was more upsetting for the internal political process than the old system in which *ladinos* occupied these posts, since it marked the beginning of *cacique* rule (*infra* p. 38 *et seq.*).

The internal politics of highland communities in the decades before 1970 involved a contest between a gerontocracy in the upper offices of the civil religious hierarchy and a cohort of young, educated, indigenous men for control over local positions in the town hall. This factional competition on the local level was not mediated through national parties in the 1950s. The clash between the two cohorts of leadership was sometimes fought out on grounds of witchcraft accusation, as in Amatenango del Valle, or in terms of adherence to tradition, as in Chamula and Chenalhó. In Oxchuc lineage elders and curers discredited their own claims of the power to control through illness that was attributed to the sins of patients. Villa Rojas (1946) attributes the massive conversion to Protestantism in the 1940s to the abuse of this power. But in many of the highland communities during the 1950s and 1960s, conflict revolved around a crisis between a gerontocracy that defended indigenes through spiritual powers, and literate young men. The mere presence of young men in high posts of the civil hierarchy challenged the principle of age authority that was intrinsic to the traditional location of power in both civil-religious and curing hierarchies.

The compromise that emerged in Chamula has served as a model for *cacique* control of indigenous townships elsewhere. Two municipal authorities served, one made up of monolingual elders who had served in lower ranks of the traditional cargo system, and the other made up of literate younger men who interfaced with the state and national officials (J. Rus 1994:15). The vote was delivered to the ruling PRI by the civil authorities, who marked all the ballots for members of the community. By co-opting the power elite, as Jan Rus (1994) tells us in his thought-provoking article on "*la comunidad revolucionaria institucional*," the PRI was able to introduce the new revolutionary order in Chamula. Youthful authorities reinforced the age-ordered hierarchy at the spiritual level by deferring to elder statesmen, or *principales,* on ceremonial occasions, and ensuring the flow of funds into religious celebrations at the same time that they were subverting the *principales'* temporal power. The legitimacy of the power exercised by *principales* derived from their performance of rituals and service in civil and religious offices. This was backed by diviner-curers who exercised sanctions through their power over sickness and death. This system was sometimes challenged by youthful *promotores,* or change agents, hired by the INI.

Amatenango conformed to the pattern of a dual partnership of a gerontocracy of *principales* who had passed through ritual offices and who maintained their authority in the town hall with a group of scribes until the decades of the 1950s. These youths, sometimes still in their teens when they were conscripted to serve in the town hall during the 1930s, served unwillingly. Ceferino López, who served in Amatenango during that period, described to me his humiliating experience as a scribe. The elders ordered him to come into the town hall and forced him to drink alcohol until he reached such a state of intoxication that he agreed to become a scribe. However, Amatenango elders never became mediators of the PRI nor did they achieve the validation of their control over the political posts and resources that reinforced the position of Chamulans through their monopoly of tradition (Nash 1970).

The contest for power with the young literate leaders took many forms. The *ejido* commission was one of the most important power bases in the pueblos because of their charge to allocate the lands to household heads. In Amatenango the curer-diviners were important players in the *ejido* commissions from the time of the first allocations of *ejido* land in the 1930s and up until the late 1950s, when I started my work in the municipality. I was not allowed to enter into the negotiations of the commission, but I heard of the proceedings. According to reports, the meetings, during which a great deal of liquor was consumed, were conducted by the *bankil u'ul* (elder curer) of each moiety in the town center. They established priorities by running an imaginary race of their *nahwal*, or animal spirit. The races apparently settled some of the contested claims within the commission, validating decisions in ways that the national government could not have imagined. As young men gained power in the town hall, they took on positions in the *ejido* commissions that were then conducted within institutional forms promoted by the PRI.

In Amatenango as well as other indigenous towns, the almost exclusively male education ensured political priority for men as Indians began to occupy local offices previously filled by *ladinos*. Political disfranchisement of women also extended to the ballot box, and no women voted in indigenous communities until 1994, when the PRI saw its control threatened by the appeal of the Party of the Democratic Revolution (PRD) to women voters. Women were reluctant to vote long after national suffrage for women was passed in 1953 with the reform of Article 34 of the Constitution, guaranteeing the vote. I never heard of any women voting in indigenous villages until after the EZLN uprising, and no women ran for office until 1980 because of the harassment or even threats by the men (chapter 3).

Cultural Involution   *indigenismo*

In the early postrevolutionary decades, a policy for gradually integrating indigenous peoples was *indigenismo,* an ostensibly proindigenous policy that envisioned the ultimate goal of cultural assimilation. This was articulated by Manuel Gamio, a major figure in the development of Mexican anthropological theory and political action:

> In order to incorporate the Indian, let us not try to Europeanize him all at once. On the contrary, let us "indianize" ourselves a little, to present to him our civilization, diluted in his. In this way he will not find our civilization exotic, cruel, bitter, and incomprehensible. Of course, one should not carry closeness with the Indian to ridiculous extremes. (Gamio 1960:96, cited in Bonfil Batalla 1996:116)

Caught up in the Western parable of unilineal evolution, the end of separate coexistence was envisioned in the assumption of the superiority of European civilization. The paternalistic denial of an authentic indigenous culture was overlooked by his contemporaries until the critique of *indigenista* policy in action by Arturo Warman and other young anthropologists in a book titled *De eso lo que se llaman antropología mexicana* (Warman et al. 1970).

The institutionalization of the Revolution thus created a contested space for indigenous cultural institutions. The vagueness of Article 4 in specifying the characteristics that constituted authentic indigenous culture and the failure to ensure juridical and political conditions for multicultural indigenous autonomy attest to the incompleteness of revolutionary advances for indigenous pueblos. Just as the ideology of liberalism served the creole elites rather than the Indians and *mestizos* following independence, so did the ideology of *indigenismo* serve what indigenous people call the *mestizocracia*—the hierarchy of elite *mestizos*—more than it did Indians after the 1910 Revolution.

As in the case of constitutional guarantees of the right to vote and of land, indigenous women were neglected when education was introduced into highland Chiapas during Lázaro Cárdenas's presidency. The neglect fit cultural priorities that charged indigenous women with the primary responsibility for enculturating children in their traditions. Parents were reluctant to send daughters to school because of their gendered responsibility of maintaining cultural distinctions, particularly the true language, or *batz'il k'op*. Since boarding schools drew children away from their communities of origin, and the schools discouraged children from speaking in their native languages, most of the interns were boys. Even when schools were introduced into the communities, parents tried to avoid sending their daughters. One of Amatenango's first bilingual mayors, who had graduated from the boarding school in Chamula, told me that they had to stay in bed all day if they spoke in *lengua*.[21]

When bilingual educational programs opened up positions in teaching in the 1970s, educated indigenous youths were preferred candidates. Even in the feminized profession of primary-school teaching, indigenous women did not gain entry because of their lack of education even in communities where schools were available. Their labor in the house, especially in artisan production, was more important in the domestic economy than that of boys, and parents often questioned the value for women of formal education. Only after the 1980s did girls gain access to primary education.

CONFLICT AND
THE PROCESS OF DIFFERENTIATION

Conflict was not only expressed occasionally but was also expected, particularly during fiestas, which were the key to restoring the balance in the world. When I lived in Amatenango in the 1960s, people seemed generally satisfied that the rains did come in time for the crops to mature, the hail and wind that damaged the milpa blew over, and illnesses were cured even if a few witches had to be sacrificed in the process.

If the spring rains were delayed, members of the community made offerings to Santa Lucía and Santiago or even made a pilgrimage bearing Santa Lucía to intercede with San Tomás in Oxchuc. In the neighboring Tzeltal town of Oxchuc, the indigenes expressed

Students in Amatenango bilingual school line up during Independence Day, Amatenango 1989.

their feelings to Alfonso Villa Rojas that the officials charged with maintaining the world in balance were deficient. He recounted the brutality of curers who verbally excoriated and even whipped patients to force them to confess their sins, since the illness was proof of wrongdoing. The excesses of lineage heads, who also served as curers, and the curers themselves provoked many of the townspeople to turn to outsiders in search of justice, calling on the schoolteachers or the anthropologist to mediate proceedings that were often marred by violence. The arrival of Mariana Slocum, a Protestant missionary, shortly after Villa Rojas began his study in 1942, provided an alternative in Protestantism for a sanctioning system that had broken down. Within a few years she had translated the Bible into Tzeltal, and in the course of proselytizing in *batzil k'op* she converted over 5,000 Indians (Villa Rojas 1990).[22]

Violence is often attributed to the differences brought about by growing wealth differences and the gap between the powerful and the subordinated within the community, or by religious conversion. The incidence of violence revealed in early ethnographies indicates that the potential for violence was there, even when these class differences were not yet manifest. It made me aware of the importance of a daily practice that maintained the balance between spirits of place and people—in effect, that restored the habitus. Disturbance of this core could happen in a "homogeneous" town such as Oxchuc, which was far more inaccessible by car before the road was built in the early 1980s, and probably

had fewer outside visitors than Amatenango or Chamula. External factors and the promotion of difference may indeed aggravate conflict, but even without the differences of
wealth, religion, or ethnicity, the important factor in maintaining a harmonious habitus,
in which individuals are willing to take on "the institution of the social" in their persona,
is a legitimated sanctioning system. In many cases, the differentiating process itself
resulted from preexisting conflict. Mariana Slocum's success in conversion to Protestantism in Oxchuc indicates the level of rejection of a harsh social sanctioning system
instituted by curer diviners and lineage patriarchs as described by Villa Rojas (1990) in
his illuminating ethnography.

Wealth Differences and the Growing Gap

In the decade of the sixties, differences in wealth, religion, and political parties were
incipient. Even prior to material signs of affluence—in tile instead of thatch roofs,
cement block walls, television antennas, or trucks parked in the patios—there were
people designated as very wealthy who showed few external signs of prosperity. Distinctions that seemed minimal to the outsider could carry a great weight within the community. A larger-than-normal house, especially one with a porch, which indicated
expanded pottery production; corn drying in the rafters long after the harvest, which
hinted at landholdings in hot country; even a greater number of dogs, indicating that residents had great wealth requiring the protection of guard dogs—all these were clear
signs of wealth. Those who were known to have gotten their wealth from the hill spirit,
a certain Don Klabil who held huge stores of wealth in the form of cattle, sheep, and
crops, were not envied because it was known that their wealth died with them. The
recipients of such wealth would also have to work in their afterlife for Don Klabil.[23]

As more resources from the central government were channeled through *caciques*, the
indigenous officials who ensured election of PRI candidates, wealth differences took on
a different dimension and significance. The wealth of these officials, who tended to be
chosen from among elite families that lived in the town center, created tensions between
the centers and peripheral settlements. Residents of hamlets were less likely to occupy
positions of power, and they lacked basic services of piped water and electricity that
began to be provided by the central government in the late 1960s. Wealth differences
arose not only because of the *caciques'* appropriation of public funds but also because of
concessions to commercial opportunities made available to indigenes through political
party connections in the state capital. Notable among these were concessions for the sale
of liquor and soft drinks that were monopolized by the *caciques*.[24] Wage labor in San
Cristóbal and even as far away as Cancun provided wage income that was sometimes
invested in trucks or grinding mills, as Collier (1990) notes. Protestant missions, which
had made considerable inroads in Oxchuc in the 1940s, were attracting converts in other
towns, particularly in Chamula and among migrants to the cities over a decade later.
Other distinctions arose as political parties were challenging the PRI monopoly over
highland communities in Amatenango, Chamula, and Zinacantán. By the end of the
1960s, with rising populations in all the indigenous communities and severely eroded

A child plays in storage room filled with commodities that are part of market exchange in the village.

lands, *caciques* began to expel members of the community accused of being Protestants or in other ways not conforming to "tradition."

The differentiating conditions that are said to be the basis for the present conflict within communities have existed for several decades. During the early decades after the Revolution, discontent within indigenous communities was still expressed in envy and witchcraft exercised within the same communities. On the one hand, the containment of discord has to be analyzed in both the structural terms that were the basis for indigenous territorial and administrative entities, and the deflection of rebellion from within and outside of communities through institutions such as the civil-religious hierarchy and the divining-curing complex. This provides the habitus where the culture becomes inscribed in the body politic of the indigenous populace. On the other hand, the eruption of discord and even violence cannot be explained in terms of external pressures alone, but has to be considered in relation to the internalization of nonindigenous behaviors and beliefs in the half, millennium of contact and exploitation by the dominant class. What is often considered intrinsic to tradition turns out to be colonial or postindependence imposition.

The Crisis of Leadership

Containment of the crisis of leadership within municipal boundaries took different forms in each community. While I was working in the township of Amatenango from 1963 to 1967 there was a marked increase in the rate of homicide: whereas six men were killed between 1938 to 1957, thirty were killed between 1958 and 1965.[25] Every weekend night, when young men of the village returned from their work in the lumber mill, I would hear shots fired, and there was at least one homicide committed during each major fiesta. Sometimes the motives would be rivalry over a girl, or cattle theft, but most were attributed to suspicion of witchcraft and envy.

Accusations that involved collective witchcraft required an investigation by the curing hierarchy from each moiety. When a measles epidemic broke out, causing the death of many children in 1966, the hierarchy of curers from each side of the dual division met in the town hall and consulted with each other as to what course should be taken. While the interrogators asked leading questions, they "pulsed" each other, a routine diagnostic procedure carried out by pressing the thumb against the artery at the wrist of the interlocutor. They used the thumb, not the fingers, to pulse a patient, they told me, when I objected to the technique as leading to confusion of their own pulse rate with that of the one being pulsed, because their blood entered into a dialogue with the blood of the patient being questioned as they tried to determine "what the heart said." When they reached a verdict as to which of the younger curers was at fault for "inviting the evil" into the town, they acted as a group. Sometimes civil officials ordered the local police to pick up the "guilty one" and put him in jail, from which his executioners would take him. At other times, relatives of the people who had died from the disease would attack the witch. This often occurred during a fiesta when most men were drunk and the noise of revelers drowned out the sound. The killer was then protected from federal agents, since the murder was considered an execution and was condoned by the town authorities. Crimes of murder were supposed to be investigated by state police, but the local officials simply complied with the letter of the law, filling out a form indicating the particulars of the crime—when it was committed, what weapons were used, how many wounds had been inflicted—but never revealing the identity of the person suspected.

Consensus mechanisms and the harmonious front presented to the outside world made the interpretation of such acts of violence difficult. Then, too, we were struggling with the inadequacies of our own paradigm of structural functionalism. Most analyses focused on the success of the people we studied in reproducing traditional ways of life, and indeed this was a miraculous accomplishment, given the meager resources directed to the pueblos. I parodied this functionalist idiom, coded in the ironic title "Death as a Way of Life" (Nash 1967), to show how the community was turning inward the violence of its reactions to changes that were initiated in the wider society.

In Amatenango, the disruption of an age-ordered hierarchy of civil and religious leaders by young literate men in the top posts of mayor and secretary caused anxiety about the ability of these men to confront the power of witches. Heat is associated with age, and only the elder leaders, or *principales,* were believed capable of confronting the power of the elder curers. One of the *principales* in his sixties told me that: "When there are young people in the *cabildo*, they can't keep control of the curers; only the old people can." The curers themselves had relaxed the seniority principle in admitting youths in their twenties and thirties who were contesting the control exercised by the elders.

After years in which no homicides were recorded, the first homicide of a curer accused of being a witch occurred in 1937. The town authorities refused to allow him to be buried in the cemetery as the widow had requested, suggesting that they agreed with the accusation that he was executed as a witch. Assassinations of curers occurred in 1943 and 1950, sanctioned by civil officials. Other deaths followed, as young men bragged of their power to kill through their *nahwal* (animal spirit). It became routine practice to go to the town hall to request permission to kill, and if evidence of guilt was convincing, the town police would bring in the accused, lock up the culprit, and give the keys to the accuser.

After describing one ferocious attack on a suspected witch with a machete and burial in a cave that had occurred in the late 1930s, my informant, a former mayor of the town who was one of the first of the indigenous officials, concluded: "Therefore, little by little, the pueblo is getting better because we scared the curers by giving permission to the president to allow the family of victims of witchcraft to kill those who carried out evil acts." He felt that this was the point at which the power of the curers was broken.

This inner turmoil experienced by communities in the 1930s and 1940s was captured by Guiteras Holmes (1961) in her monograph, *Perils of the Soul: The World View of a Tzotzil Indian*. The prevalent anxiety of Chenalhó indigenes is revealed in the high frequency of illnesses attributed to loss of soul, theft of soul, and souls in conflict that were referred to elders and curer-diviners. This was a persistent preoccupation of curers of Amatenango del Valle, who addressed these anxieties with rituals and divination. Their ultimate aim was to reinforce the identity of patients with their place of birth, thus grounding the spiritual links with the ancestors and thereby overcoming some of the alienating effects of ethnic domination. Knowing that their souls will find rest in the pantheon where gravesites are oriented in the same pattern as the living community, Amatenangueros do not fear the restless wandering of their soul after death (Nash 1970). With their umbilical cord safely buried in the *sitios*, or yards, of the houses in which they were born, Chamulans know that they will be tied to that center for life even when they are forced to seek wages in coastal plantations or San Cristóbal de Las Casas (Gossen 1974).

Esther Hermitte showed the resilience of this ethnic identification in her study of Pinola, the present town of Villa Las Rosas. She began her fieldwork in the 1950s during a cultural upheaval in which indigenous people of the town were being systematically removed from official posts in the civil and religious *cargo* system dominated by the *ladino* population. The alternation of offices between secular and sacred posts, though introduced by the Spanish colonial government, had become so deeply entrenched in indigenous governance that it was a marker for Mayan traditions validating the right to power. Hermitte's thesis centered on the restructuring of indigenous ritual and civil offices in a spirit world in which the last incumbents, upon their death, became spiritual counterparts of the *ladino* officials. In the celebration of the fiestas for Carnival and the Day of the Cross, May 3rd in the Christian calendar, indigenous participants deferred to the spiritual presence of these defunct officials. They were even more powerful in death since they did not get drunk and unruly. On these occasions, the Indians revitalized Mayan beliefs in human responsibility for keeping the world in motion, and through the rituals in which this was realized, they retained a sense of their own identity.[26]

The sense of salvation that indigenes of Pinola projected through maintaining the collective life of the community evokes the strategies of the Cancuc rebellion (see *supra*, p. 47–8) when the rebels created an orderly hierarchy of civil and religious offices without *ladino* intervention. Wasserstrom (1983a:108) interprets the logic of the earlier rebellion as a construction of native *alcaldes* and *regidores, mayordomos* and *alféreces* who yearn for the collective life of the community. Just as the succession of officials related to the ancestors took precedence over individual deaths of officeholders in the early eighteenth century in Cancuc, so did the indigenes of Pinola seek reinforcement of the spiritual leadership of their defunct *cofradía* members in the 1950s. This clearly was the concern of indigenes in the decades from 1970, on when they were forced to migrate to San Cristóbal or to the Lacandón rain forest. Even when they were expelled and converted to Protestantism or to formal Catholicism, Chamulas sought new points of reference to recreate collective ties and to resolve their union with the ancestors within the new settings (Kovic 1997; Santana Echeagaray 1996; Sullivan 1998).

Catholic Saints and Primordial Spirits

The convoluted mixture of indigenous and Hispanic beliefs and practices that makes up "tradition" is manifested in the celebrations of Christian saints identified with the community. The most important of these are the celebrations of Carnival and Easter week and the Day of the Cross, linked as they are with the collective celebrations of the communities. In San Juan Chamula, the largest township in the region and the one closest to the *ladino*-dominated city of San Cristóbal de Las Casas, the population of more than 80,000 is dispersed in many separate villages within the township and beyond in the lowlands, to which they are forced to migrate in search of work. All Chamulas try to congregate in the town center on these occasions, when men as well as women wear the distinctive tunic woven of wool sheared from the flocks tended by women (Gossen 1974). All villagers contribute money for the communal festivals related to the saints' celebrations, and officials rent houses in the center, where they expend enormous amounts of money and time hosting their fellow officials during their term of office. This sacrifice of time and money opens up the possibility of, but not the entry into, positions in the civil-religious hierarchy which validates the authority of traditional *caciques*. During the religious celebrations between Carnival and Easter, the younger men, watched over by the elder officials, reenact at least seven historical events that Victoria Reifler Bricker (1981) has identified with conquest and independence uprisings. The most outstanding one is the "Caste War" (1867–1870) recounted above. The entire event was ignored in Mexican school history books until recently, when it was treated with the respect accorded to *mestizo* national events.

In other communities as well, religious dramatizations serve as a venue for acting out subversively the latent antagonisms that have characterized relations between indigenes and *ladinos*, beneath the gaze of church and state authorities, who are often unaware of the actors' latent intent. These "traditions" have changed along with the ethnic relations on which they were scripted. For example, in Amatenango del Valle, I witnessed the Holy Week pageant of the jailing and crucifixion of Christ in 1966 and again in 1993. I perceived a shift in dramatization from a hostile encounter between polarized ethnic groups to a hilarious contest between indigenes and specific "change agents." In 1966, after the *mayordomos* attended to the crucified Christ, Judas was hung from the church belfry on Saturday "in order to show the world that he killed Christ." On the surface, the attack on his swinging body seemed to enact vengeance for Judas's role in killing Christ as it had just been described in the sermon presented by the *ladino* priest. But the indigenes' portrayal of Judas—wearing sunglasses, a cigarette dangling from his lips, and dressed in a somber jacket, shirt, pants, boots, and cowboy hat—could also be read as a caricature of a *ladino* rancher, one they might even have worked for. When they cut down the effigy from the gallows on Sunday, the *mayordomos* beat it with sticks in mocking castration of a clearly hated figure. Later it was carried around town on horseback—itself an ironic act because in early times, only *ladinos* were allowed to ride horses—while the *mayordomos* collected money from the curers to buy liquor. Finally, the assembled audience tore the figure apart, saving the wooden mask but burning the straw body. This sequence seemed to me to be a subversive attack on the dominant *ladinos*, mimicking the indigenes' own desire to kill their opponent (Nash 1968, 1994a).

The overt hatred exhibited in the attack on the effigy in the earlier ritual was absent when I witnessed the same occasion twenty years later. In 1993 Judas was dressed in a red shirt, jogging pants, and Nikes, sporting a blue helmet like those worn by engineers in the field, and carrying a plastic attaché case. When I asked the meaning of this costume, the *majordomo* told me with a smile that it represented a forestry agent. Known for their penchant for soliciting bribes from town officials for violating any one of a hundred rules on cutting trees, these agents now symbolize the quintessential corrupt representative of the government. The scene, with a hoard of children following in its wake rather than adult members of the religious *cofradías* who had attended him in the past, was a hilarious spoof of ethnic encounter, now focused on particular agents rather than an ethnic caste. Much joking and laughing ensued when the men dismantled the figure and burned the straw. They were no longer handling a figure of fear and hatred but rather a comical interloper whom they humiliated rather than attacked. Like Halloween in the United States, it had become a children's diversion.

Along with the adoption of Catholic saints as champions of their rebellions, a parallel process subversive of Catholic teachings is on going in indigenous Mayan villages. Beliefs about "our Father the Sun" and "our Grandmother the Moon," the balance of the underworld and overworld related to gender, are linked to preconquest Mesoamerican beliefs and often have more profound implications for behavior than Christian commandments do. Anthropologists working in Chiapas have found a vital cosmology that infuses indigenous cultures (Árias Perez 1994; Guiteras Holmes 1961; Gossen 1974; Nash 1970,

1997a; Vogt 1969). Some of the saints' images are masks for preconquest supernatural powers: Saint Thomas is sometimes identified by indigenous people with the rain god, Quetzalcoatl, as in Oxchuc; Santiago is equated with the thunder god, Cha'uk, in Amatenango, shown astride a horse whose thunderous hooves identify him with that power.

These equations between pre- and postconquest supernatural figures provide the continuity that is also contained in the landscape. Caves, hills, the waterfalls, and swift-flowing streams all contain the habitations of figures important in the indigenous design of life. In Amatenango, denizens of the caves found in hills surrounding the town are believed to control health and wealth, which they readily give to those foolish enough to seek it, but exact payment in the form of perpetual servitude following death. The *me'tik-tatik* themselves inhabit a cave on top of a steep hill overlooking the town. They come out to see that no evil spirits enter the streets. But even in this setting there is an uneasy sense that the gods will desert them. Some say the *me'tik-tatik* had already left in 1957 because they did not like the fiesta that was accorded to them on May 3rd. Each house contains a spirit who, I was told, looks like a dwarf *ladino* and who demands offerings with the threat that he will eat the souls of the inhabitants. These are powerful reminders of the spiritual forces people pretend to control with celebrations within the community, yet knowing that their defensive measures are themselves vulnerable.

The repertoire of spirits and places provides mnemonic devices reminding people of their cultural roots and providing archetypes of enemies and friends. Coexisting with Catholic icons of hope and redemption, these cultural archetypes can provoke fear and compromise as well as inspiration in the indigenous struggles for cultural continuity. The agents of change such as Don Klabil, the moneylender, found their place with precapitalist denizens of caves who offered wealth at the price of losing one's social relations with kin and neighbors. The fact that the wealth disappeared with the death of the petitioner, who was forced to work underground throughout his afterlife, reminds them of the evanescence of capitalist rewards and the priority of retaining collective security.

The Cargo System and Carrying the Burden of Time

The interface between indigenous communities and the dominant *ladino* society was entrusted to a hierarchy of civil and religious officials who bear the *cargo*, or burden, of carrying out rituals in their honor (Cancian; 1965, Nash 1970; Vogt 1976b). The legitimization of temporal power lay in the crossing over of indigenous leaders from religious to civil positions in the ceremonial life to promote harmony. The *principales* who had served in all the major posts also officiated in hearings related to witchcraft accusations along with the diviner-curers, or *iloletik*, literally, seers. The persisting belief in the power of the curers' mediation between the cosmos and the microcosmos, controlled and sanctioned by the *principales,* allowed Mayans to evade direct confrontation with the dominant *ladinos* as they attempted to maintain harmonious balance between people and place through their control over illness and death (Cancian 1965; Guiteras Holmes 1961; Hermitte 1992; Nash 1967; Warren 1989; Villa Rojas 1990). It also promoted the internalization of conflict, since both *principales* and *iloletik* tended to locate evil within the local context.

Differences in the functioning of the civil religious hierarchies over time demonstrate the profound differences among communities in the way people adapt to the macro changes affecting their lives and express this in traditions. Zinacantecos resolved the contradictions in growing wealth differences by richer members of the community accepting more expensive *cargos* in the cycle of fiestas in 1965 (Cancian 1965). Over twenty years later, the new, wealthy Zinacantecos, who had trucks and engaged in new, more remunerative occupations than corn farmers, still played a major role in the religious hierarchy. Cancian's interpretation is that this still served as a social investment to ensure against negative reactions to their new roles and great wealth (Cancian 1992:199). This functionalist interpretation does not fit Amatenango, but this does not negate its importance for Zinacantán. In Amatenango, the *alféreces*, or captains of the fiesta, who carried the greatest financial burden, claimed that they were the targets of witchcraft because of envy of the display of wealth. Perhaps because of the lack of reward incumbents faced, there was a great deal of difficulty in recruiting *alféreces*, and officials often coerced young men into taking on the cargoes.

When *alféreces* ceased their celebrations of the saints in 1971, a severe drought that occurred two years later was blamed on the failure to celebrate saints' days. Four *alféreces* of the four patron saints were recruited to undertake a three-day pilgrimage to Oxchuc, where the patron saint, Santo Tomás, is believed to be related to Quetzalcoatl and endowed with the power to give rain. Accompanied by scores of Amatenangueros, they bore the image of Santa Lucía who, according to local myths, was Santo Tomás's unrequited lover. The pilgrimage was a form of penance to the neglected saint, and the celebration they carried out was intended to reawaken the love between the two saints in order to bring the rain. When the rains came during their pilgrimage, celebrants felt satisfied that they had overcome Saint Tomás's anger over having been neglected by the Oxchuqueños, many of whom had converted to Protestantism.

Tradition was later seen as providing a competitive advantage in elections when the PRI faced opposition candidates for the first time in the 1990s. When the state government began to assist communities with a donation of $500 new pesos (the equivalent of US$130) for the fiestas in Amatenango del Valle, charges of misappropriation of funds disrupted the sense of the communitywide obligation to undertake the burden. The result was that no one agreed to accept the leadership of the Carnival fiesta in 1993, and the town lives in fear that there will be another drought, as happened in 1971 when the *alférez* roles had been discontinued.

Chamula's civil religious hierarchy plays a role in the validation of the privileges enjoyed by the *caciques*, but instead of leveling wealth, as a functionalist model predicts (E. Wolf 1957), the official roles enable the incumbents to monopolize the wealth flowing into the town from the PRI and to enjoy monopolies of the liquor and soft drink concessions they control. The cultural variability shown by Highland Chiapas communities in their modes of adapting to new opportunities for leadership did not universally create the conditions for *cacique* rule. It varied over time within communities and from one community to the next. The indigenous leaders who emerged in the 1940s and 1950s

were often highly motivated to bring progress, literacy, and land rights to their communities without self-gain. Manuel Árias, who served as scribe and later president of San
Pedro Chenalhó, Salvador López Castellanos, who fought the traditionalists of his time
in San Juan Chamula (Árias Perez 1994), and Ceferino Gomez, who was instrumental in
bringing the land reform to reality in Amatenango del Valle (Nash 1970:236) do not fit
the mold of opportunism implicit in the term *caciques*. These leaders resisted co-optation
into the PRI-controlled "traditions" at the same time as they resisted the loss of their
commitment to a collective responsibility.

THE MEXICAN DEVELOPMENT MODEL IN INSTITUTIONAL REVOLUTIONARY COMMUNITIES

The Mexican development ideology of *indigenismo* extolled native culture, only to rel-
egate it to the past as integration into the "mainstream" of *mestizo* society was promoted.
Manuel Gamio, who pioneered applied anthropology in the 1920s, postulated the
"incomplete character of the nation" so long as "the Indian" remained "marginalized."
This was based on the racist assumption that indigenous pueblos had to reject their culture in order for the nation to progress (Díaz-Polanco 1987: 33). In 1921 Gamio created
the Department of Education and Culture for the Indian race, and sent social action
teams into the *pueblos* to bring literacy, improved horticulture, pastoral practices, artisan
production, and to raise the living standards.

The National Indian Institute (INI)

The INI, founded in 1948, promoted direct intervention in indigenous villages under
the leadership of Alfonso Caso and Gonzalo Aguirre Beltrán. Caso defined the *indio* as one
who belonged to an indigenous community, which he defined as a space in which non-
European cultural elements predominated. This simplistic view, stripping the Indian of a
role in the class struggle and reconstituting him in bounded communities that had no
regional extension, provided the model for the paternalistic relation between the state and
the indigenous communities that was to influence a generation of developmentalists.
Although the generation of *indigenistas* are castigated as a group that denied class relations,
many of the highly motivated practitioners attracted to the field of applied anthropology
generated theoretical and practical advances. Ricardo Pozas, who became an important
force in the discipline of anthropology and in the applied indigenist program in the 1940s
and 1950s, extended the category of *indigenista*. In his view, the *campesinos* are "*indios* that
have suffered imposed changes from relations of dominance and subordination that they
have opposed, affirming themselves while maintaining their own form of economic production with a common language, that permits them to conserve their forms of thought
and to create an ethnic consciousness in spite of their exploitation" (cited in Durand
Alcántara 1994:81). Pozas's work with his wife Isabel (1971) on Indians in the social
classes of Mexico posits the "Indian problem" in class terms that emphasize the oppressive
conditions that limit their potential. Their programs for education and economic devel-

opment could still serve as a guide for promoting multicultural coexistence of ethnic groups in the national society.

It is important to keep in mind the diverse views that were contained within the institutions that promoted the hegemony of the PRI government. This provided both the strength of the central government, and its potential for divisiveness. It was marked in the operation of INI that I observed and participated in 1957 and 1958 and 1962 to 1967, which I recount below. It is also implicit in the collapse of PRI hegemony as the PRI officials disarticulate the corporate structures they helped put in place (see chapter 5).

In 1952 the INI headquarters opened up in the Department of San Cristóbal de Las Casas. Alfonso Villa Rojas was the director when I received an INI research and study grant in 1957. Innovations were adapted selectively to prevailing ways of life during Villa Rojas's leadership in the 1950s and 1960s. The selection of young indigenous men trained as *promotores* for programs in health, agriculture, artisan production, and education, who worked in their own communities, showed a rare degree of cultural sensitivity even while adhering to male priority. Having worked in Oxchuc, Villa Rojas was well aware that any change would constitute a threat to the hierarchy of *principales* and to the curer-diviners. In Amatenango, the son of a highly respected curer who was trained by INI as a paramedic shared patients with his father, who yielded to modern medicine in cases where it had proven effective (immunizing against contagious diseases and antibiotic injections for common infections), while he called on the elder curer for diseases caused by witchcraft. Compromises over innovations were often reached without bloodshed. For example, when potable water was introduced in 1962 at the instigation of the local schoolteacher, the curers who bathed their patients in the spring water objected since they were fearful of being cut off from the spring at its source. INI promoters worked out an agreement with the town officials whereby a stream of the spring water was diverted into a pool at its source to provide access for curative bathing without contaminating the water carried in pipes to the town center.

The Amatenangueros' selective responses to innovation and abandonment of old traditions during the 1950s and early 1960s are at odds with the current assessment of INI's past as an authoritarian and homogenizing scheme of ethnocide (Díaz-Polanco 1987). In my experience in Amatenango, I found that there was a great deal of latitude for local communities to select programs on the basis of a pragmatic assessment of what worked for them within their own cultural design. This was in part because programs were not as well funded as in the central and northern states. The development model pursued by INI in the San Cristóbal region during the 1950s and 1960s promoted existing agricultural techniques without highly capitalized innovation. Crop rotation, rather than expensive petrochemical fertilizers and other "green revolution" techniques, was preferred. Collective forms of capital accumulation were introduced that became a model for nongovernmental initiatives. The first INI cooperative in Amatenago was a store, which provided basic staples at modest prices. The storekeeper, a graduate of the boarding school in Chamula and former soldier, used this organizational form to start a rum shop. With four "*socios,*" or partners, he purchased a phonograph player and amplifier that attracted young men who worked at a nearby lumber company on their payday, Saturday night. He told me that he could have capitalized the venture himself, but was afraid of the *invidio*, or envy, that could cause illness and even death. "With four members," he said, "they would not kill all of us." He went on to purchase the first truck operated by an Indian in the town, with a group of 30 *socios*. Some of the cooperative members gave no more than 150 pesos (about US$15 in those days) but, as the instigator of the purchase remarked, "The more members we have, the more power it gives us." With the name of the cooperative emblazoned on the door, Cooperative of Small Agriculturalists of Amatenango, the driver did not have to fear being picked up by state police in those days. The humble reference to themselves as "small," and their deference to the superior knowledge of the state police when the indigenous driver was stopped, fed into the racist assumptions of superiority.[27] Nor did they have to fear the "risk" of making a profit; with the "social insurance" it offered, envious neighbors would hesitate to kill all of the *socios* out of envy of their wealth (Nash 1966:14).

Government programs channeled through INI tended to reinforce priorities of the communities for small-plot cultivation in a household production system. Wheat was introduced as a crop that complemented corn by replacing nitrogen in the soil for the traditional corn and bean cultivation. The fault of the program was in its failure to provide transportation of the harvest to market centers and to integrate the crop into consumption in the village by introducing ovens and training Indians in baking techniques. Forced to sell to the National Campaign for Popular Subsistence (CONASUPO) agents, the Indians encountered corrupt agents who declared their crops below standard and cheated them on the weighing of the bags.

My task for INI was to assess means of introducing a kiln for the potters of Amatenango del Valle and to demonstrate a solar cooker in the interest of saving the forests. INI showed an early concern for the depletion of the forests, and kilns would have reduced the need for wood. The women had learned to calculate the endurance of each of the distinctive clays they used to fire with the open-hearth system. This involved weeks of sun-drying the new pots in their large porches. They surrounded the fire with the new pots, tending them constantly, and turning them so they became evenly fired. When they reached a stage of firmness that could withstand pressures, women and their kin and neighbors assembled for the final mounting of the pots in a conical pyramid over the smoldering fire. As they mounted the pots, they carefully inserted an old shard to protect each pot at the point where it touched another. At the moment when the pot was done, which required careful assessment by each master potter, they dismounted the pyramid with poles. This was the crucial moment, since the greatest amount of breakage occurred then. Sometimes the men of the household helped in this very arduous operation. The kiln that was introduced was designed for clays with a higher silicon content. The pots turned to ashes in the high-intensity firing. Women rejected the innovation not out of conservative or superstitious mistrust but through an empirical assessment of the performance of the new technology. I recommended the need for an extensive process of technological modification to make the kiln serviceable, but INI did not have the resources to carry this out until the 1970s. A kiln was then introduced when the government promoted a cooperative that received major orders from museum retail shops and tourist agencies, promoting ever-greater production. Concern about deforestation may still have prompted the innovation.[28]

I was also asked to help promote a solar cooker, which was delivered to the compound in which I lived. Each morning I went out at ten when the morning mists had cleared and the sun was at its brightest. I showed the virtues of the cooker usually to an audience of children, who found it entertaining. But women had already cooked the morning meal, rising before the dawn, and by the time they needed to prepare the evening meal, the rain clouds had dimmed the sun. I realized soon that the cooker would also never work because it forced the private domestic acts into the open, where envious neighbors would see or smell what was cooking. Although these projects misfired, they showed the willingness of INI to introduce innovations related to an existing way of life that would be environmentally propitious.

Indigenous initiatives for self-development during the 1960s were toward colonizing plots of land in national lands. Amatenangueros carried out two such colonization programs in hot country, the first to the north, in San Caralampio, and the second to the east, in a colony that the town officials named "Leon Brindis," after the PRI official who legalized their claim. These colonies, in distinct ecological zones, complemented the annual cycle of Amatenango cultivators,, bringing in harvests during periods of corn shortages and maximizing the use of labor power in their own projects.

The INI projects in Chiapas during this period reaffirmed the collective strategies for the survival of small-plot semi-subsistence cultivation. The experience of Amatenangueros up until the mid-1960s contrasts with development programs more closely controlled by government agencies in the rest of Mexico, where large-scale dam projects and agroindustrial development were capitalized at the expense of the semi-subsistence sector. The convergence in Chiapas with the development models in the states of the central plateau came about over a decade later, when highly capitalized ventures became the predominant model of federal development agencies (Collier and Quaratiello 1994).

Gendered Responsibilities for the Balancing of Cultural Change

Migration was an established pattern, with men oscillating between the lowlands and the highlands as they were forced to seek wages and respond to new market opportunities (Collier 1990). Men of Zinacantán and Chamula were even more involved in wage work than those belonging to municipalities like Amatenango that had more communal land to distribute and cash income from pottery production. Women accompanied men to work in the lowland colonies to which Amatenangueros had succeeded in gaining title from the central government. Those who went without husbands were subject to rape without recourse to courts that operated in their favor in the town center. Women who marketed their own pottery beyond the neighboring towns were also subject to harassment. While they could redress their injuries in the local courts, where I have heard judges favor them over their assailants, they had to have strong family support to prove they were not "looking for a man." This is clearly a way of limiting and controlling women's movements, as Bourque and Warren (1981) show in *Women of the Andes*. If they did not have a compelling reason to cross the line between the moieties, women could be harassed and even permanently stigmatized. I learned this when the women of the Ahkolnantik moiety boycotted

a corn-grinding mill introduced in 1963 that was located in the opposite moiety of Alan-
nantik, much as they would have enjoyed using this time-saving service. It explained to me
why the woman who cared for my child when I had to be out took a circuitous route—
going down to the highway and sneaking through a little-traveled path—to the house
where I lived in the opposite moiety. Men had freer movement within the town, but could
be killed if suspected of courting a girl from the other side.

use
against
Women

Gender specialization is an important element in the representation of a distinct
ethnic identity in indigenous communities. Both men and women agreed that changes
were necessary to facilitate necessary political and economic transactions with the wider
society. The gendered responsibility was evident in most of the highland communities.
The most obvious, but nonetheless significant, example is dress. Women in most highland communities still wear the distinctive *huipil* along with skirts, which identify their
community of origin and sometimes the onset of menses (as in San Juan Chamula).
Because marriage occurs within townships, women's dress identifies marriageable partners. It also situates the woman who wears a hand-loomed and brocaded or embroidered
garment in the universe. Marta Turok captured the semiotic significance of *huipiles* in
Santa María Magdalena, where the richly brocaded central panel forms a great cross over
the shoulders, breast and back (Turok 1988:47–52). According to Turok's informant, a
diamond-shaped design in the center represents the cosmos containing the world within
it, which resembles a cube with three levels, with earth in the center between the sky
and the underworld. The colors of the *huipil*—red, black, yellow, and white—represent
grains of corn and cardinal points in the diamond-shaped world, while symbols of
death—bat, *zopilote* (turkey buzzard), and worm—represent the pueblo. A Magdalena
woman wearing her *huipil* thus situates herself in her cultural and natural world.

Amatenango women are less articulate about the symbolism of their dress. But extrap-
olating from their vision of the universe as a set of contained squares, from a sacrificial
hole in their houses (representing the house itself, the milpa, and the world), I could perceive them situating themselves in that universe when they wear the broad bands of red
and gold forming a square around the neck. The significance of this orientation occurred
to me when my *comadre* reacted with horror on seeing a Protestant proselytizer offering
free clothing from U.S. Goodwill dumpsites to townspeople. After reading Turok, I had
wondered whether the embroidered square neckline might also be a world figure. When
I asked my *comadre* if the analogy of the square world, which was the dominant image for
their thinking of the world, the square houses they built to conform to a square, and their
milpas, which they described as square, was part of their conceptualization in the design
of the blouse, she agreed heartily. Women's clothing in Amatenango became even more
richly embroidered with silk threads on backstrap-loomed cotton from Venustiano Carranza as the women acquired more income from pottery production for tourists in the
1970s and 1980s. Women prayer-makers (*resadoras*) serving the Virgin Lucía replaced her
ladino-style satin and lace garments with a richly embroidered Amatenango *huipil* and
hand-loomed skirt in the 1970s. Most of these women were leaders of the pottery cooperative that began functioning in 1970, through which they gained greater autonomy in
their control over the proceeds of their money.

Indigenous men of the highland region tend to be less traditional in their everyday clothing than women, except during ritual occasions. In the twenty-year interval between my visits to Amatenango, men stopped wearing the distinctive backstrap-loomed cotton shirts and wrapped pants in their everyday life, although they still use the *kotonchu* (tunic, literally, "heart covering"), which was made in San Juan Ixcoy in Guatemala and imported clandestinely, for ceremonial occasions. The men of Zinacantán and San Juan Chamula differ from most men in highland communities in the increasing elaborateness of their tunics, which are hand-loomed by women. In these communities, where men are forced to seek income in areas farther and farther away, elaboration of their distinctive tunics may represent an attempt by the women to "brand" their men.

The message is clearly that women's involvement with tradition is a daily aspect of life itself, while that of men is formally defined in ritual events. This is not an essentializing argument drawn from stereotypes about women's more conservative role. Rather, it is a conscientious priority adopted by women, and, as I shall show in chapter 3 in discussing the entry of Zapatista women into radical democratic change, a principal definition of their commitment. The gendered specialization of women as bearers of traditional culture allows more scope for men to adapt in ways that facilitate survival of the community. Yet traditions reinforcing gender specialization are also threatened in the current economic and political crisis, as I shall show in the following chapter.

In my recurrent field stays in Amatenango from 1957 to 1967, the "true men" (*batzil winiketik*), as the people referred to themselves, were able to mediate the changes that were occurring throughout highland Chiapas in ways that gave them a feeling of control

Women wear traditional red and gold huilpiles *as they receive food at betrothal banquet, Amatenango del Valle 1991. Their adherence to traditional dress and their sitting on the mats on the pine strewn floor contrasts with the clothing and posture of men in the following photo taken at a house ceremony the same year.*

Except for elder officials, Amatenago men wear casual clothing as they are served at baptismal celebration, Amatenango del Valle 1991.

over their destiny. The prayers of the civil and religious officials, uttered in the passing over of the *cargo,* or burden of office, reaffirmed their commitment to the past and continuity with the future. As they utter the prayer, "And so we shall be able to do what our mothers did and what our fathers did here, where our Holy Father sees us and our Holy Mother sees us, here in the eyes of the ancestors," there is a profound confirmation of the legitimacy of the new officers in their role as guardians of tradition. Yet this containment of the changes that were coming to the Chiapas highlands within a fictive corporate community carried a price. Homicide of those accused of witchcraft was one measure of the tensions, as elders curers struck out at the young contenders who were demanding priority in the curing hierarchy just as they saw young men gain prestige in civil offices. In the 1960s, the boundaries of community enabled the PRI to co-opt local officials more easily. Containment of indigenous discontent was facilitated by the community-imposed boundaries that restricted the political potential of indigenous political activity regionally.

Patriarchal control over women was threatened as women's pottery production brought in cash that became increasingly important in the household economy. The gendered division of labor, in which women accepted the responsibility for transmitting the language and practices of indigenous culture to children, succeeded in making them powerful repositories of tradition but distanced them from some of the skills and rewards of entering into greater continual contact with the dominant *ladino* society. As monolingual, nonliterate subjects, they were marginalized from power in the political and economic circuits. When they breached the boundaries that defined their sphere, the results were explosive. Rape and death were infrequent but ominous reminders of the boundaries. Discontent in the outlying settlements that failed to gain some of the benefits of development was accelerating, along with increases in the flow of funds from party headquarters in the state capital to civil offices in the town center.

The involution of rebellion in indigeneous communities that embraced an ideology of harmony and accord with the ancestors extended the control exercised by traditional leaders for more than a decade after changes began to transform the state. But by the end of my stay in 1967, people questioned whether indeed the ancestors still lived in the cave located in the hills above the community. On May 3, 1967, the Day of the Cross, when indigeneous communities prayed at each of the crosses at the exits of the town, many expressed the conviction that the ancestors had gone to live in Chiapa de Corzo because they were dissatisfied with the fiestas given in their honor. Civil officials could no longer recruit *alféreces* to carry the burden of the expensive fiesta cycle, which cost more than three times their annual income. In 1971 a drought that dried up the first planting of corn triggered alarm that the balance between the moon and the sun was upset by their own failure to continue the *alférez* roles in fiestas and provoked the pilgrimage described on pp.67–68. The identification of Saint Tomas with thunder and the power to bring rains extends the responsibilities of cargo holders to cosmic levels.

The rains followed within a few days and the crisis passed, but the *alférez* ceremonies were reinstituted. They were continued each year until another crisis related to the Zapatista rebellion occured in 1995 (chapter 5). When threats of hunger and loss of lands recurred in the following decades, indigenous communities were already organizing beyond the pueblo limits to confront powerful state and national leaders who were increasingly blamed for the impoverishment of the agrarian sector.

COMMUNITY CONTRASTS AND THE ETHNOGRAPHY OF DIFFERENCE

Ethnographic studies of communities in the region are an important corrective to generalizations of such complex processes as the transition from traditional leadership based on gerontocracy to a young literate leadership. Chamula turned to expulsions to get rid of the competitors for office. Oxchuc sought an escape in conversion to Protestantism. Zinacantecos' community celebrations retreated to the *parajes*, where the number of fiestas and *cargos* that bore responsibility and prestige expanded. In Amatenango, where an age-ordered hierarchy of curer-diviners was threatened by the competition of young leaders, the elders resorted to killing a generation that they perceived to be bent on usurping their power (Nash 1967). Reflecting on some of those leaders who were entering the town offices in 1957, two of whom were killed in the decade after I terminated my first field stay in 1967, it often seemed to me like reverse selection of the fittest: the brightest and most alert were being eliminated in order to keep the lid on the tumultuous forces set loose by rising populations and limited channels for gaining prestige, wealth, and, for some, even a bare subsistence level. Yet unlike Chamula, Amatenangeros were able to rid themselves of a *cacique* family that had abused the power of office. Family members, who had succeeded in gaining PRI backing in two successive elections in the 1970s, repudiated themselves by carrying out arbitrary expulsions from the community and killing opponents, as well as stealing town funds. A group of young men rallied around an inspiring bilingual teacher, a native of the community who opposed the *cacique's* candidacy. When the family of the disgruntled *cacique* retaliated by killing the teacher in the mid-1980s, the supporters of the latter convinced the PRI to reject him and run a candidate whom they approved.

In the context of highland Chiapas politics, where Chamula is often taken as the model of community state relations (Gilly 1994), it is important to recognize settings in which the indigenous population asserted their own agenda within the context of the PRI. We must also retain a clear sense of the changes over time and how the relations of the communities to the PRI changed. Chenalhó was once noted for the inspired leadership of Manuel Árias, who served as *promoter* in the 1950s. His nephew, Jacinto Arias, who was serving as mayor of Chenalhó in 1997, has been implicated in the massacre of 45 women, children, and men in Acteal (See chapter 5 on the Acteal massacre).

Distinct historical memories of individuals who play critical roles must be taken into account as we try to interpret the varied experiences of individuals, families, and histories related to any institutional complex. Functionalist explanations were at error not because they tried to figure out the rationale for the existence of any custom or practice within a given community; they fell short because they applied rational criteria derived from the anthropologist's own culture and expertise in a particular locality that often failed to assess the logic of the actors. This logic requires an appreciation of the history of the institution and the behaviors observed and recorded within its context.

The combined effort of ethnographers and ethnohistorians is needed to unravel the story of any institution. For example, at one moment the civil religious hierarchy might preserve harmony by leveling wealth (E. Wolf 1957), only to validate wealth differences at a later date and in a different place (Cancian 1965). Amatenangueros attempt to keep the cosmos in balance, while Indians of Pinola simply try to preserve harmony of those on earth with the ancestors. The functions of the civil religious hierarchies respond to historical changes and the new interpretations accorded to them. The new chapels built in the growth years of the agrarian sector might promote cooperative festivals through the civil-religious hierarchy within hamlets, with the effect of reducing the control exercised by the center through reciprocal exchanges during fiestas, as Rus and Wasserstrom (1980) show in their processual analysis. Zapatistas in the Lacandón rain forest are inviting ritual specialists from highland villages to teach them the customs of the ancestors. It will undoubtedly provide the continuity needed to legitimize their leadership in the transformations that are occurring today. Functionalist models are locally circumscribed and, to have any value, should be contextualized within particular historical circumstances. Since they do not and, I believe, never can address the wider context, they cannot pretend to predict change or to generalize beyond an instance, but these instances, minutely observed, are important instruments for analyzing the unfolding of culturally conditioned responses in the habitus.

The growing resistance to the paternalistic model of co-optation exercised by the ruling party as it was "integrating" these institutional revolutionary communities is the subject of chapter 3. Rejection of control from the centers of power, dominated by what indigenous leaders in rebellion call the *mestizocracia*, finds increasing expression in the emergence of autonomous pueblos and territories, discussed in chapters 4 and 5.

CHAPTER 3

EXODUS FROM COMMUNITIES:
Genesis of Indigenous Culture in Regional and National Spaces

COMMUNITIES PROVIDED THE habitus within which indigenous populations reproduced their culture and generated the adaptations that made it possible for them to survive in the colonial and independent state. Globalization processes threaten these communities as never before. Yet these same processes connect indigenous social movements in regional associations that provide a nexus for ethnic reassertion. At a moment when the terms "community," "local versus global," and the representations of spaces and changed social relations are being problematized, David Harvey's notion of the compression of time and space will help us analyze how such changes have affected Chiapas's indigenous communities over time (1989:219–221). The compression of time and space that he speaks of in global terms accelerated the integration of institutional revolutionary communities in ways that surpassed the control mechanisms they had contrived to defend themselves. These same processes provided opportunities to expand the horizons of communities and to engage in new strategies of recuperating indigenous cultures.

The changes occurring after the 1910 Revolution described in chapter 2 enabled indigenous populations to intensify cultural traditions, especially from the time of Lázaro Cárdenas's presidency (1934–1940) until the late 1960s. The acquisition of *ejido* land made it possible for small-plot cultivators to devote more of their energies to their subsistence economy, with less migration to the coastal plantations. The woven and embroidered traditional clothing became more elaborated in the 1950s, and more money was spent in festivals for the saints. Yet, at the same time as communities were able to enhance their traditional material culture with these new resources, the commodification of space and time affected the bases of indigenous institutions in unanticipated ways. The loss of reciprocal labor exchanges weakened kinship and neighborhood labor exchanges that had solidified relations. The presence of young literate officials upset the patriarchal, age-ordered, prestige hierarchy, undermining the traditional controls exercised in the household and community. The increased flow of money into the communities heightened the dependency of the communities on the federal government and reduced the level of autonomy.

The integration of indigenes in wider organizations and social spaces changed the order of priorities within communities but did not mitigate their importance. On the contrary, indigenous officials recognized the political power of communities, and used their land resources, minimal as they were, as a launching pad for making claims on the government. I recall vividly the remarks of an Amatenango town official observing the deplorable conditions of a group of deculturated *campesinos* who worked in the sawmill within the municipal boundaries in 1958: "There without our *pueblo* would be us!" The population of about twenty families of migrant laborers living in shacks above the town center had no schooling, no church, no health services, and the women and children were visibly undernourished.[1]

The political power of the community became increasingly important in the 1960s. The municipalities gained direct representation with the central government, with indigenous mayors and secretaries taking over the posts that had been held by *ladinos*. With increasing literacy, men were gaining some control over the political process, using lawyers to intercede in land disputes or cattle theft. Legal advertisements appeared in the Tuxtla Gutierrez newspapers by advocates claiming to be "Friend of the Indian." Members of the *ejido* commission and literate young officials went as representatives of their pueblo to the state capital to stake out claims to national territories opened up by highway construction in the 1960s.

Yet, so long as it was limited to bounded corporate structures, the power of communities became increasingly distorted. As indigenous communities competed with each other to win the favor of the PRI, their leaders increasingly adopted the practices prevalent in PRI hegemonic institutions. Once they accepted the structures of subordination as natural, local *caciques* tended to serve their own interests, undermining the collective concerns of the *ejidatarios,* holders of *ejido* lands, and of members of the community who shared rights in the common lands controlled by the residents of the community as *comuneros*. The increasing alienation of *comuneros* from the leadership within their own communities contributed to the breaking away of *campesino* organizations from the official corporate structures controlled by the government. Thus the PRI's success in co-opting Indian leaders ultimately weakened the control of *caciques* over their bases in indigenous pueblos.

In this chapter, I shall analyze how *campesinos* were becoming tied into regional networks and the impact this had in indigenous communities. The transformations within the postrevolutionary communities provided an infrastructure that enabled them to go beyond the structural limitations the government attempted to impose in the community model of development. In the decade of the 1970s, indigenous communities were drawn into government programs that by the 1980s were curtailed in the debt crisis. In this process, they became aware of the government's reversal of the social contract that had bound their destiny to that of the nation. A brief review of national changes will help orient our discussion of the development process in local perspective.

GLOBAL INTEGRATION AND NEOLIBERALISM IN MEXICO

The integration of Mexico into the global economy is correlated with the shrinking of national controls affecting the redistribution of wealth and the direction of development. The narrowing of the scope of national redistributive policies threatens the premises of

Mexico's "institutional revolution" that maintained hegemonic control from the 1930s until the 1990s. This was predicated on incorporation of distinct interest groups in national organizations that represented their demands, but within a control structure conforming to the priorities of national elites.

Redistribution Policies and the Debt Crisis

Mexico's corporatist state and the PRI monopoly of power culminated in the redistributional policies of Luís Echeverría Alvarez (1970–1976). Public expenditures more than doubled in the decade from 1965 to 1975, rising to 28 percent of the GDP in the mid-1970s, as Echeverría attempted to stem the rising protest brought about by Díaz Ordaz's developments-from-above policies and his fierce repression of the 1968 student rebellion (Chant 1991:36–37). Echeverría reactivated the land distribution program with the federal Agrarian Law in 1971, which distributed more financial resources to the *ejido* sector. The Agrarian Law carried its own time bomb for corporate lands, since it made possible the leasing of *ejido* lands for commercial events.

Echeverría's successor in office, López Portillo (1976–1982), pursued dual goals, one of private capitalist development and the other of redistributing wealth to the poor. His development projects became increasingly contradictory. In 1980 he introduced the Law for Agricultural and Pastoral Promotion, which provided generous compensation to large landowners whose lands were invaded by *campesinos*. He also tried to open the doors to the investment of capital in the *ejido* sector. Still adhering to populist tendencies of the PRI, he balanced this with the Mexican Nutrition System (SAM) in 1981 to promote nutrition by stabilizing subsistence production (Moncada 1983). Two years later, SAM was demobilized and the government released the brakes on programs promoting highly capitalized and increasingly privatized ventures.

Since much of the state expenditures were financed by foreign loans with the expectation of rising oil revenues, the abrupt decline in oil prices precipitated the debt crisis of the 1980s. IMF conditions for regaining creditability promoted export-oriented development policies, beginning with the presidency of José López Portillo (1976–1982), and followed by that of Miguel de la Madrid Hurtado (1982–1988). These policies set in motion the dismantling of the corporatist state and promoted free market "neoliberal" policies. The toughest sector to confront was that of the *ejidos*, which had actually increased by 1,446 *ejidos* in the period from 1988 to 1991, reaching a total of 29,504 *ejidos* (INEGI) at a time when the program of land reform was coming under scrutiny.

The rhetoric of "growth through modernization" during López Portillo's six-year term of office could not be sustained by his successor. The annual growth rate declined from 3.4 percent in his last year in office to 0.1 percent during the debt crisis that occurred in de la Madrid's presidency. Stagnation in the Mexican economy brought about by the "reform" package of privatization and liberalization of trade resulted in a minus 0.5 gross domestic product rate in the period from 1983 to 1986. The contraction was most severe for workers and the lower middle class. Wage earners suffered a drop in real wages to 66 percent of the 1978 wage index in 1988, the lowest point of the decline, and unemployment increased (Lara Resende 1995). The new private enterprises that replaced subsidized national enterprises were often export-processing assembly plants lured by government subsidies and promises of tax abatements that further undercut the redistributive role of national governments. Thus, between the periods 1970 to 1981 and 1986 to 1988, Mexico's share of social expenditures in relation to GDP fell 30 percent.[2] The earthquake of 1985 and the decline in petroleum prices expected to fuel recovery delayed for another five years the kind of stabilization that would encourage venture capitalism to invest further resources. Although the IMF conditions succeeded in ensuring the payment of foreign debt, the country suffered from recession, inflation, low productivity, imbalance in production, and severe social setbacks in health and education.[3]

What brought about decline in oil prices?

Carlos Salinas de Gotari and the New Technocrats

Despite the declining welfare of its citizens, Mexico was taken as a model of the success of the IMF debt containment conditions in 1988 when President Carlos Salinas de Gotari took over the presidency in an election that is still contested. Within his six-year term, he promoted neoliberal policies that changed the course of Mexico's corporatist government. The development priorities pursued by Salinas from 1988 to 1994 marked a dramatic departure from the model of agrarian corporatist policies promoted by his predecessors. Although he still used corporatist tactics of absorbing the opposition through co-optation and dummy organizations that pretended to respond to the urgent needs of landless *campesinos*, Salinas's promotion of the private sector oriented to export production through the Free Trade Act (*Tratado de Libre Comercio*), referred to as the North American Free Trade Agreement (NAFTA) in the United States, and his undercutting of land reform through the "reform" of Article 27 of the 1917 Constitution were incompatible with the ideology of the institutional revolution.

Throughout his six-year term, President Salinas maintained the rhetoric of corporativism while undercutting its bases. By eliminating many small-plot producers raising subsistence crops, Mexico increased the country's dependency on food imports. Although these acts confirmed policies that had been under way since 1980, the net effect of Salinas's policies was to cut the productive sector to 66 percent of levels during the preceding presidency performance while further impoverishing the low-income sector. With the reduction of agrarian supports below the levels to which they had been reduced by his immediate predecessors, Echeverría and López Portillo, thousands of *campesinos* were added to the ranks of the unemployed. Unemployment increased from a low of 1.4 million in 1982, when there were 21.5 million workers in the employed workforce, to 8.9 million in 1990, when there were 22.8 million in the workforce. Thus the increases in GDP failed to incorporate increasing numbers of *campesinos* pushed off the land (*La Jornada*, citing Banco de Mexico indicators, December 3, 1991).

During the second half of his six-year term, Salinas accelerated these processes with three major pieces of legislation. The first was the "reform" of the Article 27 Land Reform Act of the 1917 Constitution that effectively ended further entitlements when it was passed in 1991, though it did not force *ejidos* to part with existing holdings. The second was curtailment of the government's role in redistributive policies correlated with the promotion of a wealthy elite, in part through privatization of state-owned enterprises that enriched a few close cronies of the president but often devastated regional economies. The third was the opening up of Mexico's markets to global trade with NAFTA, which threatened small-plot cultivators who could not compete with U.S. subsidized agroindustrial producers. The acceleration of these trends with Salinas's initiatives is discussed below.

The Reform of Article 27. The most abrupt break with Mexico's corporatist structure came with Salinas's promotion of the "reform" of the agrarian reform article 27 of the 1917 Constitution. The original article in the 1917 Constitution represented a substantive advance in recognizing indigenous populations as subjects with legal rights (Durand Alcántara 1994:179). The reform threatened this corporate identity by allowing the privatization of collectively held *ejido* lands, opening the door to private sales.

Throughout the months after the reform of Article 27 was proposed in 1991, Salinas engaged in two quintessentially corporatist strategies. The first involved an ideological engagement of diverse interests threatened by the legislation. The second involved the restructuring of agencies dealing with agrarian conflict and welfare programs. This required a shoring up of patronage through combined public and private initiatives. He was ably abetted by intellectuals Arturo Warman and Roger Bartra, who had been on opposite sides of the *campesinista* debate in the 1970s and 1980s. During that twenty-year debate, Warman had supported the *ejido* land grant program, and Bartra opposed it as an obstacle to growth. In 1991 both protagonists in the debate supported the reform, agreeing that the new legislation would bring coherence between the reality of increasingly individual, privatized uses of *ejido* lands and a law that forbade disentailment of properties from collective management (*La Jornada* November 23, 1991).

Concomitant with these goals, the Salinas administration targeted areas of opposition to the dissolution of state paternalism that had operated within corporatist power blocks. The Permanent Agrarian Congress (CAP), a government-instigated organization, acted as a whip in promoting acceptance among its progovernment member groups. CAP used the government rhetoric, calling for greater flexibility and modification of the agrarian law, to permit free association between *campesinos* and private enterprises. Groups of "official," that is pro-PRI organizations, notably the National Confederation of Campesinos (CNC) and the National Confederation of Small Property Holders (CNPP), were trucked in intermittently during the congressional debates. The CNC returned to their bases explaining the reform bill with the rhetoric of "modernization without loss of the *ejido*." The framers of the reform were thus able to assess the support and opposition among critical agrarian sectors. CNPP raised some objections based on its constituents' concerns as *campesinos* without land. These misgivings were promptly addressed with the rhetoric of "new initiatives promoting the cooperation of private enterprises and public welfare." The bill was also modified in response to indigenous criticisms of the elevation to constitutional rank of the *ejido* commissions and the Indian pueblos. The government promised to recognize the greater freedom and autonomy of the *campesinos* in regulating the sale and purchase of plots. They also proposed a new level of organization for promoting production in commercial associations. Called the Agrarian Solicitor's Office, and with Arturo Warman named as director, it was charged with ridding the field of political favoritism and controls characteristic of the old Agrarian Affairs Office (*La Jornada* November 21, 1991). The government reaffirmed the illegality of the *latifundia*, and promised to limit the time allowed for breaking up these large holdings.

The sectors that were consistently ignored in all of these negotiations to gain support for the reform were those of the indigenous people. Peasant groups with a major indigenous component, such as the Independent Center of Agricultural Workers and Campesinos (CIOAC), whose base was with the Mayan colonizers of the rain forest, the General Workers, Campesino, and Popular Union (UGOCP), and the Campesino Democratic Unity (UCD), maintained their protests throughout 1991 and even after the Senate signed the bill on December 13, 1991. The other strong opposition came from indigenous groups: the Yaqui and Mayo marched against the reform bill on December 19, 1991, and the Tarahumara and Tepehuan pueblos registered their opposition through their bishop, saying: "We are not in accord with the change . . . . The law is always against the indigenous pueblo" (*La Jornada* January 6, 1992).

Campesino organizations brought together by the CAP, including the CNC, the CNPP, and the Union of Regional Organizations (UNORCA), signed the Manifesto of los Piños, the official headquarters of the president, on December 1, 1991, supporting the reform. It was a triumph of the old corporatist approach to gaining the neoliberal reforms promoted by the president. But the people left outside the accord, particularly those in Chiapas, did not intend to conform to the new law (Nash and Kovic 1996). Dissent grew in their representative organizations, including the CIOAC, the Union of the Ejido Unions and Groups of Campesinos in Solidarity of Chiapas (UU), and the Association of Collective Rural Interest (ARIC), to which the UU is linked. The members of these organizations became important players in the Zapatista rebellion. The dissent grew from a different logic from that of modernization and growth; campesinos, and particularly indigenes, were committed to collective control of the patrimony because of the security for the welfare of the group that it seemed to promise. The state was gradually divesting itself of this responsibility.

The most global attack on the new Agrarian Law came from the old National Indian Institute (INI). In a declaration to the press on October 19, 1991, INI warned that the twenty million hectares of temporal and irrigated land still in the hands of 360,000 *ejidatarios* would be in dispute. Of these, the INI paper declared, less than two-thirds of the *ejidatarios* had the potential to develop enterprise capitalism. By attacking this most vulnerable sector, INI declared that the new law would modify the legal basis of the state, thereby risking the social and political stability of the country (*La Jornada* October 19, 1991).

Following the passage of the new Agrarian Law, the government proceeded with a public relations campaign to get it accepted. The preamble to the law, published and disseminated by Solidarity, the usual designation for the Campesino and Teacher Solidarity (SOCAMO) group, read as follows:

> Under the principle of bringing greater liberty and justice to the Mexican countryside, the reform to Article 27 of the Constitution and the expedition of the Agrarian Law represents a change of great importance to overcome the low growth that the rural sector has had for 25 years in comparison with the rest of the economy. The recuperation of agriculture and the increase of the welfare of the *campesino* are a basic condition to modernize the region begun by the government of President Carlos Salinas de Gotari. (Procuradería Agraria 1992)

The government encountered resistance in its attempts to channel conflict cases into the newly created Agrarian Solicitors Office, along with welfare issues, bypassing the Agrarian Affairs Office. The secretariat conformed to the new technocratic image of competence. The appointment of Warman, a man who was identified with the *campesinista* position, seems to ensure its success.[4] Soon after his appointment, Warman announced to reporters that he had received few appeals responding to the new agrarian initiative under the "reform of the agrarian reform" (*La Jornada* September 26, 1992).

The process of roping in the opposition and wrapping itself in the mantle of revolutionary history while undoing the institutional base of its mandate is a stunning instance of the PRI's mastery of hegemonic rule. It took the uprising of the masked Zapatista rebels to unmask the strategy that still dominated the governing process.

The curtailment of government redistributive programs. The reduction of welfare policies and the privatization of public enterprises were two facets of the neoliberal government's commitment to reducing the public sector. Divesting the state of publicly owned enterprises had been pursued for well over a decade. Salinas's approach differed in its accelerated tempo and what Castañeda (1995:246) calls his "no-questions-asked" approach. The co-occurrence of the government's drive to privatize and the growing fortunes from drug trafficking enabled some to acquire visible overnight fortunes. Two Mexican financiers were catapulted into the Forbes top-twenty income bracket. The concerns that once tempered the policies of national banks and regional food-processing enterprises (such as the sugar mill in Pujiltic discussed below) were no longer mandatory in the operation of the public sector. These concerns once included considerations of maximizing employment, promoting credit for small-scale producers, and meeting the needs of Mexico's rural as well as urban poor.

The effects on income distribution of Salinas's privatization policies can be gleaned from level-of-living indices. The National Statistical Institute of the Government estimated that 37 million Mexicans were marginalized in 1990, with the greatest impoverishment in indigenous communities. This was the cumulative effect of the past three presidencies from 1976 to 1994, during which the PRI regimes had enriched a few while exaggerating wealth differences (*El Financiero* April 2, 1995:5–6).[5]

loyment went from 1,177,000 at the end of 1982 to six million in 1994. Real
1ich sank to a low of 66 in 1991, based on the 1978 index of one hundred, rose
1992, but never regained the 1978 level during Salinas's presidency. Even with
the recovery of the early 1990s, the sectoral imbalances in Latin America remained, with
an overall rise in unemployment, a decline in social welfare expenditures on education,
health, and the infrastructure of pure water and waste disposal, and a drop in real wages
(See World Bank *Annual Report* 1994, World Tables).

The conflict of interest between the new development policies of the government and
the small-plot cultivators was particularly strong in the Lacandón rain forest. It was clear
that if indigenous people gained control over development initiatives within their territory, neither the old co-optive politics of the PRI nor the associations of indigenous and
private enterprises proposed in the "reform" of the Article 27 Land Reform Act could
block their drive for autonomy. The Zapatista demands for a portion of the returns for
the hydroelectric power generated in the state and for the newly discovered oil were a
major threat to PRI hegemony.

NAFTA. Salinas's second major initiative was the passage of the North American Free
Trade Agreement in Mexico. The 1994 World Bank Annual Report claimed that the signing of NAFTA bolstered the long-term outlook for growth (World Bank 1994:28). The
report was published at the very moment when sectors of the Mexican population most
affected by the agreement, that is the semi-subsistence producers in rural and particularly indigenous areas, were rejecting the agreement in armed uprisings and massive
demonstrations. Yet upbeat pronouncements persisted. In response to the rhetorical
question posed: "Does globalization hurt wage earners?" the editors of the Inter-American Development Bank responded: No (June 1997:8), but a growing portion of the
labor force without the necessary skills have been permanently left out of the job markets. The plight of Mexico's indigenous population is steadily declining in relation to
other sectors and even to their recent past conditions (Inter-American Development
Bank 1997:150). The failure to address this growing gap between the rich and the poor
during the recent recovery suggests that the long-term trends toward a declining standard of living (Beneria 1992; United Nations Development Program 1991) will persist
for the one-third of the population that fell into impoverishment during the crisis.

The North American Free Trade Agreement introduced more risks into an economy
weakened by over a decade of debt crisis and belt-tightening. The sectors most threatened were the small entrepreneurs who faced greater competition from the offshore
production enterprises that were attracted in increasing numbers to Mexico, and the
indigenous cultivators. The promise of free trade was negated by the political climate of
injustices in a society that prevented democratic change from overcoming the structural
inequalities (Castañeda 1995).

Zedillo's New Economic Plan

Despite the dismal results of austerity policies in the 1980s, the current "solutions" for the debt crisis of the 1990s in Mexico are more of the same measures, with austerity measures and cuts in social welfare threatening the stability of the country. During the first hundred days of Ernesto Zedillo Ponce de León's presidency, the government faced the worst crisis since the 1982 debt crisis. The country suffered an extreme drain on its reserves in the transfer of office from Salinas to Zedillo when the low reserves and imbalances were made public at the end of 1994. Gustavo Saouri (*El Financiero* April 13, 1995:3A) attributes the loss to the natural economy of almost $46 billion in the five-year period from 1989 to 1994 to payments of interest on external debt as well as flight to safer markets, given the climate of uncertainty during the last year of the Salinas administration. Even before the *peso* was devalued on December 20, 1994, billions of dollars left the country, with bank failures adding to the vulnerability of the economy.

Zedillo's New Economic Plan, introduced in March 1995, called for a 35 percent increase in gasoline prices and a 20 percent increase in electricity rates and propane gas. The plan limited wage increases, which had scarcely risen during the past decade despite inflation in all sectors, particularly energy, which is produced domestically. A 15 percent sales tax passed in the Mexican Congress raised protests among consumers of all classes. This spelled the end for industry, according to the editorial opinion of *El Financiero Internacional* (March 15, 1995:21). The prediction proved true in the short run, with many bankruptcies recorded for national small industries, but transnational firms promoted by NAFTA picked up some of the slack in intervening years.

Labor was further alienated by the 9.8 percent reduction in public spending, with slashes in government payrolls and across-the-board decreases in state-provided services. Real wages, which had been declining throughout Salinas's administration, dropped precipitously in 1995, the first year of Zedillo's administration (Ramirez 1997:139), and with rising inflation, the minimum wage could buy only 56 percent of the basic food basket for a family of five. With rising inflation caused by the devaluation of the peso in international financial markets, the 10 percent hike in the minimum wage was not sufficient compensation to forestall protest. As Mexico entered a new election process in 2000, the "Chiapas problem" was not resolved. In fact, it had spread to neighboring states with high indigenous populations.

The Mexican crisis that began with the transfer of power from Salinas de Gortari to Ernesto Zedillo Ponce de León in December 1994 set off shock waves throughout Latin America. Even while state officials in Venezuela, Argentina, and Brazil were denying that the "Mexico Effect" would have an impact on their economies, these countries were, in fact, experiencing shortages of credit and devaluation in their currencies (*La Jornada* December 26, 1994:29). With the austerity measures that President Zedillo initiated when he took office in December 1994, the government could not even fund operating costs for the National Solidarity Program (PRONASOL), which was his predecessor's principle co-optive mechanism.

58

nstrations against these policies occurred throughout the nation. Thousands of
s, small businessmen hit by rising interest rates and doubling of their debts with the
devaluation and flight of capital, and workers left unemployed descended on the Mexican
capital, where they overflowed the *zócalo* in protest marches during the spring of 1995.

NAFTA under Zedillo. Since the passage of NAFTA in 1993, Mexico has increased
imports of corn and beans, with disastrous effects on the grain, surplus-producing states
such as Chiapas. Sold at lower prices than Chiapas farmers can produce these crops, these
federally subsidized crops from the United States may well put out of business the few
remaining producers of subsistence products. Price controls on subsistence crops have
caused further deterioration in the economic position of Chiapas producers, leading to
seizures of the headquarters of the National Campaign for Popular Subsistence (CONA-
SUPO) to protest controls that threatened the 1995 production (*El Financiero* March 15,
1995:25). The twelve and a half million agricultural day workers and small-plot holders
in the countryside have been caught in the stagnating economy from December 1994,
when the devaluation occurred, to the present. Prices rose, but the increases benefited
the middlemen, because most of the producers sell their products without any processing, either to CONASUPO or to commercial intermediaries since they lack money to
transport their harvest. Inefficient as it was in its later days, and as subject to corruption
and underpaying of the low prices accorded to producers, CONASUPO at one time provided an essential service for producers who had little access to alternative markets and
who lacked storage facilities so that they could take advantage of price fluctuations. The
lack of credit to plant, and even the money to migrate, made it difficult to exercise other
options as well, according to Rafael Jacobo, president of the Independent Center of Agricultural Workers and Campesinos (CIOAC) (*El Financiero* March 15, 25).

By the year 2000, the weakened CONASUPO had ceased to function, and the estimated 450,000 cultivators of subsistence crops experienced the worst crisis of their history. With huge imports of beans from the United States in 1998 and 1999, the price for
producers fell 30 percent, hardly covering the cost of production. Yet the prices to consumers were still too high to meet the real demand, since only the intermediaries benefited. Farmers were left with 80,000 tons unsold in the spring of 2000. This oversupply
was equivalent to the import of beans in 1999, in accord with NAFTA agreements.
According to a study made by the Autonomous University of Chapingo, the inability of
the producers to sell their beans will threaten the self-sufficiency of the country in this
critical subsistence crop (*La Jornada* March 12, 2000:1,7).

At the close of the millennium, when subsistence producers were losing ground in the
global marketplace, the PRI government was benefiting from the highest oil prices since
the 1970s. Yet none of these benefits were redistributed to sectors that were failing in the
global economy. The Petroleo Mexicano strategy of permitting foreign investment in
modernizing productive strategies has eroded the national base of the company that was a
symbol of sovereignty from the time that Lázaro Cárdenas nationalized petroleum production in 1938. Celebrating the second anniversary of the nationalization of petroleum,
Cuahtemoc Cárdenas made a campaign issue of the threatened dismantling of the national

company in his bid for presidency under the banner of the PRD, but the ruling party was listening more attentively to warnings from the United States that investments for Mexican export processing industries that had benefitted from NAFTA would diminish if oil prices remained high (*La Jornada* March 19, 2000:4).

As Mexico loses its self-sufficiency in the production of basic subsistence commodities, indigenous cultivators find themselves in a critically precarious situation. The coincident loss of control over the petroleum resources threatened what many Mexicans considered to be a pillar of national sovereignty. Where enormous wealth and power differences exist within a country, neoliberal practices exacerbate economic and social inequalities that make the play of the market a game between life and death. When those nations pretend to be players in global capital arenas, they can be destroyed by sudden changes in their investment ratings.[6] Those losses are frequently shifted to the poorest producers in the nations.

NAFTA sucks for them too

Welfare trends in the 1990s. In contrast to the reversal of long-term trends in health and education that occurred during the 1980s in most countries of Latin America, Mexico showed a rise in infant mortality beginning in 1986, after years of improvement prior to the debt crisis.[7] The latest available estimate (Interamerican Development Bank 1997) indicates improvement, with infant mortality rates back to 33.0 per thousand in Mexico, and life expectancy up to 71.9 years. Illiteracy declined by almost 2 percent from 1990 to 1995, from 12.5 to 10.4 percent in the nation as a whole. But high mortality figures, high illiteracy rates, and a lower life expectancy persist in Chiapas and other states with large indigenous populations. The effect of subsistence insecurity on the quality of life is immeasurable.

Widening gaps within the nation occurred during and after the recovery of 1990, with indigenous regions consistently showing the greatest impoverishment. Of the total 2,403 counties in Mexico, 803, or one-third, have more than 30 percent of Indian inhabitants. The predominantly indigenous villagers live in the most severe and inhuman conditions of marginality and poverty: illiteracy rates of 43 percent, three times the national average; 58 percent of children five years of age do not attend school; and nearly a third of the population from six to fourteen years of age do not know how to read or write. Rates of unemployment are dramatic—with up to 60 percent for those twelve years old and over (*Proceso* no. 984, September 11, 1995:23–24). Analyzing the impact of neoliberal reforms on Chiapas and South Mexico, Michael E. Conroy and Sarah Elizabeth West (1999:41 *et seq.*) attest that the human development indicators show a widening gap between the southern indigenous states of Oaxaca, with an index of 0.16, and Chiapas, with an index of 0.209, compared with the rest of Mexico, with an index of 0.804 (with 1.0 being the highest attainable).[8] The fact that government spending in the period 1988 to 1992, when President Salinas's touted Solidaridad program was in place, was skewed in favor of states with low levels of impoverishment indicates that redistribution was not high on the PRI agenda.[9]

These structural changes in Mexico's economy caused a seismic shock in the indigenous communities of Chiapas. I shall pick up the story from chapter 2 of how some of the "institutional revolutionary communities" developed into what I call "communities and

Table 3-1
Poverty Estimates in Mexico, 1984–1999

	1984	1989	1992	1999
% of total population				
living in extreme poverty	15.4	18.8	16.1	28
living in extreme and in intermediate poverty	42.5	47.7	44.0	43
% of rural population				
living in extreme poverty	25.4	27.9	25.7	na
living in extreme and in intermediate poverty	53.5	57.0	54.9	na

Source: INEGI-CEPAL 1993 and Banamex 1998, 1999, adapted from Tanski and Eber n.d.

regions in rebellion." In this story, we begin to see how the habitus of indigenous culture relates to the hegemonic institutions of the PRI government.

FROM INSTITUTIONAL REVOLUTIONARY COMMUNITIES TO COMMUNITIES AND REGIONS IN REBELLION

The agricultural crisis of the 1980s released new social forces promoting agrarian reform programs that did not keep up with the growing political discontent. The state population doubled between 1970 and 1990, going from 1,569,053 to 3,210,496, with the indigenous population increasing by more than half of its 1970 population of 502,097, rising to 847,751 in 1990 (INEGI 1991). The fact that two-thirds of the households of the highland indigenous communities had less than two hectares of land, considered the bare minimum for producing the required for staple crops of corn and beans, suggests the urgency of the need. The population expansion beyond the production capacity of small-plot intensive-cultivation practices led to a variety of responses by the state and local governments. The erosion of the subsistence base of the Chiapas rural economy produced tensions that were addressed by a combination of co-optive processes and repression. The exercise of these options depended both on the acuteness of land shortages and the availability of alternative cash earnings, as well as the socio-political dynamics within each municipality.

causes of shift

Some indigenous municipalities of the highlands chose to limit competition for *ejido* and communal land by expelling dissidents on either religious or political grounds. Other municipalities chose to increase their collective holdings when roads opened up in national territories that were not allotted either to *ejiditarios* or large landowners. Still other municipalities expanded their land holdings by purchase or by gaining *ejido* grants. In the decades of the 1970s and 1980s, all of the highland municipalities intensified their cultivation practices with chemical fertilizers and pesticides, taking advantage of the increased credit that was made available to rural smallholders in Banrural, the national credit bank. Men increased their migrations in search of work in neighboring towns and more distant sites, while women became more active in seeking sites for the sale of their artisan products.

Collier

I shall expand the discussion of these options and their effect on state and local relations in the case of Amatenango where families exercised all of these options. During the 1960s, Amatenango was able to gain *ejido* titles in two sites as highway construction opened up access to national territories in that decade. The first site, called San Caralampio, is in the lower altitudes. It opened up when the road to Venustiano Carranza was under construction. The other, called León Brindis after the Tuxtla Gutierrez state official who helped the local land reform commission gain title to the land, is on the Pan American highway, extended past Comitán in 1966. I visited both these sites in 1966 and spoke to householders who felt very isolated from their families in Amatenango, although they were within fifty miles of their home town. Few vehicles drove into the rough countryside, and I was able to make it only with a four-wheel drive vehicle. The rich virgin land in these lower altitudes enabled families to plant two crops of corn and beans with harvests in distinct seasons that enhanced the productive capacities of household production. In San Caralampio, men often chose to plant some sugar cane, which was grown in the area and sold in Pujiltic, a hamlet of Venustiano Carranza. The Amatenangueros often processed it as liquor in their own stills in the highland municipality, selling the product locally and to surrounding indigenous villages, as well as to coastal plantations to which Indians migrated seasonally. Women were unable to find clays suitable for pottery production and often returned home rather than settling permanently in these colonies.[10]

Highway
Belize

Land ownership was becoming polarized, but not to the extent of neighboring localities. Comparing the two censuses I carried out in the town center, the first in 1958 and the second in 1987, we can see the shrinkage of *ejido* lands and the growing importance of private ownership (Table 3-1).

In the 1957 census, all households in the town center held at least two hectares of land, while thirty years later this was reduced to a half a hectare. The two censuses taken thirty years apart show a reduction of 4 percent of households with *ejido* plots, with an

Table 3-2
**Land Ownership and Ejido Holdings in Amatenango Center,
1958/1987**

Number of Hectares   **Number of Households Possessing Land**

	Ejido Only	Purchased Land Only	Ejido and Purchased Lands	None	Total	%
1958						
/hectare	26	14	—	—	40	13
fi hectare	33	28	28	—	89	30
fl hectare	15	13	29	—	57	19
1 hectare	13	17	38	—	68	23
1 and fi		6	25	—	31	11
2 hectares	1	3	4	—	8	2
3 hectares	1	1	1	—	3	1
5 hectares		1		—	1	0.3
No land					—	—
Total	89	83	125		297	
%	30	28	42		—	100

	Ejido	Bought	Ejido & Bought	None	Total	%
1987						
/hectare	26	14	—	—	40	13
fi hectare	48	41	61	—	150	43
1 hectare	13	29	61	—	103	30
2 hectare	1	3	17	—	21	6
4 hectare	1	1	1	—	3	1
5 hectare		1		—	1	0.3
No land				24	24	7
Total	89	89	140	24	342	
%	26	26	41	7		100%

overall 7 percent landless rate. The gap in land ownership has not increased significantly: 96 percent had less than 2 hectares in 1957, compared with 93 percent (7 percent of which have no land) in 1987. In the higher landholding levels, from 2 or more hectares, 3 percent holding 2 to 5 hectares in 1957 has increased to 7 percent in 1987. The wealth increases are not nearly as marked in landholding as in total wealth, which would include those owning trucks and other consumption goods such as televisions and cement-block houses. It is more than likely, however, that respondents did not include plots of land purchased out of town or held in the lands Amatenango has colonized in the hot country.[11]

Like neighboring municipalities, Amatenango expelled some families that converted to Protestantism in the 1970s, although not on the scale of Chamula. Over a thousand of the expelled families sought refuge in hamlets of the municipality and in the neighboring town of Teopisca. There the Protestant mission bought a parcel of land that became the site of Betania, with populations of expelled Protestants from Chamula and Zinacantán, as well as Amatenango. The original evangelical church separated into three churches that responded to the ethnic origins of the converts. Like most of these exile communities with limited communal lands, the colonizers intensified commodity production, particularly charcoal production, and fruit cultivation.

Individual solutions to the land pressure included migration of indigenous men to the coastal plantations and wage work in neighboring cities to make up for diminishing subsistence crops. With a greater land base, Amatenango men did not engage in these migrations on a regular basis, as did men in other highland municipalities (Collier 1990; J. Rus 1995:77). It was predominantly a recourse for young men intent on raising money for bride price exchanges and ceremonial obligations as *alféreces*. The women of Amatenango were in the forefront of the intensification of artisan production, especially after 1971, when the government helped promote artisan cooperatives (Nash 1993; Eber and Rosenbaum 1993; D. Rus 1997). When I tested Chayanov's (1966) hypothesis that peasant households intensify artisan production with increasing numbers of dependents in the family, I found a negative correlation, since the artisans were women. Women with young children were not able to maintain high production rates. In fact, the highest producers were single women, either separated, never married, or widowed.

The short-term solutions to land shortages delayed, but did not eliminate, the threat to the survival of semi-subsistence communities. The federal government made the national lands in the Lacandón available for settlement with the promise of *ejido* titles, thereby stimulating large-scale migration in the 1970s. The growing political conflict correlated with changes in the labor market, and the decline of corn and cash crop prices was further exacerbated by the influx in 1982 of 150,000 Guatemalan refugees. Since Guatemalans worked for half the minimum wage of Chiapas *campesinos* (about US$1 per day), they took over many of the plantation jobs that highland indigenes had relied on. Mexican indigenous populations in the Lacandón colonies on the Guatemalan border were harassed by National Immigration Service agents, along with the Guatemalan exiles, making them feel like enemies in their own homeland.

The transition from institutional revolutionary communities to communities and territories in rebellion is related to the contradictory trends of government programs in the 1970s and 1980s. Some programs fostered the creation of an elite of *caciques* within the pueblos, while others promoted outward migration to solve the problems that were emerging. Gendered differences were enhanced as men and women sought distinct ways of earning income, thus putting stress on the household organization of production. Given the divergent claims of indigenous and nonindigenous sectors, and the marked difference between the genders, government policies were often contradictory and short-run solutions responding to the political exigencies described below.

Government Co-optation and Containment

The co-optation process in Chiapas accelerated in the 1970s as more funds were made available to indigenous communities. This promoted centripetal tendencies, with local officials in the head towns of communities responding to federal initiatives through the PRI outreach. These initiatives were offset by centrifugal tendencies in municipalities and hamlets that government-funded programs for potable water, paved roads, electricity, and expanded educational and health services failed to reach. Since most of the funds that came from the central government stayed in the head towns, hamlets expressed disaffection with PRI officials by joining opposition political parties or by converting to new religions that addressed their needs.[12] The new government initiatives often promoted political action as *campesinos* reacted against the oppression of their traditional *caciques*, who maintained their allegiance to the PRI. Expelled Chamulas in the Hormiga settlement in San Cristóbal recovered their sense of community in Protestant evangelical churches and often turned to opposition parties to gain control over their precarious economic situation (see chapter 5). This was also the trend in the case of expelled Catholics of the Christian Base Communities inspired by Bishop Samuel Ruíz's liberation theology. The explosion from the defensive boundaries of landholding communities was the culmination of intensified commercialization and resource exploitation, during which communities attempted to adapt to the new conditions of land scarcity, diminishing productivity, and increasing populations during the last three decades (Nash et al. 1995c).

PRODESCH. The Program of Economic and Social Development of Highland Chiapas (PRODESCH) superceded INI as the principal conduit for government funds in 1971. INI retained only a minimal presence in its compound in San Cristóbal, where a few staff members had their offices and where the bilingual program for indigenous schools under the aegis of the Secretary of Public Education (SEP) was lodged. Cancian (1992:38) enumerates the wide variety of programs undertaken through PRODESCH during the Echeverría Alvarez (1970–1976) and the López Portillo (1976–1982) presidencies, when public spending multiplied eightfold nationally.

The change in government spending was even more dramatic in Chiapas, where government expenditures multiplied the flow of capital by twenty-five during Echeverría's presidency alone. Roads were the principal investment, with over 3,000 kilometers of roads built in five years, often to the detriment of other programs. Christiene Deverre (Groupe d'Etude des Relaciones Economique Internationales February 1978) notes that this emphasis came with the sacrifice of other programs, such as wheat production, that were related to bolstering the subsistence economy. The PRODESCH ministry under Luis Echeverría introduced cash crops such as coffee, fruit trees, and vegetables in highland towns, as well as cattle production and forestry. It continued to promote commercial agricultural production during the presidency of President de la Madrid, making the indigenous population vulnerable to price fluctuations during a period marked by wild inflation. The construction of schools, clinics, and administrative buildings, often embellished with the PRI logo, supplied emblems of the party's power and control of the countryside. They were not always adequately staffed or supplied with materials and medicines to work. Since accounts of expenditures were not carefully reviewed, the money often promoted private expenditures by local officials, with the new *caciques* in Zinacantán (Collier and Quaratiello 1994), Amatenango, and Tenejapa investing in consumer durables such as cement-block houses and television sets, as well as trucks used for personal profit. At the same time, consumption of Coca Cola and other consumer "needs" were promoted by *caciques* who obtained the monopoly of such refreshments as well as liquor through their contacts with PRI leaders in the state capital.

Connecting pueblos to other centers. Roads were one of the major efforts carried out by PRODESCH in Chiapas. When I arrived in Chiapas, none of the highland indigenous communities were connected by paved roads, and few were connected by roads that could be traveled by vehicles year-round. Within twenty years, the Pan American highway was paved all the way to Guatemala City, and roads connected highland villages to each other, to lowland areas, and to the gateway cities to the Lacandón rain forest.[13] Buses provided passenger service every two hours to the major cities of the state. Electricity was installed by the end of the 1960s in the town centers of many highland municipalities. This remarkable expansion of the transportation and communication infrastructure was tied to developmental schemes that followed in the 1970s and 1980s, opening up the rich resources of Chiapas to national and international exploitation, with few of the revenues benefiting the people.

When I lived in Amatenango in the summer months from 1962 to 1967, as the Pan American highway was being paved, I was more concerned with the progress in highway construction from the perspective of my own problems of getting to and from Amatenango and beyond, than as a problematic for anthropological observation and analysis. At that time, when I was teaching the first Indian driver how to drive[14] and advancing small amounts of cash when the trucking cooperative in town had unexpected expenses, my interest was in ensuring backup transportation when my Scout International Harvester broke down. In retrospect, I can reflect on how the roads began to affect local peoples' use of space.

Prior to 1965, roads were of value primarily to *ladinos*, since they were the only ones who owned wheeled vehicles and controlled the traffic on them. Indians preferred using the walking paths connecting villages to paved and even unpaved roads because of their

fears of vehicles and of the *pukuhetik* (evil spirits) said to travel on them. When indigenous people began to take advantage of the roads in the mid-1960s, the gendered practices that prevailed in communities extended to the roads, highways, and urban settings.
In the early years, men rapidly accommodated to the new roads as pedestrians, bicyclists,
passengers in buses and trucks, and eventually as drivers of their own vehicles. Women,
who were more confined by tradition to the home site or nearby gardens, continued to
fulfill their daily chores of drawing water, collecting firewood, and bringing clay from
distant sites by walking and carrying loads on a tumpline. They often walked the four
miles to the town of Teopisca in order to sell their pottery and pick up food supplies,
even after buses became available in the mid-1960s. In the latter part of the 1960s,
women began to accompany their husbands on the buses that began operating after the
mid-1960s, often travelling with large loads of pottery on top of the buses to sell in San
Cristóbal. Chamula women had limited access to the city of San Cristóbal until some of
them were expelled as Protestants. Forced to live in the "misery belts" that grew with
the expulsions in the 1970s and 1980s, they became directly involved in the marketing
of their handicrafts, as Amatenango women had been a decade earlier in the 1970s.

The flows of goods, money, people, and labor increased not only in speed and
volume, but also in the direction, with the improved transportation. Amatenango potters transported their wares to San Cristóbal and Teopisca by bus, but soon there were
enough trucks running from the town to accommodate pottery cargo. A cooperative of
31 Indian members was able to purchase a truck on credit from the Tuxtla Chevrolet
dealer that went into operation in 1965. This was a spectacular breakthrough, opening
up a lucrative occupational and entrepreneurial outlet to Indians that could not have
been imagined before. By 1985 all the highland indigenous communities were connected by roads and many had regular bus and truck service available. Mail began to be
delivered to highland communities at least once a week, and the first post office opened
in the house of the town secretary in 1969.

Some indigenous market centers, such as Oxchuc, Tenejapa, and San Andrés Larrainzar, flourished with the construction of connecting highways in the 1980s, and *ladino*
market centers such as Venustiano Carrazanza expanded the size and variety of their consumer markets. Some products, such as local contraband liquor, found new market outlets as far away as coastal plantations that hired indigenous labor. Sellers of patent
medicines would arrive in town to sell their potions. By the 1980s, when candidates for
state offices began to arrive in town to give their pitch, Amatenangueros called them
"medicine sellers" (*ya schan posh*).

The roads and the rest of the infrastructure promoted regional and national traffic, but
were of little interest to global investors until the exploitation of forest and water
resources attracted their attention. With the discovery of vast reserves of oil in the
Lacandón rain forest that was made public in the early 1990s, political attention began to
focus on the area. Construction of the barracks, "Nuevo Rancho," 12 kilometers from
San Cristóbal began in the latter part of the 1980s, and in the following decade militarization of the Lacandón rain forest and the northern region of autonomous villages hastened the construction of new roads for military vehicles, a story I will pick up in chapter

5. In this chapter, I shall reflect on the regional and national integration that was occurring in the compressed time frame of three decades.

THE "CRISIS OF CORPORATIVISM"

The disaffection from official *campesino* organizations resulted in what Neil Harvey (1991:57) calls "the crisis of corporativism," a period in which the corporate groups developed by the government became the base for articulating new and more strident demands and sometimes led to the formation of indigenous organizations independent of government structures. The PRI government attempts under Echeverría (1970–1976) both to contain the independent *campesino* mobilization and to reinvigorate agricultural production with the Federal Agrarian Reform Law had a direct but contradictory effect in Chiapas. These programs consolidated *ejido* plots and revitalized the subsistence small-plot cultivation, but at the same time provided credit for cash crops through the creation of the Rural Credit Bank. This had the unanticipated effect of undermining the communitarian basis for institutional revolutionary communities. The government-sponsored Mexican Coffee Institute (INMECAFE) and Mexican Tobacco (TABAMEX) encouraged the commodification of agriculture by promoting the cultivation and sale of the new cash crops (Harvey 1990:188). These trends are detailed below.

Breakaways from Official Organizations

With each attempt to rein in the growing disaffection, indigenous initiatives went beyond the national corporate organizations that claimed to address their needs. The ferment of *campesino* movements that rose outside of the "official" or government-sponsored organizations preceded, and was in turn promoted by, the National Congress of Indians (CNI) in 1974. Organized by Bishop Samuel Ruiz, who was commissioned by the governor of Chiapas to carry out the task of bringing together Indians from throughout the country, the congress provided indigenous people with the opportunity to share perspectives on common problems. Shortly thereafter, indigenes and *mestizos* formed independent *campesino* organizations that trespassed on the boundaries of corporate communities as they engaged in land struggles, commercial expansion, and wage labor disputes that expanded their social and political horizons.

The *comuneros* of the Casa del Pueblo (House of the People) in Venustiano Carranza are a case in point. They had already broken their ties to the National Confederation of Campesinos, and in 1977 formed the Coalition of Independent Revolutionary Campesinos (CCRI), a group that was integrated in the statewide organization of the National Plan de Ayala Coalition (CNPA) in 1977. This provided the basis for the Emiliano Zapata Campesino Organization (OCEZ) in 1975. With each step of the *campesinos* toward independence, the government formed opposition groups. Harvey (1991:61) details how the government tried to respond to the needs of disaffected members sponsoring new official organizations. The Independent Campesino Center (CCI), the Confederation of Campesinos and Leagues of Agrarian Communities (CCLCA), and the

National Confederation of Small Property-Holders (CNPP) were all attempts by the PRI to organize agricultural workers without land in regional confederations, along with small property holders. This ploy failed to attract the increasingly disaffected *campesinos*, though, who formed the Independent Center of Agricultural Workers and Campesinos (CIOAC). This breakaway also occurred in the case of the organization United by Our Force, which started as a government-sponsored cooperative. Its indigenous name, *Kiptic Ta Lecubtesel,* was a savvy attempt to promote hegemony among increasingly rebellious Indians. Breaking free from state intervention, the union formed three branches of *Kiptic ta Lecubtesel* in 1980, in the municipalities of Ocosingo, Margaritas, Simojovel, and Huitiupán became a dynamic force for indigenous cultivators as they were drawn into commercial crop cultivation. In order to recapture the force released in these indigenous *campesino* organizations, the government formed the supreme Tzeltal Council, with which they began to divide the groups between those who relied on government support and those who opposed government intervention. By 1980, the Union of Ejido Unions and Campesino Solidarity was the largest group in the region.

The trend toward organizing across community boundaries in regional or even national coalitions increased during the debt crisis of the 1980s, as *campesinos* tried to counter government policies. President de la Madrid's government persisted in its support of populist programs to reinforce the dwindling hegemonic accord with *campesinos*, but these government programs often provided the context in which increasingly rebellious *campesinos* formed alliances with others to subvert the government programs to their own ends. The unions of *ejidos* and cooperatives which the PRI Governor Velasco Suárez promoted later became part of an umbrella organization, along with 180 communities from fifteen municipalities called the Unión de Uniones (Harvey 1990:188). This organization pursued the combined objectives of the growing independent movement of *campesinos*, those for land tenure and for the promotion of cash crops and credit.

Commodification of artisan production. Women's organizations of artisan cooperatives emerged in the 1970s with the intensification of artisan production. Women in villages which had never commercialized their weaving on backstrap looms began to seek markets for their products, creating new items that attracted the attention of the foreign tourists (Eber and Rosenbaum 1993). The dual thrust toward commodification of women's artisan products and migration of men threatened the complementarity of gender relations within households (Nash 1993). Marriages were contracted later, as measured in census data in Amatenango del Valle and in Zinacantán. In comparing censuses I did in 1957 and in 1987, the marriage age had moved up a decade: whereas 47 percent of men between 15 and 20 years of age were married in 1957, only 10 percent of the same age group were married in 1987. For women, this marital contract was even more dramatically related to increasing age: whereas 69 percent of women were married in the 15 to 20 year old group in 1957, only 18 percent in this group were married in 1987, and in the older group of 15 to 25 years, the percentage of married women dropped from 86 percent in 1957 to 52 percent in 1987. The increasing age levels also indicate a structural change in the degree of control by the parental generation over children, since marriages were initiated more often by the parents in my earlier field stay than in the later period. It may also be related to increasing education, although most girls finish school before their late teens. Collier (1990) shows the same progression toward later marriages in Zinacantán.

The Amatenango pottery cooperative provided an arena for women's participation in politics. These organizations are rarely addressed by analysts of the *campesino* movements, yet by targeting a sector of *campesinos* that had been ignored by independent as well as official organizations, they offered the potential of doubling the strength of *campesino* organization. This was not overlooked by the PRI, who proceeded to stimulate the organization of cooperatives through INI in communities with artisan traditions (Nash 1993) in the 1970s. Women's artisan production provided an increasing portion of family income, as the pottery they fashioned brought in cash that was increasingly important as indigenous people became dependent on chemical fertilizers and other capital inputs in agriculture. Potters, who once feared that they would never become betrothed if they fashioned anything more than the conventional repertoire of water jars and carriers, began to make an imaginative array of animals, birds, flowerpots and

Women in a weaving cooperative in San Andres Larrainzar compare designs for huipiles *sold in San Holobil Cooperative.*

Women of Zinacantán form an artisan cooperative at headquarters of the government in the transition following the August 21, 1994 elections.

candleholders to lure the tourist trade. The development of cooperatives for the sale of artisan products in museum outlets and tourist centers increased the prices they commanded. Several women in the cooperative disclaimed any interest in, or intention, of getting married.

The political arena provided by the cooperatives that were promoted by the PRI government in the 1970s sometimes had explosive consequences. The president of the women's pottery cooperative in Amatenango, Petrona Lopez Bautista, with the encouragement of women in the PRI in Mexico City, ran for the post of town president. She was killed during her election campaign after she criticized the expropriation of funds meant for community improvement by her predecessor, who was also of the PRI. Women who were in the cooperative at the time of her death recognized the threat to all of them. They tried to gain the assistance of PRI leaders in Mexico City, but their calls were not answered. Some fled to other towns, and others lived in fear of provoking authorities by remaining in the cooperative.

When I returned on a brief visit to Amatenango in 1982, two years after Petrona was killed, the incumbent president assured me that she had to be stopped because she was organizing only women who were not married or widowed, and that it upset the household unit. The transgression of norms of behavior for women, combined with her attack on the local *caciques* during her campaign, meant that her murderer was never indicted, although most townspeople knew the identity of the man hired by her opponent to assassinate her. It wasn't until 1995 that the women began to mobilize a new cooperative, this time under the auspices of the PRD, which is discussed in chapter 5.

Rebellion in the municipalities. Municipalities of predominantly indigenous populations were also struggling for independence from the dominant *ladino* groups in their town centers during the 1970s. Indigenous people of San Andrés Larrainzar began their revolt in 1974 following a drought and famine. The federal army entered to protect the interests of powerful landowners. When they left, the indigenes began a campaign of intimidation that forced the *ladinos* to sell their properties in the center and to move away. Gradually, the public spaces of the church and town hall reverted to indigenous control. Similar confrontations occurred in Simojovel, Teopisca, and Venustiano Carranza. Chenalhó moved against the plantation owners who remained in the township, attacking the owner of El Carmen for transgressions against townspeople, and seeking an increase in the *ejido* Los Chorros from the land belonging to Rancho San José (Groupe d'Etude des Relacions Economiques Internationales, Institute Nacional de la Recherche Agronomique. Economic et Sociologie Rural, February 1978). Chalchihuitán and Mitontic followed with threats and expulsions of the *mestizo* population.

Homero Waldo Rubín Bamaca (1999:25) calls this process of political reassertion the "reindianization" of the population. The census reports affirm this, with figures showing marked decreases in the proportions of those who did not speak an indigenous language (i.e., *ladmos*) living in highland Indian townships. The 1970 INEGI census of the population in the nine rural municipalities in the 05 electoral district surrounding San Cristóbal (Zinacantán, Chamula, Larráinzar, Chalchihuitán, Chenalhó, Mitontic, Pantelhó, Tenejapa, and Huixtán) registered 16.2 percent as non–indigenous language speakers. Twenty years later this percentage of non–indigenous language speakers had diminished to 2.04 percent. The marked decrease was a gradual process of ethnic cleansing, as indigenous populations increased their presence as well as control of the highland pueblos. Some of the communities in the 05 district, such as Chamula, had never allowed non-Indians to stay overnight in town.

The compression of space was, clearly, a two-way process, with indigenes increasingly asserting their priority in regions where they were a majority. This had been a factor when I lived in Amatenango in the 1950s. Aside from the schoolteacher's family, I was the only non-Indian living in the *cabecera* of Amatenango. However, I was identified as an *alemán,* or German, rather than a *ladino;* although that category was often associated with bitter experiences with plantation areas in the coast, it at least distanced me from the *mestizos,* whose proximity made them a more threatening presence. I was aware of the problem in other towns without any nonindigenous residents. The killing of a German tourist in Chamula shortly before my first extended stay in the region convinced me to take that prohibition seriously. What was happening in the 1970s and 1980s was a concerted takeover of the spaces occupied by *ladino* populations in mixed ethnic municipalities.

Wealth and the Changing Logic
of Indigenous Society

When I returned to do fieldwork in Chiapas in 1987, nearly 20 years after I had terminated my previous study, I was impressed with both the continuities and the changes. The town center in Amatenango seemed to have preserved the semblance of its corporate character while pushing the problems to the hamlets in the periphery. The old thatched-roof town hall had been replaced by a modest adobe building during the 1980s, which was in turn supplanted by a two-story building modeled on those being constructed in PRI-dominated towns throughout the highlands in the 1990s. A tiled plaza, ringed by shrubbery and shade trees, gave the impression of a *ladino* town as one entered on a paved street from the Pan American highway. The kiosk that had been the pride of the *ladino* schoolteacher in the 1960s was painted with graffiti, with CIOAC, PRD, and OCEZ slogans predominating, while the public buildings built by the PRI government were emblazoned with the red, green, and white logo of the party.

This transformation in the plazas of indigenous municipalities was superficial evidence for profound changes that were affecting most of the indigenous townships, with the increasing influx of money and attention from the central government during the 1970s and 1980s. The plazas still served as ceremonial spaces for religious celebrations of local saints and inaugurations of civil officials, but secular cultural activities became increasingly prevalent. They continue to serve as assembly sites for the male populations of the towns when policies affecting the *ejido* lands or other issues are aired on public address systems. But opposing political party candidates also come to address the voters, and women now join the assemblies, sitting on the perimeter of the plaza. Schoolchildren present patriotic programs that demonstrate their allegiance to the nation, but the new bilingual schools, which postdate my earlier field stays, present self-consciously "ethnic" programs, with children dancing what the school teachers believe to be authentic indigenous dances. Vendors and traveling salesmen come regularly, selling patent medicines, ice cream, and soft drinks that could never have been afforded except during fiestas in my earlier stay. Tourist buses now arrive, and troops of little girls armed with baskets of miniature pottery items descend on the tourists who venture onto the plaza.

Representations of status differences have been gradually admitted into the public spaces of the Indian pueblos. The homogeneity in dress and housing that was the norm when I lived in Amatenango in 1958 has been breached without fear of envy and witchcraft. Institutionalized *envidia* is no longer as threatening, and the rewards are more worthy of the risk (Foster 1965, Nash 1966). Although most women dress in the red-and-gold embroidered *huipil*, there are marked variations in quality and condition.

Changes in the material culture of the towns signify profound transformations in social relationships. When I visit my friends and *compadres*—ritual coparents—in Amatenango, I now enter through high adobe walls, often with bolted, metal doors, into yards that separate households. A community that was once unified in opposition to the outside world of *ladinos* has by this time been differentiated by clearly marked political and class distinctions. Cement-block houses, often sprouting television aerials from corrugated metal roofs, predominate, with only occasional reminders of the wattle-and-daub houses with thatched roofs that once prevailed. Sweat baths, which were still in frequent use for ritual purification when I lived in Amatenango, are no longer in evidence. The impressive thing to me was not the material evidence of wealth, but the open display of it. When I lived in the town in the years 1963 to 1966, no one would dare reveal possession of even a radio. By the late 1980s it was possible to flaunt a dish antenna or even a truck in the patio. Individualism, expressed in consumerism and patterns of interaction, was given a far wider range of expression. This signaled the end of communal censoring of differences that threatened a collective spirit predicated on homogeneity. The large complex of buildings that served as production and sales headquarters for the pottery cooperative that had flourished during the 1970s was now converted to a primary school.

These signs of material wealth revealed the extent to which a community that was still involved in household production of pottery and small-plot cultivation of corn was also becoming integrated into world markets. The external signs of modernization—electricity, paved streets, cement-block houses, television aerials—exhibited the growing dependence on external markets and the federal government. Even more significant was the integration of prices and currency with regional and national changes and with reevaluations of the currency in international finance markets. When the price of gasoline rose in 1986 as the Mexican government tried to pay back its debt by increasing revenues from the national refineries, transportation costs doubled, and artisans, many of whom traveled by bus or in hired trucks to sell in neighboring cities, found their earnings reduced.

Semi-subsistence farmers experienced ever-diminishing returns with rising costs of cultivation. In Amatenango, each family's share of *ejido* lands was reduced to a quarter of the holdings in 1967, from 2 hectares to one-quarter of a hectare, and 7 percent of the families in the town center had no land (see Table 3-1). With the rising population, the intensive cultivation of land required greater inputs of fertilizers and pesticides. With increased prices of petroleum products, the costs for chemical fertilizers and pesticides also doubled in price, and farmers throughout the area were forced to purchase on credit. The San Cristóbal director of the Ejido Bank told me that up until the late 1960s they could not prevail upon farmers to take on loans, but by the 1970s they did not have enough capital from public sources to meet the demands.

Participation in a financial credit system intensifies the compression of time, since interest rates of 55 percent annually, charged even by the government-subsidized *ejido* credit banks, mount up fast. This enhanced, in turn, the importance of women's income from pottery production, effectively tipping the balance in the household organization of production in favor of women. Their contribution is symbolized in women's participation in planting, with women adding the fertilizer that their income from pottery supplied when the corn and bean seeds are sown. Women's work was not just a supplement to men's production in the subsistence economy as it was when I lived in the town, but the major determinant in whether they could continue as small-plot cultivators.

As a result of the diminishing lands available for households, men were forced to seek wage work regularly. Instead of going only seasonally to work in distant plantations to pay for betrothal celebrations or religious cargoes, most young men, in the 1980s and 1990s, were seeking regular employment in nearby towns and the city of San Cristóbal de Las Casas, or, with a very few, as far away as Cancún or Mexico City. Chamulans and Indians of other neighboring towns with less land or fewer resources go even farther afield, to regional centers, tourist meccas (Collier 1990), Mexico City, or even the United States, where they learn new trades and adopt urban behaviors. At the same time, wealthier members of the community—usually those who had served in town offices—own trucks that provide transportation services to Teopisca and San Cristóbal.

With the closer relation between the state and indigenous townships in the 1970s, another level of wealth distinction was created with a class of loyal PRI supporters who no longer represented their constituency. When I worked in Amatenango in the 1960s, town officials, including the mayor and secretary, were receiving salaries comparable to those of schoolteachers. In the next decade, public expenditures on streets within the town center, schools, and potable water increased exponentially from nothing to thousands of pesos a year. These funds could be tapped for personal use without much fear of disclosure, since the state and federal governments were concerned primarily with the delivery of votes to the PRI. A wealthy elite emerged in office in most of the highland towns, with capital to invest in trucks, land, and other private property that ensured lifelong returns.

NEOLIBERALISM AND THE CHANGING MODEL OF DEVELOPMENT IN CHIAPAS

Development projects initiated by the government in Chiapas from the 1970s to the 1990s have been on a far greater scale, using high-capital investment. In contrast to government programs of the past that pretended to redistribute wealth, the new development projects openly aggravate the wealth differences in the regional economy, siphoning revenues from the state of Chiapas. The construction of La Angostura Dam in the township of Venustiano Carranza is a case in point. The dam, built between 1969 and 1974, flooded over 5,000 hectares of rich arable land and forced the relocation of over 20,000 people (Cancian 1992:37; Collier and Quaratiello 1994). The government paid the ousted landowners only seven million old pesos, about US$2,500, and most of that had not been paid in 1991 when I visited the Casa del Pueblo with National Science Foundation students. The town was later split in two when the government gave 120 *comuneros* some lands, seeds, and tractors, and left hundreds of claimants without any compensation.

These development projects rarely benefit the indigenous people. With all the development of hydroelectric generating plants, the state produces 52 percent of the electricity generated in the nation, but to this day, 34.92 percent of the residents in the state do not have electrical energy. The recent discovery of what some call "an ocean of oil" under the Lacandón rain forest is already committed to payment of the debts incurred by the Salinas government. The very presence of these resources helps explain the militarization of the state in the face of increasing pressures by militant colonizers and *campesinos* to redistribute some of the proceeds from the sale of oil, hydroelectric power, and lumber. Salinas's development policies had particularly negative consequences in Chiapas, where *campesinos* organized massive protests throughout his presidency. These were met with increasingly aggressive military force, now quartered within easy reach of the areas of protest, by the PRI governor of Chiapas during the Salinas presidency, José Patrocinio González Garrido.[15]

One example of the changing objectives of regional development projects is the sugar refinery in Pujiltik, a hamlet of Venustiano Carranza. Run as a private enterprise by the Pedrero family from the 1960s to the 1970s, it dominated the purchase of cane and sale of liquor throughout the region. When a campaign carried out by state police troops failed to eliminate the production of alcohol in the Indian towns, Pedrero lost the monopoly of liquor production. He later sold the company to the government in the 1970s at a time when prices for sugar were low. For the next decade, the government operated the refinery in order to sustain the cane growers in the region. During Salinas's presidency, when this was no longer a priority, the government sold the operation in 1990 to a consortium of Japanese and Mexican operators. The Mexican owners, who operated a shipping fleet of trucks, were primarily interested in selling the Cuban sugar stored in warehouses. When this was sold, they sold the company back to the government. With little development of the refinery, it was falling into bankruptcy when the government again reclaimed it and continues to operate it in the 1990s.

Commodification of Crops and Artisan Products

Salinas promoted capitalist development programs that enriched the friends of the PRI but increased the vulnerability of the *campesino* economy to national and even global fluctuations. The *campesinos'* experience with cash crop cultivation is a case in point. Throughout the 1980s the cultivation of coffee had been promoted by the Mexican Institute of Coffee (INMECAFE), which provided the seedlings, credit for fertilizers, transportation facilities, and technical assistance. Salinas extolled the advantages of intensive cultivation of cash crops when he advanced the reform of Article 27 and promised new initiatives. Instead he withdrew the infrastructure for existing commercial crops, leaving agronomists and extension agents stranded in the field. Pedro Farias, a City College undergraduate student in the National Science Foundation's Research Experience for Undergraduates program, accompanied some of these agents in Chiapas in the summer of 1991. He found that the *campesinos* had great difficulty in getting their crops to market and were consequently the victim of "coyotes," or middlemen, who came to take advantage of their isolation. The *campesinos* summarized for him their dilemma in attempting to raise cash crops in response to government programs: "The more we grow, the more the prices fall for all of us." As a result of this experience, the *campesinos* were reluctant to believe Salinas's promises to support further cash crop cultivation with the passage of the reform of Article 27. They concluded: "What we must do is diversify crops to avoid the fall of prices, because without organization with other *campesinos,* we will be competing with each other." The reduction of field staff agents in the producer unions such as INMECAFE and CONAFRUT from 1991 and throughout the second half of Salinas's presidency confirmed their fears.

The women had similar experiences, as they competed with other artisans for a limited market for their products. Women in the artisan cooperatives, which were organized with the help of INI and some international NGOs in the 1970s and 1980s, supported the PRI candidate for the gubernatorial elections in 1988. However, when Salinas entered office, Chiapas state programs sponsored by the Integrated Development of the Family (DIF) agency undercut prices given to the cooperative organizations. The story is worth telling because it illustrates privatizing within publicly funded operations. Mercedes Arias, the leader of one of the largest cooperatives of weavers which included women from Chenalhó, Pantelhó, Las Margaritas, Tenejapa, and San Andrés, agreed to convoke the artisans during a visit with the mother of Salinas and the wife of the Chiapas PRI candidate for governor, Patrocinio Gonzalez Garrido, to promote his candidacy in 1988. Over 200 women congregated at the gathering for the candidate's wife and mother, which was widely publicized to show indigenous support for the party. When the governor was installed, his wife became the titular head of the DIF. Through her brother, who was the Mexican representative for the World Bank, she promoted a grant of three million dollars, which was invested in tourist shops throughout the state. The DIF then bought weavings from individual sellers, bypassing the cooperatives, which charged higher prices that provided the women with much needed money. When challenged as to why she did not patronize the cooperative, Señora de González replied that those women could take care of themselves, and she wanted to help the truly needy.

Chiapas was also the state most severely affected by the reform of the Agrarian Law of Article 27. Soldiers from the Nuevo Rancho garrison just outside San Cristóbal confronted the protests of *campesinos* who were adversely affected by the new Agrarian Law. These protests, mobilized by OCEZ, ARIC, CIOAC, and the Union of Ejido Unions and Campesino Solidarity Groups of Chiapas (UU), engaged in massive marches of people from the gateway cities of the Lacandón rain forest to San Cristóbal, and on to the state capital to present their case (*La Jornada* April 12, 1991).

When the reform act was passed at the end of 1991, a new bureaucracy called the Agrarian Solicitors Office was instituted. The continued preference on the part of indigenous *campesinos* for the old bureaucracies, paternalistic and corrupt as they were made out to be by the new technocrats, suggested the reluctance of indigenes to conform to the new order ushered in by the reform of Article 27. We[16] noticed in our visits to the old and new headquarters of agrarian affairs that *campesinos* from indigenous communities continued to go to the Office of Indian Affairs in San Cristóbal with their land problems, while the newly renovated offices of the Agrarian Solicitors were completely empty of clients. When we visited the newly opened office in 1993, we were ushered into the office of a young lawyer, who was settled uneasily at the polished, uncluttered desk. There were no files, and the young agents knew nothing of the history of land reform in Chiapas. In response to questions about the background of the new law and why it was needed, the young lawyer had no response, not even the usual bureaucratic evasions. He referred it to another clerk, who also lacked an answer. Finally he stated: "You see, we are all young here and we do not know anything about the past."

Salinas clearly wanted to start with a clean slate in his new ministry, but he could not wipe out the historical memory of the *campesinos*. We accompanied a young agent to San Mateo, an *ejido* of 300 inhabitants in the municipality of Villas Las Rosas, for one of the few cases that came to the attention of the Agrarian Solicitors in the spring of 1993. The *ejidatarios* were objecting to the actions of one of the constituents of their *ejido,* who wanted to cultivate his allotment individually without submitting to the collective constraints of the *ejido*, including that of pooling the harvest and dividing it up. The *ejido* was located at a distance of a two-hour walk up a steep escarpment that effectively cut it off from wheeled vehicles. We were supposed to have been met by a guide, but after waiting a half hour we proceeded up the hill on our own. When we arrived, after getting lost on several byways in the second-growth forest, we saw an extremely impoverished settlement of the Santa Rosa *ejido.* It was clear that the small gathering of twenty *comuneros* lounging in the basketball court, emblazoned with the PRI emblem linked to Solidarity, had little expectations of what they could gain from the new Agrarian Solicitor's Office. A few poorly dressed women, unable to afford the elaborately embroidered blouses worn by indigenes of the municipal center, peered at us from the cookhouse. We were ushered into the schoolhouse, where we waited over half an hour for the dissident who wanted to farm his land separately to show up. The women served us some cold scrambled eggs and dried-up tortillas. When the dissident arrived, the young agent, following the new manual he brandished, informed them of their legal rights in terms we could hardly understand, let alone the nearly nonliterate and barely bilingual group he was addressing. He described the objectives of the Agrarian Solicitors Office as to "promote agrarian justice and guarantee the legal security of the land," and then went through a list of the benefits of the new agrarian legislation (the reform of Article 27). After he spoke, with the men listening intently, two of the *ejidatarios* asked him how the new laws would affect their village. He was unable to respond to the questions they posed.

The impasse in communication created by the new organization with its inexperienced staff and its negation of historical memory was clear. Yet the expression of concern for the sectors disprivileged under the old paternalistic system—women, youths, wage workers, and urban migrants—could have shifted the support base for the new government agrarian program if the projected goals of the Agrarian Solicitors Office were carried out as they were stated in its brochure (Procuraduría Agraria 1993:8;13). These include the rights of women to land, and the growth and development of the small landholders addressing the decapitalization and growing impoverishment of this sector. It also promises low-interest credit loans for improving production and advancing new ventures. But the kind of transformation projected depends on the democratic participation of the rural smallholders.

Ejido commissioners, whom we interviewed in Amatenango and at the old Office of Agrarian Affairs, were raising questions about the reform of Article 27: What would happen if the new private initiatives, using public lands that were part of the *ejido* allotments, were to go bankrupt? And how would the subsistence needs of the families be addressed if there were not enough lands remaining after the private initiatives advanced? The head of the Ejido Commission in Amatenango told me that they intended to boycott the new legal entity and to prohibit any sales of *ejido* lands.

National Solidarity Program (PRONASOL)

Salinas's flagship organization for rural development was the National Solidarity Program (which I refer to as Solidarity) to construct over a thousand basketball courts and hundreds of buildings that were to house schools and clinics. Solidarity programs have exceeded past efforts in addressing local needs in short order while giving less power to local *caciquismo*. Bypassing the institutions of the state, whose corruption was well-known, they delivered direct remedies on the demand of local officials who supervised the production and control the financing in cooperation with national agents. As Christopher Wood pointed out (*The Economist* February 13, 1993:14), the personality of the president was salient in the attention given to petitions from local officials. In the case of states near the Federal District, Salinas received each contingent of project applicants personally and appeared in the village where the project was delivered, thus bestowing credit on himself rather than the PRI as a party.[17] He did not attend to the progress of Solidarity in the state of Chiapas until trouble started to develop in 1992, as we shall see below.

Solidarity exemplified the streamlined approach of the Salinas administration. Set up to assist all *campesinos,* indigenous as well as *mestizo,* it also embraced urban barrio dwellers. The young director with whom we spoke in Tuxtla Gutierrez emphasized that Solidarity programs differ from earlier development programs by overcoming the paternalism that characterized past relations with government. Under Solidarity, a community is able to select the project that will serve its needs. Also different from earlier programs is the highly public manner in which Solidarity operates, giving the PRI the greatest visibility for spending money in communities. Solidarity funds projects such as the construction and rehabilitation of mills, roads, and bridges, irrigation projects, potable water, population control projects, health centers, and school classrooms. Communities that desire funds from Solidarity must form an assembly that selects the project. Once the mayor signs the request, it is sent to the Development Planning Committee (COPLADE) for approval. A very competent and knowledgeable agent of COPLADE in Tuxtla Gutierrez, whom we interviewed in 1993, explained that Solidarity has been more successful in carrying out public works than past organizations have, since projects are completed quickly. In fact, according to its regulations, Solidarity will fund only projects that can be completed within a year.

Agents process requests from communities directly, assessing the proposals in a short period of time and cutting through the bureaucratic red tape that had caused delays and misappropriation of funds from the national, state, and local administrators. Further, the maximum cost per project is 100 million pesos (roughly US$33,000). The Solidarity projects are visible public works that benefit many members of the community. Completed projects bear a sign announcing the project with the president and governor's names, the number of people the project will benefit, and a Mexican flag. Hence the school buildings, health clinics, municipal installations, and basketball courts serve as monuments to the national concern for remote areas of the nation. Even though the programs are often funded by international agencies such as the World Bank, Solidarity has effectively drawn them into a redistributive network that garners support for the PRI. While some projects (such as potable water) are essential to the people living in the villages, others (such as the construction of elegant municipal buildings) demonstrate that the bureaucrats are often divorced from the needs of the people. The window-dressing projects fail to address the rising demands for land titles and cash crop assistance in credit and marketing among the indigenous peoples who had been lured into cultivating them. The infrastructural improvements in road building and establishing power lines serve the agroindustrial development sector, while most local communities in the colonizing area are left without electricity or subsidies to assist them in marketing their crops.

Solidarity promoted itself as making a break from the overly bureaucratic and corrupt institutions of the past. The literature on Solidarity described its programs as honest, efficient, and clear, emphasizing that they strengthen the government's responsibility to society and promote community participation in all stages of the project. To overcome the corruption characteristic of government spending by previous administrations, Solidarity tightened up control over the disbursement of funds through three subagencies, the Federal Secretariat of General Control, the Secretariat of Programming and Budget, and the State Board of Inspection. The irony is that, while Solidarity supposedly represented a break from the corrupt bureaucracies of the past, the National Solidarity Program itself became yet another bureaucracy that failed to address the real needs of the indigenous communities.

Announcement of the new projects was a highlight of visits of the governor or president, as the PRI mended its fences in preparation for the 1994 elections. Recognizing the conflictual situation as well as high growth potential of the southern frontier, President Salinas made two trips to Chiapas in the spring of 1993, the first to Oxchuc and Ocosingo and the second to Tuxtla Gutierrez. In Oxchuc, a Tzeltal-speaking township in the highlands, every detail of the visit was well orchestrated, from the arrival of the helicopter 15 minutes before the ceremony to the flag-raising drill. Thousands of Indians from nearby villages had been bused in at government expense to watch the ceremony, announced as the *abanderamiento* (salute to the flag). We stood in the hot sun watching the Indians practice the simple routine of raising the flag on command for over an hour. When Salinas arrived, he strode swiftly up to the platform with only a few plainclothed attendants. In his speech, the president announced that Solidarity was giving one billion pesos for the economic and social development of the area, emphasizing specific projects such as providing potable water to overcome pressing health problems. During the speech, a group of Indians calling themselves Abuxu (The Ants), who had marched on foot, were detained outside Oxchuc, where we saw them as we left the town. The marchers held placards protesting that none of the Solidarity funds were going to the northern part of Chiapas, claiming that over 50 percent of the Indians living there had "never seen the famous resources of the National Program of Solidarity so celebrated by the authorities." Because they were not allowed to enter, Salinas's visit went smoothly, with no visible dissent.

Later in the day, Salinas lunched at the Lion's Club in Ocosingo, the *ladino*-dominated center of a township that includes Tzeltal villages, where he announced that funds were to be given to develop tourism on the main route to Palenque. His visit later that week to the Lacandón rain forest, where colonists had been protesting both the lack of government services and the corruption of forestry agents for years prior to the uprising on New Year's Eve (Nash and Sullivan 1992), was a further demonstration of his attention to potential areas of dissension. Shortly after the visit, the state governor announced the allocation of 3,800 new pesos (approximately US$1,200) for the paving of the highway to Palenque, and 800,000 new pesos (about US$266,000) for potable water in Pakal Na, a jungle colony (*El Tiempo* May 4, 1993). Given that this is where the uprising later occurred, Salinas's visit was indicative of the PRI's awareness of conflict and a desire to co-opt leaders, or at least mend fences, but clearly it was a matter of too little, too late to stem the tide of rebellion.

Despite claims to the contrary, Solidarity benefited communities supportive of the PRI. The fact that the municipal president has to approve the plan can cause problems, since these officials are in most cases PRI incumbents. We were informed of a case of a barrio of San Cristóbal de Las Casas making a request for potable water from Solidarity that was never filled because the municipal president did not complete the proper papers. The municipal president was from PRI, but the barrio was PAN-dominated. The failure in communication demonstrates the control that the PRI held over who would benefit from Solidarity funds.

The old programs fostered by Salinas's predecessors languished, with reduced budgets and often incompetent administrators. Already weakened by the charges of misappropriation of funds and loss of key programs to the Integrated Development of the Family (DIF), INI was reduced to a shambles of agencies that lacked coordination and funding, while the Secretary of Agriculture and Water Resources (SARH) competed with several parallel development agencies. Both INI and SARH had been reduced in budget and personnel through the 1970s and 1980s as new agencies relieved them of their missions. PRODESCH did not have even the reduced stature of INI or SARH, and by the end of the 1980s the offices were abandoned. The buildings of all these old agencies still stood as sentinels of past attempts by the government to integrate indigenous populations into its schemes of modernization. Occasionally, the INI buildings hosted bilingual programs in education or refugees from municipalities in conflict. Solidarity buildings were little more than billboards to carry the slogans of the PRI. Most of the agronomists contracted to work in agricultural and outreach programs had left, and only a handful of devoted professionals were working without salaries to keep contact with desperate *campesinos* whose crops were rotting in storehouses. The patients of the doctors were left without recourse to medicines or attention.

Redistribution of public funds in areas undergoing rapid development or posing conflict continues to be a key element in the hegemonic control exercised by the government through the PRI and the constituent agencies. Mayans, like the Mexican nation of which they are a part, are beginning to operate in a world of debt and runaway interest charges that leaves them indebted before they even begin the new year's sowing, dependent on wage work that is often not available near home. The changes in their lifestyle are clues to their greater integration as consumers, producers, and debtors in markets far beyond their lived environment. Instead of sponsoring effective redistribution programs, the government now adds to the wealth differences that are dividing the polity.

FROM RESISTANCE TO PROTEST

Fragmentation of the municipalities reflected the decentralization that was occurring in national political life in the wake of neoliberal assault on welfare policies and corporate controls in the 1980s and 1990s. The processes set in motion by the debt crisis of 1982 upset the hegemonic base of PRI control over the agrarian sector and the urban barrios to which the uprooted *campesinos* migrated. This was marked by political competition in the form of opposition parties that broke the monopoly of PRI power. It was further exemplified in the breaking away of hamlets and barrios within municipalities as the PRI elites were challenged by residents of barrios and hamlets who felt ill-represented by the officials in town centers.

The monopoly of power that the PRI had enjoyed since its inception in 1928 began to erode with the neoliberal policies introduced during the debt crisis of the 1980s, and this only accelerated during Salinas's presidency. In highland indigenous municipalities, the *parajes* were breaking away from the centers, and in the Lacandón canyons, sectors of the settler populations were disputing land claims because of contradictory government allocations.

Pluripolitical Competition and Decentralization in the Highlands

Frank Cancian (1992) records the rising conflict in the municipality of Zinacantán during the 1980s and 1990s, when Zinacantecos broke away from the PRI to elect a president who was a candidate of the National Action Party (PAN) in 1982. The new president and his followers found themselves locked out of the town hall on the day of inauguration, and multiparty affiliations continued to fragment the municipality in the following years.

Separation from the PRI monopoly of political power followed a conversion from PAN opposition to *campesino* organizations, and then to Cárdenas's PRD following the failure to seat Cuahtemoc Cárdenas in the presidency he had won in 1988 (Collier and Quaratiello 1994). Political power shifted from the center to the hamlets as opposition grew. The PRI cut dissidents off from the resources that flowed into municipal government, and deprived political opponents of basic services such as writing out birth and death certificates. The PRI governor, José Patrocinio González Garrido, instituted ever more repressive measures, increasing penalties for opposition groups and ruling out the autonomy that hamlets had enjoyed in electing their own authorities (Collier 1994).

The same process was visible in other municipalities. Hamlets broke away from the town centers where local elites backed by the PRI had monopolized all the federal resources that had flowed into the town as the PRI attempted to control the erosion of its power. With the growth of opposition parties in the 1980s, fragmentation along these lines became widespread, penetrating municipalities that had always delivered the vote to the PRI. Amatenango and Chenalhó followed this pattern, with hamlets giving their votes to the opposition in 1988 and 1994. The breakaway in the Lacandón rain forest that led to the Zapatista movement was, from the local perspective, a revolt of communities left without rights, resources, or basic services in established townships within which the new territories opened up for colonization had been incorporated. From this perspective, the rebellion was an attempt to gain the local autonomy indigenous pueblos had in fact enjoyed during the colonial period, but now extended beyond the boundaries of the community to embrace regional administrative units. This expansion responded to the *campesino* organizations that had expanded the range of indigenous political activities.[18]

Conflict and Competition in the Lacandón Rain Forest

The regional organization of *campesinos* was most marked in the Lacandón, where they were not bound by the closed corporate communities established during the colonial period. The Lacandón rain forest began to be colonized soon after independence, as private companies started to exploit the land for lumber, chicle, and oil, and to introduce coffee and cattle. Few indigenes arrived until after the end of World War II, when colonies named after their places of origin—Morelia, Chihuahua, and Pozo Rico—were established. Tzeltales from nearby townships in the department of Ocosingo began to establish the colonies of Nueva Esperanza, El Lacandona, ll de Julio, and Ricardo Flores Magón. Other colonies were established still later by former agricultural workers of coastal plantations during the presidencies of Adolfo López Mateos and Gustavo Díaz Ordaz, both of whom emphasized *ejidos* over large landholders to promote basic production of subsistence crops (Arizpe, Fernanda and Velázquez 1993:82). Colonizers after 1970 came from Guerrero, Puebla, Oaxaca, Michoacán, and the highlands of Chiapas. Along with a grant of fifty hectares of land, the *ejidatarios* received cattle credits and a promise that the state would buy the wood they cut.

Contradictory government policies. Government policies vacillated between concessions to the colonizers and those to environmentalists. The initial rules regarding the cutting of the rain forest promoted deforestation at a rate so alarming that the situation attracted world attention. In 1971 Echeverría issued a presidential decree that gave 688,000 hectares to sixty-six Lacandón heads of families. The land was already settled by a dozen Tzeltal families that had founded five communities in 1934. The donation simultaneously made it easier for lumber companies to bypass national laws controlling lumbering, since concessions were to be mediated by indigenes who were expected to respond favorably to money offered by private companies. Simultaneous delineation of a biosphere reserve in the central-west jungle impeded the sale of lands in a restricted area while it deprived existing colonizers of the rights to the lands they had settled. This exemplifies the conflict inherent in land claims based on simultaneous donations and promises to different groups of settlers that has culminated in the land problems experienced at the end of the century.[19]

Over 200,000 *mestizos* and Mayans were settled in the area by the 1980s, where they were in conflict with oil explorers and cattle ranchers, who were buying up plots of land from the indebted colonizers, and Lacandón Indians, who had been there since the colonial period. Indigenous communities that had lost their lands with the hydroelectric power installations were joining *campesino* organizations that had struggled for decades to gain the land promised in the 1917 elections. These indigenous people, along with *mestizos* who had lost their lands in past struggles, promoted the social movements for land and social rights in the area (Nash and Sullivan 1993; Collier and Quaratiello 1994).

Conflict had thus been developing in the Lacandón rain forest for decades before the Zapatista uprising. The division of national territories here, as elsewhere in Chiapas after the Revolution, allowed prosperous landowners to acquire large holdings because each member of the household could claim his or her share, along with that of children and collateral relatives living together. Latent conflict between interests of large ranchers and smallholder cultivators broke into the open as ranchers hired their own gunmen, who often harassed the cultivators as the ranchers asserted their rights over large territories.

The contrast between municipal center and outlying hamlets noted in highland municipalities prevailed in the settlements in the Lacandón rain forest, as each new colony was put under the administration of one or another of the gateway cities dominated by *ladinos*. The disparities between the new settlements and the center were particularly pronounced in Las Margaritas, Ocosingo, and Palenque, where the municipal centers controlled large areas of settlements. The roots of revolt that culminated in the Zapatista uprising in 1994 lay in these marginalized settlements, neglected by the federal government and abused by elites controlling the funds and decisions affecting the municipalities.

In contrast to the marginalized settlements under the control of gateway municipalities, the colony of Marqués de Comillas received its titles in an earlier settlement with direct benefits mediated by the National Confederation of Campesinos. Lacandón Indians benefited from government patronage directly from the biosphere reserve, which assured them 614,321 hectares of land.[20] This contradictory allotment of land, which had already been settled by Tzeltal Indians as early as 1934, sowed the seeds of conflict that the government stimulates periodically for its own end.[21]

The experience of the colony Marqués de Comillas in the Department of Ocosingo encompasses most of the problems affecting indigenes in the new environment. Even though the colony, composed of four *ejido* plots located in the Montañas de Oriente on the banks of the Usumacinta River, was favored from the time the land was allotted in 1963, conflict arose when new immigrants began to encroach on colonies established prior to 1972. The region now includes Ch'oles, Zoques, Nahuas, Chinantecos, Tojolobales, Tzeltales, and Tzotziles, along with *mestizos* and *ladinos* settled on *ejido* land.

The ambiguities and contradictions inherent in government policies regarding resources in the *ejidos* led to a protest march in 1991 by over 150 colonizers from Marqués de Comillas. The government ruled that the trees cut by the colonizers to plant their crops could not be sold. Without warning, government trucks arrived, loaded up the wood the settlers had cut to clear their land, and carried it off to sell for its own profit. The various groups colonizing the area joined a march of men, women, and children, prepared to go all the way to Mexico City to protest government corruption. They were met by 700 federal troops stationed in Chiapas, and men, women, and children were imprisoned in Palenque and Tuxtla jails, where they were held incommunicado for several days, without being allowed to take the food offered by relief agencies. The coincidental meeting of a United Nations group in Mexico at the time of the jailing led to a declaration calling for their release. Despite this experience, the same group mobilized several months later to protest the government's failure to uphold the terms of the agreement.[22]

This unprecedented protest action by culturally distinct indigenous groups including women and children signified the movement to collective political action in the region. The colonizers succeeded in mobilizing people who spoke different languages and who came to the jungle from widely separated villages. They were able to maintain an orderly confrontation against the massive military opposition. It was a preview of the growing opposition to government policies in the rain forest.

Adding to this latent conflict among colonizers with contradictory claims to land was the influx of Guatemalan Mayans, when over 50,000 were forced into exile by the war in Guatemala during the early 1980s. The exiles competed for the same jobs and resources as the colonizers. Both populations were harassed by the Mexican National Immigration Service, which often ignored the citizenship rights of Mexican Mayans as they detained and jailed them when they did not carry identification papers. Since the municipal offices of the towns in which the Lacandón settlements were included were dominated by *ladinos* who favored the ranchers, indigenous *campesinos* often found it difficult to obtain a birth certificates establishing their citizenship. When we spoke with a group of Mexican Mayans in a clinic in the hamlet of El Porvenir on the Guatemalan Mexican frontier in 1991, they claimed that they fared worse than their Guatemalan neighbors did. They pointed out that the latter received stipends from United Nations sources as refugees, while they were abandoned by their own government and treated like exiles in their own country. Both groups of Mayans were in conflict with oil explorers and cattle ranchers who were buying up the plots of the indebted colonizers.

The growing protests demonstrated the political potential of these settlements even before the uprising. Despite the diversity of Mayan linguistic groups in this new setting, they have shown a greater ability to coordinate political action than the corporate communities they left behind. The general poverty of the colonists contrasts with the growing differences in wealth in corporate communities, where "tradition" is invoked to validate the arbitrary rule of *caciques*. The neglect of the Lacandón colonies by the federal government, which had never even delivered voting urns to the settlements before the uprising, meant that none of the co-optive strategies that divide the highland communities operate in this context. The shared poverty creates a class solidarity that reinforces ethnic identity as indigenes rather than as members of distinct communities.

Religious roots of communal action. From the early days of the colonization of the Lacandón rain forest in the 1960s, the Order of Maristas stressed the key of communal action based on a shared religion, reaching out to other Catholic communities in the region. Pilgrimages from one to another settlement and to highland villages promoted interrelations among the communities far more than had ever occurred among highland villages. Intermarriage between members of different communities, which was strongly prohibited in the highland communities, knit together the multiethnic settlements of the Lacandón. Women became the primary agents in promoting these ties before and during the uprising.

The pastoral role of catechists provided the linkages among distinct groups in the category of "brothers," achieving unity through the theology of liberation (Leyva Solano and Franco 1996:125). The key biblical theme that provided a common identification was the biblical story of the Exodus of the Israelites from the desert. Former serfs on the old plantations identified themselves with Israelites in the desert who gained their freedom in the Exodus (ibid.:159). Regional unions of *ejidos* and production units, such as the Rural Association of Collective Interest (ARIC), thrived in this pluralistic society, fighting under the banner *Kiptij ta Lecubtesal* against *ladino* ranchers and liquor sellers.

María Eugenia Santana (1996) describes the collective basis for Christian Base Communities in the community of Flor del Rio, where she worked in 1983 and 1984. When I visited Flor del Rio with her in 1994, I was struck by the greater impoverishment in the colonies than in any of the highland pueblos where I have worked in the past three decades. The school is a crude wooden shack and is rarely staffed by teachers. Villagers have to walk two hours to get to the nearest clinic, where a doctor occasionally appears, and where the lack of medicine is deplorable. Although high-power lines that draw electricity from the hydroelectric plants of Chiapas run directly overhead, the town has no electricity. The gifts we brought—rubber boots for every member of the community, along with medicines and food supplies such as matches and cooking oil that they could no longer get because of the harassment community members experience when they go beyond the military lines established by the cease-fire—were stored in the community storehouse to be shared equally. So great were the needs of the colonizers for almost anything—from soap to cooking oil to matches—that we were embarrassed to retrieve the few personal belongings which had inadvertently been stored along with our gifts.

The Marista mission, which founded the community, taught the Agrarian Law and the rights of Mexicans in the course of teaching the catechism. Santana quotes one of the community members' statements about weekly meetings in which they carry out "a communal study of our life in confrontation with the Word of God, especially the deeds of the apostles and their teachings on the first Christian communities. This makes us see the road to be better and we understand that this road is to share what we have and all have the same."

I was able to appreciate this collective approach espoused by the colonizers in all dimensions of daily life during our visit. The community as a whole takes an active interpretive role in its approach to the doctrine. Each Thursday, Bible study is led by alternately a men's and a women's group. People spoke of their ideals of communal sharing in relation to the chosen text, relating the text to the collective aspirations that find a base in the communal land reform. They also related their struggles to those of the Israelites against the Egyptian pharaohs, and how the freedom they found in the canyons was threatened by the "reform" of Article 27 of the 1927 Constitution. The next day we saw men and women working side by side in the fields, where all plots are cultivated in common and the harvest of subsistence crops, as well as the money from cash crops, is shared equally. The community buys fertilizers with credit from the credit union linked to ARIC, sharing it in common. With the earnings from coffee cultivation, the community of Flor del Rio purchased a truck which serves the community as a whole.

Women's Protests Against Subordination. Women's participation in the cultivation of the principal commercial crop of coffee is greater than in subsistence crops because of the intensive labor demanded in harvesting the crop. Women have a greater share in decision-making than in highland villages, and as a result are more assertive in demanding their rights in the family and community. We joined the women in the church, the only large-scale building in the village. There the women spoke to us about their attempts to change the patriarchal relations in the home. They challenged practices of wife abuse and control over the movements of women that are considered "tradition" by some indigenous males. Seeing them articulate their claims, it was clear why Zapatistas have put women's demands for change in all their negotiations (Rojas 1995; Santana 1996). Despite their collective liberation movement, they feel strongly about the need for separation of the sexes in their discussion groups and in daily life. In the celebrations I attended in Flor del Rio and in Patihuitz, I noticed that the women preferred to dance with female partners.

The change in Article 27 regarding claims to land had a greater impact on the colonizers in the Lacandón rain forest than on the indigenes in corporate communities. Since many of the settlers lack title to the lands they have been cultivating for more than two decades, it dashed the hope that they would ever obtain legal rights to land. The reform of Article 27 also re-creates the conditions for large landholding, since titleholders are able to include allotments for children and spouses as part of a single domain, just as in the Agrarian Law of Chiapas in 1921. Some of the cattlemen have been able to take over as much as 250 hectares of irrigated land, 20,000 hectares of wooded land, and up to 300,000 hectares of pasturage. Without any of the infrastructure promised to the colonizers, many small-plot holders have been forced to sell to the cattlemen. The colonies settled by former plantation laborers in the canyons of the Lacandón rain forest became the crucible for the protest movements that culminated in the 1994 Zapatista uprising. Their efforts to redefine tradition in a revolutionary setting is described in the next chapter.

CONCLUSIONS

Stimulated by the National Indian Congress, independent groupings of *campesinos* emerged out of the government-sponsored confederations. Among the most important of these in organizing communities of the rain forest have been the Independent Center of Agricultural Workers and Campesinos (CIOAC), OCEZ, and ARIC.[23] These organiza-

[handwritten annotations: "Can we make (imply) causal links to rebellion?" "I would apply a dif. set of questions — how did they do it? Hegemony over most. What issues took the forefront"]

tions were constantly under siege as official channels fought with the left wing within the groups to control the social forces released, using tactics of *cacique* intervention and corporatist approaches. In the communities of the rain forest, government co-optation was not even attempted, and the emergent independent organization took deep roots.

In the years just before the rebellion, Chiapas *campesinos* had extended their organizations beyond local bounded communities and state boundaries, and had drafted petitions presenting their position in concrete terms. They demonstrated this growing unity with national organizations in April, 1991, when they joined *campesinos* of Chihuahua, Sinaloa, Zacatecas, Oaxaca, Guerrero, Veracruz, Mexico D.F., and Morelos to protest the reform of the Agrarian Reform of Article 27 of the Constitution of 1917. The group drafted a document asserting that the privatization dynamic in the field affected the integrity and operation of the *ejido (La Jornada* April 11, 1991*)*. The *campesinos* present at this meeting pointed out the failure of the government to settle the land claims: there existed 3.5 million solicitations for land that were left in abeyance, and 200 resolutions not executed by then-president Salinas, with 7.6 million hectares in litigation and more than 8.7 million hectares conceded to ranchers for cattle pasturage against the minimal allotments established in the rules for colonies in national territories. They indicated that technical assistance and credit were lacking in over half of the *ejidos*. Fifteen million *campesinos* received less than the minimum wage of two dollars a day. Continual violations of human rights confronted individuals and organizations that sought redress for these problems. Based on these failures to execute the laws of the land, the *campesinos* claimed that the government in fact was subverting the Constitution. They called for revision of the agrarian legislation, support for commercialization of crops, credit opportunities, social services, and the recognition of their human rights and constitutional rights. Salinas responded to this indictment only with the rhetoric of modernization, ignoring repeated pleas throughout his six-year term.

The storms of protest were rising, yet the government seemed unable to act. By 1991, government funds rarely reached the agents working for the government (N. Harvey 1994:30). Instead of responding to their demands, the governors of Chiapas, General Absalón Castellanos Dominguez and his successor Patrocinio González Garrido, and the state of Chiapas resorted more and more frequently to outright repression by the army.

The ideology of a corporate community founded in the rituals carried out by religious *cofradias* continues to legitimate behavior, but now in a system of class stratification in which an exploitative *cacique* elite exists among the indigenous populations. The *caciques* still appeal to tradition to support their arbitrary rule, taking advantage of the funds dispersed by the PRI, which relies on them to deliver the vote. But this monopoly of power is shaky. Exodus from the communities contributes to the genesis of regional and national associations of indigenous and *campesino* organizations.

Although not all of the indigenes remaining within these communities perceive their troubles as coming from external sources, those who have been forced to migrate to colonizing areas of the Lacandón rain forest have begun to organize to defend their rights to the land in collective terms independent of co-optive government organizations. Indigenous people, including Choles, Zoques, Nahuas, Chinantecos, Tojolobales, Tzeltales, and Tzotziles, along with landless *mestizos*, have joined the Lacandones who lived there even

before the conquest (Arizpe et al. 1993). There they fight for survival, competing for limited land resources and rudimentary medical and educational facilities. Their presence in
the rain forest is contested by the rising concerns of environmentalists, who charge them
with destruction of the forest and the attendant grave dangers to the global environment.
Much of the destruction of the forest is a result of clear-cutting the forest by cattle ranchers who hire paramilitary bands to prey on the settlers. According to official figures, only
one million hectares of forest, of the 15 million hectares existing a decade ago, survive,
with an estimated 400,000 hectares destroyed each year (Sedue 1987, quoted in Gonzalez-Ponciano 1995).

There is also a diaspora from communities caused by *caciques*, who have for the past
three decades been expelling Indians from the land-poor Tzeltal and Tzotzil communities.
Thousands of people from Amatenango del Valle, Mitontic, Zinacantán, and San Juan
Chamula have been forced to leave their homes, land, and animals, and have gone to live
in the "misery belts" growing around San Cristóbal and eastward along the Pan American
highway. Hundreds of others have formed new rural communities of exiles on land purchased by the Protestant groups, which they have joined. Their lands and houses in their
natal communities are seized and distributed among the *caciques*, who control the administration of the *ejido* plots allotted to household units as well as communally owned and
operated woods and pastures.

Wealth differences, combined with an erosion of subsistence strategies, have undermined
the code of reciprocity and upset the balance of the moral community. Membership in the
closed corporate community, with its internal sanctioning system and norms of shared
poverty, brings heavy penalties for innovation. One outcome has been violence turned
inward. This has occurred at different time levels throughout Mexico. Homicide and the rule
of *pistoleros* were marked in the central plateau and northern states during and after the Revolution, as community studies in Tarrasco and Morelos indicate (Romanucci-Ross 1976).

I witnessed this explosive potential when I was living in Amatenango in the 1960s. It was
later confirmed by the homicides that occurred in Amatenango in the 1970s and 1980s,[24]
targeting the most innovative and forceful leaders whom I had known in the years of my
participation in community life. This was an index to the pressures experienced internally,
as the artificial boundaries of the village were maintained by the assassination of men and
women who threatened it. Petrona López, the leader of the pottery cooperative, challenged
male authority in household production by offering direct sales to regional and national
markets and a political base with PRI leaders for women. Simón Perez Kantirón and Mar-
iano López Lin met their death, after they had succeeded in introducing the first cooperative of indigenous truck owners, thereby gaining control over one of the most important
sources of profit in the commercialization of agricultural and artisan products, formerly
dominated by *ladinos*. In a community dominated by envy and retribution against those who
prospered more than their neighbors, they all recognized the potential of the cooperative
in overcoming the risk of making a profit by sharing the returns of such enterprises. But the
power that they assumed, and possibly their own improved standard of living, exceeded
communal norms based on homogeneity.

What happens when we exclude voices
EXODUS FROM COMMUNITIES *from a* 117
Study on globalization
Who can theorize about globalization? Clearly

The new social forces released by the National Indigenous Congress and the bishop's *not*
outreach in the Christian Base Communities, in conjunction with increasingly independ- *the*
ent *campesino* organizations, provided an alternative to co-optive government policies. The *Zap.*
emergence of these alternatives was coincident with the withdrawal of funds from government agencies that had contained the unrest. The Salinas government's increasingly
close alliance with highly capitalized, export-oriented sectors was concurrent with the
retraction of government programs for *campesinos*. The "Reform of the Agrarian Reform
Act" passed in 1992 was taken to be the death knell of state paternalism. In the decade of
the 1980s, the many *campesinos* killed by paramilitaries were the martyrs to changes
brought about by the explosion of communities.[25]

The threat to the survival of indigenous communities as distinctive cultural entities
became increasingly evident in the following years. The adaptations in wage work in
coastal plantations, the intensification of subsistence cultivation, and artisan production
were no longer adequate. Prices for subsistence surplus cultivator's crops did not expand
with the increase in the cost of living, since they were kept artificially low by federal pur-
chasing agencies. Forced to compete with redundant labor of people expelled or forced
out from their own communities by landlessness and that of Guatemalan exiles and land- *outlaws*
less migrants, Chiapas *campesinos* felt like outlaws in their own country. Although the
population increased at a lower rate after the 1990s, it still exceeded the capacity of
indigenous communities to survive with the given technology. This was notable in the
Lacandón, where birth rates were high and contraception not available.

The agrarian movements of the 1970s and 1980s drew upon the struggles of indigenous communities but went beyond them to develop a multiplicity of *campesino* and
comunero organizations through which they confronted landowners and the transitional
corporation government favored by the elite. Alliances with civil society strengthened
the movements of indigenes as they linked their objectives with those of *ladinos* and *mes-*
tizos, who were also rebelling against the monolithic control of the PRI. The Lacandón
rain forest provided an expanded setting for the resurgence of indigenous consciousness.
In these new conditions, the Zapatista rebellion took root in this new settlement, where
colonizers who had escaped the enslavement of the plantations and who had never been
yoked to the *caciquismo* of corporate highland communities engaged in collective forms
of production that became an incubator for the rebellion. Their demands for democracy
and dignity appealed to broad sectors of the Mexican population when they voiced them
on New Year's Eve of 1994. That historic moment and the aftermath of peace negotiations and dialogue are the subject of chapter 4. The new political space that they created
for "people without faces and without voices" has subsequently been placed under siege
in a counterinsurgency war mounted by an armed force of 60,000. The ensuing contest
between civil society and paramilitary and armed forces is the subject of chapter 5.

CHAPTER 4

RADICAL DEMOCRATIC
MOBILIZATION, 1994–1996

*use this
in paper*

Silence has translated to injustice and has been the germ of conflicts for Mexicans; this
has been particularly prejudicial for indigenous pueblos throughout the country. Their
language, the center of a universe of thought, is silenced: their isolation is both effect
and cause of poverty; from it stems impunity, impeding awareness by the rest of society
of the conditions of life and problems of indigenous pueblos. The dialogue here is prov-
ing that we Mexicans can acknowledge our differences and overcome our conflicts
through a peaceful road. May it never again require an armed uprising as the condition
for dialogue and tolerance becoming the instruments of relations among Mexicans.

Fifth Group, Dialogue between the Zapatistas and the
Mexican Government, *El Tiempo*, November 2, 1995:21.

assimilation

NATION-BUILDING OFTEN assumes the assimilation or even annihilation of marginalized cultures. Colonialism in the fifteenth to nineteenth centuries was premised on the
superiority of European nations in terms of conquest and the "civilizing mission." Following independence in the Americas in the early nineteenth century, imperialism confirmed a hierarchy of power conforming to racist ideologies. As we enter the third
millennium, the assumptions that underwrote that hierarchy are under attack. The challenge comes from subordinated societies that survived as enclaves within European
empires and the nation-states in which they found an uneasy accommodation after independence. In this chapter, I address the Zapatistas' challenge to the new world order conceived in racist and ethnocentric terms, and the collective strategies for survival they
propose for the coming millennium.

COLLECTIVE STRATEGIES FOR SURVIVAL

The very survival of collective bases of work and beliefs among indigenous societies
represents the antithesis of white European supremacy and control that dominated
colonies and empires. Indigenous efforts to define cultural *autonomía*, or autonomy—
self-determination for multiple, coexisting, and autonomous entities within nations in

which they find themselves—are so distinct from Western models of society that we lack the vocabulary to encompass them. The First Continental Meeting of the *pueblos indios* drafted the "Declaration of Quito" in August 1990 that defined the indigenous vision of a pluricultural state. Self-determination was at the heart of it, defined as the "right that *pueblos indios* have to the control of our respective territories, including the natural resources of soil and subsoil and air space. The defense and conservation of nature, . . . the equilibrium of the ecosystem and conservation of life and the democratic constitution of our own governments." (*Servicio mensual de información y documentación, Separata num.* 130 ALAI, Quito, Agosto 1990, cited in Díaz-Polanco 1997:16fn).

If we translate the term *autonomía* in English as self-governing, we leave out of consideration the generative basis of culture encompassed in the indigenous understanding of autonomy. In their expanded definition, they reach for terms such as "attaining dignity." This is a more radical concept than that of self-determination, which implies yielding personal self-will to a constituted authority elected through some form of plebiscite. The indigenous definition also includes, by extension of autonomy to pluricultural coexistence, the rights of all people to dance to their own music.

This fundamental premise of autonomy in the right of pluricultural coexistence is acted out when indigenous peoples congregate. I began to understand this as I watched the concluding plenary session during the National Indigenous Forum in January 1996. Before the assembly was called to order, delegates of the Ch'ol Brotherhood (*Hermandad Ch'ol*) from the Northern Autonomous Region, the group that had declared their autonomy on October 12, 1994, marked out a space in the vast hall with candles, incense, and pine needles and then proceeded to invoke the spirits at each compass point. Another moment occurred at the Intergalactic Convention at Oventic in July 1996, as I watched a variety of indigenous groups from Chiapas and other states of Mexico as they arrived at the stadium. Each group spread pine needles, lighted up the pitchpine incense, drew out their instruments, and danced a few steps on the raised platform. No one applauded, but everyone appreciated that they were making that space theirs for the moment. It had become their habitus. By defining the space in their own traditional ways, they asserted their autonomy while accepting that of other groups to do it in their own way.

Indigenist movements in countries with high proportions of indigenes, as in Guatemala and the Andean countries, are proposing the political premises for autonomy. Kay Warren (1998) provides an insightful analysis of the process now under way in Guatemala, where Mayans have emerged out of three decades of a genocidal war with a mandate to found a pluricultural basis for civil society.[1] Xavier Albó (1995), who is well acquainted with indigenous "nations" in the Andes, has said these small groups not only manage to survive but may also "constitute the basic cell of the social regeneration of the continent." Díaz-Polanco, who has participated in the dialogues on indigenous autonomy in San Andrés, writes that the movement for indigenous control over their territories in Mexico during the 1980s and 1990s is now coalescing in a "unifying project for governing autonomous communities and regions" (Díaz-Polanco 1997:16). As this unifying project transcends the political limits of old empires and nations, it clearly has the potential for redefining the geopolitics of space, not only in the Western Hemisphere but worldwide.

The pluricultural base of Mexico, as in many other states of Latin America with large indigenous populations, was treated as an obstacle to modernity. The *indigenista* ideology that ostensibly embraced indigenous cultures only promoted policies that induced them to give up their distinctive identity. The critique of *indigenismo* by Latin American scholars (Warman et al. 1970), along with the revindicative movements of indigenous people, has led to the current recognition of the importance of these resistant cultures as alternative cultural models. Bonfil Batalla (1996:94) expressed this most poignantly in his book, *México Profundo*, when he wrote "The stigmatized and devalued cultures are in truth a vast reserve of alternative cultural resources whose value, denied until today, would be absurd to ignore."

The awareness of the profound roots of indigenous culture in Latin American identity developed with the social movements of *campesinos* and *comuneros* in the 1970s and 1980s. From October 12 to 15, 1974, 1,230 indigenous people from throughout the state of Chiapas assembled for the Indian National Congress (CNI) in San Cristóbal, convoked by Bishop Samuel Ruiz. The ferment of activities in the following decades prepared the organizational base for demonstrations during the 1992 quincentennial year of the arrival of Europeans in the Americas. On that occasion, indigenous peoples throughout the hemisphere celebrated the survival and persistence of many small and diversified nations not, as in past years, their "discovery" by the Spaniards. In San Cristóbal, as many as 10,000 indigenous people from throughout the state of Chiapas marched through the streets of the colonial city to the Dominican convent. Without fanfare, one of the marchers climbed up to the monument of the conqueror of Chiapas, Diego Mazariegos, and struck the statue off its pedestal with a mallet.

The act signaled the end of indigenous peoples' tolerance for secondary citizenship. In the following two years, mobilized *campesinos* and *comuneros* throughout the state attempted to change the relations of subordination with peaceful protests. Repeated mobilizations of the settlers in the Lacandón jungle sought redress for the injustices and unequal treatment they endured (Nash and Sullivan 1992). The state of Chiapas responded with repression and militarization of civil society. The Center for Human Rights, "Fray Bartolomé de Las Casas," recounted 56 incidents of violations of human rights, affecting a total of 1,036 people in the state of Chiapas, in the six months just prior to the uprising (Centro de Derechos Humanos Fray Partolomé de Las Casas 1993). The office of the Secretary of the Agrarian Reform accumulated over 3,000 petitions for land by indigenous pueblos who were attempting to regain lands lost during the Porfiriato. In the course of demanding their human rights, distinct ethnicities have come into coalitions with other ethnic groups that have been similarly deprived. These movements for pluricultural coexistence of indigenes within Mexico gave rise to the Zapatista rebellion and reinforced the demands made in Chiapas throughout the nation.

I have argued that in their search for peace with justice and their invention of new democratic forums in the years following the January 1, 1994, uprising, Chiapas Mayans are demonstrating that enclaves of distinctive cultural formations may be the best prepared to usher in a postmodern world of pluriethnic and pluricultural coexistence (Nash 1997b). The dialogues between the EZLN and the government team of the Commission for Agreement and Pacification (COCOPA), mediated by Bishop Samuel Ruíz and the National Commission of Mediation (CONAI), increasingly focused on autonomy as a necessary precondition for achieving their desire for justice and equality as culturally distinct entities. That effort appeared to reach an accord in the San Andrés agreements on February 16, 1996, when the government signed the plan for autonomous regions made up of indigenous cultures based in communities. Their vision of autonomy includes cultural plurality as an integral part of the nation (Stephen 1997b).

This chapter touches on some of the encounters in which indigenous people defined their own objectives as they fashioned the accord. The PRI government countermanded its own commitments to a negotiated settlement by reinforcing the military presence in the Lacandón rain forest and cutting the Zapatistas off from their growing support in the highlands and in the nation. The opposition of these two currents, one moving toward democratic reform supported by a heterogeneous civil society, and the other directed toward repression and even elimination of the agents of change through militarization, will be discussed in following chapters.

RADICAL DEMOCRATIC MOBILIZATION 1994–1996

The explosion of indigenous communities from the defensive boundaries in which they were incorporated is the culmination of the intensified migration, commercialization, and resource exploitation discussed in the previous chapter. In their opposition to contradictory policies pursued by a government that claimed to be following the mandate of the 1910 Revolution while undermining semi-subsistence producers, indigenous people of Chiapas have forged alliances with *mestizos* who share their poverty, at the same time as they have challenged the control by *caciques* within their communities.

The armed attack and seizure of the town halls in San Cristóbal and three other cities on New Year's Eve of 1994 was the culmination of months of peaceful protests and years of gathering resentment to the government's denial of human services and political rights to the settlers in the Lacandón rain forest. An EZLN armed force of about 2,000 men and women seized and ransacked the town halls of Altamirano, Chanal, Huistán, Las Margaritas, Oxchuc, Ocosingo, and San Cristóbal de Las Casas. They entered the barracks of Rancho Nuevo, where thousands of federal troops were quartered on the outskirts of San Cristóbal, seized guns and amunition, and freed 179 prisoners from the maximum security jail. Announcing an end to five hundred years of immizeration and injustice, they declared war on the government, appealing to the Geneva Conventions of War. After twelve days of combat with the 12,000 federal troops mobilized in the area, President Salinas called for a cease-fire and promised to negotiate with the leaders (Collier and Quaratiello 1994:3–4).

The two weeks of active combat by the EZLN troops, made up of Tzeltal-, Tzotzil-, Chol-, Tojolobal- and Mam-speaking men and women, gained worldwide attention for what has been called the first postmodern revolution.[2] It served as a catalyst for social movements for land, religious freedom, and democracy within and beyond the boundaries of community and the region. Less attention has been paid in the press to the social movements of indigenous and *mestizo* supporters of the uprising in the years following the armed uprising than to the armed encounter that lasted only two weeks. Yet the importance of these movements in charting an historic change in the relations between indigenous peoples and the state is recognized by Mexican social analysts and their colleagues throughout the world.

In the wake of the uprising, organizations of *campesinos* and popular fronts of *comuneros* have tried to further the demands of the EZLN for integration as culturally distinct ethnic groups in the Mexican State. The demands of the neo-Zapatistas reflect the roots of the movement in Zapata's Plan de Ayala, promulgated in 1911, and the subsequent Zapatista Agrarian Law of 1915, drafted by radical intellectuals who joined the movement. Like the earlier Zapatistas, they are calling for autonomy of democratically organized communities with rights over economic resources, the judiciary, and other political and social institutions.[3] But the new movement is more radical in its claims: it demands land and the right to determine its distribution within self-governing regional bases that go beyond the municipal limits defined in the colonial era. It also seeks a percentage of the returns from natural resources of the subsoil and waterpower. The educational reform it seeks does not stop at a bilingual program using indigenous languages as a crutch toward gaining literacy in Spanish and entry into modernizing programs. Rather it is directed at restoring indigenous history as a continuum with pre-Hispanic civilizations, with indigenous cultural premises central in the organization of studies. Women's voices are being heard for the first time in the new Zapatista movement, and they often contradict the pronouncements made by men. This was explicit at many moments in the conventions called by the EZLN, particularly as the demand for autonomy coalesced.

The indigenous movement in Chiapas has taken decisive steps toward realizing its goals of autonomy and self-determination. Indigenes began to occupy town halls soon after the uprising and, following the elections of August 1994, they opposed PRI incumbents who had often gained their office by electoral fraud. They have taken over lands for which they have been petitioning for decades but were denied by the reform of Article 27 of the 1917 Constitution, which went into effect in 1992. Some of the activists in the independent communal organizations that split from corporatist organizations controlled by the ruling party over two decades ago are now incorporated in the Party of the Democratic Revolution (PRD). Others are active in Civil Society, a loosely associated group of activists that supported the first dialogues for peace between the Zapatistas and government representatives in March 1994 and followed up with the National Democratic Convention, hosted by the EZLN in the Lacandón rain forest shortly before the August 21 elections. The constituents of Civil Society organized the campaign for Amado Avendaño as governor of Chiapas in 1994.[4] Since then they have been instrumental in coordinating the many forums and congresses that have mobilized indigenous, *mestizo*, and international support for the Zapatistas.

At the center of the storm in the political ferment following the uprising were the populations of the Lacandón rain forest organized as municipalities and territories in the rebellion of the EZLN (Municipios y Territorios Rebeldes del Ejército Zapatista de Liberación Nacional) and the Pluriethnic Autonomous Region of the northern area

(Region Autónoma Pluriétnicas). They inspired the rebellion of highland municipalities that formed town councils (Consejos Municipales) recognizing the parallel government of Amado Avendaño, the gubernatorial candidate of civil society and the PRD in the contested election of August 1994. The common goals of these diverse groups include autonomy and an end to the fragmentation of indigenous society and control from above by the PRI. I shall describe these multiple sources of ferment in the pluripolitical and pluriethnic communities of Chiapas, and analyze their converging attempts to transform political life in dialogues with the central government.

The Reform Movement Against
PRI Monopoly of Power

Two distinct movements for change among indigenous peoples that emerged in the highlands and Lacandón rain forest began to converge during and after the Zapatista uprising. In the highlands, the politics of co-optation carried out by the PRI government with indigenous municipalities kept the lid on transformative changes. So long as *caciques* continued to deliver the vote to the PRI, the monopoly of power paraded as tradition in indigenous communities masked the class conflict and ethnic reassertion that were the outgrowth of contradictory development policies pursued by the government. As we have seen in chapter 3, the ferment from within the communities constantly threatened to blow off the lid. *Caciques* responded by expelling opponents on the charge that they were Protestants, even when political differences or the desire to take over their lands were the underlying motivation. The federal government constantly built up the military presence throughout the state of Chiapas from the latter part of the 1980s, building residential quarters for increased numbers of troops in Nuevo Rancho, just twelve kilometers from San Cristóbal. There, within close range, the government constructed a maximum-security prison in readiness for the conflict that was coming.

The diaspora from the communities that began in the 1950s, when the existing *ejido* lands became too limited for the growing population, was swelled by the more than 35,000 indigenes expelled as Protestants or political dissidents. The federal government responded to indigenous demands for land by opening up national territories in the Lacandón rain forest. These temporary expedients became the basis for further discontent in the 1990s, particularly after the passage of the "reform" of Article 27 of the Constitution, which opened up the *ejido* lands to privatization and rejected further claims. This defeat of the hopes of the colonizers to gain title to their lands, combined with the opening up of the markets to foreign goods through NAFTA, which was to go into effect on January 1, 1994, culminated in the uprising.

Following the Zapatista uprising, discontented groups in municipalities throughout Chiapas openly challenged the PRI monopoly of power in the state, sometimes seizing town halls or engaging in marches to the state capital in Tuxtla Gutierrez to demand the resignation of mayors and other officials whom they charged with fraudulent election practices. Very often the leaders of these demonstrations were inhabitants of the rural hamlets who fought the control by officials in the town centers, charging them with favoritism in the distribution of *ejido* lands and failure to provide basic services such as safe water, paved roads, or electricity.

Even with manipulation of the August 21, 1994, elections, which most observers felt was more flagrant in Chiapas than elsewhere in the country,[5] the PRI lost mayoralty elections in 25 of the 111 towns in the state. In the following months, as towns took individual action against their municipal leaders, the figure rose to 35. In all of these municipalities, the demands were for profound democratic changes directed toward exercising new forms of democracy. Towards this goal they are formulating their own laws and are reordering the territorial patterns in a new relationship between the governed and the governors.

Following the election of August 21, 1994, after which Ernesto Zedillo Ponce de León took office in December 1994, exposure of the depths of the budget imbalances resulted in the flight of capital and a state crisis. Even before the currency was devalued in late December by more than half its value, billions of dollars controlled by PRI elites left the country. The country was forced to accept an even more onerous austerity program than in 1982, when the IMF set the course of neoliberalism. Zedillo increasingly relied on force to face down indigenous opposition and competition from adversarial parties.

The rebellion took two directions in responding to these two forces. The reform movement sought democratic changes to seat candidates who had won elections where incumbent PRI candidates remained seated. Working within the framework of political parties, these towns chose to carry out plebiscites to determine the vote, often with the result that they were governed by municipal councils made up of two or more political party representatives. The reaction in these towns was limited to municipal boundaries. A more radical wing took the form of municipal and regional declarations of autonomy, with governance as municipalities in rebellion, within autonomous regions governed by indigenous parliaments. These distinct directions are described below.

Municipalities in Rebellion

Teopisca was the first town in which residents of hamlets took over the town hall after the uprising and deposed the mayor on February 9, 1994. Tila and Simojovel had already petitioned the State Congress to remove their mayors on February 8. *Comuneros* of Tenejapa renounced their mayor on March 2, and Chenalhó followed their example with the election of a new mayor on March 17. In March, over a thousand members of the State Council of Indigenous and Campesino Organizations (CEOIC), an organization formed in January, 1994, and represented 280 indigenous and *campesino* organizations, marched into the city of San Cristóbal de Las Casas. They called for the removal of all 111 municipal officers in the state, urging the formation of municipal councils that would include *campesinos* and indigenes. The Union of Organizations and Political Parties of Venustiano Carranza demanded the removal of the mayor for fraud and misappropriation of funds on April 10, 1994. Zinacantecos ousted their president in June, 1994 when they discovered that he had confiscated public funds for his own use (Collier 1997:19). Many other towns that rejected the elected authorities as fraudulent continued to stage protests and urge further removals. As indigenous people began to gain a sense of their rights, they proceeded to rid the municipality of officials they considered to be fraudulently elected throughout the months of April, May, and June, 1994, bringing the number of towns in which actions were taken to 28.

The new President, Ernesto Zedillo de León, was faced with a major financial crisis caused by the discovery of huge deficits and the need to devalue the peso. *Subcomandante insurgente* Marcos addressed his communiqué marking the first anniversary of the uprising to the weekly news journal, *Process*, the newspapers *El Financier* and *La Jornada*, and the San Cristobal de Las Casas *El Tiempo*, expressing surprise that the supreme government blamed the Zapatistas for the devaluation of the new peso. With characteristic irony, he admitted his popularity in financial circles, and promised a campaign to raise the emotion of risk and uncertainty, and to move people to buy new pesos. However, he complained about the constant buzzing of helicopters, planes, and tanks, as well as the incursion of dogs that government troops had sent in to hunt the Zapatistas (*Expreso*, Tuxtla Gutierrez, December 31, 1994:7).

The lack of what was called "governability" was pronounced when the newly elected local officials tried to take office and were blocked by municipal takeovers. The town officials sometimes chose to carry out plebiscites to determine who should occupy the presidency. Once the vote was tallied, the state legislature would assist representatives of the contesting political parties to constitute municipal councils. Unlike the territories in rebellion discussed below, these reconstituted town governing offices were represented by political party candidates of the PRI, PRD, and/or PAN, and were recognized by the PRI government. This was probably the first election in the state of Chiapas in which the ruling party in effect admitted fraud in the elections by yielding to local claims for a recount.

Amatenango chose this path after the takeover of the town hall on January 2, 1995, by members of the PRD. The PRD claimed to have won the mayoral contest in the August elections, but leaders of the PRI prevailed upon the PRI incumbent to stay in office, even though he did not want to.

Field notes on the inauguration, January 1 and 2, 1995. I attended the inauguration of the incumbent mayor of Amatenango on January 1, 1995, with students who were part of the National Science Foundation training grant.[6] We watched the *mayordomos* playing traditional music of drums and flutes in the church plaza, and saw the civil officials march around the plaza with the banners of the local, state, and national governments. Except for the absence of *alféreces*, whose *cargos* had not been undertaken because, according to the opposition PRD, the mayor was a Protestant, the inauguration was carried out just as I had seen it done in the 1960s when I did fieldwork.

When we arrived the following day, we saw the PRD supporters pushing the municipal vehicles from the patio of the incumbent president. Knots of PRI supporters stood on the church side of the plaza while the PRD officials who claimed to have won the elections were holed up in the town hall. We spoke with some of the young PRD supporters warming themselves around a bonfire in front of the town hall. They told us that the PRD mayoral candidate and his supporters broke the window of the town hall the night before and

*Newly elected officials march around the plaza in January 1, 1995 in Amatenango del Valle
after taking their oath.*

entered the premises, where they stayed. Posters tacked on the wall of the town hall appealed to militants of the PRD and the police of both sides of the division to support them. Like many supporters of the PRD, the youths were from the hamlets, which had rejected the control over money and power by PRI officials in the center. The PRD mayoral candidate was from the center, chosen because the party leaders felt that he would enhance their chance of winning the election. He was, in fact, the son-in-law of my landlord and, in the 1960s had struck me as an intimidated young man very much under the control of his powerful father-in-law, who was the *bankil u'ul,* or elder seer, of the lower moiety. It struck me that politics had really taken the place of divining and witchcraft as the locus of power.

The plebiscite was set for January 13, and representatives of the PRD stationed themselves in the town hall day and night until that day. When we arrived at 10 A.M. to see the action, the plaza was full of indigenes, along with international and national reporters and television crews. Just scanning the crowd of indigenes, who were lined up on either the church or the town hall side of the plaza, in accord with their affiliation with the PRI or the PRD, it looked as though the PRD would win. The PRD lineup had a clear majority of women, standing with their babies in the shade of trees on the town hall side of the plaza. PRI supporters noted this and sent out men to round up the women in the nearby households in the center, most of which supported the PRI. The apparent preponderance of women in the PRD fold proved to be the case. After a time-consuming count, with women and men counted separately as each voter walked through a narrow channel formed by the distended bellies of the state congressman and local PRD and PRI officials who performed their own counts, it was announced that, while the PRI had 892 votes, 324 of which were women's, the PRD won with 1,095 votes, 600 of which were women's.

Later, in conversation with my *comadre*, whose sons occupy important posts in the PRI local government, I asked why she thought people were turning to the PRD. She discounted the trend as the preferences of people from peripheral hamlets that she clearly thought should not have a voice in town affairs. These people are not, she declared, descendants of the "original" townspeople. The town was, in fact, a product of the colonial *reducción*, when scattered populations were settled in hamlets around what had been the core community. As for the preponderance of women in the PRD support group, she attributed it to disgruntled widows and other women without men who wanted the

Women of Patihuitz carry water from open cisterns, since they have neither drainage systems nor electricity in their homes.

Kay — ┌ rebellion as a method of healing,
June – casal effect   └ making meaning out of violence

town to respond to their needs, particularly in reference to the *ejido* plots which were allocated to male heads of families. She herself had been widowed when her eldest son was 14 and was able to hold on to her husband's *ejido* plot only because of him. Some of the hamlets had never received potable water or electricity, and their residents had never served in the lucrative posts with salaries and disposable funds in the town center. *Defers author to anthro.*

I asked what influence she thought the EZLN uprising had on local events, and she responded with the ambiguity PRI supporters feel about the event. She admired their courage, and said that many people considered "Marcos," the EZLN *subcomandante*, to be the *"Rey Cha'uk,"* or King of Lightning, a term applied to outstanding curer-diviners who had powerful *nahwales* or animal spirits. But because of the disruption to her own sons' political future, she felt uncertain about whether she should support them or not, and wanted to know my opinion.

Despite the vote, the PRI officials contested the results. The final decision by the State secretary of government and a congressional committee in Tuxtla Gutierrez was that the town should be governed by a council of three PRI and three PRD officials, with a seventh member chosen by these officials, until a special election could be held in November 1995. This proved to be an uneasy truce, interrupted by frequent threats of assassination of the leadership by their opponents. In October 1995, the elections proved decisively that the PRD mayor had the majority, and he was inaugurated on January 1, 1996, with the full panoply of rituals officiated by the *alféreces*, just as he had promised in his campaign.

This sharing of leadership in councils that included diverse political party leaders proved to be the solution taken in other hotly contested municipalities. The threat of violence was endemic in these situations, and state troops were frequently sent to patrol the area. Amatenango differed from other municipalities such as Chenalhó, which will be discussed in chapter 5, in resolving the crisis internally. The PRI officials withdrew from political life, thus avoiding the divisive actions promoted by the PRI.

EZLN Territories in Rebellion

The government of the state of Chiapas was in disarray after the elections, with many municipalities claiming electoral fraud. Dissent coalesced around Amado Avendaño, a former director of the Human Rights Center, "Fray Bartolomé de Las Casas," and candidate for civil society. While Avendaño was still recuperating from the injuries sustained when his car was forced over a precipice while he was campaigning,[7] his wife, Concepción Villafuerte, held a press conference claiming that the governor-elect, Roberto Robledo Rincón, was fraudulently elected. Following his recovery, Avendaño set up offices of a parallel government in the old buildings of the San Cristóbal INI. This government in rebellion was recognized in 32 municipalities, mostly located in the EZLN territory of the rain forest and in the Northern Region, which formed the core of the municipalities in rebellion. There, as the elected candidate of civil society, Avendaño adjudicated claims to land and other issues of the municipalities that recognized his government. The government was, for a brief time, carrying out the mandate of autonomy, with the ultimate goal of creating thirty new municipalities to be governed by the *pueblos* and communities designated as the bases for EZLN support (*Expreso* February 3, 1995:7). The governance of these municipalities in rebellion did not respect preexisting political divisions. In Ocosingo, for example, there were eight municipalities in rebellion. Their charter as autonomous indigenous pueblos was drawn up in the act of the General Executive Council of the Autonomous Regions of Chiapas realized in San Cristóbal on January 20, 1995, fulfilling the constitution of autonomous regions projected on October 12, 1994. They are the core of the contested governance that provoked the armed invasions of June, 1998 (chapter 5).

These autonomous regions are formally included in municipalities of Ocosingo, Las Margaritas, and Altamirano, all of which encompass vast territories extending into the rain forest. The opening up of national territories in the Lacandón rain forest during the period from 1940 to 1970 relieved the pressure for land by settlement in virgin lands that did not infringe on the large landholdings of the large landowners who had seized communal lands during the liberal period and refused to yield them after the Revolution of 1910–1917 (Reyes Ramos 1994:59). Following the January 1994 uprising, the settlements in the Lacandón rain forest, along with the autonomous regions and the municipal councils that recognized the government in rebellion of Amado Avendaño, the gubernatorial candidate who claimed fraud in the PRI victory, were designated as Territories in Rebellion of the Zapatista Army of National Liberation (EZLN).[8]

A new political dynamic developed in these communities distinct from that in the highland communities. Nearly abandoned by the central government, these communities have in fact been exercising the autonomy that many dissidents throughout civil society aim for in the future. Thirty of these 32 municipalities calling for independence are creations of the EZLN and are governed by civilians who constitute their support group. The self-constituted authorities act in accord with the Constitution of 1917, in addition to the new laws ordained by the Zapatistas, including those proclaimed by women, and laws drawn up in local municipal committees and ordained by popular vote. They hold their meetings in separate spaces from the formally constituted authority, which is drawn from the *mestizocracia,* the elite made up of ranchers and entrepreneurs who do not represent the concerns of the smallholding settlers. Las Margaritas, for example, contains within its limits self-constituted autonomous regions of El Valle Tojolabal, comprised of 37 pueblos with 1,800 indigenes who support the "parliamentarians" who work full time in the offices of the *ejido* house and Santo Domingo Las Palmas. In the course of settling land disputes and adjudicating other issues at the local level, they are trying to put into practice a new relationship between the indigenous pueblos and the state (Nash et al. 1995).

Indigenous parliaments. The State Board of Indigenous and Campesino Organizations (CEOIC) represented the Territories in Rebellion located in the municipalities of Ocosingo, Altamirano, Las Margaritas, and the Northern Region. The CEOIC chose the October 12, 1994, Dia de la Raza, or Day of the Races, to declare these regions in the north of the state and on the frontier as autonomous. On January 20, 1995, indigenous parliaments constituted the General Executive Council of the Autonomous Regions of Chiapas in San Cristóbal. In the act they signed, the originators stated:

[margin annotation: isolation gave autonomy]

Autonomy is the basic condition and necessary for the life of a pueblo. Without autonomy no pueblo can exist. Without our autonomy, the indigenous pueblos will disappear. (*Expreso*, February 1995)

Eleven of the autonomous indigenous parliaments were located in the Northern Region, and ten other indigenous parliaments existed in municipalities of the highlands and in the rain forest. The 21 autonomous parliaments that existed in 1995 carried out judicial proceedings, charged fines, and paid for electrical energy. The indigenes demanded that the federal government recognize the parliaments of the autonomous regions by the inclusion of a new chapter in the Constitution which would establish the rights of the Indian pueblos to these governing bodies and would transfer the infrastructure and resources of the INI to them (*Expreso*, February 3, 1995:7). This would have given formal recognition to the parallel government that Amado Avendaño had in fact been leading. In response, the government reinforced the military presence in the region.

In Las Margaritas, a gateway city to the *ejido* lands opened up in the Lacandón rain forest, conflicts between the dominant cattlemen in town leadership and the poor set-

Dawn in the Lacandón canyons, May 1995.

Families in the Lacandón rain forest live in wooden houses with thatch roofs.

tlers of the rain forest were continuous, waged by *campesinos* against the hired guns of the ranchers. On April 3, 1995, militant *campesinos* of the PRD seized municipal offices. Three days later, members of the Organization of Tojolabal Pueblos named five commanders and forty police, "in accord with their traditions" *(Expreso,* April 7, 1995:l). This seemed to signal the end of one-party control in this municipality.

When the Tojolobales who carried out the revolt in Las Margaritas failed to gain recognition of their act, and the PRI president of the town, whom they accused of ordering the assassination of two of their indigenous leaders, remained in power, the Independent Center of Agricultural Workers and Campesinos (CIOAC) and members of the PRD organized a march of an estimated 1,000 to 1,500 Tojolobales from Las Margaritas to Tuxtla Gutierriez, starting out on April 28 and arriving on May 3, 1995. At a rally in the San Cristóbal plaza halfway to their destination, I heard the group's leaders, including women and men as well as Amado Avendaño, who had joined them, speak of the fraud perpetrated in the August 1994 elections and their desire for democracy. They called for an end to domination by *ladino* cattlemen and the *mestizocracia* (mixed-blood elites) that dominated political life in the town centers of Las Margaritas and the other gateway municipalities. Some carried placards of the PRD, OCEZ, and CIOAC, which had organized the march. The group of *campesinos*, which included men, women, and children, many of them barefoot and wearing much-mended clothing, was a community in motion. They embodied the metaphor they often use for themselves, the Abuxu, or Ants.

When the group arrived in Tuxtla Gutierrez, Placido Morales Vásquez, the PRI director for the state of Chiapas, assured reporters at a press conference, held while the dissidents were crowding the municipal plaza, that there would be "clean and transparent" elections in all the municipalities of the state in October, 1995. The agreement reached in Tuxtla Gutierrez was to establish a municipal council for Las Margaritas, with equal numbers of PRI and PRD representatives who would serve their term and run for reelection the following year. This left the question of indigenous autonomy in abeyance, along with the hundreds of other claims that were accumulating. These multiparty councils put in place by the state government in highland municipalities, such as Amatenango del Valle and the Tojolobales of Las Margaritas in the Lacandón, were an uneasy solution to the problem. They provided the fissures for further dissension with the buildup of military and paramilitary forces described in the following chapter. They also fail to address the issues indigenes were raising about regional representation for the indigenous municipalities.

In the struggle to maintain their position in the semi-subsistence economy of small plot cultivation, indigenous people have forged alliances with *mestizos* who share their poverty. At the same time, they have challenged the control by indigenous *caciques* within their midst. Jacinto Arias Perez (1994) shows how, in the process, "the limits of Indianness have widened, and are less definable in themselves now that many of those who were considered Indian have as much of the outlook of conqueror or invader." While he occupied an important position as secretary in attendance to the indigenous pueblos for the PRI government in Tuxila Gutierrez, he distanced himself from the government's position by supporting these movements for cultural autonomy. At a meeting of the Center of Research and Higher Studies of Social Anthropology (CIESAS), he stated that "autonomy was a right of the pueblos guaranteed in the 1917 Constitution" (Arias 1994). But autonomy limited to the boundaries of the municipalities could no longer address even the minimal needs of the people.

In order to achieve cultural rehabilitation, indigenous people are rejecting the *indigenista* ideology of the PRI, which they criticize as an ideology that co-opts elements of indigenous culture only in order to create hegemonic control over them. They are, at the same time, reinventing the meaning of pluriethnic governance in terms that they claim are more related to ancient Mayan practices.

Our categories for thinking about ethnic groups are transformed by the struggles of the indigenous movements now actively seeking to define a new relationship with the state.[9] The discourse of the Zapatistas reflects primordial roots of both inspiration and

identification; their strategies reflect a sure sense of the political process in which they
are situated and which they are trying to push to new levels of pluricultural coexistence.
By tracing the programmatic statements made by Zapatistas and their supporters during
the National Democratic Convention of July 1994 and in the dialogues that took place in
March 1995 through September 1995, culminating in the National Indigenist Forum of
January 1996, I hope to show their distinct approach to a pluriethnic society that eludes
Western categories of thought.

DIALOGUES FOR A NEW DEMOCRACY

Our path was always that the will of the many be in the hearts of the men and
women who command. The will of the majority is the path on which he who
commands should walk. If he separates his step from the path of the will of the
people, the heart that commands should be changed for another who obeys.
Thus was born our strength in the jungle, he who leads obeys if he is true, and
he who follows leads through the common heart of true men and women.
Another word came from afar so that this government was named and this
work gave the name of "democracy" to our way that was from before words
traveled. (Translation of an EZLN communication from the jungle, published
in *La Jornada*, February 27, 1994:12)

This communiqué from the Indigenous Clandestine Revolutionary Committee of the
EZLN shortly after the uprising expresses its purpose in words that echo ceremonial language I have often heard. The cadence of the speech and the imagery of the language
reflect Mayan poetics even in translation. The repeated references to what the heart says
reflects a belief that true language—*batzil k'op*—issues from the heart. Diviner-curers
gain access to the language of the heart of patients by means of pulsing them. This is done
by holding a thumb over the throbbing pulse in the wrist of the patient while they utter
provocative questions. When the pulse leaps, the curers who listen and feel—the verb,
awayi, is the same for both verbs—know where the problem lies. This rhetoric resonates
among the poor of Mexico and the world audience it is reaching.

Dialogue in the Cathedral

The EZLN delegation of 15 Zapatistas arrived for the first dialogue with government
representatives in San Cristóbal de Las Casas on March 8, 1994. Much to the conster-
nation of a group of "*autenticos coletos,*" the self-designated term for descendants of conquerors in San Cristóbal, it was held in the seventeenth-century cathedral, with Bishop
Samuel Ruíz presiding as negotiator for the National Commission for Mediation
(CONAI). Supporting the peace talks was a Civil Society group, which maintained a
twenty-four-hour vigil around the cathedral in order to prevent attacks on the negotiators. These security lines were an important base for the increasingly solidified cohort

that called themselves "Civil Society" in the elections of August 1994 and in the many congresses and conventions that followed.

Among the demands of the Zapatistas were the following, which I have summarized from reports of the discussion groups, or *mesas*:

1. Autonomy of indigenous villages, with the right to use their own language in schools, public contracts, courts, and the media. As one step in the democratization of government and the recognition of pluriethnic groups, the Zapatistas proposed a decentralization of the government at every level, overcoming "presidentialism" as well as control by the federal district over the entire country. They called for a redistricting of electoral districts conforming to the reality of the constituencies. From the very beginning of the talks, *subcomandante* Marcos made it clear that the Zapatistas were not demanding a racially representative leadership. This in itself does not ensure responsiveness to the interests of indigenous people, as five hundred years of *caciquismo* proved. Rather, the desire was to have representatives who fulfilled the will of the people, rescuing democracy from co-optation by false leaders.
2. Redistribution of large landholdings to the smallholding villages, and government support for those who work the land, including agricultural machinery, fertilizers, insecticides, credit, technical aid, improved seeds, and cattle. Assurance of just prices for crops is a prerequisite for commercial production in the international market, since Mexican farmers now face competition from subsidized U.S. products.
3. Support for housing, health, education, recreation, communication, and other necessities for overcoming cultural marginalization. The Zapatistas demanded services equivalent to those accorded to other communities and towns throughout the republic, such as electricity, potable water, sewage, roads, telephone communication, recreational centers, and sports facilities.
4. Recognition of the rights of women and attention to their special medical needs, and support in gaining access to markets for their artisan production. Zapatistas are credited with raising the issues of women's rights to national attention.

The negotiations in San Cristóbal in March 1994 received favorable attention from then-president Carlos Salinas, who admitted publicly that in the drive for modernization he had given insufficient attention to the needs of the people. The Zapatistas terminated the first phase of the dialogues in March, announcing that they had not reached any agreement, despite the attempt by the government to assert a successful outcome. In a strong denunciation of the "lies" and "deception of the government" on March 15, 1994 (EZLN 1998:197), the Clandestine Revolutionary Committee's Indigenous Command declared that the government had not seriously entered into negotiations, and that they were unwilling to pursue the dialogues until government negotiators indicated their commitment. But other events distracted the attention of PRI leaders from carrying through on the negotiations even if they had the will. The assassination of Donaldo Cola-

more than ~~govts.~~ *resistance*
~~distracted~~

sio during his campaign for presidency in March 1994 and threats to PRI hegemony in other states revealed the deep levels of dissension in the party. Salinas left the problem for his successor, Ernesto Zedillo, to handle.

During the transfer of power to Zedillo in December, the new president had further preoccupations with the peso crisis and growing financial instability. The dialogues were not reconvened until April 1995. During the interim, the head of the National Commission of Mediation (CONAI), Bishop Samuel Ruíz, undertook a hunger strike, which was joined by many people throughout the country, calling for a resumption of peace talks. Indigenous people from throughout the state came to show their support for the bishop's initiative in the peace move. On December 27, 1994, a delegation of Tzeltales from Oxchuc, dressed in their striking handloomed garments, engaged the bishop in a dance to the faint, almost insect-like buzz of homemade harps, drums, guitars, and gourd rattles. The images of the bishop, flittering in the midst of the thirteen men and thirteen women dancing in the cathedral's chapel of the Virgin Purisima, were a vision of how one might settle discordant social relations in a postmodern world.

Despite the pressure to reconvene the dialogues, the government was apparently unwilling to enter into further negotiations. Weakened by the disarray caused by the devaluation of the currency, the economic upheaval resulting in the flight of an estimated

"Monkey dancers" of San Juan Chamula performing for Bishop Samuel Ruíz during his fast in December 1994.

US $10 billion of capital, and the political turmoil caused by municipal takeovers where elections were contested, Zedillo's government feared any confrontations in the new year.

INVASION OF THE LACANDÓN RAIN FOREST

Peace was not on the agenda of Zedillo's weakened government. On February 8, 1995, the prosecutor general's office issued a warrant for the arrest of terrorists, among them Rafael Guillén and others.[10]

With the pretext of seizing the "terrorists," on the following day, 60,000 soldiers broke the cease-fire agreement with the Zapatistas and invaded the Lacandón rain forest. The pretext was falsified by the actions of the armed forces themselves, as they deployed an estimated 60,000 soldiers who invaded houses, ransacked the possessions of the people who fled to the canyons, sprayed their food supplies with insecticide, killed animals, and destroyed all the supplies of the colonizers. The army then proceeded to destroy Aguascalientes, the site of the first National Democratic Congress called by the Zapatistas in July 1994, and constructed a permanent military installation. No press representatives, human rights observers, or even the Red Cross, were permitted within the army lines, posted at the gateway cities to the jungle. *How did they rally int'l support?*

The presence of international NGOs was especially felt during the tense months following the February 9, 1995, invasion by federal troops of Zapatista territory in the Lacandón forest. Groups from the Midwest and West of the United States arrived in San Cristóbal, where they were met by Global Exchange and International Services for Peace, which coordinated work with local organizations such as the Coordination of Non-Governmental Organizations for Peace (CONPAZ). As patrols of soldiers harassed visitors throughout the zone, detaining *campesinos* as though they were foreigners and making their presence felt to tourists in the nearby Maya ruins, and with helicopters and military observation planes equipped with sensitive observation technology provided to narco-traffic units flying over the villages of the conflict area, the Pastors for Peace followed the troops into action.

I joined the Pastors for Peace on February 9 when they tried to gain access to the conflict zone. The group included laypeople as well as pastors, who were well informed by CONPAZ. We were stopped by armed guards who demanded to see our identification papers and laboriously made a list of all of our names. For the Mexicans, it could have resulted in detention in the political prison in Tuxtla Gutierrez, and for nonnationals it might have meant summary dismissal from the country, an experience that was later accorded to Catholic priests. One of the pastors in the group sought an interview with the commanding officer but was refused. We later learned that other peace NGOs, including the Caravana Mexicana and national groups organized by CONPAZ, as well as Red Cross and international press representatives, were also refused entry into the conflict zone from the first day of the February 9 invasion.

When these peace groups and media representatives finally gained entry to the villages on February 13, they spread the word of how federal troops had burned houses and

Not rebels supporters

raped women. Their reports indicated that 20,000 men, women, and children were forced by the troops to flee into canyons that cut through the territory. Some of the peace groups and alternative media people filmed the return of the colonizers over a week later to find all of their food supplies contaminated with pesticides, their clothing and furniture destroyed, their animals killed or stolen, and all of their tools stolen. Several women who had fled to the canyons reported on their return the spontaneous abortions that some had as a result of their flight, and increase in respiratory diseases and diarrhea that children experienced from their ordeal. In the following weeks, the food rations of the colonizers were entirely used up, yet the army detained the trucks with relief supplies sent to alleviate their distress. Flor del Rio, where I had visited a few months before, reported that the army had stolen the town's collectively owned truck.

In his February 9 communique from the jungle, *subcomandante* Marcos again demonstrated the power of the movement to shake the financial world upside down:

> The Zapatista uprising raised the price of the blood of indigenous Mexicans. Formerly it was worth less than a chicken, today their death is the condition for the most ignominious loan in world history. The price of the Zapatista's head is the only one that remains high in the rise and fall of financial speculation. Mr. Zedillo started the payment of the debt. His message is clear: either speak submissively on one's knees in front of the supreme government or, with the backing of my congressional accomplices, we will annihilate you.[11] [Author's translation]

In a paean of praise to the Zapatistas, Marcos reveals his command over language, as he excoriates the government for their attack on "those who teach the present governors what they cannot learn in postgraduate universities and what has not yet appeared in textbooks with which they diseducate the Mexican children: That is a shame, to the dignity of human beings and the love of country and its history."[12]

effects on stock market / globalization

The political upset following on the militarization of the Chiapas conflict brought about major disturbances in the stockmarket. Four days after the order to seize Marcos was given, the stock market dropped 1.94 percent, and there was a marked increase in speculative purchase of dollars. The following day, the peso declined 3.04 percent and stocks lost 0.47 percent. On February 15, financial markets "suffered the second most difficult day of the new government, characterized by the lack of confidence, nervousness and speculation provoked by the management of the conflict in Chiapas," which resulted in a severe drop in the stock market of 6.41 percent and a fall in the value of the peso to 6.10 pesos to the dollar. *El Financiero* calculated that $2,500 million left the country (February 26, 1995:57). In short, Zedillo's attempt to show the Chase National Bank and the United States the strength of his government in taking military action failed to impress them. After the army invasion of the territory in February, the Mexican stock market fell to its lowest point, along with the value of the peso. Given the fact that the EZLN is positioned precisely where the richest oil wells are being discovered in Chiapas, Tabasco, and Veracruz, what happens to this movement will have resounding implications for world financial interests for years to come.

In the months following the February 9, 1995, invasion of federal troops into the jungle, the presence of NGOs in "peace camps"[13] throughout the conflict zone may have made the difference between the Mexican army's low-intensity warfare and the Guatemalan war of extermination in the 1980s. Religious and secular NGOs worked with Mexican Civil Society groups, organizing outside of political parties, to bring the government to the negotiating table after the interruption caused by the assassination of PRI candidate, Luis Donaldo Colosio, in March 1994. This resulted in the meetings in San Miguel, followed by those in San Andrés Sacam Ch'en de los Pobres (as San Andrés Larrainzar was renamed in anticipation of the meetings[14]) in March and April, when the government reluctantly agreed to attend.

FIESTA OF THE WORD

Despite the many provocations within the territory designated as Zapatista throughout the spring and summer of 1995, the Clandestine Committee of the Revolutionary Indigenous General Command, which was the decision-making core of the EZLN, persisted in its attempts to negotiate with the government. The first encounter in San Miguel in March 1995 after a year's hiatus was able to come to an agreement only on a time and place for another meeting. The negative reaction by Civil Society to the army invasion of the Lacandón rain forest forced the government to resume the dialogues.

The San Andrés Dialogues

Conditions for the dialogue were less than propitious. *Subcomandante* Marcos was still in hiding, and the lives of the seven-member delegation led by *comandantes* David, Tacho, and Trini were endangered. Wearing ski masks, they were escorted by Red Cross workers into the basketball court, on which the meetings were staged in an improvised dwelling flanked by the two baskets.

The choice of the town of San Andrés Sacam Ch'en de los Pobres was symbolically apt, even though Zapatistas stated a preference for a site where they would have greater access to popular movements and communication media, such as Mexico City or even San Cristóbal. However, the strongest basis for Zapatista support in the highlands is found in San Andrés Sacam Ch'en de los Pobres, which was founded in the last quarter of the sixteenth century during the colonial concentration of Indians. The Tzotziles began an intense stage of resistance and battle in 1850 when large landholders Ramón Federico and Manuel Larrainzar, whose surname was given to the town, acquired village lands. The rejection of the appendage of this surname "Larrainzar" is related to that history. Indigenes confronted *ladino* landowners in the "Caste War" of 1867–1869, and also in other highland towns, particularly Chamula, when the region was opened to commercial agriculture that employed Indians as artisans, laborers, and mule drivers. The consolidation of *ladino* power led to the dislocation of Indians from the town center and to their subordination economically and politically. The indigenous community was able to recuperate its forces after the National Indigenous Forum in 1974, and then initiated actions for the restitution of communal lands. These actions convinced many *ladino* families to abandon their landholdings and houses in the center, leaving indigenous religious officials in charge of the church and the town hall. Yet some residents of the center of town remain less supportive of the uprising than those in the surrounding hamlets. The rebellious character of the town was also indicated in the election of a PRD candidate for mayor in the August 1994 elections, which provoked the government to send in troops late in 1994. In 1995, the army, which had been posted in the town ever since the New Year's Eve uprising, withdrew to the present barracks, only four hundred meters from the center of the town, in partial compliance with the conditions for the dialogue. Even the selection of the basketball court as the locus for the house constructed for the dialogue was symbolically appropriate. Like their ancestors, Mayans again played out their political fate on the court, willing to take the risks of death as the outcome, just as ancient players submitted themselves to ritual death when they lost a game.[15]

At 10 A.M. on April 12, 1995, I joined the "security belt" of international observers from the United States, Germany, and France, along with national observers, college students from branches of the Universidad Nacional Autónoma de Mexico throughout the country, artists, development workers, teachers, merchants, and housewives, some of them with their children—all of whom had come to support the Zapatistas and discourage an attack by the Mexican armed forces stationed just 400 meters from the town center. Over 450 press, television crews, radio reporters, and photo journalists from around the world who had registered with the government's Commission of Agreement and Peacemaking (COCOPA) were positioned just beyond the ball court with a huge dish antenna set up in the plaza to relay their news to the world.

The most extraordinary presence was that of the indigenous people. Throughout the morning, quietly and without any disturbances, over 7,000 indigenous people who had congregated from the hill communities and *ejido* settlements in the rain forest filed into the roped-off section between the Red Cross and international observers. Carrying food supplies and boiled water, since cholera was rampant in the countryside, they settled in with their children for a long wait. Villagers who had for hundreds of years defended their separate identity within the boundaries of their corporate communities were joined together in the "security belt" created to defend the Zapatista negotiating team. They were here in a festive mood, optimistic about the success of their venture. In their hand-loomed *huipiles* and tunics, they were a living embodiment of the movement for a pluricultural, democratic society, tolerant of differences and respectful of others.

Throughout the day they waited for the arrival of the government representatives of COCOPA. The Zapatista delegation remained inside the hastily constructed hut for fear of an attack; the National Commission of Mediation (CONAI) members moved restlessly in and out of the improvised hut on the ball court; indigenous security guards occupied themselves reading copies of *El Tiempo* and preparing their food or nursing babies; press representatives were drinking, dozing, and testing their equipment.

Late in the afternoon, word came from the government representatives, who claimed that the indigenous peoples' signs of support for the Zapatistas were a violation of the agreements for the peace talks. *Comandante* Tacho's response pointed to the paradox that

Women from Chenalhó await government officials in San Andrés, April 1995.

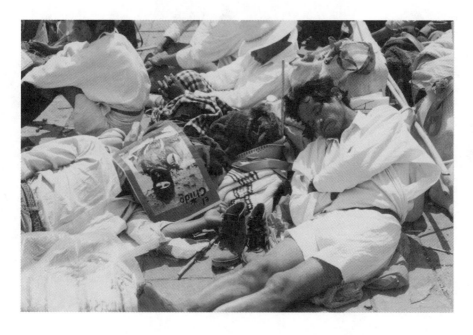

Men passed their time reading or sleeping as they awaited government officials in San Andrés, April 1995.

Media from throughout the world came to the meetings in San Andrés in April 1995.

Child selling belts outside the forum in the Municipal Theater.

Women from the pottery cooperative "H'pas Lumetik" of Amatenango del Valle join thousands of leaders of highland indigenous villages to participate in the dialogue with the government in April 1995.

government representatives, not the Zapatistas who were under attack by the military and the white guards of the cattlemen, were the ones who expressed fear "in the presence of thousands of unarmed indigenous men, women, and children." He urged the thousands of indigenous supporters to leave, in accord with the COCOPA government representatives' refusal to meet until they had gone. Indigenous leaders of the State Democratic Assembly of the Chiapas Pueblo (AEDPCH)[16] defended the mobilization of indigenes: "We came here of our own will and with our own resources. We came because those who took up arms and shed their blood are here awaiting the disposition of the federal government to dialogue. Because the demands of the Zapatista Army of National Liberation are ours, our cause is the same: democracy, justice, liberty, and peace with dignity" (*La Jornada* April 22, 1995:14).

Responding to the urgings of the EZLN commanders and the CONAI, the indigenes withdrew to their communities. When they left, the government representatives finally agreed to come into the basketball court at 7:15 P.M. and, after a brief exchange, agreed to return the next day. On the following day, when I arrived in town, I found it had been transformed into a military field. Two hundred and sixty military police stood with rain capes draped over their meter-long billy clubs, with crash helmets in position, two feet from one another, one faced forward and the other back, circling the basketball court and conference house as well as the town hall, forming a third ring outside the Red Cross and "security belt" of peace forces. Two of their commanders communicated to the troops and to the high military command located in their base camp with advanced radio communication technology. Red Cross and peace security force participants had to step inside a

A campesino *passes through military lines to attend dialogues in San Andres, April 1995.*

metal detector armed by several military police wearing crash helmets in order to take their places. These were the only conditions under which the governmental delegation would consent to speak.

The leadership shown by the State Democratic Assembly of Chiapas Pueblos (AEDPCH) in the tense 48 hours of the dialogue was an impressive demonstration of democracy and restraint in the face of immense provocation. The government, in contrast, presented its demands in an intransigent manner, leaving little room for negotiation. In the final statement for easing the conflict (*distensión*), the government rejected the Zapatista demand that the zone be demilitarized and yielded only to positioning army troops outside the centers of the towns in which they were stationed. Government representatives claimed that they would suspend the investigation of members of the high command, end the orders of apprehension, and permit the surveillance of the area by the National Commission of Human Rights (CNDH). The militarization of the zone remained intact, with substantial barracks in Altamirana and Las Margaritas, where most of the armed encounters occurred during the twelve days of the uprising, along with San Andrés, Simojovel, and Tenejapa. Patrols were actually increased after the dialogue in May, "putting at risk the dialogue and the peacemaking process," according to the Coalition of Nongovernmental Organizations for Peace (CONPAZ) (López and Correa 1995).

During the slump following the aborted dialogues, the EZLN carried through one of the most innovative acts undertaken by a revolutionary force. In June, it called upon "the citizens of Mexico and the world" to participate in a plebiscite concerning the new relation between indigenous people and the state. Initially, six questions were phrased at a meeting on June 27 in San Andrés Sacam Ch'en, with opportunities for each network to delineate its own programs. The plebiscite was to be enacted by email, fax, and plebiscite tables within Mexico, as well as conventions called by support groups throughout the world. In the call, the EZLN starts out with this declaration:

> We are Mexicans and we have a national proposal: to struggle for, and achieve, democracy, liberty, and justice for all the men and women of this country. We are here to say that we are human beings and we have a worldwide proposal: a new international order based on, and ruled by, democracy, liberty, and justice. [Flier, author's translation]

I attended one such session at Hostos College in New York, organized by Courtney Guthrie, who was a member of the National Science Foundation research training group of City College of New York in 1993. The most crucial alternatives were phrased in question Numbers 2 and 4: "Should the different democratizing forces [in Mexico] unite in a citizens' broad-based political and social opposition front and struggle for the 16 principle demands? Or should the EZLN convert itself into a new and independent political force without joining other political organizations?" The other questions were mostly rhetorical: "Do you agree that the principal demands of the Mexican people are land, housing, jobs, food, health, education, culture, information, independence, democracy, liberty, justice, peace, security, combat of corruption, and defense of environment?" "Should Mexicans carry out a profound political reform which would guarantee democracy?" and so on. The questions, designed to garner support as well as to gain feedback, provided an index to the extent of support for the movement. The votes counted in August indicated that a million and a half people worldwide supported these propositions, and the interest created in the plebiscite probably convinced the government to go back to the table and talk.[17]

With the resumption of the dialogues in September, 1995, also held in San Andrés Sacam Ch'en with a heavy military presence, the Zapatistas succeeded in moving the process for peace with democracy to a new level. The participants engaged in six sessions: community and autonomy, justice, political representation, situation and rights of women, access to media, and the promotion and development of indigenous culture. The report of the table on autonomy was developed on the basis of proposals of both the State Council of Indigenous and Campesino Organizations (CEOIC) and the State Democratic Assembly of the Chiapas Pueblo (AEDPCH). The draft for the agreement succeeded in formulating the intermediate units needed to govern the autonomous pluriethnic regions. This was put into action on January 21, 1995, with the creation of the General Council of the Autonomous Pluriethnic Region (RAP) for the northern region, which had declared its

autonomy on October 12, 1994. The RAP elected an executive council with 24 parliaments distributed in 12 commissions (Díaz-Polanco 1997:70).[18]

The government representatives, who were not nearly as well prepared as the EZLN,
did not want to deviate from their prepared program; their intermediaries, the PRI-
appointed agents of the National Indigenous Institute (INI), were ignored. The indigenous representatives made it clear that the relations between the state and *pueblos indios*
(the term applied repeatedly in the context of the negotiations) "could only be resolved
in the framework of a profound reformulation of the state, modifying at the root the
daily forms of public life that generate and reproduce domination, discrimination and
racism" (Ce-Acatl 1995:6). Given the shaky condition of the PRI government, with
Zedillo commanding only a 12 percent approval rating, the government could not afford
a public rebuttal of its position, and so it yielded on most of the points.

Autonomy of indigenous pueblos became the center of the debates concerning the
new relationship with the state. Clearly this required a careful reassessment of what the
concrete provisions guiding the new relationship would be. After all, indigenous people
had, for the 500 years of colonization, defended themselves against *ladino* domination in
the context of fragmented communities with leaders co-opted by the state. In the current struggles, indigenous people had begun to unite in regional and national movements
such as the Nation of Purepecha, the Guerrense Councils of 500 Years, the Pueblos of the
Northern Sierra, and the Autonomous Pluriethnic Regions (RAP). They had arrived at
some consensus at meetings in Sonora, Baja California, Oaxaca, and the State of Mexico
(N. Harvey 1994; Stephen 1994), but it remained to be seen whether they could unite
for sustained, long-range governing of the constituent groups.

Much of the discussion focused on the constitutional changes needed to reformulate
state-local relations in such a way as to recognize the pluriethnic character of the nation.
The Zapatistas pointed to the need for a reformulation of Articles 4, 73, 115, and 116 of
the constitution to establish autonomy of indigenous communities recognized as juridical entities. The reformulation of Article 4 was required because the existing Article 4
pretended to recognize the political, economic, and legal rights of indigenes, but was not
enacted, while that of Article 115 was necessary in order to establish a new balance of
power among the federal, state, and local authorities, and to address the needs of the
autonomous pluriethnic regions. The Zapatistas argued for a return to Article 27 as it had
appeared before the "reform" during the Salinas government that had, in effect, abolished the land reform program and allowed for private use and sales of existing *ejido*
grants. This reform, passed in 1991 (Nash and Kovic 1996), was one of the precipitating
causes of the Zapatista uprising, since it in effect abolished the basis for communal smallholder agriculture (see also chapter 3).

Autonomy was the key demand in the Zapatista attempt to gain recognition of the
plural character of society with harmonious articulation, rather than the old domination
of *pueblos indios* at the core. In the discussions, the qualification of the meaning of equality made by Don Antonio—the indigenous savant often quoted by Marcos—was
invoked. In the past, the Zapatistas pointed out, equality has been interpreted as same-

ness, not allowing for differences. While they agreed that economic and social inequalities ought to be eliminated, the goal was not to arrive at cultural sameness:

> There are no cultural universals, no concepts or criteria based on universal culture. Any time that anyone thinks or feels, when s/he conceives of the other or him-herself, they do it from their culture, from a specific manner of being in the world that no one can elude, and that characterizes the fundamental plurality of social reality. (Ce-Acatl 1995:22)

In a phrase that catapults the Zapatistas into the postmodern condition, they conclude that: "We are all Mexicans, but each lives and feels his/her Mexican-ness differently."

The autonomy that the Zapatistas seek is not the cosmetic autonomy of local rights but a recognition of regional institutions to resolve agrarian conflicts peacefully and legally, to give men and women (who had always been excluded from the land reform of the 1910 Revolution) access to land through the offices of an Agrarian Tribunal that would be funded adequately in order to purchase an expanded *ejido*. This would provide the material base for a fortified autonomy.

Another significant change posed by the Zapatistas involved the political process itself. They rejected the electoral process through parties dominated by the *mestizocracia*, calling for a return to indigenous practices related to the civil religious hierarchy. Considered the key institution in defining Indianness, the civil religious hierarchy was in fact introduced by the Spaniards during the colonial period. The system has alternately been condemned for draining social surpluses from the community, and extolled for its success in enabling indigenous people to resist the domination of *ladino* institutions. Since there is an element of truth in both these positions, it is extremely difficult to assess the political outcome of such an approach. It would certainly reinforce the gerontocracy that characterized indigenous political life, but by bringing together the young and old, a dialogue between generations within an autonomous indigenous action group might overcome the tendencies to co-optation and *caciquismo*.

Autonomy was also the basis for development programs for the *pueblos indios* on the basis of funds allocated for growth, from a percentage of the Gross National Product. The most provocative material demand related to autonomy in development in regards to the rights to resources of the soil and subsoil. This means, in Chiapas, returns from the ocean of oil on which the Zapatist territory sits, as well as from the swiftly flowing rivers, which produce 52 percent of the electricity for the Mexican nation. Education and health programs were to be self-administered in programs that would ensure the valorization of the history and cultures of *pueblos indios*, as well as their knowledge of medicine and herbs. This aspect of development was vigorously expressed in the session on the rights of women, who asserted the contribution of native practitioners in midwifery (Ce-Acatl 1995:32).

In addressing the human rights of women, the text of the Zapatista negotiations recognizes (but very summarily) the potential conflict between autonomy and universal rights. In the summary report of the women's rights platform we find a statement that:

violence against q not expressed

"The practice of local customs should never validate violations of women's rights" (Ce-Acatl 1995:44), but the question of violence against women in the often patriarchal *pueblos indios*, and the abuse of power by diviner-curers or those who claim to possess three or more souls, is not addressed.[19] In workshops organized shortly after the Zapatista uprising, the women of Chiltak, CONPAZ, and the Diocese Coalition of Women (CODIMUJ) considered questions of human rights in the 1917 Constitution and in the revolutionary law of the EZLN. Their considerable input into these documents is a rejection of the position of many guerrilla movements that dismiss women's claims as the expression of Western feminism or domination by an alien culture. But they insist that the issues must be dealt with in their own terms. Rejecting the tendency to justify all customs in terms of tradition, indigenous women drew up a list of customs that they liked and those that they did not like. They firmly opposed patriarchal practices that included parental forcing of daughters to marry early and to a person not of their own choice, forbidding girls to attend school or political meetings, drinking and abuse of wives, forced pregnancies, and polygamy. They expressed the will to take on public offices and to be active participants in building democracy (Lovera and Palomo 1999:70 *et seq.*).[20]

The Zapatistas made it clear during the September 1995 dialogue that alternatives to government plans for development cannot be realized within the existing neoliberal framework of an export-oriented cash crop and privatized economy. The attempt by representatives of the government to limit the dialogue to the state of Chiapas was clearly overcome in the September meetings and their follow-up in November. In the talks that terminated a six-day negotiation on September 10, 1995, the government responded to Zapatista calls for a peaceful settlement with less truculence. Beleaguered with problems of a mounting recession, the government made concessions that people hardly dared consider possible. Zapatistas expressed satisfaction in the agreements that opened up the lines of communication for future conversations, with the EZLN acting as a political rather than a military force (*La Jornada* September 11, 1995:5). The negotiators agreed to a commission to consider human rights of indigenous people, and to a center for "Maya" education of indigenous people. The fund that they hoped to establish from the sale of natural resources in the Lacandón area would provide the basis for nongovernmental programs of social and economic development (*La Jornada* September 11, 1995:3). The meetings were hailed by both sides as the most successful since the preliminary meetings in March 1994 (*New York Times* September 11, 1995).

When we take into consideration the tensions that were building in Chiapas, with federal troops deployed throughout the Lacandón rain forest and with military patrols outside many indigenous communities, it is remarkable that there was no violence. Much of this can be attributed to the presence of national Civil Society groups. They ensured security lines at all the meeting points and monitored the participants from foreign countries as well as Mexican nationals, providing identification badges for everyone who attended the meetings. Civil Society groups organized press conferences in the Center for Human Rights, "Fray Bartolomé de las Casas," in San Cristóbal. These were attended by a large contingent of press representatives from Europe who were more responsive than the U.S.

press. The U.S. media tended to paint a picture of economic recovery and investment opportunities, culled from financial headquarters in Mexico City, whereas other components of the international press relied heavily on the information coming in through their own reporters on the scene (Nash 1997c).

The peace lines in these dialogues were made up of sectors of *campesinos*: ARIC, Las Abejas, and other indigenous groups of men and women, as well as members of mobilized sectors of Civil Society. They surrounded the Red Cross, which took the inner ring, with international observers and other Mexicans in the outermost ring. We were registered and instructed in the behavior expected of observers by the National Commission of Mediation (CONAI) (see chapter 5).

The Zapatistas celebrated the second anniversary of the uprising on New Year's Eve in four newly constructed Aguascalientes, the site of the first National Democratic Convention in August 1994. This structure was completely destroyed when government troops invaded the Lacandón forest on February 9, 1995. As the inhabitants of the four sites worked on the construction of their amphitheaters, military vehicles tore through the sites and soldiers harassed those assisting in the work. In one case, women and children of Oventic, the site called for one of the celebrations outside of San Andrés Sacam Ch'en, surrounded a jeep bearing artillery weapons, and shook their fists at the soldiers, telling them to leave. In another encounter, townspeople surrounded a lone soldier, whose accent revealed that he was from San Juan Chamula, berating him for being in the army and fighting his own people. The New Year's festivities proceeded without major incidents, and the hosts invited their guests to attend the National Indigenous Forum in San Cristóbal that began January 3, 1996. My field notes of the event that Tacho called "The Fiesta of the Word" are recorded below.

The Fiesta of the Word – meeting

The four-day meeting of the National Indigenous Congress, which *Comandante* David called "the fiesta of the word," was attended by indigenous people from throughout the country and visitors from Argentina, France, Switzerland, the United States, Canada, Germany, Holland, Ireland, Spain, and Italy. It signaled the birth of a political front named the Zapatista National Liberation Front (FZLN). In *Subcomandante* Marcos's words, the FZLN was to be "a civil, peaceful organization, independent and democratic, Mexican and national, that fights for democracy, liberty, and justice in Mexico" (*Cuarta Declaración de la Selva Lacandona* January 1, 1996, flier).

The excitement of the event was palpable as security lines surrounded the House of Culture (Casa de Cultura) in San Cristóbal. *Subcomandante* Marcos was the least seen member of the EZLN.[21] All of the sessions were led by one or another of the indigenous *comandantes*, and Marcos appeared only briefly on the second day. While the Zapatistas handed over their arms, the government continued to carry out the low-intensity warfare in the rain forest.

My request to attend the forum, approved by Marcos and registered with COCOPA, enabled me to join the 400 or more indigenous representatives from throughout the nation who attended, along with academics, writers, and supporters from civil society. The agreements reached during the September dialogue were summarized in the presence of 24 members of the Zapatista high command, four of whom were sitting at each of the six tables. The Zapatistas still wore ski masks since they were still threatened with apprehension or even assassination attempts. They spoke only at the plenary and the beginning of the discussions at each of the six tables. They were there to listen to the discussion by indigenes from other regions.

Tacho addressed the assembly on January 3, 1996, urging the indigenous people of Mexico to speak with their own voice without asking for permission, and to join in constructing a world where everyone loves without the need to dominate others. Chiding that "[T]he government that we have now has wanted to kill, buy and silence us," he declared that "now we must form a new Nation." He invoked the meaning of being indigenous in this new movement.

> We are indigenous people; we have suffered centuries of rejection, of persecution, of abandonment, of death. Many times the oppressor has had white skin, but other times death and treason has had dark skin and our same language. The good path also takes on the word of men and women of white skin and of a different language. In the world that the Zapatistas want, all skin colors fit, all the languages and all the paths. The good world has many ways and many paths. And in those paths there is respect and dignity. [Author's translation]

The speech was signed with the names of *Subcomandante* Marcos, David, and Tacho (Internet, Cecilia Rodriguez, moonlight@igc.apc.org).

Tacho set the stride with his opening attack on the neoliberal policies of the government, a theme that was picked up by an indigenous woman leader from Oaxaca, Bartola Morales García. She excoriated a government which represents only capital interests, while indigenous people have suffered more from the reductions of the past ten years than any other group. The newly reconstituted Commission for Agreement and Pacification (COCOPA) celebrated the formation of the Zapatista movement as a political force, and the leader of the group, Dr. Castillo, promised to bring the results of the deliberation to the legislature. This was a welcome change from the position of COCOPA that presided at the April dialogue, but many who attended the meeting criticized the COCOPA's failure to censure the army's continued presence in the rain forest.

Throughout the five days of meetings, all who attended were allowed to speak, even foreign visitors. The Zapatistas came as listeners and watchers, and except for the opening speeches, they remained an alert audience for what their invited guests said. In the compulsive speechifying of modernizing political life in Mexico, as in the United States, this is a remarkable stance. This, too, is a custom of village politics: each evening *principales* and police officers sit quietly on the benches at the town hall, watching and listening to the people.[22]

The wide range of representation was evident, as people who had never attended a national meeting spoke of conditions in their pueblos for the first time, in the presence of leaders in the popular movements who had been active in politics since the revolutionary decade of the 1920s, along with academics and intellectuals. Denunciations against the government's mistreatment of people were heard in all the sessions. The contingent from Guerrera, who had fled as mounted police rode into their villages, spoke of the massacre of their people. The women's session was the most contentious, with charges of domination by *mestizas* present in their session.

People were careful to include nonindigenous along with indigenous needs in their statements. A leader of the indigenous proletarian organization called for indigenous representation on the councils; a Huichol asked that their pueblos be freed to practice their own religion[23] and called for the self-management of their language; a representative of the Autonomous Pueblos of Chipango talked of the loss of the youth who migrate for lack of land; a representative of the homosexuals of Oaxaca proposed that there be translators in all places of justice, and that the abusers of women and minors should be brought to justice. The impressive variety and forcefulness of these popular representatives were an embodiment of the aspirations for a pluriethnic and pluripolitical governance of the country.

Sunday's plenary session was marked by the sacred atmosphere typical of village celebrations, with pine needles strewn on the floor of the Casa de Cultura, potted palms, and copal incense swung by officiates to purify the air as the people congregated in the large auditorium. Government representatives of COCOPA and CONAI took their place at a semicircular podium. The 24 Zapatistas who filed into the room with the women who acted as their security guards joined them and, as they took their seats, Marcos arrived suddenly and without fanfare. Security precautions were more pronounced in his case, and we were told by members of the security guards outside the Casa de Cultura that they were not allowing Marcos to leave the premises for fear of an assassination attempt.

Forum for establishing a new relationship with the state opens in July 1996.

In his opening address, Tacho reiterated the desire of the EZLN that the struggle for land would continue without fratricidal warfare as they sought a harmonious recognition of cultural variety. He summed up the constitutional changes needed to arrive at an autonomous, pluralistic form of jurisprudence and administration by indigenous pueblos. Self-organization, self-definition, and self-rule were the themes in the Carta Magna of the future, as discussed in the preceding sessions. Marcos spoke very briefly, referring to the rainbow they saw as they rode out of the jungle that portended a peaceful outcome of the conflict.

David opened the plenary session on Monday, January 8, with what sounded to me like a counterpoint to Tacho's opening remarks on January 3, stating that the assembled group did not have to seek the permission of the government to speak their own words, and instead asked permission of *Tatik Dueño de la Creación,* the Lord Father of all Creation, to begin *"la gran fiesta de la palabra en el gran país de México,"* (the great Fiesta of the Word in the great country of Mexico). Each of the raconteurs for the six sessions summarized their discussion. Antonio Hernández Cruz of the third session on Indigenous Political Participation invoked the great tradition of treating political authorities as parents as he outlined the new political pact with the state in the framework of a new constitution: communication between government agencies and local authorities should be promoted with provision for conferences of indigenous pueblos in regional assemblies and settlement of land conflicts with autonomous regional councils. He summed up the specific changes called for in the session: changes in the electoral law to include indigenous customs in the choice of their representative, constitution of autonomous regions embracing *pueblos indígenas,* participation of women in government at all levels, and an ongoing critique of the methods and practice of self-government; the rights of women in employment, and of those who were forced to migrate, should be recognized and made explicit in the governance of pueblos.

Tuesday's program opened with a quasi-spiritual ceremony conducted by the Hermandad Ch'ol, Sisterhood/Brotherhood of Ch'ol speakers. They were a motley group, with some of the women dressed in the *ladina* clothing of poor countrywomen, others wearing the backstrap-loomed woolen skirts of Chamulas, and two men with ponchos and straw hats typical of the northern states. A very tall, almost gringo-looking young man carried an incense pot with copal, while some carried candles and flowers. Almost as in a pageant celebrating multiculturalism, they circled the room, stopping to pray at each compass point. Facing east, they prayed, "For the new day, the new light, as the Father-Sun teaches us to be brothers, as we show and share this work, so we all benefit"; facing west, they invoked the "Lord who will listen to our prayer here in San Cristóbal, thanks to the Lord Father, thanks to the benediction of justice and dignity, the Father Sun who rules us, directed us to pass here and raise ourselves up, the sun who is the one who created this sun; we unite in this fight, if there is no food there is no peace," facing north they spoke, "Those who came here from the north to see our misery, taught us this religion. They established their superiority over us. We now say they are not superior; the north is no longer a symbol of superiority. The north is now converted to a symbol of equality, the place where a new life in which we live in equality will come"; facing south, the *hermandad* prayed, "The god of the south comes with the true voice, we ask him to help our siblings." One of the women then spoke in Chol, saying, "In this forum, let us walk together," then uttered the Lord's Prayer, ending with, "In the reign of peace with justice and dignity," and a song in Tzeltal. Bearing aloft a flaming candle, a woman spoke what an Indian sitting next to me called the "*snichinal k'op*," the flowery word:

> The whites came 503 years ago to destroy us, but the *Chiba* (sacred plant of the Maya) was not destroyed since its roots are deep. May all its flowers flourish; with water, it can kill us or it can save us. We live from the fruit of the land that comes with water. If there is no water we do not live. The light signifies the life from the night that might kill us. Some who have an evil heart must change; those who want to stultify our work cannot do it. Thus we carry this light so it is not put out. With our money, with our desire, we will light our way with this light. We will go forward to progress. We speak to the Mother Earth, the Father Sun through the media of the roots, which are the passage to make us siblings. The Mother here holds the land that is a gift that she gives with open hands. We speak with the youths who help us with the writing, with the ancients who have the gift of their experience in the school of life. To the siblings who convoked this assembly we unite with our creation, Lord the Father Lord the Mother (*Tatik Tiosh, Me'tik Tiosh*), the movement of liberation. [Author's translation]

This stunning pageant, wedding together five hundred years of traditions retained from the Mayan past and imposed by the Spanish conquest, embodied the pluricultural society the assembly called for. The diversified genetic pool, including indigenes from throughout the country, and with visiting delegates from the hemisphere and Europe, with young and old, men and women, sitting and standing together, unlike the age-, ethnic-, and sex-segregated villages, marked the successful unification of the emergent civil society. In the final plenary session, the "word" was passed to Bishop Samuel Ruíz, who in his own lifetime traversed the road from conventional Christianity to liberation theology and an awakening to his indigenous parishioners. He spoke of "the road of difference, the road of enrichment," invoking the same couplets that are a part of all Mayan prayer forms:

> In our living together, working for change, with the participation of women, all are signs of change in our life and not only in our hope. The pueblos that live together, those of the north who live in "the time of the Indian," we thought they would die, but they are surging forward. The old say it will not happen in two or three days. Some who continue with their own language have reinforced it. Others who have experienced change, reinforced it. In this continent and in this world, we do not speak of fantasies, but of reality. We are making history. The search for peace is not lost. The road is much broader than contemplated. We live now in the firm hope for open spaces for a long peace.

The harmonious interweaving of several layers of culturally differentiated syntaxes, with the mingling of Spanish with Chol and Tzeltal resounding in the cavernous space of the overflowing auditorium, was a living expression of the aspirations of the forum.

A month after the forum in San Cristóbal, Zapatista leaders announced in San Andrés Sacam Ch'en that they would sign an agreement with the government clearing the way for a final peace accord. Tacho indicated that the group that represented the Zapatistas in San Cristóbal had consulted with thousands of the colonizers in the rain forest, and that 96 percent of them had endorsed the accord (*New York Times* February 15, 1996). The accord charts "a new relation between the state and the indigenous people" throughout Mexico, requiring changes in practice at state and national levels as well as constitutional reforms. Recognition of the "autonomy" of indigenous pueblos, their right to "multicultural" education, including teaching in their own languages, and "adequate" representation in local and national Congresses are the basic conditions in this accord, which is only one of six sets of negotiations under way (*New York Times* February 15, 1996). Specifically, indigenous communities will be exempt from the national requirement that they must be members of a political party to present candidates in elections. The Zapatistas made it clear to reporters that they "want to shift from an Indian army to an unarmed leftist pressure group" (*New York Times* February 15, 1996), a change in status which was in fact achieved during the January 1996 forum. Further negotiations over issues of land, resource shares for the riches contained within indigenous areas, and social justice regarding human rights violations were expected to take months to reach a final accord.

FORGING A NEW FEDERALISM

I wrote the following passage in 1996, shortly after the February accord:

> In the pluripolitical, plurireligious and pluricultural settings in colonizing areas of the Lacandón rain forest, and in the urban barrios to which highland indigenous people who have dissented with *caciques* have been forced to migrate, we find the social movements that are forging a new understanding of what modernist values of liberty, democracy, and equality might be in the postmodern world. The paradoxical emergence of the most marginalized sectors in the global capitalist system as the center of opposition to neoliberal advance is a response to the latest and most predatory stage in the advance of late capitalism (Nash 1997b).

Like most of the delegates to the National Congress of Indians, I was filled with optimism about the potential of the movement. But after signing the agreements of San Andrés, President Zedillo pursued the military solution of the conflict that he had begun in February, 1995. Despite the fact that the military buildup to 60,000 troops effectively renounced the conditions for a negotiated settlement, he asserted his desire to reactivate the dialogues. Blocked in their attempts to proceed with the agreements, the Zapatistas called together their national and international forces for an Intercontinental Encounter against Neoliberalism and for Humanity, analyzed below.

Intercontinental Encounter
against Neoliberalism and for Humanity

In an attempt to break the stalemate caused by the government's failure to imp
the San Andrés Accord, Zapatistas and their supporters organized a series of events in
July 1996 culminating in the International Encounter against Neoliberalism and for
Humanity. Civil Society leaders organized the Forum for the Reform of the State that
brought together workers, *campesinos*, and intellectuals, along with leaders of the PRD,
PAN, and the PRI, to consider how to unite the democratic movement of *campesinos* and
indigenous agriculturalists. This was to precede and provide the substantive basis for dis-
cussions in the following Intercontinental Encounter against Neoliberalism and for
Humanity in the rain forest. International intellectuals Eduardo Galeano and Alain
Touraine met with Mexican intellectuals Pablo González Casanova and Carlos Monsiváis
to discuss the course of events in Mexico City and then again in Chiapas at the beginning
of July 1996. They were later joined by Danielle Mitterrand, the wife of the former
French president, and James Petras, a Binghamton professor of sociology, who journeyed
to La Realidad in the rain forest for the intercontinental event later in the month.

I was able to attend the Forum for the Reform of the State in San Cristóbal at the Universidad Autónoma de Chiapas with students in the National Science Foundation Research
Training project. Some of the participants emphasized the philosophical and constitutional issues at stake in reformulating the state to embrace pluricultural entities. In a synthesis of the implications of "autonomy," Héctor Díaz-Polanco, a participant in the 1995
dialogues that led to the San Andrés Agreements, indicated the importance of articulating
collective rights with individual rights and particular premises within universalities.[24]

This new perspective, called for by the speakers, requires a shift from Cartesian
dichotomies of culture versus rationality and collectivity versus individuality. Locked into
the absolutes of particular versus universalistic dichotomies, Western-dominated discourse has rejected the possibilities of embracing pluralistic values. This Cartesian discourse, opposing nature and culture, linking female with emotional and irrational
premises in contrast to male rational premises, supported male-dominant Western modes
of thought that were transferred through conquest to most parts of the world. The
"native" became categorized with the irrational, feminine principles that became another
component in the white man's burden to tame and civilize. These premises were challenged in the 1970s by feminists[25] and in recent years by indigenous peoples throughout
the world. The prejudicial indictment of indigenous people as unable to govern themselves was the ideological framework in which their loss of autonomy was justified as a
necessary condition for the civilizing mission.

The call for the Intercontinental Encounter from July 27 to August 3, 1996, posed the
Zapatista program for peace in its most global terms, as a plea for human survival against
the death of humanity implicated by neoliberal policies. Like the first National Democratic Convention hosted by the Zapatistas in the rain forest two years before, it summoned a worldwide congregation of intellectuals and activists along with indigenous
participants from throughout the hemisphere. Since the original site of Aguascalientes

.d been destroyed by the army after its February 9, 1995, invasion, the encounter was to take place in the four new "Aguascalientes" that had been constructed to celebrate the second anniversary of uprising in the Lacandón rain forest. I attended the first session in Oventic just outside San Andrés Sacam Chen de Los Pobres, described below.

The encounter was to be a celebration of the transition from the armed fight to democracy, with the transformation of the EZLN to the Zapatista Front for National Liberation formally declared. President Zedillo was reported as having applauded the transition of the EZLN to a political "front" (*La Jornada* July 6, 1996:ll), but he did nothing to implement the accords in more formal terms.

Field notes on the International Encounter against Neoliberalism and for Humanity. Security was more marked than during previous forums and congresses called by the Zapatistas because of the increased violence provoked by the presence of the army and paramilitary forces throughout the region. Guards recruited from the Zapatista ranks checked the luggage of delegates and guests carefully; they even took my penknife, which they promised to return upon my departure. The main staging was built on the same model as the first: a large open shed with wings that was the stage for the speakers and performers, and folding chairs arranged in the open auditorium. I watched the congregation of indigenous groups as they entered and carried out their own ceremonies before the evening plenary. Groups from Chenalhó, Tenejapa, and Oxchuc arrived with musicians and prayer makers climbed up the stage and performed a dance. It was not an exhibition for the audience, but a communal act, much like the celebrations for a saint's day. Delegates from around the world chose their sleeping spaces in the campsites, about twenty log cabins with metal roofs. As evening approached, the distinguished guests, including Eduardo Galeano and Alain Touraine, arrived. I saw clusters of North American Indians, indigenous groups from the north of Mexico, and the Argentinian Madres de La Plaza Mayo. Each of these groups represented both a distinct political identity and a merging with the collective identification of Latin American political life. *Comandante* Tacho welcomed the participants in the program by first introducing the EZLN. The lights on the podium were dimmed as the hundreds of Zapatista supporters—men, women, and children carrying lighted candles—wended their way down the hilly path into the arena of the stadium. The response of the crowds below awaiting their arrival was electrifying with the shouted *Vivas!* to the Zapatistas. Like the first National Democrat Convention in August 1994, the theatrical impact of the slow descent of youths, some in uniform with guns and others carrying wooden rifles, and women with babies, was a bodily manifestation of what the "army" was about.

The evening closed with a speech by *Comandante* Ana María. In a masterful weaving together of the past and the present, she summed up the history of the encounter between the guerrillas and the colonizers of the Lacandón in a mythopoetic rendering of Mayan traditions and the postmodern discourse of rebellion that is analyzed in chapter 6.

The following day, each of the preliminary tables addressed the agenda, for the next two days related to the Zapatista counterproposal to the neoliberal agenda. Autonomy and the transition to democracy took first place. Self-determination signified full control of the lands in which the people are located, liberty for political self-determination, autonomy to ratify organization of the form of government of their choice, economic growth, and social and political autonomy. The discussion sessions reiterated the proposal of the CIOAC on the use and exploitation of their resources by the *campesinos* of the Autonomous Pluriethnic Region (RAP). Introducing the RAP statement with a strong endorsement of the conservationist practices endemic in the indigenous areas, the RAP leaders concluded that *campesinos* should decide on the plans for the development of ecology, services, and education.

The women's session was the only one in which I heard dissent during the discussion about autonomy. They pointed to the subordination and abuse of women in what masqueraded as tradition in indigenous communities, and called for autonomy of women as subjects of their own destiny. They succeeded in specifying the agenda for discussing women's issues in each of the seminars that were to take place in the following two days.

Touraine's talk the following day in the Zapatista village of Realidad in the Lacandón rain forest reveals the basis of the appeal of Zapatistas to French intellectuals:

> Now it is a question of going from revolutionary to something that does not have a name yet, but that ties democracy to the defense of cultural rights, the capacity of communication to the defense of diversity. The union of identity is that of specificity with the universal. I believe that international opinion appreciates a great deal what the Indian communities of Chiapas are—located in a space, a time, a culture, they speak a universal language. In some way, the ski masks signify "we are you," the universality. I am at the same time a member of my community but with the voice of my mountain I speak with the phrase, *I am you*, that, along with the phrase, *to command while obeying*, is of the greatest definitions of what is democracy. [Emphasis in original; Author's translation; *La Jornada* August 10, 1996: 11][26]

In Touraine's vision of three possible outcomes for the process set in motion by the Zapatistas, the first is chaos, which signified narcotraffic, brutal violence, and social disruption; the second is militarization, which has increased each year since the February 9, 1995, invasion of the Lacandón rain forest; and the third is democratization (*La Jornada* August 10, 1996:11).

CONCLUSION

The presence of international and national peace NGOs was essential for the organization and registering of thousands of witnesses, participants, and observers. There were no outbreaks of violence, despite the frustration of people who had walked for hours to be part of the historic occasion. Indigenous people learned of the widespread support for their movement, and international observers were impressed by their commitment to a radically new form of government. The people's emergence in these settings indicated their changed status, even without their having gained the compliance by the government: they were no longer perceived by the representatives on both sides of civil society—the government and the supporters of the EZLN—as marginalized "tribal" or "peasant" populations. The international visitors heralded the indigenous organizers as the innovators of a changed state indigenous relationship by large sectors of Mexican society.

Zapatistas and their supporters are living simultaneously all three outcomes—chaos, militarization, and democracy—envisioned by Touraine. Narcotrafficking and internecine violence have increased; government troops have spread the war of low intensity from the rain forest to the highland indigenous pueblos, as civil society has become divided and militarized; at the same time, democratization in elections ensures the most contested election in Mexico's history in the year 2000. The playing out of this triple and contradictory process is analyzed in chapter 5.

CHAPTER 5

CIVIL SOCIETY IN CRISIS
The Contest for Peace and Justice, 1995–2000

THE DEMANDS OF the Zapatista Army of National Liberation (EZLN) for land titles and development programs, which had initiated the ferment of *campesino* mobilizations, broadened as the movement defined its objectives as a new relationship with the state. In the course of the dialogues described in the previous chapter, the Zapatista uprising became the apex of *campesino* and indigenous struggles in a variety of civil society organizations that expanded the horizons of the movement to include justice and autonomy for indigenous peoples in self-governing territorial units. Indigenous groups, such as the Plural National Indigenous Assembly for Autonomy (ANIPA), that grew out of organization of the quincentennial celebration in 1992, responded to the Zapatista call to unify their efforts to renegotiate the relationship of indigenes with the state. The communication between indigenous groups and the EZLN was interrupted when the PRI government increased the deployment of federal troops and paramilitary forces in the Lacandón rain forest and highlands of Chiapas. Yet the force of the movement resulted in the signing of the San Andrés Accord in February, 1996, and some indigenous communities began to enact the principle of autonomy included in the agreement.

With the enactment of autonomy at a local and regional level, indigenes found themselves on a collision course with the PRI government, especially in communities of the northern region, which had constituted an Autonomous Pluriethnic Region on October 12, 1994. Although their expressions of autonomy consisted of relatively minor challenges to state sovereignty, such as issuing birth certificates and adjudicating disputes, the communities have been subject to constant harassment from paramilitaries since that time. These paramilitary groups differed from the old gunmen hired by large landowners, since they were made up of indigenous PRI followers calling their group Peace and Justice. They constituted a vigilante group that preyed on their indigenous neighbors who engaged in acts considered inimical to state policies.

When communities in the Lacandón rain forest asserted their autonomy in July 1996, they were subject to more direct sanctions from the federal and state security forces rather than the paramilitary forces operating in the Autonomous Pluriethnic Region. At that point, the contest for legitimacy in the exercise of power moved from political parties and formal governing institutions to a mobilized civil society confronting military and paramilitary forces. With the arming of PRI supporters in the highland municipalities and in the northern region, especially after 1996 when negotiations broke down, the PRI

xtended the scope of counterinsurgency warfare beyond the Lacandón rain
expanded conflict zone, the Zapatistas, their supporters, and the govern-
the same ideals of peace and justice while contesting the practices for
ach... ...m.

def civil society

By civil society, I refer to the associations of people outside the arenas of formal governmental institutions who are attempting to change the discourse and practice of the
political process. This encompasses many distinct sectors of society that may find
common cause in times of social transformation. What differentiates the emergent civil
societies of Latin America, Asia, and Africa from those of seventeenth-century Europe,
when Locke (1690)[1] envisioned their role as a counterpoint to government institutions,
is that civil society no longer represents a single dominant ethnic group, but now
embraces a multiplicity of ethnic groups once incorporated in colonial states. It also

gender

includes women and the working classes, whose voices were not heard in the coffee
shops and inns where a narrow elite of men pretended to influence the direction of
public affairs in the seventeenth century. In contrast to the rational discourse about civil
society in the eighteenth and nineteenth centuries, when Locke and Hume left little

religion

room for spiritual sources of inspiration, civil societies of Third World countries today
are strongly influenced by religious institutions.

assimilation ≠ paper

During the century of Western liberal governance, the integration of ethnic minorities as participants in civil society was at the price of divesting themselves of many
aspects of their cultures, at least in public life. The indigenous groups of the hemisphere
are contesting these Eurocentric premises of a political process that have persisted long
after independence.[2] Women are not waiting for the revolution to succeed to voice their
goals, but are demanding inclusion in the process of transformation. Even more transformative is the fact that civil society now spills over national boundaries, energizing collective aims endorsed by human rights advocates in transnational, nongovernmental
organizations (NGOs).

Civil society is not an ascribed category waiting for actors to enter into preordained
roles; it comes into being with the emergence of new social actors who challenge the
status quo, and with the reinvigoration of civic consciousness among those who see their
values or premises denied. Just as the notion of civil society from the time of the Romans
came from those people with their own legal codes living within the Roman empire
(Lipschutz 1992), so do the social movements for inclusion in the political arena generate the changes that redefine civil society today. The class struggle of the nineteenth century was as much motivated by the desire of workers to become full citizens as it was to
gain decent wages and working conditions, thereby generating socialist and communist
alternatives to "bourgeois class society" that excluded them (Montgomery 1993). The
redefinition of civil society has also occurred in our times, with the women's movement
and the civil rights movement (Cohen and Arato 1992). It is an ongoing process, now
energizing indigenous societies that are demonstrating the possibility of multicultural
coexistence throughout the hemisphere.

A half-century ago, the extensive networks of indigenous and *comuneros, campesinos,* and
ejidatarios that now constitute civil society in Chiapas could hardly have been imagined

[handwritten: autonomy]

[handwritten: Where is the nation state]

[handwritten margin, right: 162]

by them or by us as anthropologists. The political imagination of most indigenes circumscribed by the boundaries of the municipalities, the plantations to whic were forced to migrate seasonally, the markets where they sold their products and bought the few necessities they required, and the few colonies carved out of national territories for which they had fought in the 1960s. As the Zapatistas say of themselves, they were people without faces and without voices in national spaces—postcard representations of a generalized Indian. *[handwritten: people w/o faces]*

Until the early 1970s, few indigenes read newspapers, and news of indígenes was never published in the papers or broadcast on radio or television. Native-language radio stations began in the 1970s, and only one TV program in Tzotzil is available in Chiapas. *El Tiempo* was the first newspaper in Chiapas to publish news of indigenous people. Concepción Villafuerte, the editor with her husband, Amado Avendaño, of *El Tiempo,* told me that before the National Congress of Indigenes in 1974, they rarely featured news of indigenes, but during the organization of that event, they began to report the preliminary events and continued to feature news of indigenous movements that were beginning to change history (Nash 1997c). *[handwritten: global integration → transnational civil society indig. movts,]*

The emergence of indigenous movements along with global integration is not coincidental. In the name of sovereignty, nations have served as the locus for the repression of groups that lacked representation in the political process. Indigenous appeals to NGOs in their struggles to define the parameters of this new polity provide us with an understanding of the generative potential for transnational civil society in the making. In the last three decades, many Latin American countries have yielded control over their boundaries and citizenry to transnational corporations, global banking and finance institutions, communication media, and policing operations such as the drug control agencies. The weakening of national prerogatives in a globalized world (Appadurai 1996; Arrighi and Silver 1999; Rudolph 1997; Sassen 1998[3]) is contingent upon the "deterritorialization" of capital, labor, and the very institutions of family and community that once ensured cultural reproduction. These are the conditions, usually taken as a given in globalization studies, in which civil society is mobilizing to defend itself against what is seen as a threat to national and cultural identity. At the same time, counterhegemonic groups within nations are seeking incorporation into the wider civil society without the loss of their distinctive ethnic identity. The struggle for land by indigenous groups throughout the Americas is carried out in terms of a defense of their distinctive way of life. In that process they have learned to constitute new bases for mobilizing social action beyond the level of communities.[4] *[handwriting in right margin: drug, CRUX]*

[handwritten vertical left margin: Borders more defined, less present]

[handwritten vertical left margin: Not assimilation]

Civil society emerged as a self-conscious grouping in the two weeks immediately following the uprising. The concern that brought together disparate groups and individuals from throughout Mexico was to prevent a genocidal bloodbath. The group calling itself the Coalition of Nongovernmental Organizations for Peace (CONPAZ) succeeded in getting both sides of the conflict to sign a cease-fire agreement within a fortnight after the uprising. Since that time, other groups of citizens distancing themselves from the government and political parties have developed an agenda in support of a restructuring of state and indigenous relations that will be detailed below. The State Democratic Assembly of the Chiapas Pueblo (AEDPCH) has been instrumental in defining the juridical status of this emergent civil society. Others, such as the State Council of Indigenous and Campesino Organizations (CEOIC) came into being to facilitate the settlement of land claims that provoked the crisis. This organization yielded to the criticisms of the colonizers, who claimed they favored PRI supporters, and failed to resolve many of the conflicts between settlers and ranchers in the Lacandón rain forest. The Independent Center of Agricultural workers and Campesinos (CIOAC) emerged as a central player when CEOIC dissolved. The Civic Alliance (AC) promoted democratic procedures in elections and other civil actions.

These civil society organizations support the human rights of indigenous activists who represented many distinct trends. Some are attempting to reclaim the ground they lost in the decades following the debt crisis as they try to restore the commitments of populist governments to the agrarian sector. Others, such as the National Coalition of the Ayala Plan (CNPA), joined by more radical wings of the above organizations, are addressing radical issues of democracy, discussed in chapter 4.

The Zapatistas, particularly during the five years following their uprising, served as a catalyst for the *campesino* and indigenous organizations that had come into being during the debt crisis and the mobilizations for the quincentennial celebration. They demonstrated their effectiveness in communicating the more radical dimensions of their cause in terms that resonate with a wide support group within the nation and throughout the world at conventions and through opinion polls conducted by civil society. The 1,200,000 respondents to the first poll conducted by civil society organizations such as Alianza Civica in July, 1995, registered over 90 percent approval for their attempts to reform democratic institutions and construct a broad opposition front. The second polling in April, 1999, when five thousand Zapatistas left the rain forest to fan out across the country and appeal to people to cast their votes, reached over two million people, who registered approval for the settlement of conflict and demilitarization of the rain forest. The national respondents represent a cross section of professionals, clerics, students, homemakers, and workers who counter national governing policies on moral grounds. Along with the 55,000 foreign supporters contacted by electronic ballots, they represent an emerging global civil society which supports the call of the Zapatistas for a changed relation between the central government and ethnic groups. Their views are not predicated on unique class positions nor constrained by particular economic interests.[5]

This appeal to radical democracy is opposed by *caciques* within indigenous communities, as well as by *ladinos* who, as the power of the state wanes, feel the loss of privileges they once enjoyed. As the state mobilizes military and policing power to oppose the more radical position, some groups within the Zapatista territories in rebellion have begun to break away from the central command of the EZLN. Given the desperate economic and social situation of those living in the Lacandón rainforest, the government has been able to gain adherents within indigenous communities through various strategies of divide and control.

In this chapter, I will analyze the constituent bases of civil society in religious groups and in *campesino*, indigenous, and women's movements. These bases are made up of networks of fluid and volatile protagonists who are changing social structures as they seek a position in political arenas that once rejected them. They respond to changing opportunities in ways that cannot be predicated on class or ethnicity. They are monitored and abetted by transnational human rights groups and by national activists in civil society, who

[handwritten marginalia: Polling as a method for getting peoples ideas — not class based]

have become increasingly vocal as the process of changing the state relationship indigenous groups deepens and broadens. I shall argue that the proliferation of both religious and secular NGOs is correlated with the inability of neoliberal states such as Mexico to maintain hegemonic control because of the concessions they make to transnational financial and corporate institutions. In opposition to rising protests, the PRI government in Mexico is increasingly relying on military intervention, with soldiers taking on policing and welfare roles as they disrupt daily subsistence routines and try to make indigenous communities dependent on their assistance. Resistance to the militarization of society by the colonizers in the Lacandón area is countered by the government arming its supporters in highland communities. Groups within the same pueblo are pitted against one another in the name of the same goals of *"peace and justice."* Civil society within the nation is expanding its networks with international human rights groups that are attempting to promote grounds for a political settlement in a society racked by violence and discord.

In this chapter, I shall assess how dissent is mobilized by religious and *campesino* organizations, as people enter into and constitute themselves as activists in civil society. What is often called "identity politics" considers the role of consciousness and its political construction as working-class, feminist, or ethnic movements. I propose that the focus on specific identity often loses sight of the amalgam of religious and secular groups that foster these identities as they promote the moral and ideological basis for civil society in opposition to the increasing militarization of Mexican society. I shall first assess the religious mobilization of dissent in the Catholic diocese and in Protestant groups. I shall then assess how the indigenous groups that have coalesced in the context of *campesino* and class-based organizations are becoming the driving forces for indigenous autonomy that postulate a new social pact between the state and social groups in society. Finally, I shall analyze the role of transnational and national human rights agents in disseminating information on the abuses of power and in opening a political arena for dissent.

RELIGIOUS MOBILIZATION OF DISSENT IN CIVIL SOCIETY

Religious beliefs and rituals provide a matrix for social formations that transcends national boundaries. The revitalization of religion is found within the Catholic Church as well as in the evangelical missions that compete for souls in Latin America. In their migrations to the Lacandón rain forest and to urban barrios, Chiapas Mayans continue to draw upon primordial sources of cosmology and belief as they reconstruct their collective lives in the new settings. Collective action is deeply embedded in these spiritual sources for promoting consciousness of identity.

The Catholic Diocese and Liberation Theology

Living in San Cristóbal during the eventful months of 1995 and 1996 was almost like reliving a fifteenth-century drama while fast-forwarding into the third millennium. The Catholic Church still plays a major role in establishing the civil basis for governance, just as it did during the colonial rule of New Spain (Casanova 1997). The contradictions played out within the Catholic Church as a major hegemonic institution were still unfolding, almost as they had done in the sixteenth century. Bishop Samuel Ruíz, who retired in 1999, has played a major role as defender of indigenous people, just as Bartolomé de Las Casas did when he was bishop of the diocese of San Cristóbal de Las Casas. Like Bishop Samuel Ruíz, Bishop Bartolomé de Las Casas was reviled by the *coletos*—those who claim direct ancestry with the conquerors—of San Cristóbal and by his opponents within the Catholic Church itself. Conversion to the doctrines of liberation theology is almost as dramatic as conversion to Protestantism.

These divergent forces within the Church continue to vie with one another in the region today as they did 450 years ago. The contemporary Church, like its colonial predecessor, is still internally divided between those who want to dissociate themselves from programs for social change and those who respond actively to the needs of the people who live in the countryside. The bishops and priests who support liberation theology address the concerns of the poor, while the papal envoys, the *nuncios,* represent the Vatican to the power elites. The clash between the two has been increasingly sharp as the present Mayan conflict has developed.[6]

Liberation theology offers the clearest theological doctrine for advancing social welfare programs undertaken by the NGOs, whether linked with the Church directly or not (MacShane 1993). Pope John XXIII set the Church on a new course with his pronouncement at the Second Vatican Council of 1962–1965, in which he reconceptualized the pastoral task as one engaged in social movements of redistribution instead of the dispensation of sacramental grace. These orientations, explored in the Latin American Bishop's Conference in Medellín, Colombia, in 1968, encouraged priests to move the faithful away from fatalism and the acceptance of poverty and marginalization in life on earth and towards becoming collaborators with God in the fulfillment of their destiny. This trend toward promoting change in the world rather than focusing exclusively on the hereafter was sharpened after the Latin American Ecclesiastical Conference (CELAM) in Puebla in 1979. There the recognition of the dignity of humans and the rights of the poor was cast in terms of a harsh judgment of capitalism, Marxism, and the support for military dictatorships as essential for national security (Collins 1995).

These proclamations changed the relations of priests to their parishes throughout Central America in the 1980s. The clergy was urged to address the social suffering and inequity generated by free-market economics and to encourage people to be agents of their own history in the kingdom on earth. The action orientation of the clergy working in Christian Base Communities combines the principles of democracy from below and learning from the grass roots to counteract the hierarchical leanings of most international organizations. The address of Pope John Paul II on the occasion of his visit to Mexico in January 1999 is the latest invocation by the Church of moral issues related to the growing gap between rich and poor in the global economy. Coming at a time of political and societal demoralization, his critique of capitalism and its attack on the poor may reinforce the crusade of liberation theology priests in Latin America.

Bishop Samuel Ruíz was responsible for redirecting the diocese of San Cristóbal de Las Casas toward liberation theology. He remarked in an interview with me in 1991 that in the course of assembling representatives of communities from throughout the country for the first National Congress of Indigenous People ordered by the governor of the state of Chiapas, his growing awareness of the poverty and suffering of the indigenes transformed his own consciousness. Since that historic congress took place in 1974, the bishop and the Church have become the center of the storm in the diocese of San Cristóbal de Las Casas, over which he has presided since 1959. Bishop Ruíz called for a new kind of missionary organization and action for the marginalized people of modern Latin America. "If the task of the primitive Church was to baptize the converted, our task today is to convert the baptized," he said at that conference.[7]

The bishop's approach, like that of the many priests who served in Central American countries during the 1980s (Berryman 1984), was to cultivate forms of analyzing the situation of impoverishment among the people while actively supporting the justice of their demands. Working with priests and deacons selected from the Christian Base Communities that are located in the Lacandón rain forest and urban belts of poverty in San Cristóbal, he put into action the Vatican II doctrine. Much of the work in development and human rights derives from NGOs supported by Catholic Charities.

A crucial arm of the bishop's program in the diocese was the creation of the Human Rights Center "Fray Bartolomé de Las Casas" in 1989 with funding from the church and its members. The center continues the tradition of the sixteenth-century bishop for whom it is named. The center became directly involved in agrarian problems addressing the torture, expulsions, and assassinations of peasant leaders. The director, Padre Pablo Romo, defined three areas of action in which the center is involved: 1) diffusion of information gathered on complaints, 2) legal aid for those involved in cases, and 3) education.[8]

In their efforts to diffuse information on human rights violations, investigators from the center collect testimonies of the principles in the case and check these against government reports. They bring food and assistance to *campesinos* held in jail, providing an important communication link between the prisoners and their families. They then bring their findings to international human rights organizations, such as Amnesty International America Watch, and hold press conferences to further disseminate the news.

The center provides legal assistance without charge for those identified as victims of human rights abuse. Sixty percent of the cases reviewed in the center in the first two years were related to land ownership, including evictions, conflicts among *campesinos* who had been allotted the same land by government agents, and forced labor on the plantations. One of their most celebrated cases was that of the Venustiano Carranza *campesinos*, who had invaded lands for which they had petitioned since the 1940s and were evicted from by the state police in 1991. Expulsions of indigenes by their own *caciques* was another important source of litigation. At the time of my interview with Padre Pablo Romo in 1991, the center was addressing the abuses of the human rights of over 15,000 indigenes expelled from their communities since 1964, when the practice had begun. Another arena in which the center has been involved is political rights, such as those of some residents of Zinacantán who complained of electoral fraud against candidates and their supporters who were not affiliated with the PRI. Over the years, torture and unjustified detention in prison have become an increasing focus of concern. Attention has also been directed to violations of women and the abuse of children that have come to the fore as indigenes have sought assistance beyond their towns.

Education is a persistent concern, as personnel from the Human Rights Center inform individuals who come to them with questions and as they address collective groups in various communities. The center personnel have taught the constitutional laws that are relevant to the concerns of the people, and they draw examples from the collective memory of the community. Padre Pablo illustrated this with the example of *campesinos* of Venustino Carranza, who are able to present visitors with a veritible archive of their experiences, demonstrating the root causes and cases of human rights violations. The government's Secretariat of Public Education has not allowed the human rights center to give courses in the schools.

Christian doctrine promotes a general sense of self-worth that contributes to the spirit of rebellion today as it did in colonial times. During the spring of 1995, the history of the Cancuc Rebellion of 1711 and of the War of the Castes in Chamula in 1867–1869 (chapter 2) was often invoked in discussions of the Zapatista uprising. Parallels were drawn between the religious inspiration in these rebellions, inspired by miraculous appearances of the Virgin and talking saints, and the Zapatista uprising that some attributed to the preaching of the bishop's lay deacons in the Lacandón rain forest. Just as these earlier rebellions held the inhabitants of San Cristóbal de Las Casas in fear of an invasion for weeks before the rebellion was overcome, so were many contemporary *ladinos* dismayed by the thought of hoards of Indians taking over the streets as well as the cathedral and its plaza. *Ladinos'* fear of Indians adds to the hostility in the racism that characterizes ethnic relations throughout the state.[9]

The spiritual basis for the rebellion is particularly evident in the Christian Base Communities in the Lacandón rain forest, although the message does not advocate armed violence, as the bishop's opponent's claim. The colonies in the canyons of the Lacandón rain forest, settled by former laborers in the plantations and cattle ranches, became the crucible in which the bishop and the San Cristóbal diocese attempted to carry out evangelization that responds to the needs of the people.

Liberation theology departs from the paternalistic Western faith that dominated Christian Catholic missions of the past. In the Lacandón settlements, the deacons and catechists developed their own lessons, emphasizing faith in the community. The emphasis is on salvation in this world, gained through everyday commitment to communal life. Learning itself is redefined in the catechist sessions, conducted in whatever language is that of daily parlance. In Flor del Rio, a relatively young offshoot of an older Tojolobal community settled in the 1970s that I visited with anthropologist María Eugenia Santana (see chapter 3), Spanish is the universal language, used in Bible sessions as in daily life. In Patihuitz, where I went as a poll watcher in 1994, Tzeltal is the predominant word. Syntheses of the catechists' discussions reaffirm the faith of the community shown in its struggle for freedom.[10] Unlike highland communities, where each parish is locked into municipal and sometimes even hamlet boundaries, settlers in the jungle circulate among neighboring settlements. Pilgrimages among the rain forest settlements and to the Christian Base Communities in bordering highland municipalities cultivate a broader base for civil association.

The Exodus from Egypt in the Bible was a model of communal identity for the colonizers who, like the Israelites, crossed a wilderness to escape enslavement (Leyva Solano and Franco 1996:159). María Eugenia Santana Echeagaray (1996:196 *et seq.*) vouches for the importance of the worship services of the Word of God in the development of collective life in Flor del Rio, where she worked. The oldest man in the village, Don Lucas, told her of the communal values that were at the core of this practice:

> Little by little the road of reflection was brimming over, so much so that in June, 1982, we started a communitarian study of our life in confronting the Word of God, especially as illuminated by the Deeds of the Apostles and their teachings on the first Christian community. When we took into account our differences, to see that some of us have many and large milpas, others few and small, that there were some with coffee cultivation and others that had nothing, we decided to put in a common holding what we had, and we began to cultivate in common. Then with a great milpa and a great bean cultivation, we weeded our gardens in common, we harvested, dried and sold our coffee. [Author's translation]

The collective emphasis found in these rural Christian Base Communities is carried over in the urban sectors to which many indigenous people have been forced to emigrate. Christine Kovic's thesis (1997) on one of these communities of expelled Catholics in San Cristóbal reveals the communalistic norms embraced by parishioners who have "converted" from folk Catholicism to liberation theology. These are expressed as "walking together as one heart," and are literally undertaken by the congregation in the form of frequent pilgrimages to other parishes. The same conformity to collective goals is found by Kathleen Sullivan (1998) in urban Protestant communities in San Cristóbal. Some of these communities have actually expelled members from their homes when they have converted to another church. Thus the adherence of the expelled to a rule of religious conformity within the new parish contradicts the human rights principles they evoked in their opposition to their own experience of expulsion from their indigenous communities because of conversion. *land/religion*

The habitus created by pluriethnic groups in the Lacandón rain forest generated a new faith in their custodianship of the land. Drawn to the theme of the Exodus in the Bible, the catechists living in the settlements drew parallels between the colonizers and the Jews. Both had escaped the forced labor of their overlords and were destined to reach a land that promised food, dignity, and liberty (Leyva Solano and Franco 1996, Villafuerte Solis et al. 1999:39). This "sacrilization" of the right to land for those who work it empowered the indigenous settlers to defend it from the encroachment of cattlemen and those who wished to exploit the natural resources of oil and water power.

As with all movements of social transformation, the new approach to evangelizing by indigenous deacons trained in liberation theology generated opposition. This came from within the Catholic hierarchy at the national level and from elite parishioners in Chiapas. Threatened by the revolutionary trends that were sweeping the state, many blamed Bishop Ruíz for the ferment. The former papal *nuncio*, Girolano Prigione, tried to promote an investigation of the Bishop by the Holy See in 1993. But, perhaps because the Vatican was reluctant to start an investigation of a bishop who enjoyed the support in the Bishops' Episcopal Conference of Mexico (CEM), the *nuncio* himself was withdrawn. Moreover, the bishop's appointment as head of the National Mediation Commission (CONAI) to settle the Zapatista conflict demonstrated that he enjoyed the respect of both parties (Casillas 1995:274). The current *nuncio*, Justo Mullor García, was aware of the political vacuum that would result if Bishop Ruíz were to retire in 1995, but he, the cardinal, and other members of what is referred to as "the Club of Rome" urged the bishop to withdraw from "political and ideological dialogue" (that is, the CONAI) and concentrate on promoting jobs to benefit "*esos hombres indígenas*"(these indigenous men) (*Proceso* April 5, 1998, No. 1118:6 *et seq.*). The bishop withdrew from CONAI in June 1998 when it became clear that the government did not intend to follow through on any of its commitments to the negotiations and that the negotiations themselves had become a sham that allowed the PRI administration to claim it was trying to settle the conflict.

Bishop Ruíz's enemies within the diocese include the cattle ranchers of the Lacandón rain forest as well as the commercial bourgeoisie of San Cristóbal. Both sectors blame him for the economic stagnation and chaos that have plagued the area since the upheaval in the countryside and the resultant decline in tourism. His defenders assert that the militarization of the area may have far more to do with the flight of tourists than the uprising does. Supporters of the bishop assert that if the government were to legalize the land claims of the colonizers as promised, the violence in the countryside over land seizures would abate.

The opponents of the bishop carried out public protests throughout the years following the 1994 uprising, as the bishop vainly tried to bring the dialogues to a peaceful settlement (*cf.* chapter 4). The demonstrations against the bishop for his championing of the indigenous cause reinforced the vigilance of members of civil society from the time of the first dialogues between government leaders and the Zapatista leadership in March 1994. When the bishop conducted a hunger strike to hasten the peace process in the closing weeks of 1994 and January 1995, civil society members maintained a constant guard around the cathedral. Contingents of indigenous ritual officials visited him, dancing and praying to animate his spirit as he meditated. Oxchuc supporters, numbering twelve men and twelve women, came with their home-made harps, flutes, and guitars, dancing in the flickering candlelight as he sat in an easy chair in the sanctuary of the church. Chamulan "monkey dancers," in their version of the French brigade uniform, showed up on the plaza of the cathedral the bishop as he fasted. This was a daring step for ritual leaders in a town where *caciques* punished dissidents with expulsion. Many of the bishop's supporters slept in the cathedral throughout this period because of the death threats against him. The cathedral, once the domain of *ladino* elites, became an arena of indigenous dissent as the people previously excluded from civil society were finding space within it. Increasing numbers of middle-class parishioners joined the security lines of *campesinos* mobilized by the OCEZ and ARIC.

positions religion as a motivating force → dangerous b/c it feeds into stereotypes about natives

On March 8, 1995, Women's Day mobilized thousands of women in San Cristóbal, terminating with speeches in the central park calling for peace and with *Vivas* for *Tatic* Samuel. The death threats continued, provoking two simultaneous rallies at the end of the month, the first a women's march for peace and the second a countermarch of cattle ranchers calling themselves the National Confederation of Small Propertyholders (CNPP). The speeches culminated with the burning of a satanized image of the bishop. As I walked around the plaza taking photographs, I saw men wearing dark sunglasses holding ferocious looking guard dogs on a tight leash at the main streets leading into the plaza. Simultaneously, the predominantly indigenous women's group, bearing white flowers and smoking incense, congregated in front of the cathedral. Suddenly the ranchers began to converge on the plaza of the cathedral. Some of the women took refuge inside, while a group of older *mestizo* women planted themselves at the door as if to defend it from the ranchers' group, which also included women.

People started pelting vegetables, eggs, and garbage at the women defending the cathedral door, while a group of indigenous men started to pile up the chairs and tables that were used in their nightly vigil as fortification at the door to the cathedral. There were no police in sight, but a uniformed soldier on the roof of the City Hall seemed to be manning a machine gun. I went to the police station to call for guards, but found the door locked. When I returned to the plaza, the television camera crews that had been parked in their huge trucks outside the cathedral during the weeks of tension had moved in with their cameras as they filmed the action. Often called the "third army" in the undeclared war, they indeed seemed to have an overwhelming impact on the crowd. The belligerent attackers, who had already lit a fire presumably to burn the door of the cathedral, fell back as they realized they were being filmed. Several shots rang out, and the crowd started to disperse. It was hours before the state police, summoned by a citizens' group's call to Mexico City, arrived.

Bishop Samuel Ruíz sensed the central role of indigenous people in the transformation of the state and the nation sooner than anyone else. In 1972 he stated:

> The Indian problem is the crossroad of all problems in our society, and we cannot expect a solution without the solution of the problem of our society. Therefore, one can say the resurrection of our society is in the resurrection of the indigenes. More than speaking of the resurrection of the indigenes, I speak of the resurrection of our society, which lies in the resources of our indigenous situation. Thus the community is a means of reaching out to embrace this resource. (Ruíz 1972:46–47, cited in Villafuerte Solis 1999:43, author's translation)

Religious convictions generate a dynamic that cannot easily be controlled by state power or the rational ordering of values in civil society. It may have been for this reason that the early proponents of civil society preferred to leave religious inspiration out of their analyses. But for people who had been deprived of their own sense of self on the plantations, religious input enabled them to redeem their sense of humanity. It was a short step to go further and rebel against the dehumanizing conditions of their life.

Protestant Evangelizing
and the Challenge to Catholicism

Protestants found an uneasy base in Mexico as early as the colonial period. Their numbers increased during the Mexican-American War of 1845, when the United States promoted missions as a means of undermining Mexican resistance (Levine and Stoll 1997;
Sullivan 1998:113). The "historic churches," that is, those that had been in the country
the longest, such as Presbyterians and Methodists, were often sponsored by Latin American governments to curb the power of the Catholic Church during the liberal period,
when the nations of Mexico and Central America sought a territorial rather than a religious basis for unity.

The Pentecostal churches expanded Protestant conversion, especially after World War
II, through evangelizing that promoted spontaneous participation in worship. Due to their
remarkable ability to promote a sense of community among people disrupted by forced
migration and economic turmoil, the number of Protestant evangelical churches in Latin
America more than doubled from 24,000 in 1953 to 54,000 in 1985 (Rudolph 1997:14).
Their success inspired changes in Catholic practices, but convergence in pastoral methods
has as yet failed to develop a common ecumenical platform. Occasionally, Catholic liberation theology and evangelical Protestant groups support specific issues related to the human
rights of indigenous people, as in the expulsions from indigenous communities in the Chiapas highlands (Tickell 1991). Bishop Ruíz was one of the strongest critics of the expulsion
of Protestants by Chamulan authorities. The *caciques* responded by expelling the resident
priest, Father Leopoldo, replacing him with a visiting Orthodox Greek Priest in 1984.

The Catholic population has declined in the state of Chiapas during the period in which
the bishop has presided over the diocese, but follows national patterns. The 1990 census
reports that 67.33 percent of Mexicans are Catholics, 16.25 percent are Protestants, and
12.73 percent reported no religion. In Chiapas the percentage of Protestants has doubled,
going from 8 percent of the population in 1970 to 16 percent in 1990 (INEGI 1991).
Protestant conversion is currently most active among the evangelical churches of Pentecostal and "para-Christian" faiths, rather than the Presbyterian, Methodist, and other
churches that predominated in the first half of the century. Commitments to either
Protestantism or Catholic liberation theology warrant expulsion from the indigenous
municipalities that proclaim their allegiance to traditions rejecting the changes within the
Catholic Church as well as those from Protestant conversion. For many of the indigenous
people who were expelled, conversion to Protestantism came after their expulsion and
was a means to find a sense of community in the urban setting that had been lost in their
own pueblo (Sullivan 1998).

The influx of Protestantism in the Lacandón rain forest is in part due to conversion by
exiled Guatemalans. There investigators have found Presbyterians, Seventh-Day Adventists, Baptists, Pentacostalists, Column of the Living God, Light of the Good Pastor, Light
of the Lord, Church of God of the Prophecy, and many other sects. This is often attributed
to isolation and ignorance of the colonizers. This ignores the many currents of political as
well as religious currents conveyed by *campesino* organizations, NGOs, and opposition par-

ties. Despite their relative geographical isolation, these colonizers were actively searching for alternatives and were more tuned into the currents of change than most Mexicans.[11] Though they are remarkably successful in proselytizing in impoverished communities, Protestant evangelical churches lack the coherent political ideology of the Christian Base Communities. Their commitment to individual self-expression leads them to eschew political action as redemption. The Protestant migrants, who for the most part are nonliterate, do not have the support structure available to Catholic catechists. In San Cristóbal, the titles of the lands on which they build their houses are often held by schoolteachers or the pastors of the churches they form, and their monthly payments contribute to the mortgage holders' ownership, with little legal assurance that they will indeed benefit. Problems connected with this communal model are frequently encountered in urban congregations.[12]

As a result of their insecure status, the expelled Protestants in San Cristóbal formed the Regional Organization of the Indigenes of the Chiapas Highlands (ORIACH) in 1980 to defend the rights of their members and to document violations of human rights. Many of the members belong to one or another of the Protestant churches found in La Hormiga, the *barrio* of San Cristóbal in which they reside. When political disagreements arose among the members, Domingo López Angel, a Chamulan who was exiled because of his political challenge to the traditional elites and who converted to Protestantantism after his arrival in San Cristóbal, formed a new group, the Council of Indigenous Representatives of the Highlands of Chiapas (CRIACH) (Sullivan 1998).

The secularization of organizations such as ORIACH and CRIACH that began as defense systems for the migrants is related to the lack of hierarchy and control from above in Protestant sects. The CRIACH takes a more partisan political position than ORIACH in its programs for the economic defense of the exile community. Allied with the PRD, it was able to elect its leader, Domingo López Angel, to the state congress. The organization now includes *mestizos* as well as Indians, Catholics as well as Protestants, and they number in their membership long-term residents of San Cristóbal as well as the exiled indigenous people. Some of the CRIACH members have accumulated property, trucks and small businesses, and a great number are employed as drivers of trucks, vans, and taxis. Equipped with citizen-band radios, they communicate among their comrades, calling for aid when any of the frequent assaults on chauffeurs by highway brigands occur, or when the army or state police harass drivers. They have been accused of exercising Mafiosi tactics in the defense of their members and of expanding their territorial control, in the marketplace and through their network of drivers. Like most newcomers to political arenas of power, their experience as outsiders provokes strong reactions. In April 1998, the Chiapas prosecutor's office charged some of the CRIACH leaders with trafficking in armaments, and issued a warrant for their apprehension that provoked a massive police and military operation involving over a thousand army and federal and state police in Hormiga (*La Jornada* April 9, 1998:1–3, 7, 8). A year later the leaders who had been seized, including Domingo López Angel, were still being held in Cerro Hueco, the state penitentiary in Tuxtla Gutierrez.

Protestant denominations are also at a disadvantage in their international operations compared with the Catholic Church. Some have turned to the transnational spaces being opened up by NGOs and ecumenical groups for their mobilizations on broad sociopolitical issues. Pastors for Peace is one such example. Organized in recognition of a minister killed in Central America, Pastors for Peace have engaged in an investigation of alleged massacres by the army. The member groups that organize delegations through a variety of networks with local parishes in the United States funnel aid that poured in from many parishes throughout the United States during the Central American wars of the 1980s. They continue to coordinate the work of groups that play the role of witnesses in encounters between civil society and repressive governments. After the Zapatista uprising in 1994, Pastors for Peace concentrated their witnessing in Chiapas, where their member organizations provide much-needed resources to the communities that remained within the conflict zone in the Lacandón. Their testimonies were crucial for disseminating throughout the world news of the February 1995 invasion and the subsequent military occupation of the rain forest.[13] The international caravans they organized have brought hundreds of thousands of tons of humanitarian aid to the Lacandón rain forest and to the northern Autonomous Pluriethnic Region (RAP), where the paramilitary group Paz y Justicia has fired at them.

Pastors for Peace is exceptional among Protestant groups, many of which have no interest in promoting human rights agendas in an international setting or who take partisan positions supporting U.S. intervention.

The presence of multiple and competing ecclesiastical groups has promoted more dialogue among and between groups than when the Catholic Church represented a monolithic presence in the spiritual world. Protestant congregations develop secular organizations that enable them to confront the entrenched elites in urban settings. Expelled indigenes of both Protestant and Catholic churches relate to civil society or to opposition political parties, rather than the PRI or national institutions, as they consolidate their position in urban society. The new alliances they have made with NGOs have assisted them in reconstituting a sense of community in urban settings. Their forced separation from the communities of origin was in a sense as liberating as the exodus from the plantations had been for the colonizers. This is discussed in the following section.

INDIGENOUS MOVEMENTS AND
THE COALESCENCE OF CIVIL SOCIETY

In the aftermath of the Revolution of 1910–1917, indigenous peoples of Mexico participated in the nation as subordinate groups to *mestizos*, who expropriated the indigenous past and constituted themselves as the hegemonic power through the ideology of *indigenismo*. Indigenous populations began to mobilize politically as distinct groups in the 1970s. The Mixtecans of Oaxaca mobilized on a statewide level sooner than did Mayans in Chiapas. Mixtecan consciousness of collective identity was stimulated by the alliances they made in their migrations to the United States. This coalesced in the Indigenous Oaxacan Front and other groups that maintained transnational alliances among indigenous people in both nations (Nagengast and Kearney 1990; Stephen 1997b). Indigenes from Oaxaca and the northern states who settled in the rain forest often reinforced their in identity in the new settings outside their state or local pueblos. Since fewer Chiapans have experienced foreign migration, their awareness of distinct identity deve later than that of Guerrero or Oaxaca.

The defining moments for Chiapas Indians came during the mobilization of the National Congress of Indians in 1974, when they encountered leaders of ethnic groups throughout the nation, as described below. Since then, indigenes have expanded their activities, moving beyond but not abandoning national class-based *campesino* organizations seeking restitution of land, to coalitions of indigenous activists in civil society mobilizations.

The Independent Campesino Movement

Campesino organizations that broke away from official corporatist organizations developed an alternative to monolithic control by the PRI, particularly after 1970. Here I shall sort out from the political economic developments promoted by *campesino* organizations noted in chapter 3 those that contribute to the coalescence of civil society dedicated to the formation of a new relationship between ethnic groups and the state. The member organizations derived some of their resources from these national organizations as they promoted the struggles for land that had deep roots in the Chiapas indigenous *campesino* movements. As indigenous groups that coalesced around the organizing for the 1992 celebration of 500 Years of Resistance proliferated, parallel groups that emphasized the control over territory developed a programmatic position and took legal steps to attain autonomy.[14]

The fissioning and fusing that took place in indigenous movement during these years of ferment are difficult, if not impossible, to comprehend in the Aristotelian and Cartesian traditions that dominate Western perspectives. In this framework, hierarchy and opposition are the framework for thinking about social mobilization. Continuity and persistence of the same organizations are applauded, and the shifting processual "coming into being only to become something else" is often considered a sign of failure. The closest we come to appraising the subtle maneuvers of oppressed people who are trying to make a bid for change is through the Marxist dialectical approach that sees contradictions within a structure as the emergent framework of opposition. Even within that framework, it is almost impossible to conceptualize the fluid and often acephelous organization of *campesino* mobilizations. Self-designated names for their resistance groups and settlements, such as "Abejas" (Bees), "Hormiga" (Ants), and "Kiptik ta Lecubtesal" (United by Our Strength), give us clues to the collective base of their organizational practices.

The indigenous people of the northern frontier are explicit in the metaphoric connections for the name of their organization, "Abejas", though each locality in which it exists differs in denoting how it came about. The "official" version, as published in *Sipaz*, is the following:

> We came together in 1992 because we are a multitude and we want to build our house like the honeycomb where we all work collectively and we all enjoy the same thing, producing honey for everyone. So we are like the bees in one hive. We don't

allow divisions, and we all march together with our queen, which is the reign of God, although we knew from the beginning that the work would be slow but sure. (Members of Las Abejas, cited in SIPAZ April 1998)[15]

The group of about fifty Chol and Tzeltal men and women marched all night from Tila in March 1993 to protest the neglect of their communities in basic human services and development programs. We[16] caught sight of the Abuxu when they were detained outside the town center of Oxchuc, when Salinas arrived to promote interest in his development programs for the area.

The Abejas formed a Christian Base Community in the municipality of Chenalhó but were forced to abandon their homes when they were severely harassed by the PRI mayor. In their new hamlet, called Acteal, they were brutally attacked by paramilitary forces in what is now called the Acteal Massacre (see p. 203 *et seq.*).

La Hormiga, or the Ant, is an apt term for the community of expelled Chamulans in the "misery belt" in San Cristóbal, where they have taken up residence in exile. The steep hillside indeed looks like a gigantic anthill occupied by the thousands of families who have recreated village life in this inhospitable setting. The root metaphor of ants derives from the prevalent myth among Mayans about the advent of corn. The ancestors (*me'tik-tatik* in Tzeltal, *totilme'il* in Tzotzil) prevailed upon the ants to bring out of primeval rock the kernels that became the seed for this most important crop. Mayans recognize the energy of ants and of bees, as they show in their myths, in which the collective strength of these small creatures overcomes formidable opposition. They also recognize the fact that ants, like bees, proceed about their business without deterrence because their actions are often not detected.

Operating within existing organizations, *campesinos* develop opposition positions that then become the basis for new organizations in an ever-renewing cycle. *Kiptik ta Lecubte-sal*, a Tzeltal phrase meaning "applying our strength for a better future," is another independent organization that developed in the Ocosingo area. Like Tierra y Libertad and Lucha Campesino in Las Margaritas, which were recognized by the Ministry of Agrarian Reform (SRA), they provided the social bases for the unions of *ejidos* (N. Harvey 1998:79). The names evoke the collective action of ant and bee colonies that clearly inspire the unremitting determination of *campesinos* to gain justice in the face of massive repression. Sometimes the PRI has recognized this and promoted what appeared to be breakaway organizations in an attempt to capture opposition, but the dissident groups frequently attain an independent life.

I shall pick up the story of the multiplying *campesino* organizations from chapter 3 to show how they were attaining a pivotal position in civil society. It is worth decoding the maze of acronyms that proliferated in the decades of the 1970s and 1980s because it reveals a new kind of politics promoted in indigenous mobilizations. The initiative for independent indigenous movements, like that which proliferated in independent *campesino* movements, often came from the PRI as it tried to co-opt dissidents.

Two key umbrella organizations, the National Coordinating Committee of the Plan de Ayala (UNPA) and the National Union of Regional Autonomous Campesino Organizations (UNORCA), developed as coordinating groups for existing *campesino* organizations in the early 1970s. The UNPA drew its membership from a strong independent regional association, the Emiliano Zapata *Campesino* Organization (OCEZ), in the Venustiana Carranza area. As a government-created association, UNORCA drew upon producer organizations started by the PRI government, such as the Association of Rural Campesino Interests (ARIC) in Las Margaritas. Xóchitl Leyva Solano (Levya Solano and Franco 1995:204) estimates that a majority consisting of 85 percent of the 23,330 indigenous colonizers of the 137 settlements of Las Cañadas belonged to the ARIC in 1990.

In Venustiano Carranza, the group of men and women who congregated in what came to be called the Casa del Pueblo (House of the People) waged a continuing struggle for control over the communal lands that were granted by presidential decree in 1965 but never passed over to titleholders. Members of their group were killed by gunmen hired by the large landowners or jailed in the state prison by state police. The Emiliano Zapata Campesino Organization (OCEZ) was formed in 1982 by the imprisoned commissioners while in the state jail of Cerro Hueco. The extraordinary support for the imprisoned activists by those united in the Casa del Pueblo raised the awareness of people throughout the region as to how the PRI government supported the interests of the large landowners against the *campesinos*. OCEZ continued its struggle to reclaim lands taken during the Porfiriato and to regain lands compensatory for those seized from *campesinos* in the construction of the Angostura Dam (N. Harvey 1998:108 *et seq.*). OCEZ, like other member organizations of UNPA, derived some of its resources from the national organization as it promoted the struggle for land that has deep roots in the Chiapas indigenous *campesino* movements.

The second umbrella organization, UNORCA, was developed during López Portillo's government in 1985 as an adjunct to the producer cooperatives. UNORCA linked two or more Unions of *Ejidos* (UE) with a third level called the Rural Association of Collective Interests (ARIC) (Harvey 1998:193). These became the basis for other support structures in credit, especially for coffee producers in the Las Margaritas ARIC. Other producer organizations developed in the diocese of Tapachula, such as San Isidro Labrador, San Francisco de Asis, and still other producer cooperatives such as UNCAFESUR and Majomut, sought autonomy and provided a thick and interconnected network that reinforced civic action.

Independent Indigenous Movement

The independent indigenous movement also owed much of its impetus to government initiatives that inspired organization at wider levels. Instigated by the PRI government, the National Indigenous Congress (CNI) convoked the Chiapas meeting in 1974 and the Patzcuaro meeting a year later. In the course of promoting the meeting, the indigenous leaders developed an independent agenda from that envisioned by the PRI. Dissidents from within this group formed the National Plan de Ayala Coalition (CNPA) in 1979 (Mattiace 1997:39). Regional congresses of the 56 participating linguistic groups became the nucleus for the National Council for Indigenous Peoples (CNPI) (Díaz-Polanco 1992:153).

The regional indigenous and *campesino* organizations provided a civic network that fed into broader political actions throughout the state of Chiapas. This introduced a plurality of visions that posed new modes of civic action, overcoming formidable opposition through their collective strength. Margarito Ruíz Hernández (1999), an activist in these organizations and a state representative of the PRD, describes the dynamic of this new paradigm:

> The plurality of autonomous perspectives of the distinct organizations and leaders with whom we have debated these initiatives [in the autonomy proposals] since 1994 has been a substantial underpinning on which the autonomy formulation has nourished iself and that has permitted the advance and enrichment of the proposal. This process of construction never was lineal. As with every process, it had fluctuations, although characteristic of the period from 1990 to 1993 was the multiplication of indigenous organizations that grew in distinct regions of the country like mushrooms after the rain. Little by little, many of these new organizations were convinced of the strategic importance of the indigenous struggle and of the relevance of the modifications in the laws at a national and international level that had to be resolved immediately in the daily life and situation of our pueblos. This was seen as an indispensable condition to initiate the process of modification in this life setting. [Author's translation]

His sense of the history of this process as a multicentered, pluralistic organization clearly defies unilineal progression typical of Western modes of thinking. It exemplifies the collective inputs of many active agents that provide the resilience and flexibility enabling the movement to survive even when leaders are killed or imprisoned, or when dissidents are co-opted by the state.

Civil Resistance of Independent Campesino and Indigenous Organizations

Following the Zapatista uprising of 1994, these organizations provided the vanguard in civil resistance actions that were directed toward realizing the aims of the organizations. The claims for land title that had been central to the EZLN demands from the first dialogues with the government resonated with *campesino* organizations throughout the state and the nation (chapter 4). The State Council for Indigenous and Peasant Organizations (CEOIC) came into being in late January 1994 and became an important level for coordinating 285 *campesino* organizations such as OCEZ, ARIC, and other organizations that were breaking away from PRI control. It became the democratic and public presence of a movement that supported the aims of the Zapatistas, calling for a peaceful settlement of the war and "elaboration of a global proposal for the integrated growth of our pueblo" ("*Resolutivos del Encuentro de Organizaciones Sociales de Chiapas, por la Paz, la Democracia, y la Defensa de Los Derechos Humanos,*" January 13, 1994, cited in Villafuerte Solis et al. 1999:167). CEOIC was successful in its negotiation of a cease-fire and amnesty for EZLN in the early weeks of the uprising, and its call for a political resolution of the conflict gained wide support. The organization included both moderate as well as confrontational organizations during the tumultuous years following the uprising. Its presence as a pluri-ethnic regional representation of indigenous and *campesino* interests maintained support for the autonomy of indigenous communities and the municipalities and regions in which they constituted a majority (N. Harvey 1998:211–212).

CEOIC was also instrumental in promoting land takeovers in Chiapas during the stalemate of government institutions following the uprising, when *campesinos* were taking action into their own hands on the thousands of pending land claims that were not addressed by the government. Some of these involved civil disobedience that contributed to an ambiance of "ungovernability." This was the case with invasions of plots that had been in dispute since the Constitution of 1917 introduced land reform, which became institutionalized during Lázaro Cárdenas's presidency. The government policy of buying the lands in dispute and redistributing them to peasants in the PRI-sponsored organiza-tions, which was pursued during the first year after the uprising, backfired when the independent organizations that had engineered the invasions objected to the deception. The independent organizations also objected to the government's subsequent trusteeship program in 1995, which distributed lands bought on credit to groups of *campesinos* that were not defined within organic entities formed at the grass roots.

The very diversity of interests and origins resulted in fissures within CEOIC. The pro-EZLN group within the organization joined with 120 other social organizations to create the State Democratic Assembly of the Chiapas Pueblo (AEDPCH). This organization was the driving force behind the candidacy of the Civil Society nominee for governor of Chi-apas, Amado Avendaño. When his campaign faltered after an accident that nearly cost his life, the PRI candidate Robles was declared victor. On the evening of the vote, when Avendaño was still recovering from the accident, his wife, Concepción Villafuerte, declared the elections a fraud at a press conference held in the new municipal theater in San Cristóbal. Although dozens of reporters, including representatives of media from the Western world, attended the press conference where Concepción Villafuerte demon-strated falsified ballots and tallies, few followed up on the story. Upon his recovery from the severe concussion that he had sustained, Amado Avendaño set up a parallel govern-ment in the old San Cristóbal INI headquarters, where he conducted affairs as governor. AEDPCH served as the major group coordinating civil society groups of *campesinos,* pro-fessionals, and trades people in the actions taken by the parallel government.

The indigenous *campesinos* within the state of Chiapas distanced themselves from gov-ernment agencies as official organizations increasingly discredited themselves by their own practices. Villafuerte Solis and colleagues (1999:165) advance the proposition that land as a means of work and subsistence receded, as land as a space or territory generat-ing new symbols and cultural imaginaries for a change in governance became central to the objectives of a conjuncture of diverse social entities. The new, more complex con-juncture of interests and motivations related the gathering struggle of the *campesinos* of Chiapas to a national level as they became the core for even larger groups that consti-tuted the civil society opposition to the PRI government. The presence of these adver-saries in the political arena is a tribute to the hegemonic capacity of the PRI in forseeing opposition and engineering a corporatist takeover, but also a condemnation of the party's shift to neoliberal policies that caused the *campesinos* to break away from the party. Left without resources from the central government to carry out their functions, some of the technical agents and administrators within the agencies still retained a strong commitment to the small-plot cultivators with whom they had worked. Some official agencies initially structured by the PRI, such as the Union of Unions, turned over their organizational capacity to the independent *campesino* movement and burgeoning civil society mobilization. Others, such as Campesino Teacher Solidarity (SOCAMO), were crucial in stirring up conflict in the northern Pluriethnic Autonomous Region. *Campesino* groups such as Xi'Nich, the Altamirano Campesino Alliance and the National Independent Campesino Emiliano Zapata Alliance (ANCIEZ), operated independently of government and PRI in the rain forest, the northern region, and the highlands.

Coordinating the interactions of *campesinos* and indigenes as a working-class and civil society sector is the Independent Center of Agricultural Workers and Campesinos (CIOAC). This national organization originated in the Campesino Independent Center (CCI), formed in 1963, which split into two wings, one the "official" party organization and the other one communist. The communist wing was renamed CIOAC in 1975, but was later expelled from the Maoist Política Popular, along with leaders of *campesinos* in the rain forest.[17] This expulsion probably freed the energies of these rural workers and farmers to pursue the uniquely indigenous practices and goals that characterize CIOAC's actions. CIOAC counts about 300,000 heads of families as members, predominantly in the poorer states of the southeastern part of the country. They were among the first to engage in the takeover of land claims that had not been adjudicated by the government in the year following the uprising. Disdaining the PRI tactics of trucking in *campesinos* for their demonstrations (called *acarreados*), the CIOAC members walk hundreds of kilometers to bring their claims to state and national capitals. In March 1995, hundreds of CIOAC and PRD members from the *ejidos* of the municipality of Las Margaritas joined their demand for legal titles to land with that of autonomy.

More than any other contemporary *campesino* organization, CIOAC embodies the aspirations and strategies of the Bees and Ants as they rebuild society from the bottom up.

Indigenous Women's Entry into Civil Society

Indigenous women's participation in civil society lagged behind that of men. Women did not gain suffrage until 1953, and no women voted in national or local elections in indigenous communities of Chiapas until the 1994 elections. In some communities, men were also disfranchised, since *caciques* filled in the ballots, as in San Juan Chamula. The PRI finally responded to female suffrage when the opposition PRD began actively to involve women in the election process. Few women in highland Chiapas Indian villages spoke Spanish until the 1970s, when they began to attend school in larger numbers. Women still represent over two-thirds of the nonliterate population of the state of Chiapas and are sometimes prevented from attending school not only by an indifferent state but also by their own parents.[18] Their movements, restricted as they were to household activities and occasional trips to the market to buy supplies or sell their artisan products, also inhibited their circulation in the political currents of change.

Artisan cooperatives were among the first arenas in which women of the highlands experienced and participated in political action. The PRI government, which had promoted an indigenous artisan production cooperative through the National Indian Institute (INI) in the 1970s, withdrew monetary support for women artisans in the 1990s. Instead of direct action mobilizing women, the PRI chose to extend the operations of the official bureaucracy, Integrated Development of the Family (DIF), opening retail outlets that sold the products of individual artisans, bypassing the cooperatives.

The cooperatives promoted through international NGOs such as Sna Jolobil and the Catholic Church in Tenejapa and Venustiana Carranza survived and remained an important basis for women's political organization. Shortly after the New Year's uprising, Amatenango women potters associated with the PRD reconstituted the cooperative for the sale of artisan products, which they called the J'pas Lumetik (Potters' Workshop), in Amatenango. The leadership was entirely new, since the women had been profoundly frightened by the assassination of the former leader. Some had fled town and continued to live in San Cristóbal, where they were employed; other former leaders produced for the DIF, which allowed them preferred access to more profitable markets through the party-controlled outlets. The organization of San Cristóbal artisans, J'pas Joloviletik persisted, even after an internal split in 1995 that threatened to destroy the organization.

Artisan cooperatives clearly expanded the women's political interests. I have noticed that women who are representatives of the pottery cooperative J'pas Lumetik in Amatenango appear as a group in the security belts along with indigenous men and international peace observers during the dialogues and international congresses (chapter 4). Christian Eber also found that the weavers' cooperative in Chenalhó provided women with the political experience and resources to assert their concerns in other settings. The organization of women called Palabra de Dios (Word of God), inspired by liberation theology, provided another arena for Chenalhó women to participate in the political life of their pueblo (Eber 1998). Women in the support groups for the Zapatistas are working out cooperative efforts to allow some to become leaders by assisting them with their domestic obligations. They have mobilized support for those women who fled Acteal, a neighboring hamlet of Chenalhó, after the massacre (see below).

Women's organizations on broader fronts appeared, first with the Group of Women of San Cristóbal, Comrades (Chiltak), and Land of Women (K'inal Antsetik). Like the agrarian umbrella organizations, these groups also acquired regional representation in the Independent Organization of Indigenous Women (OIMI), which expanded activities for women in health, savings, and legal affairs. The Coalition of Nongovernmental Organizations in Support of Peace (CONPAZ) and other civil society groups have provided important support for the women's organizations. Though rarely discussed in the literature on agrarian conflict and political organizations, these women's groups represent the most revolutionary change in Chiapas society, bringing the half of the population that was restricted from political participation into active civil society roles. Since women were marginalized and restricted to roles in the subsistence and domestic sector, they bring an important perspective, because this is the sector most threatened by neoliberal policies.

Marta Figueroa Mier, a San Cristóbal lawyer and civil rights activist whom I interviewed in April 2000, was among the feminist activists who formed the Group of Women in the 1980s to address the rising problem of violence against nonindigenous as well as indigenous women. The office and homes of the Group of Women have been repeatedly robbed, and the women are subject to threats and physical violence that, according to Figueroa, differ from those accorded to men's political organizations. Sometimes the women receive flower arrangements, but the flowers are marigolds, associated with death, and the note contains a death threat if they continue activities. Among items robbed are intimate clothing, along with the theft of computers and other articles with a presumed resale value; vandalism includes attacks on furnishings related to sexual encounters: beds are smashed, intimate arenas of home life violated.

Marta Figueroa Mier noted that women are often unsympathetic toward women assaulted after engaging in public demonstrations, saying that if they stayed in the house it would not have happened.[19] The women who take the courses in women's rights and legal advocacy offered by the Group of Women sometimes find themselves ostracized in the indigenous communities when they try to stand up for the rights of other women. People will say, "Why look for others' problems?" In her experience, Marta Figueroa finds that in indigenous communities there are great inequalities between the punishments that are imposed on men and women for the same crime, despite their supposed equality under law. Women can be severely punished for adultery, whereas men are given a minor fine. Women can be banished from the house their husbands often own, and left without compensation for their children. Indigenous lawyers, both men and women, who have received training with the Group of Women organization have difficulty confronting local authorities who respond on the basis of different sets of customs. Their work often has to be clandestine if they wish to remain in the pueblos. Marta Figueroa has found that the people at the Human Rights Center, "Fray Bartolomé de Las Casas" respond less aggressively to cases of violence against women—even those that are politically motivated, and not domestic abuse—than to those against men. When women are detained in prison, the center is lax about gaining compensation for women's time lost for unjustified imprisonment, since staff members accept the sexist tradition that women do not work.

One of the greatest changes since the EZLN uprising is the greater participation of indigenous women in political movements. Of the 15,000 soldiers in the EZLN, 40 percent are women. Single, divorced, and widowed women, who enjoy few of the benefits of patriarchal society in their pueblos, are particularly energized by the new vision of femininity demonstrated by *comandantes* Ramona, Ana María, and Trini in the high command of the EZLN. The demands that Zapatista women elaborated before the uprising, in March 1993, enjoined all Mexican women to participate in the Revolutionary Laws of Zapatista Women:

> "Do not leave us alone!" is the cry of the women of the EZLN. Their cry to Mexican women is not for them to take up arms, rather it is that they support the proposed changes in the Revolutionary Law of Women and their demands in consideration of

[handwritten margin note: violence against 9 activists]

equality, justice, health, education, and housing within their own spaces. [Author's translation]

The laws were simple and definitive: 1) women, regardless of race, creed, color, or political membership, have the right to participate in the revolutionary fight in the place and to the degree that their will and capacity determines; 2) women have the right to work and receive a just salary; 3) women have the right to decide the number of children that they can bear and care for; 4) women have the right to participate in the affairs of the community and hold office if there are free and democratic elections; 5) women and their children have the right to medical attention and nutrition; 6) women have the right to education; 7) women have the right to select their own partner and not to be obliged to marry against their will; 8) no woman shall be beaten or mistreated physically, by either family members or strangers. The crimes of attempted rape as well as rape will be severely punished; 9) women can occupy leadership positions and military duties in the revolutionary armed forces.[20]

Comandante Ramona embodied the courage and determination manifested in the women's revolutionary demands. Inspired by her example, indigenous women's participation in political mobilizations increased after 1994. In March 1995, women were organizing their own parades and public assemblies in the interest of peace and justice. I witnessed the second of these marches organized for the International Day of Women, March 8, 1995, when hundreds of women—indigenes and *mestizas*—and a few men circled the city of San Cristóbal and ended up at the kiosk in the *zócalo*. The speeches by indigenous women as well as *mestizas* focused on peace and the settlement of the conflict in Chiapas. Two weeks later, hundreds of women congregated again for the March for Peace and Justice in support of Bishop Samuel Ruíz, shouting for peace and urging the government to withdraw troops from the Lacandón rain forest.

Traditional behavior denied women access to political activities in public spaces. The first time I saw large contingents of women as active participants with men was in the protests that emanated from the rain forest. The women who had joined men in the Marqués de Comillas march in 1991 were jailed in the Palenque prison and held without food or water for days (chapter 3). Yet women still experienced constraints despite their growing participation in economic and political life. Even after publicizing their demands and organizing to defend their rights, men prevented women from attending meetings, asserting that it was only they who had the right to go and speak. Women also complained that they were subject to control over their movements not only by their husbands but also by their sons. One woman was killed by her husband for attending a meeting (Lovera and Palomo 1999:70–71).

The demands articulated by Zapatista women in 1993 were followed by other declarations. In response to the men's initiatives in reviving traditions in the movement for autonomy, women prepared a list of customs that they liked and those they did not: they rejected the custom of fathers obliging daughters to marry at ten or eleven years of age and preventing their daughters from attending school. They objected to the customs of husbands preventing their wives from going to meetings, of men drinking excessively,

[handwritten top margin: "9s attempts to change → violence against 9"]
[handwritten: ", nothing"]
[handwritten: "No, clearly mens reinvestment in patriarchal, etc"]

often following up their indulgence by abusing women, and of forcing them to have more children that they wanted (*ibid.*: 71–72). Women wanted control over land, training in health care and medicine, and the right to work and receive a salary (*ibid.*: 79). *Comandante* Ramona embodied the valor of indigenous women in speaking out about the problems within their communities as they try to undertake political roles that relate to their condition as women. She was among the first to reject the noncritical position toward "uses and customs" prevalent in male-dominant groups. Women have picked up this point and have drawn up a list of good traditions and bad traditions, and have made clear their intention to define the criteria for what are good and what are bad traditions.

[handwritten left margin: "violence against 9 increased since uprising"]

Violence against women has increased since the uprising. K'inal Antsetik and Chiltak supported the publication of a book, edited by Nellys Palomo and Adela Bonilla (1996), noting (Palomo and Bonilla 1996:3) that in the last few years violence was increasing in all settings—community, family, and society—and that women are the most affected by the threats, detentions, and hostilities, as men seek to humiliate and degrade the human condition of women and inhibit their social and political participation. Clearly, it is women's attempts to change the structural basis of their subordination that motivates the hostility.

[handwritten left margin: "NO" and "go were men"]

Women are frequently the target of abuse by security guards when they join protest marches. In January, 1996, a woman was killed by security forces in Ocosingo. A woman who participated in the CIOAC action at the town hall in Ixtapa in March 2000 to protest the corruption of the mayor was viciously assaulted by security forces, who kicked her in the head, after which she was detained for hours without medical treatment. When the National Commission on Human Rights issued a complaint, the Prosecutor General of the State responded that she did not merit medical attention since she should not have been out on the streets (*Cuarto Poder* March 29, 2000; April 4, 2000; April 5, 2000).

Women are speaking not only of their insulting and degrading conditions, but are relating it to the root cause in indigenous cultural settings:

> We are educated to serve in our homes and in our communities. Families give preference to boys in education while girls have to leave school to work in the house. The government does not give credit or land to women. We do not work for wages, and we have nothing to pay for cultivation. When we ask for legal aid, officials ask for a marriage license, and if we are not married, they say they will not write a warrant. Women cannot be officials in their communities, and do not have the right to a voice in public affairs, and our word is not worthwhile in court. Accustomed to the bad treatment we receive, we accept rage and suffering as something normal. We seek democratic and harmonious relations with equality and without discrimination, and the sharing of household responsibilities. (Gutiérrez and Palomo 1999)

Women have formed separate groups within *campesino* organizations in order to establish their own identity, for themselves and for their reference group. Margarita Gutiérrez and Nellys Palomo, representatives in the Women's Indigenous Convention, clarify the reasons why women have had to establish their own groups while working this out:

We are convinced that all the relations in our lives are determined by the relations that we establish with men (those of our ethnicity and those who are not indigenes), and that these relations, as Marcela Lagarde says, have oppressive consequences for us and ought to be transformed. Therefore, we value the spaces that we construct in women's organizations where we construct our own identity in terms that define our gender condition and permit the flow and interaction with male and female "others," and allow us to remember a dialogue with our own pueblo, with our customs, and to make alliances and actions with women in general to demand recognition as indigenous women. (Gutiérrez and Palomo 1999)[21] [Author's translation]

Evoking the overarching indigenous value of harmony, Gutiérrez and Paloma show how the subordination of women demonstrates the lack of harmony in the relations of gender and of power in indigenous communities.

Following the invasion of the Lacandón rain forest in 1995, three organizations of women formed an umbrella organization called Xi'Nich: it included the Committee for the Defense of Indigenous Freedom, Reunion to Resolve Our Problems, and the Union of Communities of the Chiapas Forest. They anticipated even more attacks on their organizations:

We women have reflected on the situation in Chiapas. We see that the decision by President Zedillo to order the seizure of Marcos and the directors of the EZLN has worsened our conditions. We know that the government intends to destroy this organization and other *campesina* organizations. We think that the government has taken this decision because it wants to pressure Amado Avendaño's transitional government so that he cannot carry out his work, because he has moved ahead with the Constitutional Congress and because his is a government in benefit of the *campesinos*.

The PRI government wants to eliminate us through this economic crisis. We cannot pay for the debt in which Zedillo has thrust us. How are we going to pay? With the blood of the indigenes and *campesinos*. We see that there will be more suffering for our children.

Every day we live with fear of the conflict, especially because of all the rumors. The television and the radio do not broadcast the truth of what is happening to the *campesinos* and the Indians.

Yet we maintain our hope for reaching peace with our struggle. We cannot remain seated; we must mobilize people at a national level so war does not break out. Where will we women and children go if there is war?

We cannot lose heart. We have to raise the hopes of our communities so there is no fear. [Author's translation of flyer distributed by protesters]

I picked up the leaflet, a part of which is translated here, at a march for peace in March 1995. In the dark days after the invasion of the Lacandón rainforest, women carried out marches calling for peace and the withdrawal of the armed forces. On March 8, indigenous women predominated in the Women's Day March for Peace, and as the threats against the bishop increased throughout the month, they mobilized another march for peace. They developed common symbols of incense, flowers, and candles that distinguish them from men's groups and link them to religious processions, where they have always played a role.

Women's involvement in political action is promoting a greater consciousness of their own rights as human beings. Because of their responsibilities in the family and community, changes of the sort women are experiencing can radically change expectations of what behaviors are acceptable, not only in the intimate spheres of the family and community but also in the wider society. The participation of women in civil society has already transformed the action and ideology guiding political life in the state. It has also increased the fury of some sectors, particularly the male youth of the indigenous communities who sense a loss of their control over women's labor and bodies.

The National Meetings of the Indigenous Women have become an annual event since 1995. National groups are linked to the Continental Meeting of Women, which held its second meeting in Mexico in 1997, and women report their decisions to the National Encounter of Women of the National Assembly of Indigenous People in Support of Autonomy (ANIPA). The expansion of their activities strengthens the role of indigenous organizations of men and women regionally. Indigenous women can state with pride, as they did in the Meeting of Indigenous Women in 1997, "that the great cultural richness of our pueblos has been maintained, reproduced and enriched by us women." They have defined as a future objective the prevention of the exploitative use by outsiders of "this richness used in a manner foreign to our view of life" (Gutiérrez and Paloma 1999:71).

WANING OF PRI HEGEMONY AND MILITARIZATION OF CIVIL SOCIETY

I shall recapitulate here the reversals of PRI government policies in order to mark the transformation of the political process from a negotiated political settlement of the Chiapas conflict to the militarization of civil society in Chiapas. The initial turning point came with the PRI's discrediting of electoral politics by fraudulent practices carried out in Chiapas during the August 21, 1994, elections. Subsequent elections in 1995 and 1997 convinced many of the *campesinos* that they could not gain representation within conventional party politics marked by electoral fraud. The second reversal came with the invasion of the Lacandón rain forest on February 9, 1995, and the militarization of the conflict zone, when it became clear that the government would not pursue a political solution to the problems in Chiapas. The third upset came with the Acteal massacre of December 22, 1997, which revealed the complicity of the PRI in the paramilitarization of civil society. Each of these events provoked innovative responses that reveal transformative processes in civil society.

The Discrediting of Electoral Politics

The discrediting of electoral processes during the August 1994 elections has had a long-term impact, invalidating the legitimacy of the PRI in the view of many indigenous people in the state of Chiapas. The elections energized Zapatistas and their supporters throughout the state in support of the Civil Society candidate, Amado Avendaño, during the months leading up to casting their vote on August 21 (see chapter 4). The long lines of women and men, who had walked for hours to attend the few voting stations in the Lacandón rain forest, were an impressive testimonial to the commitment of the indigenous people to democratic processes, including electoral politics. I visited two of the voting sites in the Lacandón rain forest, San Miguel and Patihuitz, where I saw long lines of men and women waiting for the polls to open, hours after the scheduled opening. For some of them, the wait was in vain, since there were not sufficient ballots. Although the event was generally considered by the foreign and domestic press to have been the cleanest and "most transparent" in Mexico's history, Chiapas voters, many of whom were voting for the first time, were skeptical not only of the voting process during that election, but of the value of electoral procedures as a means of assessing public consensus.

The immediate reaction was a consolidation of popular organizations that had supported the Civil Society candidate around the charge that the elections had been fraudulent. This group formed the State Democratic Assembly of the Chiapas Pueblo (AEDPCH), which then functioned as the legislative wing of the autonomous parallel government formed by the Civil Society candidate for governor, Amado Avendaño, in August, 1994 (chapter 4).

The revolt of the municipalities during the year following the uprising was a measure of the deepening divide between the PRI government and Chiapas civil society: 88 of the 111 municipalities engaged in acts of rebellion against the state. These acts included takeovers of town halls, removal of mayors, naming of councils, invasion of cattle ranches and plantations, mobilization of traditional popular forces, removals from public plazas, municipal buildings, and lands, kidnappings, assassinations of indigenous leaders, and armed encounters between *campesinos* and white guards (*Expreso* February 2, 1995:7). The demands of the independent municipal governments that were reconstituted in the wake of these takeovers paralleled those of the Zapatista communities in the Lacandón rain forest and showed an increasing emphasis on autonomy.

The PRI government was well aware of the crumbling of its hegemony in the first two months of Zedillo's presidency. In response to the municipal revolts, the Congress of the state of Chiapas introduced changes in the Municipal Organic Law on February 2, 1995, allowing the formation of two new municipal entities that would serve as electoral districts. It seemed as though the government intended to pursue the path of conciliation that had been aborted by the breakdown of the negotiations after the assassination of Donaldo Colossio in March 1994. Governor Eduardo Robledo, whose election was contested by Civil Society, visited Chamula, one of the few towns where he could expect a welcome, on February 5, 1995.[22] Wearing a Chamula poncho and beribboned ceremonial hat, he urged an end to the discrimination against indigenes and the paternalism and demagoguery of the past. He was clearly looking for allies among indigenes. It looked good, but a Chamulan told me after I attended the event that the crowd of 20,000 indigenes had been mobilized by the *caciques* on the threat of charging a twenty peso fine, equal to more than a day's pay, for absenteeism. Yet, instead of pursuing the old PRI tactics of manufacturing hegemony that the February 5 meeting in Chamula suggested was in the offing, the PRI government chose to militarize the Lacandón rain forest and to destabilize municipalities with opposition party leanings through paramilitary operations.

As a result of this denigration of the political processes by the PRI, even more indigenous people in the Lacandón rain forest and in some highland communities chose not to vote in July 1996 than in the 1995 elections. As the election process accelerated in July 1996, I spoke with a member of the Civic Alliance, a national NGO that focused on electoral processes, who told me what the organization had attempted to do prior to the elections to ensure "transparent" voting procedures:

> We had meetings in July that included AEDPCH, the government representatives, and the Federal Electoral Institute that had assured us that the conditions for voting were untainted. As a member organization, we made an agreement with the PRD, which even loaned us their party registration list. We made several calls to the PRI urging that there be a national consultation, but they did not return our calls.

As examples of the bad conditions for carrying out a free and fair vote, the agent said that the voting booths are sometimes at a distance requiring up to two or more days of travel to get to them. Sometimes the numbering of the *casillas* where they were installed are for another voting district and cannot be shifted.

On election day I visited San Andrés and Ocosingo. In San Andrés *campesinos* had cut trees near the highway entering the town to deter government agents from entering. The town had voted against holding the elections. When the polls opened at 9:10, no one approached the curtained booth for at least an hour. Finally five or six elderly women approached the booth with great hesitation. When one finally entered the booth, we could see her through the gap at the bottom of the curtain, circling and hesitating, apparently not knowing what to do.

We noticed in the few rural hamlets we visited in Ocosingo that no one was voting. A meeting was going on in a cement-block structure marked COA, the acronym for "Coalition of Autonomous Organizations," which represented the communities of the hamlets. One of the organizers said that the organization included members of ARIC Independent, representatives of the Human Rights Center, and some opposition parties. We spoke with one of the women in charge, who told us:

> Some of us had never participated in elections before. But the urns were installed in a hamlet where there were friends of the big cattle owner. We wanted urns set where people—men and women—had easy access. Furthermore, the urns were near military garrisons and people were afraid to approach them.

One of the candidates for the PRD, who was running as congressman for the rural district, joined us. He told us, when we asked why people were not voting:

Women waited in line in San Miguel for hours to vote in the presidential elections in August 1994.

There have been many denunciations with the Federal Electoral Institute. We wanted replacement urns, and got none; we said there are no conditions for the elections; we had tried to share registration lists; we had a general assembly on July 4, and we did make an agreement with the PRD that loaned us their voting registration list. We made a last-minute attempt to get a national consultation. The San Andrés Agreement has not been fulfilled. We want people to know that our brothers the Zapatistas are not responsible for the disruption—it is the government. . . . Those who want to vote should vote. We want a peaceful opportunity to vote without threats. It is customary here to buy votes. This is the infrastructure used to gain votes, to channel services to PRI supporters.

He added that it was a group decision not to vote. Where there was a split vote, they left it up to the individual to vote or not as he or she chose. In San Pedro Carrizal, a hamlet of Ocosingo that was reputedly pro-Zapatista, the urn was stolen, making it impossible for the 2,000 voters to vote. Fifty urns disappeared, according to the Coalition of Autonomous Organizations, though the government claims 29, in one district. In other hotly contested elections, the coalition claimed 15 urns were robbed in Palenque, and 53 urns were not installed.

The confusions that resulted from the partial boycott of the 1995 elections were compounded in subsequent elections, with the result that PRI officials were installed in offices in local governments that had voted for the PRD in 1994.[23] The northern region had no opposition voters, allowing the PRI to take over all official positions, although they were in a clear minority. In 1997, the Zapatistas were fairly consistent in attempts to disrupt the vote, but by 1998 they did not take a general stand, leaving the electorate to decide whether or not to vote. The boycott spread confusion and failed to undermine the PRI. It was especially confusing since boycotting meant different things in different districts and at different times. In 1998, the pro-PRI Chamulans boycotted the elections because federal police had arrested five Chamulans the *caciques* claimed were unjustly arrested (*New York Times* October 5, 1998:A10). Although new booths were introduced in the 2000 elections, voters had serious misgivings about a process they had seen as flawed. The Zapatista announcement in July 2000 that they would not impede the voting in any way came at a time when the coalition candidate, Pablo Salazar, had a strong lead over the PRI gubenatorial candidate. Salazar won despite the fact that election results indicated that more than 40 percent of the Lacandón colonizers had abstained.

The old communal forms of democracy, wherein age hierarchies and sacred obligations legitimized the exercise of authority in communities, were abolished, but the transforming process going on was not allowed the space necessary to work itself out. The forms of traditional rule through general assemblies, biased as they were by paternalistic and co-optive processes, had ensured orderly succession in office. But the "elected" offices discredited the process itself for the new citizens who were denied their legal rights.

The Invasion of the Lacandón Rain Forest and the Militarization of Civil Society

Ever since the Zapatista uprising, the government has played a duplicitous role, engaging in negotiations for peace while increasing the military force throughout Chiapas. The estimated 37,000 troops that occupied the Lacandón rain forest from the cease-fire in January, 1994 were almost doubled in the years following the February 9, 1995, invasion, stabilizing at an estimated 60,000, until the buildup to 70,000 following the Acteal massacre in December, 1997. The conflict spread to the northern region, where paramilitary forces opposed the Pluriethnic Autonomous Region. Indigenous leaders of the PRI in neighboring highland communities engaged in homicidal struggles to maintain their position in municipalities where opposition parties claim that the PRI had lost elections.

The rhetoric of peace while pursuing war is captured in President Zedillo's speech of February 10, 1995, the day after the invasion of the Lacandón rain forest, in which he said:

I expressed my firm commitment to attend to the roots of rebellion. These roots are: poverty, absence of opportunities, injustice, lack of democracy. I have always thought that the solution to the conflict ought to be on the road of respect for law, for political causes, and by means of conciliation. Before assuming the presidency of the republic, I worked for direct negotiation with the EZLN. Since September 1994, I sent written and verbal messages reiterating my willingness to enter into dialogue and negotiation, as I continued doing from the first days of my mandate. To this overture they responded with threats of breaking the cease-fire, with armed conflict.

Despite the president's co-optation of the rhetoric of peace and justice, his actions exposed the differences in intentions of the two sides of the conflict. The EZLN has not broken the cease-fire since it went into effect in January 1994, whereas the government has doubled federal forces and has failed to intervene in the growing violence carried out by paramilitary groups.

The war on two fronts, the Lacandón rain forest and the highland indigenous communities, has polarized civil society. The process is described below.

Conflict in the Lacandón rain forest. Following the invasion of federal troops on February 9, 1995, the Lacandón rain forest became the staging ground for the current model of low-intensity warfare that minimizes body counts while maximizing divisive tactics within the civilian population. The barracks are often set up within one hundred meters of town centers, against constitutional restrictions on the deployment of the military. Patrols of soldiers in armored tanks and Humvees with mounted machine guns race through the towns, and the buzzing of helicopters and unseen surveillance planes are a constant reminder of the military presence. With the invasion of the most intimate settings of families and communities, there is a process of domestication of violence that is transforming civil society.

The invasion, briefly recounted in chapter 4, violated international covenants on warfare. No reporters or Red Cross vehicles were allowed in the rainforest for two days. Soldiers carried out acts of war that were specifically prohibited in the international covenants: they vandalized, burned, and destroyed houses, sprayed food stores with pesticides, contaminated water, and stole and destroyed tools, animals, and personal belongings. Hospitals, schools, churches, and private homes were taken over by troops for their personal use. They violated Mexican constitutional prohibitions against the deployment of military bases, establishing barracks in the rain forest in proximity to indigenous settlements; before the February 9, 1995, invasion, there were 13 military encampments in Chiapas; by June 1996, there were 44 in operation (Global Exchange 1997).

Mexican civil society reacted strongly against the invasion. Over 100,000 people filled the Zócalo in Mexico City, with demonstrators calling for justice, taunting the government ploy of apprehending Marcos with the slogan, "We are all Marcos!" (*La Jornada* February 12, 1995). Women of the Zapatista communities sent many letters to the newspapers calling for withdrawal of the troops from their communities and objecting to the occupation. Rosa Rojas, a reporter assigned to the conflict zone (1995:17), quotes from a statement of the people of Ejido Perla de Acapulco sent on February 20 saying: "The people of the community are not able to carry out their daily tasks in peace, especially the women, who cannot go out to do their work washing clothes and carrying water." Of the 140 signatures, 90 were given as thumbprints, a declaration in itself of the failure on the part of the government to educate its citizens.

The government responded with a program of "social integration." It returned 26,000 of those who had voluntarily left their homes in the rain forest after the uprising but before the invasion. Following a tactic used by the Guatemalan army in Ixcan, it located the returned settlers in the homes of those who had been routed by the army in the invasion. This divide-and-conquer strategy turned indigenous people against their kin and neighbors, ensuring the continuation of the conflict (Rojas 1995:8).

[margin note: Tactics to divide & conquer]

The military forces tried to assuage the growing clamor voiced by civil society activists calling for withdrawal of the army by providing guided tours to the "pacified zones." According to reporters who were invited in, every attempt was made to impede free access to them and to the NGOs that accompanied them (*El Financiero* February 28, 1995). Brigadier General Manuel Garcia Ruíz told one reporter that the army could not leave entirely "because the people need us" (*El Financiero* March 17, 1995:p. 45). The Secretary of National Defense aired television spots on the government-controlled news channels showing the activities of "social labor" teams carried out in dental dispensaries, food distribution depots, clinics for family planning, barber shops, and so on. Despite these public relations overtures, the people viewed the army as one of occupation. Reporters noted that women in La Realidad rejected medical attention and food offered by soldiers. Infuriated, one of the soldiers exclaimed, "Then they're asking for a good beating," while another took a bullet from his cartridge clip and showed it to the women saying, "Then they want to try this!" One of the young women defied him, saying, "Well, if you're going to shoot us, do it at once!" While she stood still in the road, the military withdrew (*El Financiero* March 17, 1995:45).

These reports of resistance have counterparts in the attrition of solidarity in the face of continued occupation. The Rural Association of Collective Interests (ARIC) split into an "official" wing that ceded space to the military in Patihuitz, where there is now an encampment near the village edge. When I stayed in a peace hut in Patihuitz in May, 1995, two of the ARIC men explained to me that they had done so in return for the army's pledge not to pillage or destroy the houses. Support for the government's military action came from sectors of civil society that coalesced in the wake of the February 9, 1995, invasion. When a contingent of the military forces occupied the town of San Andrés Larrainzar, a support group formed, representing the ranchers and propertied interests that were threatened by the land takeovers. Calling themselves the Coalition of Citizen Organizations of the State of Chiapas (COCECH), they praised the "leaders of private enterprises and agents," and showed "joy and support" for the president's actions, in the hope of "a return to the rule of law" (*Expreso* February 10, 1995, p. 8).

[margin note: complicity w/ military forces]

In the months following the February 9, 1995, invasion of the federal troops into the rain forest, the presence of NGOs in peace camps throughout the conflict zone may have made the difference between the Mexican army's low-intensity warfare and the

protection offered by human rights NGO

Guatemalan war of extermination in the 1980s. The reports of the human rights organizations from Mexico, France, United States, Spain, Italy, and Germany supplied information that was fed into international human rights agencies and affected even the Standard and Poor's stock ratings for Mexico. Civil society groups organized press conferences in the Center for Human Rights "Fray Bartolomé de Las Casas San Cristóbal" throughout the spring of 1995. These were attended by a large contingent of European press representatives, who are more responsive to human rights press conferences than are the U.S. press, and national papers and television reporters. A truck with a huge dish antenna parked in front of the San Cristoból cathedral following the invasion, and remained there at least until May to provide instant transmission throughout the world as the negotiations proceeded.[24]

I joined a Mexico City contingent of civil society activists in the peace camp organized by CONPAZ in Patihuitz in May 1995 that included a university professor, his daughter who was a teacher, and the representative of CONPAZ. We were housed in a thatched wooden shack abandoned by a family who had sought refuge from the conflict zone. The constant drone of helicopters that hovered within close range of the villages and the traffic of military vehicles speeding through the village center were a constant reminder of the presence and control of the military. The women were trying to maintain their daily routines, even as the soldiers bathed in their drinking reservoirs and accosted men as they tried to walk to their fields. Children clustered around our camp seeking diversion, since no school classes were being held.

A small celebration of Mother's Day that occurred while I was staying in the peace hut demonstrated the collective spirit of the village even under the military occupation. Early in the morning, men collected sprigs of trees to decorate the basketball court in the morning, tying streamers and balloons on the benches. As families gathered in the late afternoon, the men laid out the gifts in the center of the ballcourt. Each mother chose a wrapped gift from the pile that had been purchased by the men, which she then opened before the assembled group of about a hundred villagers. Refreshments were served and young people danced to the tapes of *rancherias* played through loudspeakers.

In my brief week's stay, I could see that the newspaper reports of conditions in the conflict zone were not an exaggeration. If anything, they underplayed the corrosive misery of living in the shadow of the military. I was able to appreciate the protests of the women against the demoralization caused by the army presence that were voiced at the State Indigenous Women's Convention earlier that year when I saw a bus unload women at the barracks. At the edge of the village, one family had opened a bar and served beer to the soldiers, a practice that had been outlawed by the Zapatistas when they were in control. A woman told me that two drunken soldiers had mounted her horse, which was pregnant, kicking the belly of the mare until she fell to her knees and died. *Zapatistas prohibited drugs*

The divisions in civil society that existed before the invasion became more pronounced with the settlement of barracks close to settlements. A contingent of about forty Protestants left to seek exile in Guatemala. They had been converted by Guatemalan exiles sometime during the 1980s, and were the first to reverse the flow of migration between the two countries. Ranchers who were engaged in long-standing hostilities with the colonizers and who hired paramilitaries to protect their interests now found an ally in the army. Divisions within even the most militant independent *campesino* organizations, such as ARIC, revealed the deep fissures exacerbated by the presence of federal troops in the colonized area of the rain forest. Women saw their hard-fought-for autonomy degenerate, as they became the target of harassment by the army and the outlet for the violence of their husbands and companions frustrated by their impotence in the face of the army. Abusing their traditional rights as fathers to force consent of their daughters in marriage contracts, some men accepted money from soldiers who "married" them and then prostituted their "wives" with their comrades in arms. The demoralization of the communities caused by these practices led to further divisions that penetrated the domestic unit.

Militarization of civil society in the highlands. A state of undeclared war exists at all levels of civil society in the state of Chiapas. The military stalemate is matched by an atrophied political process that seems incapable of governing. Governor Robledo, the PRI candidate whose election in 1994 was contested, was forced to resign in response to rising protests that culminated with the invasion of the Lacandón rain forest of February 9. His successor, Julio Cesar Ruíz Ferro, who took power as governor on February 14, 1995, was even less restrained in his use of state violence than his predecessor. Heavily armed groups of PRI supporters, such as Peace and Justice, operate in this northern region much like their counterparts Los Chinchulines in the Ocosingo area and the San Bartolomé Alliance of the Plains in Venustiano Carranza. They are not "clandestine armed groups," as the government claims, but rather "parallel armed groups," that is adjuncts of the army, according to civil society critics. Clandestine armed groups are paramilitary bands hired by private parties to protect their interests, as the ranchers and large landowners have done in Chiapas. In contrast, these parallel armed groups include indigenous members of the communities on which they prey, acting as an integral part of the action of national security counterinsurgency. Their members have an *esprit de corps* manifested in names which relate to local history (San Bartolomé, for example, was the pre-1910–1917 Revolution name for Venustiano Carranza), and they hold assemblies of their members. Formed in the wake of the disintegration of PRI hegemony in Chiapas, they have spread from the northern region, which has been the site of aggravated conflict ever since its declaration of autonomy in October, 1994, to Chenalhó. They are a segment of civil society whose characteristics are a perversion of the low-intensity warfare now in play. In the four years since the cease-fire agreement was signed two weeks after the uprising, more than 1,500 indigenous Chiapanecos have been killed (*La Jornada* December 28, 1997:6), primarily by these parallel military groups.

Violence in the Autonomous Pluriethnic Region (RAP), which includes the municipal councils of Bochil, Jitotol, Simojovel, El Bosque, Ixtapa, Huitiupán, Soyalo, and Rayón y Pueblo Nuevo, has been almost continuous due to paramilitary groups active since the councils declared their autonomy on October 12, 1994. Their autonomy is legally recognized by the local regional Congress, but not by the Chiapas state Congress. In the chaotic conditions that prevailed in most of the state during the months following the invasion of the rain forest, the Pluriethnic Autonomous Region chose to boycott elections in the fall of 1995. As a result, the PRI was able to win even in these communities where they were the least-favored candidates (Centro de Derechos Humanos "Fray Bartolomé de Las Casas" 1998:83–87). Civic Alliance, a civil society group that monitored the 1995 election, contested the vote because of manipulation of the electoral district, but the PRI victors were seated. Chol supporters of the PRD seized town halls when they served as offices after they were occupied by PRI victors of the 1995 elections, but the elected PRI officials held on to power with the help of an armed paramilitary force.

The very remoteness of this region from *ladino* townships guaranteed a measure of autonomy in practice in the past. Throughout the summer of 1996, paramilitary troops tried to crack the solidarity of Chol-speaking communities and *campesino* groups as they mobilized to demand land and other services they had been denied. This set the stage for the reign of terror by the paramilitary groups Peace and Justice and Los Chinchulines, which attacked a group of students in Tila and killed militants of the PRD and the Workers' Party in June, 1996 (*Expreso* June 21, 1996, "India" no. 21).

In June, reports of protests against the violence in the region mounted (*La Jornada* June 24, 1996). Blockades of highways and demonstrations before government buildings culminated with a march by *campesinos* to Tuxtla to complain to the governor of Chiapas about the deaths of fourteen *campesinos* killed by "white guards"—a popular term for paramilitaries—that, they claimed, "are known to be financed by the PRI authorities." Chilón, Tila, and Yajalón also mobilized protests on June 29, 1996, that were supported by *campesino* organizations and centers for human rights (*Cuarto Poder* June 29, 1996). Despite repeated protests by *comuneros*, or members of corporate land-holding communities in the area, the government did nothing to curb the violence committed by the paramilitary groups in the northern region.

The Teacher-Campesino Solidarity group (SOCAMO) of the northern Chol region continued to funnel the shrinking resources of the PRI to its supporters, some of whom joined the paramilitary organization Peace and Justice. In the violent encounters that the federal troops helped organize through their paramilitary adjuncts in the Pluriethnic Autonomous Regions in the north and in nearby municipalities of Chenalhó, they spread the seeds of factionalism and discord.

The political process set in motion by heavily armed sectors of civil society culminated in the massacre in Acteal in the township of Chenalhó. This Christian Base Community, adjacent to the Pluriethnic Autonomous Region on December 22 that called itself "The Bees," was a group of catechists that responded to the bishop's liberation theology approach.

The background to the massacre lay in the growing divisions among indigenous people, as some sectors within the communities were favored by the PRI when the government began to distribute PRONASOL funds and political power.[25] Chenalhó had lost more of its lands during the Porfirio Diaz period than most of the highland communities, and was reduced to one-third of its colonial holdings by the end of the nineteenth century. *Ladino* control of the land and of political power in the town was reinforced rather than diminished by the Revolution of 1910. Ana María Garza Caligaris, who has carried out ethnographic fieldwork in Chenalhó, compiled an account of the massacre with R.

Aida Hernández Castillo (1998:39–68) that reveals the interweaving of gender, political party, and religious antagonism. Women worked in the fields alongside men, yet they rarely gained social recognition for their contribution (Garza Caligares and Hernández Castillo 1998:42 *et seq.*). Political mobilization was restricted to men in the 1970s and 1980s, when the first challenge to the PRI monopoly came about. The contest between the parties was organized by the Socialist Workers Party (PST), that later joined with the Cárdenist Front of National Reconstruction that opposed the PRI in 1988. After the uprising, the Civil Society campaign for Amado Avendaño, who won the support of the Socialist Workers Party dissidents in Chenalhó, and the PRD were able to elect a mayor in 1995. When their candidate was not seated, this group declared Chenalhó an autonomous municipality, along with a dozen other communities (Garza Caligares and Hernández Castillo 1998).

The battlefield was set. In the next two years, violence in the northern region adjacent to Chenalhó escalated, with local Peace and Justice groups and the Chinchulines taking credit for the action. In addition, a private paramilitary group specific to Chenalhó, called the Red Masks, began to carry out aggressive actions against the opponents of the PRI. The Bees sent desperate pleas for protection to authorities, but nothing was done. They left town to escape the harassment of the paramilitary, settling in the *ejido* Acteal within the municipality of Chenalhó. Instead of responding to their alarm, the army began training local PRI supporters, including the mayor, Manuel Arias. On the day of the massacre, the assembled congregation of the Bees was engaged in praying when the Red Masks attacked.

Garza Caligares and Hernandez Castillo (1998) show that the targeting of women and their children was related to a long history of women's protest against male dominance and the drive for relations of equality in the Christian Base Community. Although the combatants on both sides were indigenes of Chenalhó, the attempt on the part of the government to call the massacre a result of "intrafamilial" or "intracommunity" conflict based on religious differences is misplaced. The PRI officials were antagonized by charges of corruption and violation of human rights made by the Bees, and by their support of the Zapatistas. The conflict escalated, with government intervention and distribution of arms. As subsequent investigation revealed, local PRI officials received weapons from the armed forces, and a sergeant and retired general were later implicated in the training of the Red Masks, the armed band that carried out the massacre.

The horror of the encounter surpassed previous conflicts. As attested by eyewitnesses (Centro de Derechos Humanos "Fray Bartolomé de Las Casas" 1997; Hernández, 1998), the attackers ripped open the bellies of four pregnant women and chopped up the embryos with their machetes. Thirty-sox of the 45 victims were women and children. Members of the armed band, some of whom were youths of 14 and 15 years of age, played a game of tossing the embryos from one machete-wielding paramilitary to the other yelling, "Kill the seed!"

Witnesses indicate that the troops were not only armed by the PRI officials, but were trained by them under a Chenalhó soldier on leave from the federal army and a retired general. Bishop Samuel Ruíz asserted in an interview in *Proceso* (December 28, 1997) that the Red Masks appeared to be on drugs. Part of their weeks of training included pornographic videos. The mayor of Chenalhó was jailed in January of 1998 and charged ' tributing arms to the band that carried out the massacre. The retired general and dier who was on temporary leave were arrested in January 1998. A year later, the general was sentenced to eight years in jail for criminal negligence. (*La Jornada* April 3, 1998:3; *New York Times* May 19, 2000).

The escalating conflict in indigenous areas in which members of the same ethnic group are turning against each other culminates decades of contradictory policies and gross neglect of cumulative legal problems related to land claims and credit distribution (*La Jornada* April 3, 1998:3; April 5, 1998:5). The militarization of PRI supporters by the government escalates the violence, bringing about the disintegration of civil society. The government has repeatedly asserted that the conflict arose from internal religious dissent, and the priests who are championing the *campesinos* are perceived as a threat. Five foreign priests, including two Americans, have been deported from Chiapas since the Zapatista rebellion. Even those who in no way support the political intent of the Zapatista uprising were sent into exile.[26]

The Domestication of Militarization – paper   Food & bombs

At the same time that it is carrying out what many call genocidal acts (Centro de Derechos Humanos "Fray Bartolomé de Las Casas" 1998), the government is pursuing a program for domesticating the military and making it a part of village life. Soldiers occupy barracks within view of the colonized settlements and highland villages. Occasionally, in an attempt to overcome growing hostility, they distribute sweets to children, pass out Mother's Day gifts to women, give handouts of food, and perform haircuts and dental services to people who have no access to medical clinics. These gifts are often rejected, particularly by the women. Paramilitary groups working in close conjunction with the military and sharing their armaments increasingly carry out the armed attacks (Comunicación Popular Alternativa, Grupo de Trabajo, December 31, 1997).

The indigenous people are showing strong resistance to the militarization of their lives. The Washington Office on Latin America reported that Zapatistas in Chenalhó refused to take the $5,000 indemnity for the victims of the December 22, 1997, massacre (*New York Times* March 6, 1998). Despite attempts by civil society to get the troops removed, the government continued to send in thousands more troops. They were met, according to reporters (*New York Times* March 6, 1998:A8), by women who marched onto the soccer field armed with wooden clubs, with which they shoved and prodded the troops. They were driven back by tear gas canisters. Men wielding machetes said, "We don't want the soldiers because they are on the side of the paramilitaries. They could try another massacre against us."

Human rights advocates from throughout the world leveled criticism at the Mexican government. The director of the United Nations Commission on Human Rights proposed opening an office in Mexico to monitor events. Madeline Albright, the U.S. secretary of state, objected to the violation of indigenous people's rights. Two Illinois congressmen, Bobbie Rush and Luis Gutiérrez, made a trip to Acteal and interviewed the survivors. Throughout the month of April 1998, the television broadcasts and some pro-government newspapers rejected the right of a foreign country to criticize the internal conduct of a sovereign power. The internal as well as external pressure on the government finally resulted in an investigation of the massacre in Acteal. The White Paper produced by the Mexican attorney general, Jorge Madrazo, on the anniversary of the Acteal massacre, December 22, 1998, blamed the violence on the creation of an autonomous municipal government that ended up with the formation of parallel governments in Chenalhó, one of PRI and the other pro-Zapatista, some of whom voted with the PRD and others who abstained from voting. The White Paper also pointed the finger at the NGOs "which brought together conflicting power groups in a series of meetings that attempted to reach an end to the chain of mutual aggression." Although the White Paper admits the investigation proved that "security officers stationed in the region prompted excessive actions" and that law enforcement institutions showed "apathy and failure to intervene in a timely manner," the conclusion is that the Acteal massacre began as an "old confrontation between rival political, economic and religious factions in the municipality of Chenalhó," and that these were simply aggravated by the structure of parallel government. The government still tried to pass it off as an internal religious conflict (*Mexican Notebook* February, 1999), but a month later 328 people were indicted, the largest number of people indicted in a civil case in modern Mexican history (*Mexican Notebook* March, 1999).

The tragedy of Acteal is not only the death of people who were dedicated to nonviolent presence, but the militarization of civil society, turning individuals within local communities against their brothers, sisters, and neighbors. Andrés Aubrey and Angélica Inda published a penetrating account of the assassins who were prevailed upon to massacre their relatives and neighbors (NACLA Report on the Americas March/April, 1998):

> Those who participate in these paramilitary groups are almost exclusively young men frustrated by landlessness and unemployment. The long-standing crisis in agrarian reform, coupled with demographic growth, have created a situation in which these young men, especially those who are married and have families, are forced to wander in search of work. Like their parents, they survive on their wits and by occasionally stealing food and animals from neighboring farms. Because they own no land and have no reliable means of subsistence, they are forced to live outside the law. Their dislocation from community life also means that they have no reason to attend assemblies, and thus have no part in communal decision-making processes. Their criminal behavior, therefore, is at least in part a product of the government's economic, agricultural and labor policies.

Military and paramilitary action is backed up by divisive political practices that have been part of the PRI corporatist strategies since its origin. The split in the ARIC threatens all the civil society groups. The ARIC-UU, or "official" pro-PRI *campesino* group, was one of the few supporters for the government-sponsored Initiative for the Rights and Culture of Indians in April 1998, which was rejected by all the opposition parties (see below).

CIOAC is constantly under siege after their effective denunciation of the PRI officials in the local town halls of Ocosingo and Las Magaritas in the spring of 2000.

The positive outcome of the turmoil in civil society in the 1990s is the growing significance of international pressure from human rights groups. Not only was the Mexican government forced to investigate and adjudicate the case, but the leaders remain accountable in the eyes of international institutions. In the spring of 2000, just after the signing of the European Union Free Trade Agreement in April, the ambassador of Great Britain visited the state of Chiapas and spoke with the governor and with Bishop Samuel Ruíz, and traveled to Acteal, where he talked with local leaders. Although he did not personally indict the political leadership of the state, three days later the head of the European Economic Union sharply criticized the abysmal level of poverty and repression in Chiapas and intimated that this would have to change if the European Union were to invest in the state. The speech, transmitted on the Tuxtla Gútierrez TV channel, will clearly have an impact in the upcoming elections in August 2000.

INDIGENOUS QUEST FOR AUTONOMY

Autonomy and the desire to govern by their own codes have been strong motivating factors in indigenous strategies ever since the conquest. Indigenous peoples of the hemisphere publicized the Declaration of Quito in August 1990 during the First Continental Encounter of Indian Pueblos, announcing that the territorial base is fundamental to constitute autonomous entities (Díaz-Polanco 1997:15). It remains as important today in generating and sustaining indigenous identity as it was when the Spanish Crown granted the rights of *pueblos indios* over water, woods, and communal lands during the colonial period. These rights, nullified during the Liberal period of Porfirio Diaz, were fortified by the Land Reform Act of the 1917 Constitution. Privatization of lands was basic to the neoliberal strategies of Salinas, who chose to "reform" Article 27 of the Constitution as a means of alienating indigenes from their lands and simultaneously from their communities.

The proclamations from the Lacandón rain forest in the early stages of the uprising were surprising in their departure from this ancient desire to escape Spanish domination by establishing autonomy. From the first National Democratic Convention in August, 1994, the prevailing emphasis was on democratic coexistence in the Mexican nation. The ceremonial unwrapping of the national flag at conventions called by the EZLN was integral to the promotion of the democratic inclusion of indigenous people in civil society. Yet the Zapatista demands for titles to the lands they colonized encompass the demand for political integrity that has always been incorporated in land. In addition to their ongoing battle to restore collective rights to land, Zapatistas have made a claim on a portion of the gains from subsoil resources for the residents. Since the expected revenues from the oil reserves in the Lacandón that have been discovered in the past decade are potentially enormous, the state is opposing the autonomy movement with all its military force; but in repressing the indigenous struggle, it is risking the claims of sovereignty that legitimize the use of force.

Pluriethnic Autonomous Regions

The Zapatista uprising invigorated the demand for autonomy that was part of the regional formations of indigenous pueblos. The National Assembly of Indigenous People (ANIPA), which developed out of the mobilization for the quincentennial celebration of indigenous resistance, became a key actor in defining and promoting autonomy. Margarito Ruíz Hernández expresses in lyrical terms the galvanizing effect of the celebration of 500 years of resistance:

> It was a basic stage that moved the spirit and the heart of the Indian pueblos to recall our history and imagine the future in a different way. This phase was a moment to remember what had been and to dream the outline of a new society, a new State, to recall all that, the five hundred years of darkness, of margination, and of discrimination. They were years of reflection, of recuperating the historical memory of our pueblos, of our ancestors. That is to say, we recalled our forms of government, of organization and of administration of the life in the communities and regions. In this process, little by little we were reflecting and debating on some proposals of reforms in the Mexican laws as a necessary road to lead to the protection of our specific rights as Indian pueblos. Between 1990 and 1992 the number of indigenous organizations increased, inspired in an important way by the hope that signified the breaking forth of the indigenous word, at the national and international level. (Ruíz Hernández 1999:25) [Author's translation]

The EZLN opened spaces for existing indigenous movements. However, it took over a year of mobilization and dialogue to persuade the revolutionary forces to adopt the ideas developed by ANIPA on autonomy for indigenous pueblos. ANIPA drafted the initial proposals for autonomy that were presented in the federal congress by PRD Representative Margarito Ruíz Hernández in 1990. The State Council of Indigenous and Campesinos Organizations (CEOIC),[27] followed by the organization that supplanted it, the State Democratic Assembly of the Chiapas pueblo (AEDPCH), along with the parallel government of Amado Avendaño, worked on constitutional resolutions to establish the legal basis for the autonomy of indigenous pueblos. In this process, working with the National Democratic Convention (CND) that convoked the huge meeting in the first Aguascalientes in the rain forest in August 1994, the indigenous groups modified and deepened their proposal for a new pact between indigenous pueblos and the nation. They defined three levels of government that would operate simultaneously: community, municipality, and regional (Ruíz Hernández 1999:33). Some of these proposals became incorporated in the San Andrés Accord, but indigenous organizations that had fought for regional representation for autonomous entities were disappointed that the regional level was not included.

The AEDPCH presented the Proposal for the Creation of Autonomous Pluriethnic Regions[28] at a meeting in the Central Plaza of San Cristóbal on October 12, 1994. The proclamation of the principle of autonomy was picked up by communities organized as the General Council of Autonomous Pluriethnic Regions. This included dozens of organizations in the region of Los Altos, in the rain forest near Ocosingo, and in the central valleys of Cintalapa, including Tojolobales and Tzeltales of San Cristóbal de Las Casas, who put the proposal into action on January 21, 1995, when they declared themselves an autonomous entity. The proclamation and the stance taken by indigenous groups was fortified by the Zapatista uprising, but it represented years of collective development by pluriethnic indigenous groups that coalesced in the monumental conventions of indigenous people and their supporters that began with the quincentennial celebration of five hundred years of resistance.

Hector Díaz-Polanco, who participated in many of the discussions in which autonomy was formulated, describes the importance of autonomous regions as follows:

> The possibility of a multiethnic state in Latin America depends on establishing autonomous regimes within a national framework. Power is organized monoethnically [in Mexico], and the recognition of multiethnicity without breaking national unity implies giving political recognition to diversity in autonomous entities. (Díaz-Polanco 1997:15)

Differences exist among indigenous people as to the extent of the autonomy they desire and the governing levels beyond the community in which it would be instituted. When the Chol of the northern region declared the Pluriethnic Autonomous Region on October 12, 1994, and followed this manifesto with the declaration of their autonomy early the following year, their demand for a regional level of representatives echoed the Indian Republics of colonial governance. The regional *campesino* and indigenous groups such as AEDPCH and CIOAC had already achieved a regional base that could provide the model for its enactment.

The parallel engagement of indigenous women in ANIPA deepened the meaning of autonomy by their assertion of the rights of gender in relation to the righs of autonomy. Their statement, formulated at the fourth assembly of ANIPA in December 1995, demonstrates the importance of defining autonomy in instrumental terms:

> The autonomy for us women implies the right to be autonomous, we, as women, to train ourselves, to seek spaces and mechanisms in order to be heard in the communal assemblies and to hold posts in office. It also implies facing the fear that we have in daring to make decisions and to participate, to seek economic independence, to have independence in the family, and to continue informing ourselves, because understanding gives us autonomy. To be able to participate in this type of reunion enables us to diffuse the experiences of women and animate others to participate.(Gutiérrez and Paloma 1999:83)

Women show a clear awareness of their responsibility in cultivating the practice of autonomy in society as well as in the home and family, since it is there that children are enculturated in the patterns that define future behavior. Women who live in fear of abuse, who accept subordination in the home, cultivate sentiments that reproduce subordination and marginalization. Indigenous women have unified their movement at a national level in the National Coalition of Indigenous Women of Mexico (CONAMIM), which also is a member of the continental organization of indigenous women.

The regional groups that had organized prior to the EZLN uprising complemented the armed uprising in promoting the agenda of indigenous people in the civil society of Chiapas and the nation. With each step away from the official organizations sponsored by the government, indigenous *campesinos* were reinforcing the potential for pluriethnic coexistence.

When the government revealed its unwillingness to implement the San Andrés Agreement by failing to withdraw the toops that had invaded the Lacandón conflict area in February 1995, the Zapatista forces responded with an agenda that emphasized autonomy. With the resumption of the dialogues between the government's representative team, COCOPA, and the civil society group, CONAI, headed by Bishop Samuel Ruíz in September 1995, the growing emphasis by Zapatistas and their supporters on indigenous autonomy was apparent. The mediations culminated in the National Indigenous Forum convoked by the EZLN in January, 1996 in San Cristóbal, where the assembled group demonstrated the consensus they had reached in elaborating the proposal for autonomy (see chapter 4). This consensus carried the San Andrés Agreement signed between representatives of the government and the EZLN in February, 1996.

The San Andrés Agreement

In the course of the September 1995 dialogues between the Zapatistas and the government mediated by CONAI and COCOPA, autonomy was the principle focus of discussion. CEOIC's proposal for the creation of pluriethnic autonomous regions that laid the basis for the autonomy of the northern region also provided the basic plan presented in the dialogue. The plan proposed pluriethnic regions made up of all the *ejidos, colonias,* communities, and other entities in a region that would require the following organizations: 1) council of representatives, (2) executive coordination, (3) municipal indigenous council, 4) general assembly, and 5) executive commission of the *ejidos, colonias,* and communities. The proposal designated that there would be participation of the indigenous pueblos in federal and state representative organizations as well as the presence of deputies of pluriethnic regions in the Congress of the Union.

When the EZLN presented its proposal, patterned on that of the CEOIC, the government argued against regional representation, preferring to limit autonomy to the jurisdiction of the community. This has always been the preference of the central authority since the colonial period, because the limitation of autonomy to communities mitigates the effectiveness of indigenous people in a wider framework. The National Assembly of Indigenous People for Autonomy (ANIPA) proposed as a compromise the formation of an autonomous parliamentary group, with communities sending representatives who would then participate as members of the federal Congress in the context of this entity. Although some of the indigenous representatives felt that this backed away from the principal objective of gaining regional representation (Ruíz Hernández 1999:52), it was incorporated in the proposal as presented in the National Indigenous Forum in January 1996, and also in the San Andrés Agreement that was drawn up a month later (Díaz-Polanco 1997:191). The PRI government hailed the Agreement as "a new social pact with indigenous pueblos."

In the months following the signing of the agreement, the PRI government never implemented the constitutional amendments or the institutional framework proposed. Instead, Zedillo increased the military force deployed in the jungle, ignoring the pleas from many sectors of civil society to implement the agreement. In order to break the impasse, the EZLN, now constituted as the Zapatista Front for National Liberation, called the Intercontinental Convention in July 1996. The impressive show of national and international delegates failed to move the PRI government to meet a single condition for resuming the dialogues. These conditions were the withdrawal of the army from the Lacandón and implementation of the San Andrés Agreement. In August, the Zapatistas withdrew from further dialogues, calling the PRI's delaying actions a sham, given the reinforcement of the military in indigenous areas and the divisions it was trying to foster between the EZLN and revolutionary movements elsewhere in the country.

As tensions increased in the rain forest, both national and transnational civil society organizations rallied to the defense of settlements in the Lacandón rain forest, setting up peace camps to monitor the actions of the army that had taken up residence in their midst. In an attempt to counter the force of public opinion in a global system, the Mexican PRI government invoked national sovereignty, as federal armed forces, backed up by the National Immigration Services and Chiapas state police, limited access of reporters and human rights missions to conflict areas. After the 1997 massacre of Acteal, all these agencies stepped up the expulsions of foreigners suspected of engaging in political activities. This applied to a wide range of activities, from serving as human rights observers in the conflict zone to taking photographs of army personnel or demonstrations in San Cristóbal.[29]

Zedillo's Indigenous Law

In April 1998, the Mexican government accelerated its divisive strategies in civil society. At the same time as Zedillo tried to disqualify the National Commission for Mediation (CONAI), a group that was charged by the Salinas government with carrying out the peace negotiations in 1994, he introduced his Initiative for the Rights and Culture of Indians, often referred to as the Indigenous Law, on March 15, 1998. It was a proposal that captures the rhetoric but denies the intent of the San Andrés Agreement since it limits autonomy to the community level. The agreement had created, according to Carlos San Juan Victoria (*La Jornada* April 4, 1998:3–5):

> . . . a juridical niche of vital importance in the present situation of migration of these pueblos and of globalization processes committed to the natural and genetic richness of their territories. On the one hand, the Agreements had established the necessity of

recognizing the legal entity of the pueblos, and on the other they attached to this status territorial jurisdiction. With this they created the possibility that the pueblos, if they wished, could control their own resources, obviously within the framework of the actual laws on property, inheritance, and sovereignty of the state; they would determine local developments, they would be associated on the level of equality with investors and have the capacity to hold back the population. [Author's translation]

Hence the government was not willing to concede to its own peace agreement to recognize the collective rights of the indigenous pueblos. The EZLN became the rallying point for pueblos, organizations, and regional leaders of Indians integrated in the National Indigenous Congress to reject the Zedillo proposal.

Broad segments of civil society rejected President Zedillo's Indigenous Law when it was first proposed in March 1998. Jurisprudence experts pointed out that changes to the Constitution are a legislative, not an executive, prerogative. The strongest reaction against Zedillo's Indigenous Law came from the Catholic clergy, which condemned the president's unilateral action for undermining the negotiations and agreement of the past four years. The archbishop of Oaxaca and of Hermosillo, the co-acting bishops of San Cristóbal, and the bishop of Tuxtla Gutierrez all indicated their support of Bishop Ruíz's work in CONAI and expressed the opinion that if CONAI were dissolved, the peace process would be set back (*Cuarto Poder* April 2, 1998:8). Independent *campesino* organizations rallied to support the San Andrés Agreement: OCEZ said there would be no peace unless the government solved the demands of *campesinos*, adding that the government had only tried to divide the pueblo by strengthening paramilitary bands like the San Bartolomé Alliance of the Plains (*Cuarto Poder* April 2, 1998:20). The Independent Center of Agricultural Workers and Campesinos (CIOAC) rejected the government proposal for Rights and Culture of Indigenous Communities, asserting that only the COCOPA and the CONAI could settle the issues. ARIC–Union of Unions (or PRI wing) was the only major *campesino* organization to support the government initiative. This organization, now split from the main wing, ARIC Independent, which is associated with the EZLN, supports government policies that are dividing the once-unified Zapatista territory. The three major opposition parties, PRD, PAN, and Labor Party (PT), expressed their rejection of the president's proposal to dissolve CONAI, with the PAN issuing its own proposal for an indigenous law, and the PRD urging the implementation of the Agreements of San Andrés (*La Jornada* April 2, 1998:7). CONAI and the EZLN stated that they were unwilling to enter into further dialogues until the government activated programs responding to the agreements and until it guaranteed the safety of the EZLN leaders.

As organized sectors of civil society were coalescing against the government's counterproposal to its own agreements signed in San Andrés Larrainzar, the government escalated its counterattack (*La Jornada* April 4, 1998:4). Under the leadership of Francisco Labastida, then secretary of the interior, government spokespersons separated the agreement from the issue of autonomy that concerned the legal status and territorial jurisdiction of the indigenous pueblos. The massacre of Acteal took on a new meaning: the image of an intense social conflict in Chiapas was no longer projected as that between the gov-

ARIC members explained why they allowed the army to settle near their village of Patihuitz.

ernment and the demands of *campesino* organizations but rather between religious factions within the communities themselves. In the broadcasts of the official news channel,
Televisa, newscasters emphasized that Jacinto Arias, the president of Chenalhó, was a
Protestant and the community of Acteal was a Christian Base Community of Catholics,
drawing the conclusion that it was a religious war among indigenes. The government
then proceeded to expand its military encampments, with an estimated 10,000 more
troops in the rain forest, highland communities, and the northern region throughout the
spring of 1998 (*La Jornada* April 2, 1998;15). The government simultaneously launched
attacks meant to discredit the mediation councils, CONAI and COCOPA. Recognizing
the intransigence of the government in failing to enact the San Andrés Agreement,
Bishop Ruíz resigned from the CONAI shortly thereafter, thus effectively ending the
mediation by an external agency.

Despite the groundswell of support for the San Andrés Agreement and the rejection
of the government's counterproposal, the government persisted with its own Indigenous
Law. Individual states proposed their laws regarding the relationship of the state and
indigenous populations. Three years after the signing of the San Andrés Agreement, with

the agreement still in suspension and many of the leaders in those communities which were trying to enact the provisions in jail, the Chiapas governor Roberto Albores Guillén proposed his own Law of the Rights and Indigenous Culture of the State of Chiapas. Like Zedillo's proposal, it was shorn of references to regional representation of indigenous autonomy and lacked any provisions for ensuring respect for rights of self determination and autonomy.

Contrasting the Chiapas initiative with that of Oaxaca, Xóchitl Leyva, Mercedes Olivera, and Aracely Burguete, all of whom have carried out extensive investigations among indigenous peoples, indicate the lack of legal specification of what the relationship between the state and the "indigenous pueblo," "indigenous comunity," and "habitat" would entail (*La Jornada* March 28, 1999). They show that the government sidestepped the legal issues involved by limiting its attention to customs and practices at a "cultural level," without concretizing steps to institutionalize the changes demanded by the indigenous movement.[30] The government ignored precedents in the International Labor Organization's Convention 169 on the rights of indigenous populations to the land and resources within their habitat. Instead, officials concentrated only on the penalties attached to committing "environmental abuses," detailing the justification for military intervention if these should occur. Recalling the forestry agent, El Señor Milagro, who was scorned for his demand of thousands of pesos in bribes in Amatenango in the 1960s, I could imagine how the law would be administered in the Lacandón rain forest!

At the height of tensions in April 1998, proselytizers of new religions were entering Chiapas. What were described in the Tuxtla Gutiérrez press as "militant groups" of Seventh Day Adventists arrived in April 1998, disseminating literature attacking "corrupt bishops," a theme which was quickly picked up by the paramilitary group Peace and Justice that was operating in the northern region. The secretary general of the Committee of Evangelical Defense in Chiapas brought legal assistance for the Protestant men of Chenalhó, who had been accused of massacring the refugees in Acteal. In addition to these new Protestant groups, "militant" Muslims arrived in San Cristóbal de Las Casas and began their missionizing (*Proceso* April 5, 1998). Domíngo Angel López, the Chamulan evangelical leader who founded the Protestant organization CRIACH, had converted to the Muslim faith and was bringing some of his followers from the Protestant church with him before his jailing. Ironically, the government, which was attributing the conflicts to religious competition, was allowing these new proselytizers to enter and to carry on their activities at a time when most foreigners in human rights groups were being restricted.

Local commentators pointed to the irony of the fact that the Immigration and National Service was granting visas to these dissident religious groups at a time when the government was still blaming the Acteal conflict on religious conflict and when international peace activists were being denied admission because of the conflict. Until 1994, the religious confrontations in indigenous communities tended to be intracommunal differences that ended with expulsions. Increasingly, the conflict among religious groups appeared to be promoted by government intervention sowing discord in indigenous communities. In the past four years, according to the director of the Center for

Human Rights "Fray Bartolomé de Las Casas" (quoted in *Proceso* April 5, 1998:6 *et seq.*), organized violence, responding to what he called "religious groups that are the instrument of governmental as well as transnational powers," has been carried out against Catholic churches, and in two cases against Protestant churches. In a report sent to the secretary of government, the diocese indicated that 36 churches had been burned or profaned, in some cases by federal troops (*La Jornada* April 5, 1998:5,6). It was, indeed, difficult to deny the allegation that the government was promoting these religious divisions.

The opposition of these religious and human rights protagonists in an enlarged arena of an embattled civil society will have profound consequences for the future of ethnic groups throughout Mexico. In the breakdown of PRI hegemonic accord and the escalating conflict experienced throughout the country, some elements of civil society have attempted to maintain space for dialogue and negotiations for "peace with justice." Opposing factions seized the phrasing in their call for "peace and justice," but it failed to legitimize the waning power of the PRI.

INDIGENOUS MOBILIZATION OF CIVIL SOCIETY

response to militarization

In the midst of this political and religious fractionating, indigenous pueblos were extending their ourtreach through their regional and national organizations. They were exhibiting new levels of restraint in the face of stepped-up military repression by the state. And despite all odds, they were confronting the power of the PRI openly, in public marches that put their lives in jeopardy. In the process of revolutionary change, they were moving forward the agenda of full participation in civil society.

Multiple Fronts and Pluriethnic Actors

With the army restricting the movement of Zapatistas out of the rain forest and inhibiting their mobilization of conventions within their territory, the EZLN tested the outermost boundaries of their political action while indigenous *campesino* groups carried out protests and civil disobedience in the pueblos. In these actions we can appreciate the significance of their collective action as "bees" and "ants," as they challenged what they considered illegitimate force.

In an attempt to overcome the repression of the Zapatista movement and the influence of the army, indigenous and *campesino* groups organized on several fronts in the spring of 1998. The National Indigenous Congress (CNI) emerged as the prime coordinating group for those pressing for the implementation of the San Andrés Agreement. At the same time as the government was escalating its campaign against the indigenous population, the National Indigenous Congress organized a major assembly of Tlapanecos, Mixtecos, Mayos, Yaquis, Nahuas, Otomies, Zapotecas, Mayans, Tzeltales, Tzotziles, Triquis, Amuzgos, and Mixes in support of the San Andrés Accord. This took place in the Mexico City *Zocálo* on April 10, 1998. Since the indigenous movement was distancing itself from government, no non-Indians were invited (*La Jornada* April 11, 1998:3). The meeting demonstrated the growing civil society initiatives of pan-Indian organizations, independent of the Zapatistas and other guerrilla groups in Guerrero and Oaxaca.

On other fronts, rank-and-file members of *campesino* organizations maintained their protests against arrests made by the government and harassment by paramilitaries. On June 8, 1998, the military directly attacked *campesinos* meeting in El Bosque, a hamlet of Unión Progreso in the northern region, killing one and taking eight men in custody. Two days later, the bodies of the eight taken to prison were returned to the village. Members of the National Commission on Human Rights delivered the severely mutilated bodies, which were in an advanced state of decay. As the villagers gathered around the vans that delivered the corpses, the lamentations of the mourners turned to rage. Clearly the government had prevailed upon the National Human Rights Commission to attend to the bodies in fear of another outburst of violence. Although some of the crowd turned against the human rights agents, the voices of two indigenous members of the community, a man and a woman, urging them to control their wrath against those who were not directly responsible, prevailed. In this incident, the army and state security agencies acted directly, and not behind the usual screen provided by paramilitary groups (Centro de Derechos Humanos "Fray Bartolomé de Las Casas" Archives).

Despite the increased severity of the repression, the jailing or deportation of members of national and transnational support groups, and the constant harassment of foreigners by government agents of the *National Immigration Service* and the military, grassroot groups of *campesinos* continued to stage public demonstrations to present their case to a wider public. On June 22, 1998, I witnessed a demonstration of about 300 *campesinos* from indigenous communities that took place in San Cristóbal. Many of the participants were from Amatenango del Valle and San Nicolás, two of the communities that had declared themselves autonomous. I saw the leaders of the local pottery cooperative with about 20 of the women members walking behind the town's garbage truck driven by the PRD president, my old landlord's formerly timid son-in-law. I understood the dangers they were facing: a military force mobilized to confront civil society directly, an enraged *coleto* society in San Cristóbal eager to push indigenes back into their positions of subordination, and the menace of paramilitaries within their own communities when they returned home.

After their march through the town, they converged on the plaza of the cathedral at sundown and presented their cases against the government. The leader of the Social Sellers, a group of market vendors in San Cristóbal, ascended the podium and spoke of the group's concern that they were being forced into the new high-rent stands in the market area built under a misguided development scheme. As the crowd of marchers found their place in the plaza, another speaker addressed them with "a manifesto against the unstated war by the police and the military against the communities of Chavajel and Unión Progreso." The speakers evoked the horror of the cadavers of indigenous leaders killed "in the style of the [Guatamalan] *kabiles* and desecrated by police [which delivered] a message of terror against the civilian population and a new stage in the war against the pueblo." Their call for respect for "the sovereignty of our state [of Chiapas] as a condition to arrive at democracy" raised the level of demand for autonomy to the statewide level. The meeting in San Cristóbal was coordinated with meetings in all the major cities of Chiapas. Partici-pating activists agreed on the basic premises for civilian consensus, stated in a flier dis-tributed to the crowd: 1) removal of the governor, Albores Guillén, 2) an end to the war and its use of thousands of military and police against indigenous populations, and 3) release of the dozens of prisoners taken in the state. A young woman ended with a pas-sionate plea:

> The government thought that civil society had ended because there have been no manifestations. We still exist! We still live! We come here from various communities: San Nicolás Ruíz, Amatenango del Valle, the barrios of San Cristóbal. We must go on although the government has made us fear for our lives! [Xeroxed flyer, Author's translation]

Although participants came from distinct organizations, the assembly was clearly a civil society mobilization with a wide range of issues and distinct levels of political conscious-ness manifested.

The Zapatistas as the Cupola of Campesino and Indigenous Movements in Civil Society

During the lull in EZLN mobilizations of civil society after 1996, it was possible to see more clearly the role they had played vis-á-vis *campesino* and indigenous organizations. We have seen how the National Indigenous Forum, convoked by the EZLN in January 1996, began the conversion of the EZLN to the Zapatista National Liberation Front. In July 1996, the Autonomous University of Chiapas conducted a series of meetings in San Cristóbal. Jorge Elorriaga, the filmmaker who had been jailed just prior to the invasion of the rain forest in February 1995, and who had just been released, took a prominent role in the forum, even upstaging *Subcomandante* Marcos. This effort to become a civilian front to forge a democratic movement culminated in the Intercontinental Encounter against Neoliberalism and for Humanity in August 1996 (chapter 4). But when the government persistently failed to implement the San Andrés Agreement, and with the ever greater encroachment of the army into the rain forest, the political transformation was cut short. The EZLN announced in August 1996 that it could no longer maintain the fiction of peaceful negotiations. In the following months, the government expanded its military operations by arming civilian adherents in the highland villages. The Acteal massacre was the startling revelation of this maneuver in December 1997. The worldwide attention to the event probably discouraged an expansion of this tactic by the government.

In order to put into effect the San Andrés Agreement to accord autonomy to indige-nous pueblos, the EZLN then took action on other fronts. On April 7, 1998, the high command inaugurated the autonomous municipality of Flores Magón, which incorpo-rated fifty hamlets, and a week later created twenty new municipalities. The government responded by arresting a professor of the Autonomous University of Chiapas who was assisting the settlers in an art project in one of the autonomous hamlets, and by expelling many foreigners. A massive force of federal soldiers and state police were deployed in the Ocosingo, area where the autonomy movement was spreading (*La Jornada* April 10, 1998:7). The official government position aired in the media was increasingly xenophobic, blaming foreign instigators for the divisions in the countryside. Communication was nearly cut off between Zapatista colonies of the rain forest and the highland communities in support.

The EZLN engagement with civil society got another boost during the spring equinox of 1999, when the Zapatistas broke free of the army encirclement in order to promote a national consultation. The event, which took place throughout Easter week, involved the mobilization of thousands of civil society activists promoting cultural celebrations and negotiations between foreign ambassadors, business leaders, and schoolteachers throughout the country. It was an extraordinary moment in Mexico's history to have such an encounter, initiated by the indigenous population. *Proceso* (March 14, 1999, pp. 32–33) called it "a rupture with the military confrontation that the government postulates as the premise for confrontation and a reinforcement of the proposals for constitutional change."

The Zapatistas supporters held meetings in the cathedral plaza throughout the week on March 21. They distributed a questionnaire designed to assess the interest in the response of citizens to the proposal that "indigenous pueblos be included in the national project, with recognition of their rights in the Constitution conforming to the Accord of San Andrés." This abrupt change in pace from the government's militarization and repression that had preoccupied the media was a welcome break, allowing people to consider alternative paths for the settlement of the ongoing conflict.

I had just arrived in San Cristóbal on March 15, 1999, when I saw a small crowd gathered to watch a tall young man wearing a rainbow headband light a fire in a brazier before the wooden cross in the center of the cathedral plaza. He announced "Now, as the sun is going down, we light the fire to ensure that it will return to give life to our crops. We will unite our force as to how we will live as a country with the opening of the *consulta*. We will not achieve peace until we recognize the indigenous pueblos. Until we Mexicans unite to make the government understand that all of us have this goal, we will not be able to achieve a just peace." He ended by saying that the consultation would continue until the equinoxon the 21st of March.

The Zapatistas, including six women and six men, arrived after this strange prelude[31] and took their seats in the tent that had been their meeting place for the months of turmoil from 1997 to 1999. It had been torn down by a relative of the mayor not long before and reconstructed for the occasion. The Zapatista representatives, wearing ski masks, began their address with a tape recording from *Comandante* Tacho. Paraphrasing his statement, he made the following points:

> Civil Society has given us the desire to unite. It was the government's failure to address the pressing needs of the settlers that forced us to rise up in arms. Through this consultation we hope to open a dialogue with you as brothers and sisters who have the

Zapatista men and women visited San Cristóbal de Las Casas for the consultation of 1999.

same problems. By uniting our force, we will organize peacefully, politically. That is why they repress us. They do not have the will for peace. We want to live in peace.

Leaflets were distributed, one with a poem of Arnoldo Chavez Rodríguez of Sinaloa, along with a statement about building society grain by grain to form a beach. The questions to be voted on in the referendum were printed on flyers that were distributed to the audience, which had grown to about fifty people. They were as follows:

- Are you in agreement that the *pueblos indígenas* ought to be included with all their force and richness in the national project and to take an active part in the construction of a new Mexico?
- Are you in agreement that the indigenous rights ought to be recognized in the Mexican constitution in accord with the agreements of San Andrés and the proposal of the COCOPA of the Congress of the Union?
- Are you in agreement that we ought to reach a true Peace by the means of dialogue, demilitarizing the country and returning the soldiers to their barracks, as is established in the Constitution and in the laws of the nation?
- Are you in agreement that we ought to organize and urge the government to govern by commanding while obeying in ALL aspects of national life?

After the ten delegates had delivered their message to the assembled citizens, a group of schoolteachers, their pupils, and residents of a barrio of *mestizos* presented a dance and poetry recitation for the Zapatistas. One of the young Zapatista men thanked the school-children, and with tears in his eyes, said that this could never have been done in the rain forest since there were no teachers or schools. In a town where racial discrimination had prevailed in its most intense forms for almost five hundred years, I saw an exchange of sympathy and goodwill between Indians and *mestizos* that dispelled the divisions that had excluded Indians from their place in civil society.

Among the many encounters between the 5,000 men and women from the Lacandón rain forest and the Mexicans during the following week, there were some crucial encounters that demonstrated significant support for the Zapatistas. A retired general in the diplomatic corp of the government admitted that their cause was just and that he favored a new role for the Mexican army. Zapatistas had a meeting that was organized by an entrepreneur with members of the Club of Industrialists. Other members of civil society organized a meeting with the ambassadors of France and Poland. The demonstration of fraternity between national and international leaders and the Zapatistas indicated that there is broad support in civil society for the peaceful integration of the indigenous as equal citizens (*La Jornada* March 20, 1999:6; March 21, 1999:14). Given their experiences with the armed forces in the rain forest, the consultation had remarkable success in underlining the Zapatistas' willingness to endure aggravated attacks to bring about a just peace. Yet despite its success, it did not divert the government from the militaristic path it had chosen. The army exerted even more pressure on the civilian population in the Lacandón rain forest, and parallel military units continued to harass the populations of pueblos in the northern region.

The CIOAC and the Bees in Multiple Confrontations with PRI Officials

With the EZLN demobilized by the low-intensity warfare, the *campesinos* and indigenous organizations took over like an army of bees and ants, mobilizing on many fronts, sustaining simultaneous actions against corrupt civil officials in countless towns, and demanding the intervention of the State Prosecutor's Office. The CIOAC was remarkably successful in sustaining participation of its pluricultural constituents during the stalemate. When the government failed to implement the principles of regional autonomy, the CIOAC became the key organization in defining forms of civil disobedience. Pushing the boundaries of its organization beyond the concern for land restitution and the specific claims of producer organizations, the CIOAC began in the spring of 2000 to demand appointments for its members in the governing bodies in the municipalities of Ocosingo and Las Margaritas.

The local-level encounters were carved out independently by CIOAC local groups but were clearly coordinated throughout the state. On March 24, the CIOAC posted guards at the Altamirano town hall, announcing that they would remain there until the mayor, Abelino López Cruz, left the building. Complaining that the mayor had diverted over $8,620,000 pesos designated for public works to his personal use, they announced that no funds were available for projects in the year 2000. On the same day, social organizations and political parties, including PRI, in communities within the municipality of Ocosingo announced that they had come to the realization that "the confidence they placed in Gutiérrez Cruz [the mayor] was lost" (*Cuarto Poder* March 24, 2000:15).

Simultaneously members of CIOAC had been carrying out similar actions for a month in Ixtapa in the Northern Autonomous Region, where they succeeded in getting one of their members included as a member of the direction of public works. The spokesman for CIOAC, Victor Pérez López, told reporters of *Cuarto Poder* (March 24, 2000:9) that CIOAC was urging the State Prosecutor's Office in Ocosingo to hold a hearing in order to demonstrate that the organization had reason to call for the mayor's dismissal. One of the CIOAC members guarding the Ixtapa town hall, Gloria Ampara López H, was severely beaten and held in the police station for hours without medical attention. Members of CIOAC brought the violent attacks to the attention of the National Commission on Human Rights and to the State Prosecutor's Office, and at the same time objected to the racism that was rampant in the treatment of *campesinos* in state offices and at the local level. During the days that followed, officials of local government allied with the mayor increased their attacks on CIOAC militants in Ixtapa (*Cuarto Poder* March 29, 2000:18).

The repression failed to deter hundreds of *campesinos* from 23 of the rural hamlets of Ocosingo from converging on the town hall of Ocosingo on March 28, 2000. There they demanded the dismissal of the mayor, Adolfo Gutiérrez Cruz, whom they charged with diversion of public funds for the purchase of a Chevrolet Blazer (the preferred vehicle of the ranchers in the rain forest), and for the sexual abuse of indigenous girls. The *campesinos'* protests against the actions of state police in the Prosecutor's Office raised, for the first time to my knowledge, the charge of racism directed at the mayor and his collaborators in the town hall (*Cuarto Poder* March 29, 2000:12).

In a state accustomed to rule by violence, these local confrontations were changing a whole paradigm of behaviors that had maintained the ruling power in control of the state apparatus. People in San Cristóbal with whom I spoke remarked that the lawyers assigned the State Prosecutor's Office were calling their critics delinquents, when those who were within the office were in fact the delinquents. Many criticized the greater attention to the safety of PRI officials than to their adversaries in the conflicts that occurred in many localities. The criticism came at a time when polls in the state gubernatorial election indicated a tilting toward the Opposition Alliance, made up of PAN, PRD, PT, and Green Action, who were maintaining a solid front to defeat the PRI. The Civic Alliance candidate, Pablo Salazar, responded to the dissent of the CIOAC, admonishing the mayor for using violence to solve the conflict rather than trying peaceful solutions to the problem.

The Bees became a leading advocate for civil rights against the paramiliatries following the Acteal massacre in which 45 of their members, mostly women and children, were killed. They played an important role in organizing the poll watchers in the elections of August 2000. A contingent of their members went to the United States on August 3, 2000, to demonstrate before the White House, protesting the presence of the former governor of Chiapas in the Mexican embassy. They also decried the role of the U.S. Army's in training officers of the Mexican army, some of whom they claimed were involved in training of the paramilitaries in the Acteal massacre. (*Cuarto Poder* August 11,

Campesinos and indigenes protest government on many fronts.

2000:23). The conjuncture of U.S. trained military in counterinsurgency operations is a new development in Mexico.

The kind of flexible networks of shifting alliances and diverse interests sponsored by indigenous *campesino* organizations were increasingly successful in confronting the PRI monopoly of power. The carefully documented criticisms and disciplined objections by CIOAC members recalled the centuries of protests by Morelos *campesinos* that Warman (1980) documented in his book, *We Come to Object*. A major difference in the presentation of their case in the twenty-first century from that of the past two centuries is the *campesinos'* rejection of the racism implicit in the official behaviors they confront. This change mirrors the transformation in self-perception among indigenous subjects that is occurring along with the increasing success of their struggles to change society.

CONVERGENCE OF HUMAN RIGHTS NGOs AND CIVIL SOCIETY

Indigenous people are increasingly appealing to human rights accords, thereby gaining support from international agencies (Kearney 1995). Third World people, and particularly the "Fourth World" (Graburn 1976) enclaves of indigenous people living within them, are just now seeking the "Rights of Man" proclaimed in the French and American revolutions. Revolutionary groups in their midst add to those proclamations of liberty, justice and equality of the eighteenth century, the collective rights to social and cultural programs that were central to the Russian Revolution in 1917. Because these populations often live in the last remaining rain forests or in sites rich in unexploited natural resources, their rights to retain their habitations are threatened by the latest incursions of lumber and oil predators. They are more likely to cast their demands in terms of global rights to peace, development, a healthy balanced ecology, and the right to share the common heritage of mankind.[32] These global rights have yet to be adopted by the United States. As civil society expands to include more populations of the "Fourth World," questions of whose values are to prevail will be phrased in terms of how these covenants will embrace pluricultural values.

The Vienna Declaration on Human Rights in 1993 challenged the concept of rights phrased in terms of individuals with its promotion of communal values. This new declaration rejects the way in which civil and political rights have been phrased by Western powers in terms of freedom of speech, assembly, and religion for the individual, since they were deemed to be antithetical to communalistic aspirations. This poses a dilemma: the communalistic aims of the dominant group within any community can, in the reinterpretation of human rights, deny what univeralistic prescriptions might consider the human rights of minority groups or individual persons within that community. As Kovic (1997:186 *et seq.*) indicates in her study of a Catholic Base Community made up of indigenous people expelled from Chamula, the very communities which were forced into exile on the basis of their violation of traditional values are now excluding other indigenous people for lack of conformity to the norms of the new community. To uphold communalistic ideals as the ultimate arbiter will inevitably result in such cross-cutting claims.

This clash between universal and particular values occurs within groups as well as between culturally distinct groups when gender and age are taken into account. I have observed that women were most frequently the dissidents in those discussions that called for a return to "tradition" during the National Indigenous Congress. For them, tradition marked a patriarchal power elite within indigenous communities that forced them to conform to the power of a male elite (Nash 1997b). When grassroots movements converge, as in the protest of June 22, 1998, that I describe above, the particular merges with the universal as the claims of poor market vendors to keep their posts in the old market merge with the plea to end the war raised by other speakers at that event. Frequently these "lesser voices" are lost as a movement gains power, but their claims are the elemental challenges for justice that ignite social movements.

An ever-present hurdle to advancing an international human rights agenda is the fact that the implementation of United Nations covenants depends on the very nation states that are often the major perpetrators of the violations. Yet the covenants provide a basis for outlawing "rogue" states in the developing global arenas, especially in trade agreements, embargoed weapons inspection, and other spaces where nations have in the past agreed to disagree. This is precisely the arena in which transnational civil society is expanding as it tries to counter the violence generated by nation-states that have lost their exclusive hold on the legitimate exercise of power. The new thrust in human rights conventions, in declaring the rights of people to peace, proposes to curb the foundations of the absolute sovereignty of nations: the use of armed force against civilian populations, arbitrary arrests, torture, covert operations, the denial of their own civil laws, and the exercise of other forms of brute force in order to maintain the power of established elites. While recognition of the economic, social, and cultural rights of all members of the human family is posed as the foundation for international peace in the Universal Declaration of Human Rights, attempts to add to this list the "Right of Peoples to Peace" as constituting a fundamental obligation of each state has never been formalized (Forsythe 1992:4). Given the proclivity of nation-states to turn to militarism in their waning days, it should move into top priority for transnational civil society, but it may never appear on the agenda of the United Nations. The potential of transnational civil society in gaining the compliance of nations with these covenants is evident in the response to the presence of international groups, as though they constitute a threat for nationalistic interests.

The transnational human rights networks established by NGOs are instrumental in alerting members of a wider public to the need to mobilize international opinion and activity. The United Nations High Commissioner for Human Rights Mary Robinson suggested that the Acteal massacre called for a special report. The United Nations considered a proposal to have a permanent office in Chiapas, responding to the many human rights abuses reported by NGOs in the area (*La Jornada* April 1, 1998:3). Throughout the month of April 1998, contingents of foreign human rights observers were detained in jail and finally expelled from the country on the charge that they were violating visa limitations, although the group of 114 Italians who were expelled on May 8, 1998, had their documents in order.[33] While the governments of countries attacked for violations see the presence of these human rights observers as a violation of national sovereignty, the "nations" they claim to be defending are often controlled by a narrow elite. In Mexico, the PRI that once stood for the nation represents a diminishing sector that lost the presidential elections of July 2000.

In the process of organizing and carrying out the dialogues with government representatives detailed in the previous chapter, a massive civil society movement has grown up, linking transnational NGOs with Mexicans. This became visible with the negotiations of March 1994 in the San Cristóbal cathedral, when hundreds of citizens took up positions in a security chain to prevent acts of violence. In subsequent dialogues and conventions, I became increasingly aware of the highly mobilized sectors of San Cristóbal society—the diocese human rights activists, educators, civil servants, and some global tourists coordinated through peace NGOs. Most of the supporters were not so much supporters of the armed uprising of the EZLN as they were sympathetic to the right of indigenous people to state their demands. In the subsequent conventions described in the previous chapter, the EZLN support group gained new adherents. The thousands of delegates that attended these events participated in the formulation of policies. A global contingent of sympathizers and supporters rallied from Europe and North and South America, as well as neighboring Central American states who maintained contact through the Internet. This virtual civil society would have meant nothing if it were not for the indigenous men and women who endured hours of standing in the blazing sun and tropical downpours that caused the tourists who had joined the lines to seek shelter. Women carrying babies, food supplies and water for their families walked hours to participate in the "fiesta of the word"—the dialogues that were to chart a new course for the nation. Many of them were for the first time participating as members of civil society. They will not easily be excluded from the pluricultural society they are helping to form.

In each of the assemblies, the participants formed bonds that affirmed their role in a broader civil society. Each of these meetings involved thousands of hours of labor to construct the shelters and provision the delegates. It brought together women who rarely left their communities and men whose political contacts with regional confederations now extended to statewide entities. From the first National Democratic Convention, the delegates supported a clear break with political parties and called for a transitional government with candidates free of party commitments. Amado Avendaño, editor of the San Cristóbal newspaper, *El Tiempo*, and former director of the Human Rights Center "Fray Bartolomé de Las Casas," who became the Civil Society candidate for Governor of Chiapas in the 1994 elections, was among the pioneers in civil society to embrace the opening of a multiethnic policy. He embodies in his own life the larger issues confronting Chiapas as civil society broke from the political parties that had dominated the public arena. From the accident that nearly took his life during his gubernatorial campaign in July 1994, to his publication of *El Tiempo* with indigenous news that has been put on the Internet and disseminated throughout the world, he and his wife are emblematic of the changing indigenous relations with *ladinos*.

With all the media attention to the conflict, indigenous people learned of the widespread support for their movement. National and international press coverage reflected a very different image of themselves from that conveyed by provincial society (Nash 1997c). The international observers were, in turn, impressed by the commitment of indigenous people and their serious intent. They no longer perceived indigenes as the marginalized "tribal" or "peasant" populations that were fixed in the public imagination by anthropologists half a century ago. The emergence of indigenes as political subjects in these settings indicated their changed status, even though the government refused to comply with the accords that the president had signed. They represent the vanguard of social transformations that are challenging the racial hierarchies of the last five hundred years.

CONCLUSION

Civil society in countries with indigenous enclaves that are demanding an equal place as citizens has a different dynamic from that which took into account only people of the same ethnic group, gender, and class. The process of gaining pluricultural recognition requires a redefinition of the constitution of civil society. Religion is often central to the promotion of the pluricultural basis for civil society, since it was one of the few institutions of Western domination that recognized the common humanity of the indigenous peoples with whom its agents worked. The objections registered by sixteenth-century priests to the unbridled cruelty of colonizers promoted legislation by the Spanish Crown that is a precursor to human rights legislation. What became the moral basis for civil society in succeeding generations often stemmed from that encounter in which the

Christian message of spiritual equality found a ready audience among indigenous leaders, who recognized in it a force for reconciliation.

The breakdown of the economic and political supports for semisubsistence small-plot cultivation that provided the substantive base for the institutional revolutionary communities precipitated the present crisis of state in Mexico. Recognizing the disaffection within official *campesino* organizations, the PRI promoted regional organizations that became the basis for opposition to the hegemonic institutions of the PRI. Divisions among sectors of civil society are now aggravated by the PRI government's arming of some of its supporters in a parallel civilian military force that extends the militarization of the state into the highlands. The instincts the PRI had shown in building consensus in the heyday of its hegemonic control over the political process continued to serve the government as it began to foment divisions among the civil society sectors that were beginning to oppose its hegemony. The militarization of those divisive sectors extended military repression by the army in the rain forest.

Civil society is acquiring a transnational base as secular and religious NGOs join organized sectors of Mexican society to renegotiate indigenous relations with the nation. After a four-year effort to document human rights violations in the undeclared war, the international NGOs, including Global Exchange, Pastors for Peace, and Amnesty International, came under attack by the Mexican government. Their challenge to Mexican "sovereignty" in the conflict zone provoked the use of massive military force to exile foreigners, including priests of long residence in the country and recent arrivals who joined the peace camps. The PRI government's attempt to curb surveillance by human rights organizations by restricting visa and harassing any foreigners who wandered beyond tourist sites ended with the inauguration of Vincente Fox on December 8, 2000. He opened the door to international observers, and reaffirmed the role of Mexican human rights groups, including the Human Rights Center "Fray Bartolomé de Las Casas", and the National Commission of Human Rights—which was a construct of the PRI government but has taken its responsibility to review violations seriously. So long as the PRI maintained a monopoly of state power, the decline in their hegemony presaged the decline of the nation. Despite the control of the party over television, and funding for political candidacies and diversion of public funds, the successful candidacy of the opposition National Action Party (PAN brought about the downfall of PRI hegemony. It is unlikely that the PRI can continue to rely on their indigenous adherents who are fearful of losing their privileged position.

Military forces in Chiapas competed with civil society as the army attempted to validate its presence through a pseudo-development role in which soldiers are taking over civilian positions. This was the Zapatistas' major condition for resumption of peace negotiations following the victory of PAN. The other conditions were release of Zapatistas imprisoned during the undeclared war, and implementation of the 1996 San Andrés Accords. The future role of the army is being reassessed as military check points are being withdrawn from the Lancandón rain forest and highland pueblos. Yet the PRI still retains control of 102 of the 111 Chiapas municipalities, and the San AndrésAgreements will not easily be passed since Fox's party, the PAN, controls only 46 of the 150 senate seats and 207 of the 500 congressional seats. By habituating people to the ubiquitous presence of the military, the government hoped to overcome the resistance of the people and undermine their ability to manage their own lives. This was combined with a concerted attempt to spread violence by arming progovernment paramilitary groups that escalate the violence against civilian populations. As Guatemala shows, the arbitrary use of violence against a population may cultivate the kind of despair that can destroy the basis for resistance (Warren 1993). Aware of the corrosive effects of militarism in counterinsurgent warfare, women's groups in Mexico, both at a national and local level, mobilized to reinforce the resistance of colonizers in the Lacandón rain forest (Rojas 1995).

In order to understand the remarkable genesis of civil society action in many areas in the world where internecine conflict is occurring, we need to cultivate a multicultural perspective. Social contract theorists from the seventeenth century to the nineteenth century emphasized rational solutions brought about through the evolution of legal codes, taking for granted the moral commitments inhering in primordial groups. The assumptions of Locke and Ferguson were that civil society represented the unencumbered will of the people. But the civil society they envisioned did not include racial and ethnic divisions, and it hardly took into account the gender and class divisions that were part of their society. As this account of the government's actions in the escalating violence following the refusal of the Zedillo government to meet the conditions of the San Andrés Accords shows, civil society can be manipulated. Elements of civil society favorable to the PRI, armed by the security agents of the national government and trained by soldiers of the National Armed Forces, were convicted for the Acteal massacre. Although indigenous people were the main victims of the violence, they undeniably contributed to the escalation of the war in Chiapas.

Indigenous people who have maintained a collective identity even within repressive states are becoming leaders, sometimes in the spaces opened up by transnational civil society and, now increasingly, in the self-constituted autonomous territories. The society of semiautonomous multicultural entities that they are seeking to construct within a national federation of ethnic groups is based on their resistance to domination in 500 years of colonization and independence. From its very genesis, women were an important constituent in formulating the indigenous version of a multiethnic society with pluricultural autonomy. This vision is more adapted to the emerging global ecumene than the neoliberal program that relies on militarized nation-states and a growing gap between rich and poor.

The conjuncture of women's demands for social justice in the home and in the wider society coupled with the forceful demands by *campesinos* for inclusion in civil society on their own terms as ethnically distinct citizens has shaken the hegemonic control of the Institutional Revolutionary Party more than at any period in its seven decades of ascendance. Indigenous women's rejection of gender subordination, which was made explicit with the announcement in January 1994 of the New Law of Women in the ranks of the EZLN, is now being played out in public and private arenas, as women address their rights while demanding greater responsibility. As they become significant agents for change in their own liberation and in the *campesino* alliances along with men, their struggles threaten the hegemonic alliance of indigenous men with power brokers in the national parties. This provokes latent gender hostility, particularly of youths who no longer can look to the patrimony of the state to secure land and ensure themselves a place in society. With few economic opportunities available, they sometimes become partisans in the low-intensity warfare waged by paramilitary and military forces. The fourteen- and fifteen- year-old youths among the men who attacked the predominantly female congregation in Acteal enacted the rage of a generation of men who can no longer count on the prerogatives of their sex or the opportunism of their elders. Whether the transfer of power from the PRI to the PAN in the year 2001 will be peaceful will depend on whether the new government will take into consideration the demands of civil society for a just settlement of the agrarian conflict.

The Chiapas case expands our view of civil society by addressing the potential for both pluricultural coexistence and divisive conflict within and between ethnic enclaves. It provokes us to develop multiple visions for transforming patriarchal and ethnic hierarchies. This will be developed in chapter 6, which will further explore anthropological approaches to the study of gender, ethnicity, and class movements in the global ecumene.

CHAPTER 6

PLURICULTURAL SURVIVAL
IN THE GLOBAL ECUMENE

ANTHROPOLOGICAL VISIONS OF the Mayans are responding to the expanding horizons of the indigenous world in the late twentieth century. Community boundaries exist as one of a number of reference points in which indigenous people establish multiple coexisting relations with regional organizations of *campesinos* and *mestizos,* national political parties, government bureaucracies, the federal armed forces, transnational human rights groups, religious sodalities, and economic enterprises that are now part of their world.

The "holistic relations" that we once pretended to comprehend in the context of communities must now take these widespread ramifications into account. This was always necessary to comprehend the forces that impinged on communities, but long before NAFTA and the negation of land reform, indigenous people carried out a local politics that denied their dependency on national and transnational levels of governance. Caught up in this circumscribed worldview that we were trying to share, anthropologists sometimes neglected the impact of a world that we, too, were often escaping. Since the 1980s, externally generated changes that had always influenced the politics of every day life became undeniable. Subsistence crops grown on *ejido* lands respond to world commodity prices, as does artisan production, once limited to personal use, now that regional exchange takes on a new importance as sales to museums and tourist outlets bring in more income for the increasing cash needs of households. Indigenous people no longer seek retreat from a threatening *ladino* presence, but their attempts to participate in civil society on their own terms have been met by increased repression. The prevalence of federal troops in barracks located in conflict areas throughout the state and of armed tanks and personnel carriers on highways is a reminder of the ongoing conflict between indigenous communities and the state, as Mayans contest the terms of ethnic gender and class hierarchies.

These changes have wide-ranging ramifications for the household organization of production, gender relations, and social reproduction. Local politics take on international dimensions as indigenous leaders bring their claims against local, state, and national officials to international human rights forums. Their struggle for land as *pueblos indios* in the context of nationalist co-optive policies is turning into a war for the autonomy of territories in the global context of human rights declarations.

The task of anthropology is no longer one of salvaging waning traditions,[1] but of catching up with the frontiers in global integration now being forged by indigenous

ments. This requires a transformation of anthropological interpretations to
f the global issues confronting the subjects of our studies. The contribution
us subjects to global studies comes from their ability to envision a world in
which distinct cultural formations can coexist within a global ecumene. The "despon-
dency" theory, as Marshall Sahlins (1998) calls the anticipated end of culturally distinctive groups, is denied by the social movements of indigenous groups that are seeking
multicultural coexistence. Even when their attempts to transform their conditions
within nation-states provoke ethnocidal and genocidal attacks, they are reasserting the
value of their cultural traditions. Guatemala's thirty-year civil war may seem to be a
warning to others attempting to renegotiate change within the nations in which they
coexist as a stigmatized minority. Yet, despite the damage that Mayans experienced in
that war,[2] they are trespassing national boundaries to forge a pan-Mayan movement and
bring their plea for multicultural coexistence to an international audience.[3]

Some indigenous movements in the Americas have achieved direct representation
within their nations as distinct cultural entities, such as the Inuit of Canada, the Miskito of
Nicaragua, the Quichua of Ecuador, and the Indigenous Territorial Entities (*Entidades Ter-
ritoriales Indígenas*) of Colombia. Many other indigenous peoples are still striving to gain
greater autonomy as pluricultural entities within the nations in which they are encapsulated. These are not static demands, and the statement of goals is a reflexive response to
the government's actions as well as to transnational indigenous mobilizations and international human rights accords. Mayans of Chiapas, who constitute a quarter of the 12 million indigenous people in Mexico, persisted in their allegiance to the state even after the
New Year's Eve uprising. This may change as their struggle for greater autonomy, which
seemed to have been realized with the agreements signed by the government in San
Andrés in 1996, is countered by military repression.

The resolution of the demands of indigenous peoples for multicultural coexistence is
critical for the transformation of nations within a global society. How we as anthropologists might develop the kind of collaborative ethnographies that will contribute to defining new ways to live in the world is discussed below.

ETHNOGRAPHY IN A POSTMODERN WORLD

When new social movements theorists proclaimed that class no longer served as an
analytic category, students writing their doctoral theses in the 1980s paused as they tried
to catch up on a new vocabulary in which to frame their field research. Circumlocutions
for class relations and capitalist modes of production were drawn from the poetics of
French poststructuralism or the deconstructive tactics of the cultural critique. *Anthropology News* even published an ironic list of "dos" and "don'ts," with suggestions as to who
should no longer be cited and what was no longer "in."

The tendency to reject the past, rather than to build on advances made in the discipline
of anthropology, often results in trivializing accounts that ignore power relations in the
political economy. Yet the postmodern attempt to go beyond the often deterministic relations ascribed to class, gender, and ethnic categories promoted strategies for capturing the

transformations occurring in the postmodern condition. Among these are discourse analysis (Foucault 1980), identity formation (Touraine 1988; Laclau and Mouffe 1985), and reconceptualizing the spatial geography of globalization (Ferguson and Gupta 1992; D. Harvey 1989; Marcus 1998). Taken as exclusive approaches, as some acolytes of these innovators tended to do, postmodern trends could subvert ethnographic inquiry. They are capable of yielding "rich," "thick" (and more often thin), or "nuanced" approaches to ethnographic observations, but by limiting the analysis to discourse, or identity, or space, they negate the "holistic" inquiry into the material conditions of life and the structural positions that relate people to significant others.[4]

The concept of habitus can rescue the notion of holistic inquiry, grounding our ethnographies in space and anchoring them in structural conditions (chapter 3 p. 81). As the "space through which we learn who or what we are in society" (Bourdieu 1977:163), habitus can also be the space where we can observe and analyze "practices that tend to reproduce the objective conditions, which produced the generative principles of habitus in the first place" (D. Harvey 1989:219–221). It is these generative principles, which in a Marxist framework derive from contradictions within a system, that are almost eclipsed in Bourdieu's frame of reference focusing on the individual. Because I chose to analyze the problematic from the perspective of societies that have maintained some forms of a collective life intact, the habitus I have concentrated on in this book is one embracing community, but extending worldwide through networks of communication we are just beginning to take into account.

Anthropologists have begun to define these worldwide interactive spaces in what Hannerz (1996) calls the "global ecumene." He defines the global ecumene as the "interconnectedness of the world by way of interactions, exchanges and related development, affecting not least the organization of culture." According to Kopytoff, this may be thought of as a "region of persistent cultural interaction and exchange." Since many people's experience of space is broken up and dispersed in the global ecumene, we cannot rely on geographically situated communities alone as sites for our observations and analyses. Both habitus, as the minimal unit for reproducing and generating cultural repertoires, and ecumene, as the setting in which diverse cultural entities unite to communicate a wider perspectives, are complementary ways of thinking about global interactions. By retaining a sense of the generative cultural practices within any given habitus and their interconnectedness through interactions and exchanges in the global ecumene, we may arrive at the structuring principles in global affairs. The flux of the human condition can be captured for each moment in a time-space continuum in a way that can illuminate the forces at work.

A new vocabulary is now developing to wed specific ethnographic observations to notions of how people's behavior is conditioned. These approaches, cast as "multi-sited" or "historical imaginaries" (Marcus 1998; Roseberry 1989), are atttempts to grasp the complexity of human interaction in global processes. In the past, ethnographers tracked informants into the many settings where they lived and worked, and tried to explore the institutional settings that impinged on them. But the new approaches force us to problematize the global dimension of habitus as it conditions much of the behavior and

globalized habitats

understandings that we observe and try to interpret. One of the ways to problematize this is through a "community of practice" approach (Ferguson and Gupta 1992). This takes into account all the places in which people who are the subjects of study engage in and interact in the process of social reproduction.

What postmodern approaches insist upon is that we avoid reifying structures and deriving cultural practices from them. This has proven to be a potentially positive contribution of the "new" scholarship. However, the tendency in postmodernism is to erect a façade, focusing uniquely on identity, or discourse, or space. This leaves out of the purview the whole history of the conflict of real material interests that are structurally sustained through the institutions of a society that we once thought of as the class struggle. It is probably not coincident that, just when indigenous people are becoming protagonists in this ongoing drama of class conflict, the pundits within dominant society have denied the existence of the drama.

In the following sections I shall try to recapitulate some of the gains from these approaches as I analyze Mayan ethnic resurgence and its relation to the Zapatista social movement. Taking a cue from Margery Wolf's (1992) illustration of new methods and approaches in *The Thrice-Told Tale,* I shall tell the tale of the Mayan uprising and its aftermath, using three different frameworks, those of discourse, identity mobilization, and the globalization of space.[5] Hopefully this exercise will allow me to go on to relate indigenous movements for multicultural coexistence to the political and economic processes of globalization that conduce to their destruction.

Discourse Analysis
and the Course of a Social Movement

The anthropology of discourse and interpretation that pervaded the field in the 1980s introduced new terms to use to talk about ethnographic discoveries. It is most productive when used by ethnologists to locate and explore the construction of hegemony in everyday interactions. Discourse encapsulates a logic of behavior that goes beyond a mere listing of the motivations for social movements, since it deals with understandings that are embedded at a nearly subconscious level—understandings that exercise a force that empowers people to take a stand. Lacking economic and political resources to command attention, powerless people often resort to symbolic systems of communication derived from these deep structures.[6] Used skillfully, discourse analysis can yield the key metaphors that allow one to assess the people's own resources and justifications for beliefs and action, and how these are communicated to wider groups.

positives of discourse analysis

This is particularly notable among Mayan indigenous groups, where the power of the word is endowed with the sacred quality of biblical injunctions, and where poetic imagery and metaphors used by all speakers of the Mayan languages are cultivated in religious rituals.[7] I shall frame my reflections on this in the opposition between what *Comandante* David of the EZLN referred to as the "Fiesta of the Word" (Tzeltal: *sk'in ta sk'oplal*), and what José Angel Gurría, then, secretary of government in 1995, referred to disparagingly as the "War of Ink and Internet." The Fiesta of the Word, celebrated in the National Indigenous Forum called by the National Indigenous Congress in January 1996, sums up the dialogues among indigenous participants and their invited collaborators (chapter 4). The "War of Ink and Internet" is a slighting reference to the communications from the Zapatistas in 1995 as they tried to make their position known beyond the military lines that surrounded them in the rain forest.

At least three practices of rhetoric enter into the communication networks that originated in the Lacandón rain forest and leaked into electronic messages and media networks that extended across the world. The revolutionary discourse itself rises from Mayan roots formulated in the five dialects commonly used in the canyons of the Lacandón rain forest, with loan terms from Spanish. A second stream is the discourse of transnational civil society, articulated in Spanish as well as English and the various Romance languages of the many foreign representatives of Church, NGOs, and revolutionaries drawn to Chiapas by the outbreak. Civil society discourse is increasingly influenced by the transnational and national NGOs appealing to universal principles related to human rights and ecological concerns but sharing in common elements of *batz'il k'op* (the true language). A third stream is the discourse expressed in modernist rhetoric of rational gain and self-interest used by political parties and development agents. Each one has its own culture, distinct history, and mode of expression, yet there are differences within each group, and in the process of mimesis, each political block responds and often co-opts the successful rhetoric of opponents.

The discourse of the rebels. The initiative in revolutionary discourse is with the indigenes, whose announcement, on the eve of their uprising in January 1994 of *Basta!*, or the end of their marginalized lives, gained a world audience. In language that is a mixture of poetry and realism, they are projecting an imaginary future without racial injustices or repression and reclaiming a past rescued from the hybridized ideology of *indigenismo*.

Press and media reports that escaped government censorship[8] were crucial in changing the perceptions that people carried, not only of the Zapatistas but of *pueblos indios* (Nash 1997c). The remarkable ability of the Zapatistas to generate support for their movement derived from the poetic imagery in which they phrased their struggle. In contrast to the rationality of scientific socialism or material determinism that marked social movements of the nineteenth and early twentieth century, Zapatistas appealed to the moral issues of the struggle against neoliberal policies and for peace with dignity. From the first negotiations in the cathedral in San Cristóbal, their rejection of payoffs or buyouts distanced them from official channels, even while it attracted indigenous and nonindigenous supporters from throughout the hemisphere.

The Zapatista movement was radically transformed in the months following the uprising by the enormous show of support within Mexico and throughout the world. During and after the January 1, 1994, uprising, their struggle was cast in national terms. Under the banner of Zapata and promoting a program drawn from the Plan de Ayala, they tried to renegotiate the promise of the Revolution framed in the 1917 Constitution: to give land to those who work it and to integrate indigenous people and *mestizos* in the national project. In the dialogues that took place in San Cristóbal de Las Casas in March 1994, presentatives presented their claims for equality along with other citizens, ttle to the lands in the Lacandón rain forest that were promised when they nese national territories, and for entitlements to medical attention, education, access to markets, and a share of the proceeds of the natural resources in the lands they colonized.[9]

In the intervening months and years since the uprising, the rhetoric shifted from this modernizing discourse to an indigenous poetics as the transformative vision inherent in the rebellion became more explicit. This vision is, in Pablo Gonzalez Casanova's (1995:344) words, "a new democracy among the revolutionaries: a plural democracy in its ideologies, in its religion, and in its politics, that is not 'necessarily' a road toward 'socialism' and in which they do not accept 'formal democracy's' only 'mediation.'" González Casanova, who served many hours on the mediating team of CONAI with the bishop and others, discovered that the indigenous conception of democracy goes far beyond that defined in modern states. They "ask for democracy with justice, liberty of the individuals and not only of the pueblos . . . not only in the *selva* (the rain forest), nor only in Chiapas, but in the country as a whole" (González Casanova 1995:355). It is, in short, a conversion experience.

It is not accidental that the transformative vision of the Zapatistas arose in the canyons of the Lacandón rain forest. Until the uprising, the colonizers lived in an isolated world in which they experienced the harsh terms of neoliberalism at a distance, but in a brutal manner. The break with their communities in the highlands left the immigrants in a liminal state in which they could experience their past and future in one moment. Simultaneously, their break from dependency relations with the government allowed them to question the state hegemonic control. In this space, colonizers of the polyglot communities were able to "reestablish a human community whose structures are for men and not for accumulation." (González Casanova 1995). Ana María expressed this in her talk in Oventic, on the occasion of the International Encounter on July 27, 1996:

> As for the power, known worldwide as "*neoliberalismo*," we do not count, we do not produce, we do not buy, we do not sell. We are useless in the accounts of big capital. And so we went to the mountain to seek relief for our pain at being forgotten stones and plants. Here in the mountains of Southeast Mexico our dead live. Our dead who live in the mountains know many things. They speak to us of their death and we listen. The talking boxes[10] told us another history that comes from yesterday and aims at tomorrow. The mountain spoke to us, the *macehualob* [commoners in Nahuatl] who are common and ordinary people. [Author's translation, copy of speech distributed in Orentic]

The true language, *batz'il k'op,* is full of metaphors, words with parallel meaning, both in Tzotzil and in Tzeltal. Only in their own words can we sense their indigenous mode of embracing the generations, capturing the past in the present with the words of the ancestors in the mouths of their children. Neither the Spanish conquest nor five hundred years of colonization have destroyed the beliefs and mode of expressing them.[11]

The point of departure for the philosophy of highland Chiapas indigenes is contained within the "true language," *batz'il k'op*. Children learn the *"k'op rios"* or language of the gods, from their parents, and youths from the elders, hearing the *pat'otan*, or prayers (literally, "behind the heart"). Their communal objective is to live as the ancestors did, attending to the words of the community authorities "below the view of the antecedents." All the prayers in Amatenango del Valle, for example, end with the words, "And so we are able to do what our mothers did and what our fathers did, here, where our saintly Father sees and our saintly Mother sees us."

This "normativity of the past," as Miguel Alberto Bartolomé (1995:365) expresses it in relation to the Tzotziles, was reinvigorated continually in the ritual cycle of the communities. Furthermore, the kind of gerontocracy that anthropologists noted in the civil-religious hierarchy gives priority to the elders and, particularly, to men. The latter priority constitutes a negation of the mythopoetic cosmological balance of the Sun and the Moon through the Mother-Fathers, *me'tik-tatik* in Tzeltal, or *totil-me'il* in Tzotzil. The loss of these principles is contingent upon a politics of domination by men over women, by elites over commoners, that is the heritage of *caciquismo*. Finally there is a politics of consensus that is practiced in the *ejidos* far from the *cabeceras* of indigenous municipalities.

Separated from their communities of origin, the colonizers of the Lacandón looked for means of reconstructing their world, giving legitimacy to the collective life. There they encountered, Ana María goes on to say (*Crónicas Intergalácticas*, EZLN 1996:24),

> . . . the powerful being who wants to dance the *x-tol* to repeat his brutal conquest. The *kaz-dzul*, the false man who governs our lands and has great war machines, like the *bo'ob*, that is part lion and part horse, that spreads pain and death among us. The false man who governs us orders the *aluxob*—the liars who deceive and relegate our people to the forgotten. [Author's translation]

There, in the canyons of the rain forest, two forces met: the political military group of guerrillas who arrived there in the early 1980s and indigenous people, many of whom had formed the Christian Base Communities and were indoctrinated with liberation theology stressing the human rights of people as they live in the world, not the hereafter. Ana María tells the story in her speech:

> The mountain spoke to us, telling us to take up arms in order to have a voice; it told us to cover our faces in order to have a visage. It told us to forget our name in order to be named, it told us to care for our past so that we would have a future. In the mountains the dead live, our dead. The Votan[12] lives with them and the Black man, the Ik'al, and the light and the darkness, the wet and the dry, the land and the wind, the rain and the fire. The mountain is the house of the *HalachWinik*, the true man, the high chief. There we learn and there we record that we are who we are, the true men.

The importance of the ancestors is notable in the communications from the rain forest. Don Antonio, the old man who figured in many of the communiqués until his death in recent years, is honored because of his age and wisdom. For Marcos, it was like encountering Don Juan, of Casteñeda's mythopoetic construction in *The Teachings of Don Juan*, who had influenced his own speech.[13]

The novelty of the Zapatista movement lies in the merging of the consciousness of indigenous people with that of a sophisticated revolutionary[14] in a setting such as the Lacandón rain forest. In the morning mists shrouding the forested canyons it is easy to feel that one is living with the ancestors. The old man Antonio was, for the young revolutionaries who arrived in the Lacandón over a decade ago, the bridge to listening and learning from indigenous people. This dialogue provoked the tension that made the Zapatistas distinct from all other guerrilla groups. Marcos says in his conversations with Le Bot (1997:145) that for him and his companions, this dialogue was "a cultural shock."

> At the time when we made contact with the communities, the indigenous element was in the majority in the political-military organization, although this was not reflected in the command structure. But, if we reflect on it, it was because of the primal cultural shock in the internal life of the group that it became necessary to assimilate, to resolve, to learn the language, but also to learn something more than the language itself: the *use* of the language, of the symbol in communication, all that.[15] [Author's translation]

Listening to the old people, particularly Don Antonio, Marcos captured the new element in the indigenous discourse on revolution:

> The idea is of a more just world, enriched with humanitarian, ethical, moral elements, more than strictly indigenous. Suddenly, the revolution was transformed into something essentially moral. Ethical. More than the redistribution of wealth or the expropriation of the means of production, the revolution begins to be the possibility of the human being having a space for dignity. (Le Bot 1997:146)[16] [Author's translation]

He does not indicate the influence of liberation theology, which obviously influenced their discourse, as I shall now consider.

The discourse of civil society. Civil society in Mexico is replete with organizations representative of the diverse tendencies that arose in the wake of the PRI's loss of hegemonic control. The most powerful of these influences is that of the theology of liberation, verbalized by Bishop Samuel Ruíz and the catechists in the Lacandón rain forest. Like Fray Bernadino Sahagun and the other Franciscans sent to analyze the spiritual premises of colonial subjects in New Spain in the sixteenth century, the adherents of liberation theology listen to and learn from the speech of the indigenous people.

The dialogue began when Bishop Samuel Ruíz, responding to the initiative of the governor of Chiapas, organized the First National Congress of Indigenes that took place in San Cristóbal from October 12 to 15, 1974. For the first time, Tzeltales, Tzotziles, Choles, Tojolabales, and Mames were united to prepare an agenda (chapter 3). A new discourse developed in the encounter between ecclesiastics and multilingual indigenous communities in the Christian Base Communities.

The principle of equality between indigenes and *ladinos* promoted in the Christian Base Communities of the rain forest had a revolutionary impact. Transposed to the rain forest, liberation theology contributed a spiritual and moral force to the colonizers, who were seeking a new relation with the state. The Order of the Maristas, who were the first to evangelize in the Lacandón, emphasized communal action based on shared religion that was extended in pilgrimages and unions in other pueblos of the rain forest (Leyva Solano and Franco 1996). In the context of the diversity of ethnic groups, which included some with rural and some with urban origins and spoke many distinct dialects, the pastoral role of the catechists was a key factor in forging interrelations and constituting a united "brotherhood" of Christians. In their communal assemblies, the men and women spoke together for two hours, expressing their concerns and opinions. The catechists synthesized the various ideas and then asked the assembly, *"Lek ay?"* (Is it good?), and then the people responded in common, *"Lek ay!"* (It is good!). The catechists also entered into other collective action groups of *ejido* unions, production societies, and the Union of Unions (UU), linked through the *Kiptik ta Lecubtesal* (United by our Strength). They are, according to Leyva Solano (Levya Solano and Franco 1995:215), "the soul of the subregional movement."

The communal discourse that permeated the daily life of men and women in the colonized area for over two decades[17] was, according to Marcos in his conversations with Le Bot (1997:322), what made them support the guerrilla movement in 1992: "Twenty years of a life sustained by communitarian ideals, ten years of reflection in the mountain where we [the guerrillas] were training the troops and exchanging ideas with the indigenes, and two years to plan the uprising." What Marcos does not indicate is that this rhetoric was also inspired by catechist faith and activity, and five hundred years of practice of resistance against domination, during which the ways of the ancestors weighed in the balance. It was in that exchange of post-Marxian revolutionary thinking, revamped in the Christine doctrines of communitarianism, that a rhetoric developed that alerted the world to a new expression of what a twenty-first-century revolution might be. Marcos does not include in the exchange the spiritual dialogue that underlay the "communitarian ideals," that primed the Christian Base Communities to accept the revolutionary message.

The permeability of discourse boundaries is most apparent in the language of Christian Base Communities and the reinvigorated Catholic Church representatives. Bishop Samuel Ruíz revealed his absorption of the patterns of the true word (*batz'il k'op*) in his address to the Forum of Indigenous Culture on January 3, 1996. I reconstructed from my notes the following fragment:

> The road of difference, the road of enrichment, goes forward. The daily living together, working together for change, with the participation of women, with the participation of men, all are signs of change. The pueblos that live together, those of the north who live in the time of the Indian, we thought they would die, but they are surging forward. The old say it will not happen in two or three days. Those who continue with their own language have reinforced the road of difference. Others who

have experienced change reinforce the road of difference. In this continent, and in this world, we do not speak of fantasies but of reality. We are making history. The search for peace is not lost. The road is much broader than contemplated, and we live now with the firm hope of finding the long peace in open spaces.

The double phrasing of ideas and the reference to the road of life are recurrent tropes in *batz'il k'op*. The reference to "the pueblos that live together" is to the plural autonomous pueblos in the northern region of Chiapas that had declared themselves autonomous and that survived the threat of paramilitaries throughout 1996 (chapter 5). The forum was a celebration of difference and unity in which the bishop's constant attempts to promote the indigenous desires for a dignified life bore fruits in the San Andrés Agreement signed in February, 1996.

The discourse of NGOs. Secular NGOs, especially those funded by international organizations, draw on a repetoire of phrases from United Nations conventions and other international circuits of exchange. Hemispheric meetings on ecology and human rights focus on the guardianship role of indigenous people over natural resources. Drawing on their shamanic and divinatory traditions, the indigenous women's groups foster the gendered equations between the earth, identified as mother, the moon, identified as grandmother and progenitor of us all, along with the sun as grandfather.

Members of civil society, both at the national and international levels, applaud revolutionary sentiments as they seek to construct an imaginary world in which they can encounter common spaces to overcome the isolation and alienation of their own societies. Attracted by the idealism of the revolutionaries and also by concern for the abysmal conditions of life of the indigenes, numerous NGOs have arrived in Chiapas since the uprising. Among them are both ecological associations and human rights groups. The current academic skepticism regarding the tendency of many NGOs to romanticize "the Indian" often rejects as "orientalism" the discourse used by both NGOs and indigenes. As Bartolomé (1995:369) says: "[the NGOs] want to align themselves with indigenes in a very idealized way . . . a way of living together with nature that does not generate its radical destruction." Yet I have found that the environmentalists' projection of a natural link between indigenes and their environment resonates with notions of custodianship that are deeply rooted in Mayan beliefs and practices. This is a two-way road in which communication is reflected by both sides listening intently to the thread of the discourse. What thrills the interlocutors in this dialogue is the spiritual empathy between humans and nature that is expressed by Mayans and is often projected into new kinds of litanies by the religious groups that come into contact with them. David Jarvis, an Anglican missionary who combined his evangelical duties with working on an agronomy project with the *campesinos* in Oxchuc and the Lacandón settlement area, found a quick response to the spiritual link the evangelists made between nature and cultivation, which then became central to his evangelical mission. As a part of preaching the gospel, the Anglicans urged conservation of forests and the natural resources in the Lacandón colonies where they worked. Adapting approaches used by the Lacandón Indians, the missionaries taught settlers from different environments to use kinds of slash-and-burn techniques that saved precious trees that were the source of medicines, and to maximize the fertility of the ashes used for fertilizer by using intense, quick-firing methods (my fieldnotes, spring 1995; see also Nahmod and Gonzáles 1988; Singer 1988).

Despite the skepticism of those who attack this kind of rhetoric as essentializing or romanticism, it is clear to anyone who has lived with indigenous populations whose environment is threatened that the people themselves feel compelled to correct the cosmic balance. The *u'uletik*, or seers, will divine the precipitating cause and suggest a remedy. This occurred during the drought of 1971 that led to the pilgrimage of Amatenangueros to Oxchuc to raise the spirits to the patron saint, whom they felt was being neglected because of large-scale Protestant conversions (chapter 3). Another crisis occurred in the spring of 1998, when the rains came late to the highlands and even the lowlands of Chiapas, and many fires started for the clearing of the land got out of control and filled the air with the fumes and heat. Chamulan *mayordomos*, or caretakers of the church, gave a fiesta to San Isidro and set his image in spring water up to his knees to encourage him to induce the rains. The logic that is implicit in normal behavior is forcefully demonstrated in such responses to crisis.

The collective responsibility of communities for their resource base is a fundamental part of the logic guiding indigenous behavior. The fact that it is now linked to the universalistic discourse of sustainable development is an achievement that cannot be dismissed by a simplistic critique of essentialism. As Rosalva Aída Hernández Castillo and Ronald Nigh (1998:144) have said, there is a more profound level in which indigenes have integrated into their discourse elements of agroecological science to reaffirm the cultural values of respect for nature. The creativity in their integration of ancient elements with those of modern and postmodern derivation lies in their linkage of indigenous respect for nature to modernist awareness of conserving natural resources that conduces toward favorable practices in agriculture. In the words of the executive director of the IUCN Inter-Commission Task Force on Indigenous Peoples: "We must ensure their [indígenes] empowerment and that we learn from them the use and conservation of resources" (Inter-Commission Task Force on Indigenous Peoples, 1997). He goes on to assert that: "Indigenous societies possess what can be described as an environmental ethic, not abstractly stated in biological terms, but built on specific experiences by a specific people living in a particular locale" (*ibid*:231). He cites as proof the biodiversity that has continued to exist in the environments in which indigenous peoples have lived for thousands of years.

This recognition on the part of the Inter-Commission Task Force on Indigenous Affairs of the need for an holistic approach has a strong basis in ethnographic particularity. The social obligation to preserve in trust the resources of a specific environment for one's children and grandchildren is evoked in every household celebration I have participated in. Corn is the flesh of humans from the gods that have created human beings, and the land itself is an extension of sacred power (Ruz 1981). Jacinto Arias (1994) notes that migration often upsets the sense of living in a sacred environment. Tales of past apocalypses provoked by the failure of humans to care for their resources are prevalent in the southern frontier, where migrations of people are constant (Ruz 1981). Alain Breton, who studied the community of Bachajón in the municipality of Ocosingo, notes the frequent desertion of town centers as a means of defense against excessive tribute during the colonial period and in the post-Independence era. Given this history of flux and migration, the indigenes of the region have contrived to freeze this motion in rituals and prayers that continually reaffirm identity between people and place. The relationship enjoins mutual responsibility between gods and humans, ensuring the trust that rises above the historical experience.

The lack of clear policies regarding the exploitation of forest and other natural resources, and the rights to the land itself, upsets the collective attempts to promote the relation of the people to the land in the Lacadón rain forest. Contradictory aims are often pursued in the colonies settled by indigenous inhabitants and in those with *mestizo* settlers new to the area. Arturo Coutino Farrera (1987) indicates that in the former case, where indigenes are settled in Flor de Cacao and Nueva Unión, they show a strict respect for the forest reserves, while in the latter settlement, *mestizos* are cutting the forest with motor saws for commercial sales, or burning woodlands for cattle pasture. The presence of Mexican Petroleum (PEMEX) and the army further upsets the colonizers' attempts to pursue their ends of improving and securing claims to the land in this highly contested area. The EZLN issued a communiqué in the spring of 2000 indicating that it was training members of the community to fight fires while at the same time the army was promoting them.[18]

The dialogical exchange in the discourse between transnational organizations and indigenous groups is also evident in the field of human rights. Claims made by indigenes are translated into legal terms that define the violations for a court audience the day the issue is raised. Indigenes are, for their part, learning what their rights are and are phrasing their political movement in terms of dignity and justice. Founded in 1989, the Human Rights Center "Fray Bartolomé de Las Casas" collected specific information concerning the repression and the betrayal by the government in the state of Chiapas. Armed with the facts on violations of human rights in Mexico, more than 60 Mexican organizations asked the United Nations Commission on Human Rights to name a special-relations group for Mexico, a request that was backed by the Mexican Commission for the Defense and Promotion of Rights (*La Jornada* April 2, 1998:3:3). The International Civil Commission of Observation for Human Rights rejected the military and paramilitary aggression in the rain forest in March and April of 1998 that, they said, "does not correspond to the provocations and attacks" (*La Jornada* April 9, 1998:4).

The discourse on human rights is global and based on universal principles addressed in United Nations conventions. But the fact that conventions have to be ratified and implemented by nations that are the violators of the rights often undermines their effectiveness. President Zedillo spoke of his "initiatives for peace" while perpetuating violence. In the contradiction of word and deed we can divine the growing distance between the rebellious indigenous population and the government.

Discourse analysis, particularly that which examines the dialogical context in which it occurs, allows us to enter immediately into the formulation of ideas and the exchanges

discourse not equal to culture

among culturally distinct people that generate collective action. But to make discourse a synonym for culture would short-circuit the social mobilization needed to change the terms of the discourse.[19] Immersed in discourse, the analyst's failure to take into account the essence of the dialogical encounter—which is listening and responding with changed behavior—can result in the breakdown of the political process. Indigenous people of the *CR of dis.* Chiapas have a highly cultivated capacity to listen and hear. The primary skill of indigenous curers is listening to the blood speak so they can diagnose the state of the heart. In Amatenango, the chief woman speaker addresses the arriving guests at a ceremony, saying,: "Speak and we shall listen." The ability to listen is, then, more highly valued than simply speaking. Indigenous leaders frequently comment on the inability of government bureaucrats to listen. As Kay Warren suggests, audience responses and resynthesis are part of a larger dynamic of reappropriation (personal communication). *Warren on reappropriation*

The effective exercise of hegemony depends on policies and practices that recognize and respond to the real concerns expressed in the dialogic encounter. The PRI has lost its hegemonic control over the nation not because of a lack of rhetorically correct words and phrases, since the PRI discourse is often phrased in the same terms as that of the people it is repressing. The duplicity with which the PRI takes over the rhetoric of the opposition and then fails to act in terms of that rhetoric is evident in its failure to generate authentic programs. Its deception robs it of the kind of receptive audience that is the basis for hegemonic accord.

Clearly the mythopoetic visionary of the Zapatistas does exhibit the power to persuade, but they themselves are very aware of the vulnerable position they and their supporters are now in. Zaptistas were kept alive by their communication network with an international audience, but the lines are fragile. When they were cut off from their daily routines by federal armed forces, that harassed men as they tried to walk to their fields and intercepted women as they tried to collect water and firewood, they had difficulty producing the bare necessities for survival. Even now they lack the material resources to ensure survival. President Fox's recognition of the need for development is premised on neoliberal investment projects rather than the collective projects they call for.

The rhetoric of political parties. The PRI government is listening to the indigenous people, perhaps for the first time in five hundred years, but listening primarily in order to co-opt the discourse, turning their words around and distorting their message as it tries to impose its own ends. The left-wing parties opposed to the PRI frequently try to channel the revolutionary themes into their own platforms.

In the old days, PRI officials intending to visit an indigenous town would find out what the people wanted, and then hasten to "make a miracle": if the need was identified as electricity, they would install the lines and officials would show up for the completion of the project, snip the ribbon, and display the miracle—a street light switched on, for instance. Salinas talked dollars and cents, or *pesos y efectivos*, in Oxchuc in the spring of 1993, when he was attempting to co-opt local politicians with his Solidarity programs by sponsoring concrete projects that generated measurable progress. He reiterated his commitment to the area by promising clean drinking water and assistance for cash crop production, but he did not utter a word about the terms of the Free Trade Act that he had just introduced into Congress, nor about the privatization of the *ejidos* that *campesinos* saw as the engines of deconstruction of their way of life. When the governor of the state or the president of the republic visits indigenous villages, he often wears an item of clothing such as a ribboned hat or serape, in order to identify with the people. Governor Robledo tried this in February 1995 when he was mending fences in Chamula (chapter 5), but the army invasion of the Lacandón three days after his appearance cut short his limited service in office, since he was made the scapegoat by the PRI in confronting the massive public outcry.

Political figures have their personal styles that differ even within the same party. In contrast with Salinas's rhetoric of modernization, Zedillo tended to expropriate the speech of his adversaries without attending to its content. In a speech delivered on February 3, 1995, he called upon the Zapatistas to negotiate a peaceful settlement of the conflict, which they had repeatedly urged ever since the rupture in negotiations in March 1994. On the day after the invasion of federal troops into the Lacandón canyons, he expressed his "firm commitment to attend to the roots of rebellion" that are "poverty, absence of opportunities, injustice, lack of democracy," reiterating his desire for conciliation. The army's rampage of pillage and destruction that was occurring on the day he delivered his speech disillusioned many who perceived a marked disparity between rhetoric and practice (chapter 5).

The PRI hierarchy continued to resort to the rhetoric of revolution taken from its adversaries in the rain forest in a bizarre attempt to reconstitute the hegemonic control that it once enjoyed. While pursuing military strategies, it asserted slogans of peace and justice at the moments when its policies negate them.

Displacement of aggression through scapegoating was another device favored by the PRI when it went on the attack after suffering a clear defeat in the popularity polls. After the massacre of Acteal on December 22, 1997, the government attacked the Catholic Church for instigating the conflict and stirring up violence between Catholic Christian Base Communities and Protestants. Its accusations came at the very moment when human rights agencies identified the perpetrators as PRI officials of Chenalhó, aided by members of federal armed forces (see chapter 5). Shortly thereafter, the government exhorted the diocese and the other churches to "end the climate of intolerance," as if the motivation for the massacre of Acteal had came from them (*La Jornada* April 9, 1998). The government support for the militia group called Peace and Justice (*Paz y Justicia*)— another usurpation of the indigenes' terms of discourse—which was operating in the northern region was made public at the same time.

A few months after the Acteal massacre, the government, in the face of mounting protests from foreign and national human rights agencies regarding the paramilitaries operating in the northern region and Chenalhó, undertook two exclusively rhetorical initiatives. Its master ploy was in taking the title of the San Andrés Agreement, Law for the Rights and Culture of the Indigenes, to designate a plan that subverted the agreement, dividing the parties and even the ranks of the Zapatistas. The plan did not address the constitutional changes needed to fulfill the agreement, nor did it provide a regional administrative level to ensure the autonomy of indigenous people, as was included in the

San Andrés agreement. Without this, the plan did little to expand the cultural rights of indigenous people already contained in Articles 4 and 39 of the Constitution as these had been amended in Salinas's term of office.

With similar duplicitous rhetoric, the governor of Chiapas launched an operation he called a "return to law," assigning a thousand soldiers and state police to seize a dozen activists of the indigenous defense organizations UNAL and CRIACH in April 1998. Federal soldiers and national police carried out this operation at dawn, without any order of apprehension, and political prisoners were retained without charges (*Proceso* no. 1128, June 14, 1998:30). Simultaneously, the government attacked the bishop's role in the Zapatista uprising, perhaps to divert attention from its violations of human rights, finally succeeding in forcing his resignation from CONAI in June 1998. Trapped in its own position of betrayal of the San Andrés Accords, the government's sole course of action has been that of furthering paramilitary and military repression.

Identity Mobilization

The interpretive focus on identity politics has its roots in European sociological analyses of the radical restructuring of production and society in the 1960s and 1970s. Reacting against the deterministic emphasis on class in the revitalized neo-Marxist theory of the 1970s, Touraine demonstrated the emergence of new premises for political expression in his study of the 1968 "May Movement" and the Polish Solidarity movement (Touraine 1988). In contrast to the class struggle that grounded conflict and its resolution in relations in production, the introduction of a social agency provided a vivid counterpoint to class struggle limited to the workplace. Touraine envisioned new relationships among a wide range of actors coming in to perform the restructuring of the economy around service and managerial positions. Laclau's and Mouffe's (1985) analysis of subject positions that make for collective action rejects any structural categories for identity formation, conceptualizing struggles on the level of discourses of identity. This limits the analysis of social movements, since it denies the culturally constructed categories such as class and ethnicity or, in Latin America, the increasingly important category of the poor, which become the bases for mobilizing action. Without a banner to relate to, groups that may become fully conscious of their subordination will neglect the structural building blocks by which they might generalize their condition and find allies.

The global shaking up of markets, production sites, and employment opportunities was met in academia with a search for models that would encompass the changing reality. Anibal Quijano (1988) finds such a model in the articulation of collective solidarity with full individual realization in postmodern settings. Elizabeth Jelin (1987) seeks it in the mediations occurring in the daily life of social movements. James Scott (1985) locates it in the resistance actions of peasant societies. But in seeking novel sites for the genesis of social movements, some analysts have lost sight of the structural conditions that ultimately set the stage for the development of consciousness and enactment of roles. They are reminded by Starn (1992:94) of the need to investigate the "particular positions within the global village" that define "quite elemental matters of scarcity and survival that drive people to act."

Advocates of the "new" social movements[20] theory, predicated on the basis of identity formation, can be criticized for some of the same difficulties that they leveled against Marxist and other structuralist positions. That is, identity formation, like class formation, is too narrowly focused and does not adequately take into account the multiple, coexisting, and often confounding identities that enter into a political consciousness. Then too, they ignore the social and cultural construction of class that, like other social constructions of identity formation, is based on particular circumstances and ideologies that are constantly changing. Hence the identity issues with which they categorize movements are "naturalized" in ways that mask their cultural confection. "The women's movement," the "gay movement," and even "the ethnic movement" are often segmented in ways that obscure the participants' common rejection of the naturalizing tendencies in such movement categories and the multiple identities that relate to diverse programmatic issues. The dynamic lies precisely in the fluid and multiple agendas embraced in the movement.

Thus what are called "indigenous social movements" are often being defined with these essentializing "postmodern" categorizations at the moment when indigenous peoples are becoming empowered as agents of their own histories. The challenge of the Zapatistas and their supporters is not directed singularly against the racist structures of their subordination but also the sexist, neoliberal, and other constructions of privilege that coexist with them. Their major goal is the autonomy for their own and other cultures within a democratic, pluricultural society.[21]

Given these caveats concerning identity formation, what can we learn about indigenous social movements from this approach? Fortunately, we have a guide in Kay Warren's (1998:178 *et seq.*) analysis of the Guatemalan pan-Mayan identity movement. Going beyond (but not rejecting) the "antiracism narratives" that see agrarian communities as centers of cultural resistance to colonial rule, the "continuity narratives" that focus on persistence across centuries, and the "*mestizaje* narratives" that stress the blend of European and indigenous, Warren seeks common ground on which to discover the truths contingent on the "transnational culture flows" in which they are expressed (Warren 1998:179). I shall draw on her strategies to analyze the Zapatista movement of the Chiapas Mayans.

Antiracism narratives. For Mayans in Chiapas, the defining moments for the social movement that called for revindication of their identity as indigenous people came in their migrations from the highland to the distinct and contrasting ecology of the rain forest. The exodus put Tzeltal, Tzotzil, Tojolobal, Mam, and Chol speakers into a new environment which tested all their capacities for survival. Confronted with difference in this new multiethnic environment, they developed a heightened sense of community, sharing a common destiny. Impoverishment and the lack of any ameliorating conditions tested to the limit their willingness to tolerate the conditions of marginalization in which they lived. This was fortified with a reevaluation of their identity as inheritors of the true word, *batz'il k'op.*

Continuity narratives. The identity issue is more complex in the case of Mayan activists than with most ethnic groups. As a people, indigenes are connected to very deep roots that continually absorbed cultural elements from a widely dispersed environment (Gossen and Leventhal 1989). I have tried to articulate the unself-conscious rooting of contemporary incidents and characters into a format that I discovered, late in my research, was based on the Popol Vuh (chapter 3; Nash 1997a). Even Marcos becomes incorporated as a potential incarnation of Tatik Cha'uk, or the Lord of Lightning, by Amatenangueros, and Mayans see everywhere the hand of their ancestors.[22] Gossen (1996:535) attests to the many instances of the symbolic and ritual traditions that are kept alive throughout the Mesoamerican area (Gossen 1986, 1998; Gossen and Leventhal 1989). Ritual itself is a way of assuring people that they are "able to do what our mothers did and what our fathers did, here where our Holy Father sees us and our Holy Mother sees us" (Nash 1970:xv). The gendered division of labor in cultural transmission ensures that women, as those chiefly responsible, do not depart from the language and customs, even when men are forced to migrate and to learn Spanish in their attempts to make a living. Protestant conversion is in itself a means by which Chamulan Indians are reconstructing the traditional basis for a spiritual community after their expulsion (Sullivan 1998).

Mayans are constantly devising new ways to live with the contradictions in their lives. Warren's (1985) exploration of cosmogenic constructs shows the intricate ways in which traditionalists work out the contradictions in their identity relations with *ladinos*. Jacinto Arias, director of indigenous affairs for Chiapas, who once spoke of Protestant conversion as the greatest threat to indigenous social and political order (Arias 1991), has revised his view of homogeneity that once seemed necessary to ensure continuity of traditions (Arias 1994). Recognizing the need for a more comprehensive understanding of identity, he stated that:

> And so those who withdraw into the fiestas, curing rituals, customs and traditions that were inherited from their ancestors are *indios*; they also are *indios* who, in their search to continue giving sense to their existence, have turned their eyes to the evangelical teachings; the PRI-istas are no more nor less *indios* than those who support the ideological platforms of the opposition parties; the schoolteacher or professional who is dressed in the *mestizo* style is no less *indio* than the one who wishes to adorn himself with the clothing that conserves part of the pre-Columbian designs and spirit. The one who reacts violently before what he considers injustice is no less a true man (*batz'i vinik*) than the one who behaves with resignation in face of it; he who turns his eyes to the past is as much *indio* as the one who arms himself with courage and wants to succeed in his search for answers to future questions not yet asked, penetrating the tangled discord of the modern world without renouncing his roots (Arias 1994:398).[23]

The recognition of heterodoxy in self-expression has important consequences for the indigenous movement. It can no longer be defined by traits as synecdoches of identification in the style of *indigenismo*. Rather, it is commitment to one's own cultural being not only in terms of the past but in their politicized engagement in the movements for respect (*bisil ta winik*), autonomy, and free expression of values that simultaneously universalize these values as they seek vindication of their own rights. It is the antithesis of *mestizaje*, discussed below.

Mestiza je narratives. The dialectic of continuity related to the ability to adopt changes that allows Mayans to remain themselves is a departure from the discourse of *indigenistas*, which assumes a merging of indigenous and *ladino* cultures that will allow the former to assimilate to the more advanced, or modern, culture of the West, but offers no entry for indigenous traits into modernization. Deeply imbedded in the *indigenista* approach are racist assumptions deriving from the colonial era, dressed in post-1910 revolutionary polemics. Superordination of the Western "civilization" and subordination of the indigenous "culture" are predicated on unilineal evolution in the *indigenista* narration of modernity. Just as the *mestizaje* narrative central to *indigenismo* naturalized the superiority, and hence justified dominance by, the *mestizo* mainstream, as Kay Warren (1998:144) demonstrates in the case of Guatemala, so does the *indigenista* approach reaffirm the need for indigenous acculturation to mainstream (read *mestizo*) culture and society in Mexico.

Warren's approaches to locating identities and assessing how they are shaped enable us to enter into the study of globalization processes while retaining an ethnographic basis for study. In the many locales in which the subjects of our studies carry out their activities, we can discover the multiple premises on which their identities are predicated. Intergenerational studies can deepen the understanding of process, particularly when the anthropologist has lived with and known each age group intimately, and can situate the changes in their life trajectories with those occurring in the nation and the world.

Cultural Production and Control over Space

I have discussed some of the local and regional implications of spatial and temporal compression in highland Chiapas communities in chapter 3. Here I shall consider the global dimensions of these changes in terms of 1) control over space, and 2) spaces of representation, production of the changing power relations in space. The compression over time and space that is the quintessential mark of globalization had begun with the development programs of the 1970s and 1980s, described in chapter 3. But while the provision of the infrastructural basis in these decades still responded to national exploitation of the rich resources of Chiapas, the intensification of these developments in hydroelectric power, transportation, and communication in the 1990s responded to growing international concerns. Chiapas was linked through highways and microwave communication towers from the Atlantic to the Pacific coast, but few villages, especially in the Lacandón rain forest, enjoyed electricity and potable water, and some people had never seen telephones. The roads and the rest of the infrastructure developed in the 1970s and 1980s promoted regional and national traffic, but were of little interest to global financial and resource enterprises until the discovery of vast reserves of oil in the Lacandón rain forest. The Zapatista uprising came close on its heels.[24] Militarization of the Lacandón rain forest and the northern region of autonomous villages hastened the construction of new roads for military vehicles. With only a little exaggeration, one could say that Chiapas was simultaneously integrated into the region, the nation, and the world as it was inundated by new social actors, new technology, and new levels of political repression.

Control over space. The large-scale development projects that I referred to in chapter 3 set in stark contrast the backward agrarian sector and the global enterprises. Indigenous people bore the brunt of the environmental contamination attendant on the oil drilling in the Lacandón and the expropriation of land inundated by the dams built on the Chicosan and Grijalva rivers, without benefiting from the proceeds. *Subcomandante* Marcos captured this territorial invasion of the colonizers' area in the Lacandón in a modernist discourse that echoes Eduardo Galeano, author of *The Open Veins of Latin America*, and one of the intellectuals he invited to the Intercontinental Convention in 1996:

> A few kilometers ahead you will leave Oaxaca and find a large sign that reads, "Welcome to Chiapas." Did you find it? Good, let's suppose so. You got here to this southwestern corner of the country by one of three prime roads: the road from the north, the one along the Pacific coast, or the one you have supposedly just taken. But the natural wealth that leaves these lands doesn't travel over just these roads. Chiapas is bled through thousands of veins: through oil ducts and gas ducts, over electric wires, by railroad cars, through bank accounts, by trucks and vans, by ships and planes, over clandestine paths, third-rate roads, and mountain passes.
>
> And what tribute does this land continue to pay to various empires? Oil, electric energy, cattle, money, coffee, bananas, honey, corn, cocoa, tobacco, sugar, soy, melons, sorghum, mamey, mangos, tamarinds, avocados, and Chiapas blood flow out through a thousand and one fangs sunk into the neck of southeastern Mexico . . . all with the same destiny: to feed the empire. The dues that capitalism imposes on the southeast corner of the country ooze out, as they have since the beginning, mud and blood.

The postmodern discourse on space loses the force captured by Marcos in his attack on the invasion of transnational enterprises in the lowlands. In the 1980s, the Lacandón rain forest was being transformed by lumber companies and oil explorations. The dirt tracks that marked roads connecting villages in the rain forest were nearly obliterated by the oil rigs representing foreign, and in particular, French companies that had acquired exploration and leasing rights. This was one of the causes for the protest by the settlers from Marqués de Comillas when the governor, González Garrido, dispatched over 700 soldiers from the newly constructed battalion headquarters in Nuevo Laredo in 1991 (see chapter 3). Even in highland villages there were discrete signs of the presence of oil exploration, as I discovered with my students when we went for an excursion to look at sheep corrals introduced by INI in a rural hamlet of Chamula.[25]

In the five years since the uprising, the army has transformed the jungle with a dense network of road and telephone communications in the rain forest to facilitate military occupation. Little of this infrastructure is of use to the colonizers, whose communally owned trucks were stolen or vandalized in the invasion and who are often prevented from moving within or beyond their settlements. Technological advances are devoted to limiting rather than to advancing the integration of the indigenous people.

The threat to indigenous control over their spaces of production and reproduction was clear as indigenous people began to respond in distinct and self-reinforcing ways in the 1990s. The first trend was developed with the 500 Years of Resistance movement that began in 1990 and continued after the celebration of the quincentennial. The second initiative was the Zapatista uprising, which combined the demands for land with the growing insistence for autonomy in territories. We can capture in the events that transpired in San Cristóbal the way in which these larger issues were addressed in symbolic behaviors related to space. I shall recapitulate this response, first by presenting how indigenous people redefined their representation of themselves to the intruders in the significant spaces defined by Spanish colonial and post-Independence governments, and second in the production of new spaces for regenerative indigenous control. Globalization affects indigenous communities first of all in their representation of themselves to the intrusive presence of tourists. With the development of the social movement for autonomy, indigenous people began to produce new sites representing the changing social relations.

Spaces of representation. The social hub of Spanish colonial rule was the *zócalo*, or central plaza. This was the center of the utopian empire in miniature, bordered with its most important institutions, the church, municipal buildings, jail, and market, surrounding the park. In my early stay in the Chiapas highlands, the open space between the church and the town hall was a place for ritual exchanges between the civil and religious officeholders. The only signs displayed in the plazas of indigenous pueblos were those of the PRI, often using the INI buildings as billboards. When the ferment of *campesino* organizations increased in the 1980s, the initials of groups would be scrawled on the buildings in the plaza, OCEZ, ARIC, EZLN, and so on, and the names of political candidates. In many towns the plaza became a contested area for the expression of pluripolitical change in the 1980s.

The first intrusion of global traffic was in the form of tourists. International tourism started late in Chiapas in comparison with the west coast beach resorts and colonial cities of the central plateau and the Yucátan that were developed as early as the first half of the twentieth century. In 1980 there were no more than a half dozen hotels that could draw an international clientele to San Cristóbal, but by 1991 there were over fifty hotels that could rank as tourist class. Tourist infrastructure was shaky but beginning to accommodate a wide range of tastes, from air tours to the ruins of Bonampak, Yaxchilán, Palenque, and the Lacandón bioreserve, to bus trips to indigenous towns. These latter trips included entry into the churches of Chamula and Zinacantán on payment of a fee, a visit to a wattle-and-daub thatch house in Zinacantán where one could watch women weaving with the backstrap loom, and to a museum that was carefully constructed according to the elders' specifications of old houses. In the city of San Cristóbal, the commercial establishments along Calle Real de Guadalupe and Insurgentes, the main streets that bisect the city's center, grew from handicraft shops making and selling goods to Indians and a few backpackers in the 1960s to sophisticated shops selling such items as designer hand-loomed and embroidered fabrics.

Indigenous towns became the sites of Mayan representation of themselves and their cultural products to tourists in the 1980s and 1990s. Traditional potters in Amatenango were beginning to respond to the tourist trade in the early 1980s, and by the latter part of the decade few potters made the standard ware of water carriers and storage pots for local markets. Most people had piped-in water by then, and the women could make more money producing figurines, candlesticks—even menorahs were available in season—and planters for display in tourist hotels. Amatenango became a regular tour-bus stop, and a small troup of little girls armed with clay animals, pots, and vases descended on the tourists with unrelenting force. Eye-catching assortments of decorated pots were placed on the Pan-American highway, and direct sales to highway traffic accounted for almost half the proceeds of households whose properties extended to the margins of the highway. Those who had house lots that bordered the highways came to take advantage of the traffic that Amatenangueros once feared.

The *pueblos indios* had always guarded their interior spaces from *ladino* intrusion. Religious officials prided themselves on retaining the integrity of the towns, particularly keeping out *ladinos* during the celebration of Easter week. Among the most adamant expressions of their control over space was the prohibition of any photographs in or near the church or of religious rituals and officials. Within the past ten years, this has become a hotly contested issue in San Juan Chamula, where officials were reputedly responsible for the death of two tourists who violated the proscription against taking photographs.

With the increasing influx of money and attention by the central government during the 1970s and 1980s, the plazas of the indigenous municipalities became sites for the merging of *ladino* and indigenous practices. Paved and tiled plazas, flowering trees, and huge town offices made government influence locally visible, but the plazas still served as ceremonial spaces for religious celebrations of local saints and civic inaugurations of officials. They also became the site for patriotic special events in which schoolchildren and others demonstrated allegiance to the nation. In addition, they served as general assembly sites for the male populations of the towns when policies affecting the lands or other issues were aired on public address systems, with all the men gathered to listen and express their opinions. By the late 1980s, Indians were asserting control over the town centers in many of the predominantly indigenous towns, as *ladinos* who had dominated them at the time of my early field trip began to abandon their houses. I found this transformation in the town centers of San Andrés Larrainzar, Tenejapa, and Chenalhó, where indigenous *cofradias* began to control the church and the plaza in front of it with festivals for the saints that they favored.

With rising protests against neoliberalism in the mid-1980s and throughout the 1990s community boundaries no longer contained indigenous practices. *Campesino* organizations mobilized marches of hundreds and sometimes thousands of men and women that converged on the plazas of major cities of Chiapas, carrying placards and banners announcing their protests and their group affiliation—CIOAC, ARIC, OCEZ, and the symbols of the PRD and PT were especially prominent. Women integrated in these groups would join the marches, but they also marched separately, as on the Day of Women, March 8, and the pilgrimages organized by the catechists, carrying candles, incense, and flowers and wearing their best traditional *huipiles*. During these years I saw graffiti on the walls of buildings in indigenous pueblos condemning the government and expressed support for opposition political leaders and parties.

Government officials tried to take back public spaces with staged mobilizations of *campesinos* bused in at government expense, as they had done in the decades of PRI hegemony in the highlands. Among the indigenous people, those who had allowed themselves to be carted in the PRI government trucks—the so-called *acarreados*—were treated with scorn. By 1993, the only indigenous communities where these staged mobilizations continued were Chamula and Oxchuc, where the local PRI officials fined any household that did not send a representative. In the spring of 1993, when President Salinas visited Oxchuc, we watched Oxchuc and Huixtán men, wearing traditional woven clothing, practice the motion of raising the flags of the state and nation (chapter 3). This exemplified the practice of instituting Solidarity programs where protest was detected, and money flowed into the PRI treasuries of municipalities. Symbolic warfare played out in town plazas became a frequent occurrence, with banners and placards of Solidarity programs vying with opposition party graffiti.

After the uprising of 1994, a new type of "political tourism" responded to the influx of human rights advocates, political activists, and members of NGOs. This new form of tourism encouraged an ongoing dialogue between indigenous activists and segments of the international audience they had attracted. A National University of Mexico student programmed a tour showing the points where Zapatista soldiers carried out their New Year's Eve takeover of the town, as indigenous history became incorporated in what had been the citadels of *ladino* power during the colonial period.

Spatial production of changing social relations. The production of the symbolic spaces of struggles that have gained international attention occurs in events when people oppose the terms of oppressive national rule on the one hand, and the destructive aspects of globalization on the other. As new centers for global struggle are being identified and marked by ritual gatherings, they often become targets of nationalist opposition. Aguascalientes, in the conflict zone in Chiapas, is now recognized worldwide, along with Tiananmen Square and the Plaza de Mayo in Argentina, as a site of encounter in the global spaces marked by confrontations that have transcended the boundaries of national states.

Aguascalientes bears a heavy symbolic burden as the site constructed in the Lacandón rain forest to accommodate an international gathering of supporters at the National Democratic Congress in July 1994. Indigenes, *ladinos*, international visitors from throughout the hemisphere and beyond, the First Nations, Native Peoples, *Originarios*, along with reporters, TV camera crews, intellectuals, and politicians took the 22-hour trip into the jungle that most described as an odyssey into another world. The separation from ordinary life as they entered into Realidad, the name of the central command post of the Zapatistas, cultivated in the participants the sense of a new dimension of life experience.[26] Realidad became a symbolic target after the February 9, 1995, invasion of the jungle, when it was destroyed by Federal troops. In an absurd appeal to the ecological NGOs, the army planted trees—to replace those that were cut down by the Zapatistas to construct the stadium, soldiers explained. Later, four new Aguascalientes were constructed for the second anniversary of the uprising.

During the three days that I spent in one of these reconstructed Aguascalientes, called Oventic, when the Intercontinental Congress for Humanity and against Neoliberalism was called in July 1996, I was able to experience a globalized space produced by indigenes in a way that conformed to their agenda. The community of San Andrés Sacam Ch'en de los Pobres (the new name for San Andrés Larrainzar) built the main auditorium, a raised platform with a gabled roof opening up to a series of bleachers. About twenty log cabin lodges were constructed to house the thousands of national and international guests. As each indigenous group arrived, the delegates stepped up to the platform and made it their sacred space by waving incense, sprinkling pine needles, striking up the handmade harps, guitars, flutes, and drums, and dancing. That evening as the invited guests arrived, I saw a contingent of the Grandmothers of the Plaza de Mayo, and Eduardo Galeano and Alain Touraine, intellectuals who have influenced *Subcomandante* Marcos and other figures who occupy the imagination of the fledgling global society. *Comandante* Ana María read the speech that I discussed above, which included a greeting to join the ranks in the fight against neoliberalism and death. In the forum of the new Aguascalientes, which Gary Gossen describes as a modern-day tabernacle (Gossen 1999), *Comandante* David welcomed the ranks of the EZLN, as men, women, and children descended from the hilltops carrying lamps, flashlights, and candles that lit the trails with a ribbon of light. As performance, the event was unparalleled.

It was the last global assembly permitted by the beleaguered PRI government, which clearly felt outdistanced by the public performance of its opponents. Having lost its command over the pageantry of public spaces, the PRI government asserted its sovereignty by severely restricting travel to Chiapas. It increased its review of documents of foreigners and began expelling foreigners with tourist visas who went beyond the usual tourist circuits. It was particularly aggressive with those who came as international human rights observers to spend time in the "peace huts" in the rain forest villages. Following the overwhelming success of the intercontinental meeting in July 1996, the Zapatistas abandoned attempts to enter into negotiations for peace with a government that refused to honor the accords arrived at in San Andrés.

Yet the public demonstrations of Chiapas civil society did not end with the stepped-up demonstrations and arrests. On June 22, 1998, a group of about three hundred protestors and Zapatista supporters whom I described in chapter 5 marched into the city protesting the killing of ten *campesinos* in el Bosque earlier in the month. Their choice of the plaza of the cathedral as the site to assert that "civil society is still alive!" is one of a series of events in which contested spaces were chosen as sites for dissent.

The following year, the Zapatista National Consultation chose this same space for its national consultation on the weekend of the spring equinox in March 1999. In the series of formal and informal encounters described in chapter 5, the Zapatistas took back some of the spaces from which the government had tried to exclude them. In San Cristóbal de Las Casas, I watched them as they took back the the plaza of the cathedral and rebuilt the tent where members of civil society sold videos and posters portraying their struggle. This symbolic representation of the tabernacle-like structure in Realidad had been torn down by *coletos* in January of 1999 and replaced with a new stand covered with a bright yellow plastic sheeting sheltering the mural of masked Zapatistas. It was similar to the structure built in Aguascalientas for the first National Democratic Convention in August 1994, and the act of rebuilding it, like the building of similar structures in the four Aguascalientas for the commemoration of the January 1, 1994, uprising, was an act of rebellion. Immediately after the vote that was part of the consultation was carried out on March 21, 1999, town officials moved in to construct a series of booths in what was declared a "Spring Cultural Festival." The DIF displayed the indigenous crafts it sells in tourist shops, arrayed on wooden dummies representing Indians dressed in ceremonial garments of indigenous pueblos in the vicinity. It was clearly a retaking of the public spaces, ironically using mannequins of Indians to make the point.

The *coletos* of San Cristóbal declared an end to the public forums that congregated in the plaza of the cathedral by undertaking a massive renovation in December, 1999, just a few days before the 75th birthday celebration for Bishop Samuel Ruíz. In the course of the next four months there was little indication of progress, except for the erection of what looked like dispersed bunkers on the perimeter of the ravaged plaza.

Zapatistas who had traveled to Mexico City for the national consultation in March experienced what it was to join in the production of national popular space in the *zócalo*. Dozens of Zapatistas marched with thousands more of their supporters to the *zócalo*, where they converged with 70,000 electrical workers protesting the reorganization of their department, thousands of students protesting tuition increases, and debtors who had been bankrupted by the 1994 devaluation of the currency. This huge public space, fronting the sixteenth-century Spanish cathedral and the ruins of the twin temple of the Aztec capital city Tenochtitlán, has become the center of many storms of protest, especially since the debt crisis of 1982. It became the focus of civil society support groups protesting military action from the early days of the uprising in January 1994. Throughout the years of civil discontent following the inauguration of President Zedillo, it served as the site of protests by the Barzonas, the debtors group formed after the devaluation of the peso in December, 1994. This dramatic incorporation of the Zapatistas in this national site for protest was a convincing prelude to their anticipated incorporation in the nation.

The spatial demonstration of solidarity is an important affirmation of popular movements; while it does not create new structures, it reinforces solidarity among the grassroots movements that enter into it. The very disparity of the groups that converge in these public spaces is a mark of the multiplicity of protests and wide range of demands in response to globalization processes that have disrupted the lives of the middle and lower classes alike. The space itself is like a mirror which reflects back to each participant the communicating groups that relate through electronic messages. Far from exemplifying the confusion or fragmentation that is often charged of globalization, each of the major gatherings has focused on specific themes that becomes the center of the dialogue and performances. In the civil society assemblies during the dialogues, the unifying theme was the aim for a just and dignified peace. Despite the extreme disruption of their lives, the Zapatistas proved in their symbolic reoccupation of public spaces that they were not alienated from the communities that gave birth to the uprising.[27]

Symbolic warfare characteristic of the pre-1994 uprising has now developed into real warfare. Indigenous people no longer tolerate the fetishized representations of themselves in government party mobilizations. With the intensified repression of pueblos that have declared themselves autonomous, army patrols hover near or in the public spaces. *Campesino* organizations often protest in front of town halls, demanding that officials who do not represent their interests leave office. These changes, discussed in chapter 5, are played out in confrontations that abandon the charade of paternalistic control by the government over indigenous people who used the town plazas to parade their hegemonic force.

The spaces of assembly became new sites of conflict. In the two years following the international protest against the Acteal massacre and subsequent human rights violations, the government extended its undeclared war to Oventic, one of the four reconstructions of Aguascalientas. Their pretense was to round up foreigners, who were often accused of being the agents who had precipitated the conflict. On the eve of the millennium, several international visitors were arrested in Oventic and detained in the immigration service for engaging in "political activity" just by being there.

The expansion of "experiential spaces" (Watanabe 1992), as indigenous people engage in political practices beyond their communities, threatens *ladino* control as never before. The presence of "monkey dancers" from Chamula and Zapatistas from the rain forest in the plaza of the cathedral shook *coleto* society to the core. Recognizing the superiority of indigenous symbolic uses of these spaces, the government resorted to military control.

In order to assess the potential of indigenous autonomy in more than the symbolic terms in which it is couched, I shall turn to the geopolitical issues of power and the innovative ways in which indigenous people in Chiapas and throughout the world are attempting to regenerate their own cultures and those of others.

GLOBALIZATION
AND INDIGENOUS AUTONOMY

In the five years since their uprising, Zapatistas and their supporters in Chiapas and throughout Mexico have expanded the scope of a movement that began by utilizing nationalist appeals to gain equal rights, to the development of a broader effort to gain pluricultural autonomy for indigenous pueblos within cultural regions. The movement itself has become increasingly split between those who would formulate their claims in socioeconomic terms and those who would pursue a new social contract between the nation and its constituent cultural ethnicities. Those who follow the latter path have forged alliances with other indigenous groups beyond the borders of Mexico and international human rights organizations, and have made other alliances designed to reinforce their rights to cultural autonomy and the freedom to express it.[28]

The innovative strategies demonstrated by the Zapatistas and their supporters in civil society are challenging the hierarchical state model extant in Europe and the constituent colonized states since the sixteenth century.[29] They have set the pace for democracy in practice that was lacking in the five hundred years of Spanish and *mestizo* domination. They are enacting the foundation for a pluricultural coexistence based on their experience as distinct indigenous entities within regions characterized by a multiplicity of languages and customs. Their exhortation to "order while obeying," is premised on relations fostered in communities where officials gain greater prestige by listening than by ordering. The cry for autonomy as distinct self-governing entities is correlated with a mode of socialization in their families and communities where respect for the will of others, including that of children, still promotes an awareness of what autonomy may mean in a collective setting.

I shall recapitulate some of the innovative steps taken by the Zapatistas to redefine their relations with the nation, and with it, their role in a history of their own making. This will take into account 1) pluricultural premises of governance, 2) human rights covenants and their instrumentation in Chiapas, and 3) the global significance of autonomy in the constitution of a pluricultural state. If I succeed in my purpose, I shall show how their struggle is addressing some of the major trends in a globalizing world, in which indigenous peoples are taking a lead in overcoming the impact of alienation, disruption of social and spatial orientation, and the fragmentation of a cultural core for regeneration itself. At the same time, they are trying to adhere to practices in their daily life that instill respect for other views of the world, and to abjure hierarchy and dominance.

Pluricultural Premises of Government

The multiclass and pluriethnic constitution of the Zapatista grassroots communities and their supporters defies analyses that fail to take into account the multiple dimensions that generate the movement. Hector Díaz-Polanco locates two of those dimensions in the class and ethnic problematic. Class movements, he notes, exclude ethnic demands as an obstacle to the greater goal of the revolution, while ethnic movements may work in multiclass groups, often promoting traditions that are authoritarian, and may undermine a lasting alliance of class and ethnic minorities (Díaz-Polanco 1995:33).

In Díaz-Polanco's analysis, the contradictions between ethnic particularity and collective norms and the universal rights of the individual are so deep that they are virtually impossible to resolve. Members of ethnic colonies are often blind to the internalization and reproduction of the very tendencies in the dominant society that have defined the ethnic oppression they experience. He proposes a research agenda that addresses the ethnic problem in relation to the struggle for coeval participatory democracy. The Guatemalan peace process indicates that this outcome not only is not inevitable, but also is antagonistic to the avowed principles of the indigenes political practices as they are now defining them (Warren 1998; Jonas 2000).

I would introduce a third dimension of identity ignored by Díaz-Polanco and other contributors to the anthology, *Etnia y nación en América* (Díaz-Polanco 1995), that of *gende*

gender. The layering of an ethnic-gender-class dynamic poses new difficulties but proposes an exit that is premised on the most oppressed sector within both class and ethnic oppression, that of women. Gender issues subvert dichotomies of class and ethnicity because they transcend both social groupings. Women have been able to unite across these divides more effectively than men, as Stephen documents in her account of women's social movements (1997a). This is also demonstrated in the Zapatista women's conventions in Chiapas (Hernández Castillo 1997). Engels proposed that the measure of democracy in society could best be assessed by the status of women (Leacock 1978). The corollary of this is that unless women achieve equality, the society will reproduce inequality by cultivating the conditions for superordinate and subordinate positions and the behaviors that reinforce them in their position as mothers and wives in the home.

I shall explore this proposition with the experience of indigenous women set forth in their declarations to the Beijing World Congress of Women in 1995. The women, who came from a hundred "nations," or distinct tribal groups, drafted a series of declarations that began with a fundamental premise which all of the delegates supported.

Article I, Beijing Declaration,
from the Indigenous Peoples Delegation

> The Earth is our Mother. From her we get our life and our ability to live. It is our responsibility to care for our Mother and in caring for our Mother we care for ourselves. Women, all females, are manifestations of Mother Earth in human form.

This declaration by indigenous women flouts the critique of essentializing that is prevalent in current anthropological debates. Yet the message of harmony that recognizes the positive virtues of their gender difference has a special authority when it represents the invocation of traditions that were nearly obliterated during the centuries of European expansion and colonization. For the indigenous women who drafted the statement, "false harmony" is based on the repression of difference, which they expose as the hegemonic denial of protest against the injustices of gender, race, and class. The novelty of their message lies in the assertion of the generative value of conflict as they seek a balance in society between genders, among races of humans and other species, and with nature. The mythopoetic expression in the phrasing of the Beijing Declaration from the Indigenous Peoples Delegation cited above contains a complex understanding of the dialectical forces in nature and human relations that could become an important principle for surviving in a multicultural society.

I will argue that the indigenous position marks a positive step in cultural revindication that they feel is necessary in order for them to play an effective role in the globalization process. The statements in the Beijing resolution resonate with those of the Mayans of southern Mexico and Quechuas and Aymaras of Bolivia whom I encountered in my field research. These are expressed in the notions of the Pachamama, the Mother Earth, and Sapuy, or Huari, among Andean people, and in the Tatik K'ak and Me'tikchich U, or

Father Sun and Grandmother Moon, of the Tzeltal Mayans. This balanced cosmogony of the Sun and Moon related to human gender differences is a metaphor for gender complementarity that is widespread in the American hemisphere. In most of the Americas, origin myths contain androgynous or dual creative powers, from Coatlicue of the Mesoamerican people, to Mama Ocllo and Manco Capac of the Andean people. Montes Ruíz (1986) sums this up for the Andean people as the opposition of symbolically sexualized entities: the sun, the mountains and the *puna*, are male, while the moon, the land, the *pampas*, and the valleys are female.

The concept of harmony that more than eleven million Quechua and Aymara people throughout the Andes share is that of a universal order and the generation of continuity in life as a product of a constant struggle of opposite forces (Alderete 1998:59–60). I found the same principles among acculturated Quechua and Aymara people who worked in Bolivian mines. Men and women retain a sense of the gender balance in their universe by offerings of liquor to the *Pachamama,* the earth-space-time spirit, and of the heart of a llama to *Sapuy*, the hill spirit, which enables them to retain a sense of their own being and its cultural regeneration (Nash 1979:318 *et seq.*).

Mayans, who were converted to Catholicism some time after the conquest of Chiapas in 1532, still believe in cosmological forces that enter into a daily contest to maintain the gendered balance achieved in the diurnal cycle. The myth related in chapter 2 about Our Grandmother Moon, Hme'tikchich U, and Our Father the Sun, Htatik K'ak, projects human behavior into the cosmic world by affirming the responsibility that humans have to maintain this balance. Implicit in this view is the possibility of maintaining distinct spheres of behavior without hierarchy. Although aboriginal American societies had developed class and status hierarchies in Mesoamerica and the Andes long before the arrival of the Spaniards, there were many societies that resisted domination by the early empires. Even within these empires, the principle of subordination based on gender and ethnicity was not presupposed, as it was in Europe at the time of the conquest.[30] The term "egalitarian" used by ethnohistorians goes far beyond that implied by "equality" in Western democracies; it refers to societies without classes that demonstrated full sexual symmetry, where individual autonomy prevailed, and the exercises of authority over others, even that of adults over children, was discouraged.

This autonomy, in the sense of the recognition of differentiation by sex and age and the necessity of giving space for its exercise, was denied in Western philosophy from at least the time of Aristotle, and even by anthropologists as late as the first wave of feminism. Implicit in this construction is the emphasis on sameness instead of the principle of difference that is so important among indigenous societies. Missionaries and conquerors interpreted the egalitarian behavior of natives as an indication of the barbarity of the people they encountered. It was taken as proof of their need to be civilized rather than as an alternative vision of how humans can relate to society. Europeans could not imagine any institutions with autonomy for all members, least of all the family (see especially Etienne and Leacock 1980; Leacock and Nash 1977). It is autonomy in this radical sense that the indigenous movements of the hemisphere are espousing.

Collective goals. The collective representation of indigenes as Bees and Ants is grounded in their fundamental mode of relating to each other as a collective people. Although few indigenous peoples in the Americas retain the collective social and production systems that once prevailed, these systems nonetheless remain the default position of the communities and come to the surface when they are under stress. Collective commitments have animated the agrarian rebellions of all the countries in Latin America that retain significant indigenous minorities. Those who have retained collective production practices with shared distribution of the harvest are the most adamant in the movement for self-determination, although they are a small minority. This will be discussed below.

What was preserved of indigenous culture was a result of the custodianship by elders, male and female, and all women charged with the enculturation of their children into these values. Perhaps because women were considered to be less of a threat to the conquerors, and because they were not as often as men obliged to leave their communities in forced labor gangs, indigenous people entrusted women with the cultivation and perpetuation of traditions. It was they who ensured the transmission of indigenous languages and cultural traditions to their children. They managed the ceremonial activities in the rites of passage celebrated within households that enabled children to mature as true men and women and that ensured the reproduction of society in accord with custom. Men were charged with public rituals conducted by the civil religious hierarchies introduced by the Spaniards that adopted Western saints. But these rituals depended on the collective work of women in the households of the officials. Washing the clothing of the saints, cooking for the fiestas, and other mundane tasks are considered sacred, with important ritual roles accorded to senior women who manage these activities (Nash 1995b).

The stereotype of women as conservative derives from this conscious and unconscious social responsibility entrusted to them. With increasing contacts and integration with the dominant society, women often sacrificed or were denied entry into mainstream career lines through education and political advancement in the new settings created by colonization and imperialism. Indeed, women bore a double burden of marginalization because of their lack of education and acculturation to Western modes. Despite this, they speak positively of this burden of responsibility.

This engendered technique of cultural survival (see chapter 3) is now threatened as never before by invasive economic institutions that undermine subsistence strategies. This is a result both of the alternative opportunities women have for gainful employment and of the commodification of indigenous products of the land and of crafts, drawing women into capitalist markets. It is also due to migration of women as well as men to cities and to colonization zones, forced by the loss of land and resources.

Finally, the militarization of the retreat zones of indigenous people that accompanies the explorations for oil, metal, lumber, and biodiversity in fauna, flora, and humans is a constant assault on indigenous ways of life. These are the sites where the intersections of gender, race, and ethnic subordination now contested, as distinct moral systems come into contact. Indigenous women's custodianship of beliefs and the social relations that constitute the indigenous ways of life are weakened in these alien settings. Women are among the chief victims of the harassment, assault, and murder meted out by soldiers and paramilitary.[31] Ethnographic studies of these sites provide us with an understanding of what is at stake in the words of indigenous women who are responding in their own terms to the challenge. They also provide a counterpoint to feminist postmodern exegeses that dismiss such radical departures as essentializing.[32]

What have the Zapatistas and their support groups in civil society taught us about the possible resolution of the contradiction? Women raised the issue of gender oppression in indigenous as well as national society at their forum at the Indigenous National Congress in January 1996, objecting to the facile assumption that their problems would be solved with the granting of autonomy to indigenous pueblos (field notes on Mesa Table 6 of the National Indigenist Congress, January 5, 1996). By raising the concrete practices of male dominance and the need to renounce them in a democratic society, they suggest a way around the polemic of tradition as an ultimate canon condoning all practices that invoke it. There are, as the Zapatista women assert, bad traditions as well as good, and not all customs should be respected.

The indigenous movement is charting a path for multicultural coexistence that proposes eradication of male dominance and patriarchy in the home and community as an essential part of the struggle for ethnic revindication. Women's demands for respect and dignity are the fundamental premises for extension to all members of the society.

Human Rights and Indigenous Participation in Governance

Indigenous peoples, as defined by the Inter-Commission Task Force on Indigenous Peoples (1997), are those that have maintained a collective identity even within repressive states and have continued to struggle to preserve control over their territories and self-determination for themselves. In Chiapas, the society of semi-autonomous multicultural entities that indigenous peoples are seeking to construct within a national federation of ethnic groups is based on their resistance to domination during five hundred years of colonization and independence. These self-constituted groups that represent a pluricultural and multicentered society that is more adapted to the emerging global ecumene than to the fading nation-states. And, because they put survival at the center of their struggle, they are attempting to protect themselves and their cultures from the destructive aspects of globalization and the exposure of their subsistence economy to neoliberal economic developments that have coincided with the collapse of the national welfare system, which had previously provided some mechanisms of support.

The logic of these indigenous societies is so embedded in cultural practices and beliefs that it requires the kind of holistic approach that was once the bedrock of anthropological inquiry to penetrate. Rituals that maintain the balanced opposition of cosmic and physical forces in beliefs and practices still pervade agricultural and artisan practices. This competition of opposed powers, played out on the Mayan ball courts or in the Andean *tinkachus* (ritualized combat), ensured the balance that gave energy to society and the cosmos. Dual models that are still found in attenuated characteristics in Chiapas moieties, and in more explicit forms in the dual models of the Andes (Gelles 1998:282), maintain difference as a generative principle to promote energy throughout the environment. The effectiveness of these beliefs and practices has been distorted by populist governments that have co-opted indígenes through favoritism. Until the present, indigenes have not directly confronted these practices, but current protests, such as that of CIOAC in Ixtapa, Ocosingo, and Las Margaritas, are exposing the corruption, diversion of public funds, and exploitation of women and girls by both indigenous officials and *ladino* superordinates. The underlying racism is being publicly denounced, along with the practices that maintain it. This is the basis for the Secretary of Indigenous Peoples of the United Nations calling for the incorporation of indigenous practitioners in developmental projects that pretend to be sustainable.

Autonomy and Self-Governance

The value of agricultural practices, medical resources, and arts of indigenous peoples is often ignored or wrested out of context. This is the body of tradition embedded in a cultural logic that is necessarily opposed to Western practices. It is a logic, as Paul Gelles (1998:236) shows in Andean irrigation systems, "that transmits and reproduces collective representations about fertility, disease, power, ethnic identity and the cosmos in general."

Indigenous women's perspectives are of particular value in regard to framing the grounds for autonomy because as they are finding their own voice, they address the multiple injuries of sexism, classism, and racism that perpetuate their marginalization (Marcos 1997; Romany 1993). They do not compartmentalize these assaults on their humanity because they experience the impact of multiple oppressions in their daily life, within the family as well as in the wider society (Article 5 of the Beijing Declaration). While the concerns for their marginalization in the wider society are central for indigenous women, they are also beginning to voice demands related to strengthening the moral core of their own societies. In combating the debilitating effects of alcoholism and violence against women within their communities, they are rejecting the imposed codes of Western powers that divide private practices from the public morality of state legal codes and theological doctrine. Women's rights to seek legal redress for wrongs committed against them by abusive fathers, brothers, and husbands were restricted in Western law courts. In the context of the separation of private and public issues in the state legal systems, women were often subordinated to indigenous men.[33] Because of their limited knowledge of the language of the courts and, even more important, their rejection of the gender subordination implicit in Western laws, women are phrasing their rights in words that evoke a primordial sense of balance on the cosmic level related to gender balance in communities.

Article 36 of the Beijing Declaration

That indigenous customary laws and justice systems which are supportive of women victims of violence be recognised and reinforced. That indigenous law, customs and traditions which are discriminatory to women be eradicated. (Turpel, 1998:100–101).

Because women in Chiapas have separate responsibilities from men in their own communities, they are distancing themselves more than men are from the national society that has
doubly oppressed them. They are seeking to redress the injustices they suffer in both settings by turning to international arenas. As they enter into struggles to dismantle the
structures of domination, they become acutely aware of their own discrimination as
women within indigenous groups. The position of native women in international settings
resonates with that of the Zapatista women in that they will not delay stating their own
demands for autonomy in the home and community until after the conflict over gaining
autonomy is resolved (Fiagoy 1990).

The Transnationalization
of Indigenous Human Rights

Initiatives to enforce the rights of indigenous people come in the encounter between
human rights activists of transnational NGOs and activists of grassroots organizations, or
GROs, who are addressing issues of the violations of human rights in their own backyards.
This is the arena for transformative change that has developed in the wake of universal
declarations.[34] It is in these arenas, often created by the disembedding of social relations
based on primordial ties, where indigenous people who are asserting their human rights
as a culturally distinct group are coming into contact with transnational groups.[35]

Some of the new directions of human rights NGOs draw on globalized religions
(Casanova 1997:126). In the zones of mounting indigenous rebellion in Chiapas, Guerrero, and Oaxaca, Catholic priests, abetted by indigenous deacons in Christian Base
Communities, propose a theological vision of liberation that motivates protest against
impoverishment and injustice. The active and vocal roles of the clergy have made many
Mexican and foreign-born priests the new martyrs of the church. The modern conventions of human rights echo papal statements, from Pope John XXIII's *Mater et Magistra* in
1961 to his *Pacem in Terris*, which was addressed to the whole world. Pope John inveighed
against the growing gap between rich and poor. The Center for Human Rights "Fray Bartolome de Las Casas" is providing documentation of human rights abuses that is disseminated to a world audience. Protestant groups, such as Pastors for Peace and Peace
Brigades International, are reinventing the role of witnessing in conflict zones throughout the Americas. Secular groups and religious groups are able to reach an international
audience of policy-makers as well as activists who are able to intervene in cases of human
rights violations.

The key word in the formation of transnational NGOs is "alternative": rethinking economic development and political institutions in new ways that reject the orthodox models
(Bebbington and Thiele 1993). By providing a political space to mobilize public opinion at
home and throughout the world, transnational NGOs are keeping alive the basis for opposition to entrenched nationalist power structures. Transnational NGOs become an
expanded arena for dissent when citizens of modernizing states lose confidence in national
law-making and -governing organizations (Landim 1987). As some turn backward to fun-
damentalist religious cults or paramilitary units to regain control over their lost privileges,

others seek more universal grounds in human rights activities. Many of these movements stem from established churches committed to making redemption meaningful in the realm of the worldly life. Operating outside of state institutions, NGOs often address the inequities that prevail with the decline in national redistributive systems, and call on the spiritual resources of indigenous people who have been marginalized from the centers of power (Nyoni 1987). They may generate alternative models for development that involve the cultivation of environmental consciousness (Bebbington and Thiele 1993; Farrington et al. 1993; Hernández Castillo and Nigh 1998; Prager and Riveros 1993). They also address the changing needs of constituencies that are losing traditional support structures. Women are now often called upon to earn wages when men are forced to migrate, or when technological innovation reduces their roles in agriculture (Landim 1987, Page 1998). In the process of addressing the immediate needs of prisoners charged with subversion of the state, or of political exiles in detention camps, transnational NGOs may create an expanded arena for political action.

The most universal role of transnational civil society is to reconstruct the moral basis for a global society. Liberal democracy and urban life tend to atomize the subject as citizen and to channel protest toward specific issues. In Third World countries such as Mexico, military repression compounds the pulverization of community. The moral basis in the emergent world order is increasingly dependent on NGO human rights and peace groups. This simulates at the international level the sense of *comunitas* that we are losing, as communities and kin groups are fragmented by forced migration and exile and military repression, as well as by voluntary choices related to employment opportunities. Few of the participants in the peace movements are connected by primal ties within the groups that assemble, yet they acquire friendships that bridge language and cultural differences as they risk their health, jobs, and even lives to bring support and encouragement to the people under fire. The majority of the participants who travel to the area are young or postretirement volunteers who are free of some of the obligations of people in their middle years, and women predominate over men. In their new international roles, they are introducing new communications technology as they break the barriers of controlled media. However, the dialectical opposition of tendencies set in motion by NGOs, that of promoting a sense of *comunitas* in a global society and at the same time creating dependencies, may cultivate rebellion while undermining the autonomy needed to realize fundamental change. It may also undermine the defensive stance of the targeted population without providing recourse to defensive measures when the human rights groups are absent. The agents are themselves often targeted by military and paramilitary bands as they reveal violations committed by these forces, and they may be deported in the name of national sovereignty.

The need for intervention is greatest where the kind of low-intensity warfare exists that is endemic in many countries where indigenous people are seeking to activate the rights that are proclaimed in international covenants. As a result, peace activists from all over the Western world[36] are drawn to support rebellions for democracy, which tend to occur in the periphery. In these conflict settings, the shift in strategy and ideology from that of the class struggles that preoccupied the nineteenth century becomes ever more evident with each manifestation. From a struggle against exploitation in the workplace to the current struggle for survival, women and children are major players. They are often confronting men of their own ethnic group and communities who have responded to their own needs for survival by integrating themselves in the federal armed forces or paramilitary groups. The low intensity warfare that has broken out in impoverished countries is often attributed to ethnic clashes. But as Miguel Alvarez Gán-dera, former secretary general of the National Commission for Mediation in the now disbanded CONAI, points out (1998), it stems from a struggle for survival in a global arena. Because indigenous people refuse to accept any longer the denial of their culture and the increasing degradation of their humanity that are the conditions for integration in global cycles, they find themselves opposed by armed forces of their respective countries. The military strength of these national forces is often enhanced by foreign funding or credit sources that are, paradoxically, often the same sources from which human rights and peace activists are drawn, from beyond their nation. Civil society is the nexus in which this strange assortment of allies and opponents meets and seeks to mediate their differences. Thus counterinsurgency warfare against people who are struggling to survive in this unequal combat with heavily armed troops brings forth a new alliance of the communities under attack with human rights activists often from the First World.

NGOs that ascribe to human rights are developing a new more flexible response that builds on the premises of both religious and secular moral orders. They are able to provide testimonies to a broader audience than that which either the nation-state or religious denomination addresses, and some of their agents have legal training. The role of international observer reinvents in these novel settings the witnessing that is a hallmark of face-to-face "folk" communities and of religious proselytizers. As Susanne Hoeber Rudolph (1997:12) indicates: "New alliances and goals become possible as domestic civil society joins up with transnational civil society to challenge states, and as states in concert employ elements in transnational civil society to limit particular state sovereignty." The effectiveness of the transnational human rights groups can be measured by the opposition they encounter from rogue governments that decry their presence in the name of sovereignty. Yet their vulnerability is still attested to by the many abuses of the human rights of agents who are subject to national sanctioning power.

CONCLUSIONS

The internationalizing of indigenous movements is a response to the acceleration of capitalist penetration after World War II, as indigenous people found themselves dislocated by enterprises that threatened their environment. They often despaired of gaining help from national governments that rejected populist claims in the name of neoliberal policies of development. Instead, they turned to international NGOs and the United Nations, where they found allies among other indigenous groups facing similar problems. The ethnic reawakening in the 1960s and 1970s throughout the world began to address common problems through united action (Stavenhagen 1996).

Indigenous peoples of Mexico experienced these dislocations, particularly in the decades of the 1970s and 1980s with the expansion of oil exploration in the Gulf, the Yucatán Peninsular, and Chiapas. Their fight to gain titles to the lands they were promised when they migrated to the Lacandón rain forest has expanded into a quest for cultural autonomy. This reawakening of indigenous identity is coming to fruition in Native American movements for multicultural coexistence throughout the hemisphere.

Semi-subsistence producers in Mexico, like those elsewhere in the continent who are increasingly forced to compete in international markets for the sale of their subsistence crops and artisan products, are seeking political alliances and markets beyond the old regional and national boundaries. The 1994 uprising was, as Collier and Quaratiello (1994) and others have shown, a warning to the Mexican government that the colonizers in the Lacandón rain forest could no longer support their marginalized conditions of life. In the intervening years, protracted delays in negotiating a settlement have expanded the scope of the problem.

hidden benefits
of globalization

A hidden benefit of global integration is the opening up of local protests against growing inequalities to a worldwide audience. This depends on a conscientious press whose reports are made available to a wide audience. It also depends upon data collection agencies inspired by human rights concerns. The conjuncture of these two conditions made the Chiapas uprising available to a wide reading public throughout the world. The press and human rights NGOs provided both a mirror for the indigenous people to perceive how the world was responding to their protest and a catalyst to world opinion. The most persuasive reaction was a volatile stock market that reacted negatively to the militarization of the conflict and to the massacre of *campesinos* in Acteal, and responded positively to negotiations for peace. An increasingly organized civil society orchestrated the intervention of a wide variety of international agencies that recognized the importance of cultivating world attention to indigenous *campesinos* who were once the most marginalized sector.

The messages of the Zapatistas have had a resounding impact throughout the world. Zapatistas are, like many of the cultivators and wage workers from Guatemala to East Timor, seeking democracy as they try to balance their subsistence needs with entry into cash crops or wage work in international markets. The new trade agreements have further marginalized them as their own nations have withdrawn the supports once offered by populist governments and abandoned them to the vicissitudes of free trade. The Chiapas Mayans are realists, in that they know they cannot return to the isolation in which they once lived, and their demands are modest. But in taking their stand, they are projecting a new vision of what democracy might be: coexistence, with their own languages and customs functioning along with those of others whose differences they have always respected, and participation in the decisions that affect their lives. They do not seek power for themselves but rather to ensure democratic processes for all people. Their armed uprising was only the last recourse to draw attention to the daily violence they face when all other protests failed. They now seek a peace that promises justice and dignity for all.

If 1994 will be assessed as the year in which free trade was embraced throughout the world, it will also be known as a time when capital markets responded negatively to government actions that allowed social discontent to reach the boiling point of uprisings. Fear of falling stock markets may yet become the most powerful force backing redistributive measures to ensure a favorable climate for investment. With Wall Street monitoring the uprising in Chiapas, the movements of EZLN forces in thirty-eight towns on December 1995 lent power to their demands for negotiating peace with the Salinas government and his successor Zedilla. When the government turned to a military solution in February 1995, increasing the federal armed forces and arming civilian bands, indigenous organizations persisted in their drive for a peaceful settlement. The failure of the government to comply with the agreement reached in San Andrés *Sacamch'n* in February 1996 caused a stalemate, but President Fox has placed indigenous autonomy on the agenda of the new congress. However the negotiations proceed, Mayas have forever changed the perception of indigenous relations with the state.

The Zapatista confrontation now poses dilemmas for all indigenous peoples in globalizing processes that threaten pluricultural coexistence and the capacity of humanity to generate differentiated cultural forms. Mayans are forging ties with other indigenous groups through the National Indigenous Congress. The demonstrations throughout the hemisphere on the quincentennial of the day once celebrated for the discovery of the Americas reinscribed October 12 as a day for the celebration of a plurality of ethnic groups. Mayans have not turned back from the course they took on that day when they demolished the statue of the conqueror of San Cristóbal. They are turning to alliances with international organizations as they experience confrontation with an increasingly repressive state power. These alliances will help to open space for the development of a transnational civil society that cultivates multicultural coexistence. But the realization of this potential ultimately depends on the mobilizations in civil society at the level of communities and regions. It is there that the organizations of women and men of indigenous societies are defining what they need to live in the world. When others appreciate that this opens up their worlds as well, we can begin to perceive the challenge for the coming millennium.

GLOSSARY

abanderamiento, raising flag ceremony
abejas, bees (**abuxu** Tzotzil)
acarreados/as, campesinos bused in for PRI assemblies
aguardiente, distilled cane liquor
alcalde, mayor; **alcalde mayor,** lord mayor
alférez, captain of fiesta; pl. **alféreces**
aluxob, liar
awayi, Tzeltal, verb to feel or to hear
bankil u'ul, Tzeltal, elder brother curer
barrio, neighborhood, **barriadas,** city wards
basta, enough
batz'il k'op, Tzeltal, true word or language
batz'il winik, true man or person; **winiketik,** men or persons (Tzeltal)
batz'il vinik, true man (Tzotzil)
bisil ta winik, respect for man
cabecera, center of a township
cacique, Arawak term for indigenous leader serving state, currently party boss
caciquismo, institutionalization of state co-optation of indigenous leaders; bossism
calmecac, Nahuatl term for school
calpul, Nahuatl term for kinship-based territorial unit
campesino/a, agricultural smallholder and/or laborer
cargo, burden or office
casa de cultura, house of culture, or cultural center
Casa del Pueblo, House of the Pueblo, Venustiano Carranza *campesino* center
casillas, voting lists
cha'uk, Tzeltal, lightning ray; **Tatik Cha'uk,** Lord of lightning, term for *subcomandante* Marcos
chinamit, Cakhiquel term for pueblo
Chinchulines, paramilitary group
cholos/as, people of indigenous descent in the Andes who are partially acculturated
cofradia, brotherhood sharing responsibility for fiestas of a saint
coletos, those who claim descent from the original conquerors, referring to hair worn in a pony tail, or **coleto, coleto auténtico,** or authentic
colono, agricultural wage laborer
comadre, godmother; **compadre,** godfather
combi, van used as bus
comisión ejidal, ejido commission
comunero, resident of indigenous community with access to common lands
comunidad, community
compadrazgo, kinship alliance based on ritual relationship of baptism
concentración, bringing together distinct populations
concejo, council

confederación, confederation

consulta, consultation (applied to the meeting of Zapatistas with the people to
receive their advice

coyotaje, reign of wolves

creoles, offspring of Spanish parents born in New Spain

deletrar, read haltingly, letter by letter

ejidos, from Latin, land at exit of town; Spanish term for lands donated to *campesinos*

encomienda, grant of tribute; **encomendero** recipient of **encomienda**

envidia, envy

hacienda, landed estate

halach winik, high chief (Tzeltal)

hectare, land measure, equal to about 1.6 acres

hermandad, brotherhood

huipil, indigenous woman's blouse

idioma, Spanish term for European languages

ik'al, black man, fearful large men who figure in Indian mythology, possibly related to
slaves who escaped from coastal planations

ilol, literally seer, pl. **iloletik**

indígena, Indian

indigenismo, ideology apparently pro-Indian but bent on acculturation

indigenista, pro-indigenous

indio, indigenous man, **india,** woman

kabiles, Guatemalan paramilitary units

Kiptik ta Lecubtesal, Tzeltal, United by Our Strength, peasant producers union

k'op rios, word of god (Tzeltal)

k'otonchu, Tzeltal, literally heart cover, man's tunic

kurik, Tzeltal, rustic person

ladino, bearer of Western culture and language

lek ay, it is good (Tzeltal)

latifundia, extensive landholding by a single owner or family

lengua, tongue, Spanish term for indigenous language

macehualob, commoner (Nahuatl)

mayordomo, religious officeholder, or caretaker

mestizo, mixed blood; **mestizocracia,** mestizo elites

me'tik, Tzeltal, mothers; **metik-tatik,** or **me'il tatil,** ancestor

municipio, township or municipality composed of two or more settlements

nahwal, Nahuatl term for animal spirit; Tzeltal, **wayohel**

paraje, subdivision of a **municipio** or township

pat'otan, Tzeltal, prayer, literally behind the heart

posh, medicine; **ya schan posh,** selling medicine, a reference to political speech-
making

principal, top-ranking officials

promotores, agents of change

pueblos, community in the sense of town as well as locus of nationalistic or broader
identification, **pueblos étnicos or pueblos indios,** indigenous pueblos

pukuh, evil, devil; pl. **pukuhetik**

reducción, reducing territorial base of population

regiones autónomos, regions with self-determination and government

resadoras, women prayermakers

selva, forest or jungle

sexenio, six-year term of president

skil ha', Tzeltal, cold water, reference to liquor
sk'in ta sk'opal, fiesta of the word (Tzeltal)
snichinal k'op, Tzeltal/Tzotzil, flowery speech of ceremonial language
socios, member of an association
solidaridad, solidarity
tatik, Tzeltal, father; **htatik,** my father
Tatik Dueño de la Creación, syncretic term for Lord God of Creation
tierras baldias, fallow land
tlaxilacalli, Nahuatl term for subdivision of town
totil-me'il, mother-father (Tzotzil)
u'ul, Tzeltal, curer-diviner; pl. **u'uletik**
wayohel, Tzeltal, animal spirit, or **nahwal**
zócalo, central park or plaza
zopilote, turkey buzzard

NOTES

Preface

1   Each year from 1988 to 1991 I was able to bring eight undergraduate students to Chiapas on the National Science Foundation Research Experience for Undergraduate grants. In 1993 I received a National Science Foundation grant for training graduate students and was able to bring two successive groups to Chiapas, the first in 1994 and the second in 1997. I am grateful to the NSF for making this possible and to the director of the Anthropology Program, Stuart Plattner, who had the vision to fund training in ethnographic field methodology.

Chapter 1
Indigenous Counterplots
to Globalization Processes

1   I am using the term substantive economy as defined by Polanyi (1957), who distinguished the actual economic behavior in areas governed by kinship structures and in past systems characterized as feudal or early empires. This contrasts with formal economic claims that deduce rational behavior in relation to market calculations. Mayan rebels are asserting the viability of collectivist noncapitalist alternatives in semi-subsistence cultivation coexisting with capitalist exchange. This challenges assumptions about lineal evolution and the single dominant mode of production that were central to both Marxist and liberal economic theory. The Noble prize in economics awarded to Amartya Sen for his work in the economics of social welfare in 1998 suggests an awakening to these substantive aspects of economic analysis ignored by mainstream economists. So, too, are the events surrounding the World Trade Organization meeting, November 30 to December 3, 1999, in Seattle, Washington, where a crowd of an estimated 10,000 protested the trade policies that ignored the needs of people throughout the world. A series of full-page ads sponsored by environmental and alternative trade policy groups in the *New York Times* before, during, and after the meetings dwelt on substantive issues of food, water, and air, as well as human rights of workers that should occupy the attention of those involved in trade negotiations.

2   Katherine Bowie (1992) has demonstrated the mythic dimensions of subsistence society, using Thailand as a case in point. Implicit in this myth is the "image of the Thai peasantry as homogeneous, egalitarian, self-sufficient, non-market and unchanging" (Bowie 1992:797). This myth has pervaded the histories of other third world countries. In contrast to subsistence societies, substantive societies can be characterized as feudal or early market, and apply to kingdoms as well as religious orders where class and status privileges prevail. What is signaled here is the orientation of those engaged in economic pursuits that rejects or abjures the profit rationale. The medical profession was guided by a nonprofit ethic until only recently, and while many of its practitioners may have been motivated by profit, the profession curbed for-profit practices.

3   See especially Comaroff and Comaroff (1992), and the review of the literature on resistance to global integration by subsistence economies in Nash (1994d).

4   Contrasts in the responses of nations during the financial crisis in southeast Asia in the summer of 1997 reveal the powerful dynamic of national and global financial interaction. The King of Thailand responded by shoring up the subsistence sector, urging a return to the land and promotion of food production during the restructuring of the capital sector. In contrast, the intransigence of Prime Minister Suharto of Indonesia in addressing the corruption endemic in his regime culminated with public demonstrations that toppled his government in 1998 and continued protests of students (*The New York Times* May 24, 1999).

5   During this period, the Dow Jones lost 6.06 points in a drop attributed to the situation in Mexico (Agencias, Washington, December 29, 1994, reported in *La Jornada*, December 30, 1994, p. 28). From

Christmas Eve to New Year's Eve, ten billion dollars left the country, according to German Gonzalez Quintero, president of the Confederation of National Chambers of Commerce (Concanaco), leaving national enterprises without dollars to cover their foreign obligations (Roberto Gonzalez Amador, *La Jornada*, 30 December 1994:26). U.S. mutual funds investment corporations lost heavily in this period. Financial analysts envisioned an inflationary future in Mexico given the instability of the peso and the lack of reserves (Josephine Jimenez, analyst of Montgomery Assets Management, interviewed in New York December 29, published in *La Jornada*, December 30, 1994, vol. ll, no. 3703, pp. 1–28).

6   Kearney (1996) has pointed out the inadequacy of the term "peasants" in the context of Mexican and Latin American indigenous cultivators.

7   Eric Wolf (1982) went on to rescue "the people without history" from this static world where history was written only by Europeans, giving special attention to the peasants and their role in the major revolutions of the first half of the twentieth century. Jane Schneider and Peter Schneider (1976) expanded the horizons of peasant studies in time and space to show how marginalized peasantries of Sicily played important roles in "successive world systems."

8   Sidney Mintz (1977), William Roseberry (1989), and Carol Smith (1984) provide the ethnohistorical studies that broke the spell of core capitalist dominance in the global economy. Jane Schneider (1977) raised the possibility that a world system existed before capitalism and proceeded to demonstrate the global scope of mercantile trade in luxury goods.

9   See Enloe 1983; Nash and Fernandez Kelly 1983; Ong 1982; Roseberry 1989; and Safa 1981.

10   See for example Schiller et al. 1992; Grasmuck and Pessar 1991; Nagengast and Kearney 1990.

11   Massey (1987) has remarked on the complexity with which Somalian agropastoralists respond to a high level of uncertainty in their arid environment before the shrinking of pasture lands required an intensification that devastated the soils. Posey (1983) has documented the ingenuity with which the Amazonian Kayapo exploit their environment without despoiling the delicate balance of faunal and floral resources. Walker (1985) has shown the balance maintained by Southeast Asian hill tribes as commoditized ventures such as poppy cultivation became part of their survival strategy. Okoko (1987) indicates the contradictions for Tanzania's socialist regime in a time of increasing scarcity, restricted growth, and government spending.

12   Among those studies are Arhem on Tanzanian agropastoralists (1984), Barkin on Mexican cultivators (1987), Corea on Sri Lanka (1975), Mencher (1978, 1985) on the impact of the green revolution and the loss of a subsistence base in India, and Pryor on Malawi and Madagascar (1990). With the Latin American debt crisis, many commercial entrepreneurs and even professionals sought subsistence strategies to survive (see especially Hans and Judith-Maria Buechler's 1992 study showing the remarkable ingenuity of small-scale entrepreneurs in deploying their families in various activities to maintain subsistence levels during the 1980s. In Bolivia, I knew many families of miners who were laid off with the closing of the mines who went to Cochabamba to work in harvesting crops and were repaid with a portion of the crop.

13   Li (1991) has assessed this potential in the Tinombo region of Central Sulawesi.

14   The "Gini coefficient" measures the distributional inequality in income and the UNDP provides indicators that measure educational and health levels and provide a clue to distribution of resources. Reference to comparative levels are made in assessing Mexico's development and its consequences.

15   The king of Thailand has reinforced his commitment to a plan strengthening the subsistence sector of small-plot farmers first proposed in 1994. Urging farmers to fortify their bargaining power through collective transactions, the King hopes to overcome individualistic approaches to capitalism by "rediscovery of the cultural capital of local communities." The ideology governing this recovery of collective petty commodity production, according to Vasana Chinvarakorn ("A New Theory," *Bangkok Post*, November 8, 1999:1,8), is that of the Buddhist *sammaditthi*, a key element of the road toward the end of the suffering, called the Eightfold Noble Path. Other signs of the recurring interest in addressing the substantive interests of people include the award of the Nobel prize in economics in 1998 to Amartya Sen for his work on the economics of social welfare. So, too, are the events surrounding the meeting of the World Trade Organization, November 30 to December 3, 1999, in Seattle Washington, where thousands of protestors from unions and environmental and human rights groups marched to protest trade polices that ignored the environmental impact of enterprises and the conditions of workers. A series of full-page ads sponsored by alternative trade organizations and environmentalists appeared in the *New York Times* before, during, and after the meetings, dwelling on substantive issues of food, water, and air, as well as human rights of workers that they claimed should occupy the attention of trade negotiations. Excoriating the World Trade Organization's censuring of nations that rejected biogenetically altered foods, the ads predicted that the next great war would be fought over water.

16 A sophisticated analysis of the current debate on the cultural criteria of ethnic identity is contained in Kay Warren's analysis of indigenous movements in Guatemala (1992). She assesses the dilemma of Mayan scholars in seeking traditional roots to underwrite a new relationship with the state, discussed in chapter 5 of this book. I am grateful to Lynn Stephen for bringing to my attention the analysis of Les Field (1999) that distinguishes "essentialist" and "constructionist" approaches to ethnic identity. Essentialist determination of identity, i.e., the reference to a set of essences, is more a part of common parlance than the constructivist approach that asserts the social construction of identities involving collaboration between subjects and anthropologists. Field defines essentialism as "the entrenched anthropological predilection (in both evolutionist and antievolutionist theoretical currents during the century) for describing the ethnic identification of a particular group of people in terms of a set of essences." The fact that this form of essentialism can be used to establish rights to a territory makes it an extremely useful term of self-representation, yet, as Field points out, one that threatens identification if the assigned essences are lost or abandoned. Kay Warren's (1998) engagement with Mayan intellectuals enables her to raise the critique of essentialism to a new level. She shows how charges of essentialism have become a polemical tool in debates to disorient social culturalism and indigenous political organizing.

17 Appadurai (1996), J. Friedman (1994) and Hannerz (1991) have staked out the anthropological domain in these global sites.

18 The importance of these linkages is shown in studies of gender and reproduction that use social indices to document comparative statements (Bose and Acosta-Belen 1995; Chant 1991; Collins and Gimenez 1990; Nash 1990; Stephen 1991, 1997a, 1994), of race and ethnicity (Mullings 1989), and of the underclass (Susser 1997; Vincent 1991).

19 Tarn (1991) rejected the "widespread empowerment of the critic at the expense of the poet" implicit in the cultural critique launched by Clifford and Marcus (1986). His imaginative reconstructions of Mayan cultural processes before and during the genocidal wars of the 1970s and 1980s (Tarn and Prechtel 1997), and that of Dennis Tedlock (1993), are based on years of ethnographic study that enable the authors to unlock the mysteries contained in complex metaphors.

20 Carol Ann Ready's thesis (1999) shows how women's coming to consciousness during and after the war in El Salvador is making appreciable changes in their political participation through the DIGNAS feminist movement. In contrast to feminists of the North, Salvadoran women retain their identification in maternal and familial roles within and beyond the organizational structure of feminist activism.

21 See Collier and Quaratiello (1994), and Womack (1999) for detailed analyses of the precipitating events for the Zapatista uprising.

22 Lynn Stephen (personal communication) describes the routing of messages sent from the jungle by couriers who then fax them to the newspaper, La Jornada, that puts them on the Internet.

23 The reference to a mirror is a frequent figure of speech in Don Antonio's narratives that relates to collective representations. It appears in the Popal Vuh as a master motif defining the gods' ultimate control over their "manikins," the human species, by casting a cloud over the mirror of their perceptions.

24 I first noticed the turn to this new direction in 1974 when the peasants of Cochabamba, Bolivia became the protagonists of change. Angered by edicts of the military regime of Hugo Banzer that drove the price of their surplus products below the costs of production, campesinos staged a road blockade that halted north-south movement on the main communication artery from Santa Cruz to La Paz. The campesinos's appeal to the right to live contrasted with the miners' opposition to forms of exploitation at that moment; later, when the miners joined forces with campesinos to oppose the New Economic Program that simultaneously closed the nationalized mines and taxed agricultural production, the right to live became a mutual banner. It continued to be the basis for successive protests against the conditions of the International Monetary Fund imposed by Paz Estenssoro's government in 1985, the most impressive of which was the March for Life and Peace in 1986 (Nash 1992a). Their movement was intercepted by an armed force of 8,000 national troops, refurbished, trained, and armed with financing for nacrotraffic controls. This scenario has become familiar in Colombia, Venezuela, and Ecuador, as well as in Mexico (Nash 1992a).

25 This parallels a similar address by Daphne Ale of Bougainville, who represented her people at the Women's Forum in Sydney, Australia in 1996 (Vinding 1998:12). "We are the custodians and the life line of our societies through our maternal heritage and in our positions in society," she told her audience of indigenous activists. Women like Daphne Ale, who still have the memory of a gender-egalitarian past, are not inhibited by postmodern fears of essentializing their positions as they speak from their experience of the problems they face. In a similar vein, Leonore Zabalata Torres, spokesperson for the Arhua-

can of Colombia (Vinding 1998:24), asserts that "Women have many things in common, and I deeply believe in what we conceive of as tradition: that the woman is the mother of the land, and similar to Mother Earth, she is productive, gives refuge and warmth."

26 The tendency to characterize as "essentializing" women's political action as women, as we discussed in Note 25 in relation to indigenous movements, reveals the failure in universalizing propositions that reduce the moment of coming to consciousness of subordinated groups. See Micaela di Leonardo's (1985) review of the positions of feminists regarding essentializing positions.

Chapter 2
Indigenous Communities

1 Laura Nader (1990) has shown how the ideology of harmony promotes these fictions at both local and national levels in Oaxaca. She found that the Zapotecs of Talea present a front of harmony as a shield to defend their autonomy from outside interests, while national leaders appeal to harmony in order to promote the power of the state over localities. This parallels what Kay Warren found in *The Symbolism of Subordination* (1989) along with a strategic syncretism to protect self-determinism within ethnic boundaries of domination. Florencia Mallon (1995:66) demonstrated how the negotiation of conflict during the nineteenth century created "vital, changing institutions through which people constructed and modified communal political culture."

2 My census of 1967 indicated that 87 percent of marriages adhered to the rule of moiety endogamy. When I returned in 1987, it was more frequently violated, but marriages contracted across moieties were usually elopements and caused uneasiness for the partners and their families. In the period from 1938 to 1965, for which I have all recorded homicides, three were the result of fights over a girl, in two cases a resident of the opposite moiety.

3 During my field sessions in the summers from 1961 to 1965, three deaths resulted from the interdiction against betrothals across moiety lines (Nash 1979).

4 Bishop Samuel Ruiz, who has had over three decades of acquaintance with indigenous people of the Diocese of San Cristóbal de Las Casas, interprets this to mean that what is behind the heart is transferred by prayer to be what is in front of the heart, or in Spanish, word and deed are *transparente* (Lecture at the University of Chicago Divinity School, May 24, 2000).

5 Myths recorded in other Mayan communities of the region state that the ancestors made people out of clay or even a series of different materials including wood and, finally, corn. In the pottery-making village of Amatenango, clay is the material used in all three creations, with earlier models lacking a leg (discarded because "their manikin couldn't work in the milpa"), genitals (discarded because "their manikins couldn't reproduce themselves") and a heart (discarded because "their manikins couldn't talk," since all communication comes from the heart). For these potters, the material clay remained a constant, and only the form differed.

6 It occurred to me when I learned of their deaths in 1986 within a few months of each other that the disease might have been precipitated for both of them by the use of chemical fertilizers which the local distillers began using especially in the 1970s to accelerate the process of fermentation. No men have succeeded them in their position of *bankil u'ul*, although several women curers have become practitioners.

7 The community setting maintained a central place in the next generation of anthropologists. Sol Tax of the University of Chicago, in collaboration with students from the Instituto Nacional de Antropologia e Historia promoted studies of municipalities undertaken by Fernando Camara in Tenejapa, Calixta Guiteras Holmes in Chenalhó, and Ricardo Pozas on Chamula. A second generation of University of Chicago students arrived in 1957 to carry out community studies in diverse ecological settings in the Tzeltal region of highland Chiapas (McQuown and Pitt-Rivers 1970) that resulted in two monographs (Hermitte 1992; Nash 1970) and essays focused on aspects of medicine, economy, political authority and social control, archeology, and history. In the diversity of cultural and ecological settings present in the western highlands, with five distinct dialects and altitudinal ranges from one to seven thousand feet, the municipal base provided a contained setting for preliminary investigations of a nearly unknown region. Evon Vogt arrived in 1957 to advance community studies in the Tzotzil region, and ethnographies proliferated as his students produced holistic studies in a wide range of monographs (*cf*. Vogt 1994). Guatemalan ethnologists recognize the vitality of communities, which were subjected to the long civil war and are now recuperating this base as they reassert indigenous identity (Carlsen 1997; Warren 1998; Watanabe 1992).

8 Contributors to *La Explosión de Comunidades* (Nash et al. 1995) observe the process of transgressing com-

munity boundaries by social movements mobilizing indigenous people in Chiapas since the uprising.

9   Tejeda Gaona (1995) rejects current approaches to resurrecting *comunidades indigenas* as yet another ploy to establish political spaces that generate linkages of cohesion with NGOs and government agencies with resources to distribute. By focusing on the "tattered vendors of ancient traditions in urban streets," he waves away the hundreds of thousands of mobilized *campesinos* and *comuneros* who assert their presence in communities as a viable alternative way of life. They are now seeking wider regional associations that will permit them to break out of the boundaries that limited the scope of their political action. Confusion of the inner boundaries constructed by communities to keep the outside world at bay and the boundaries imposed by the state to prevent concerted action in rebellion persisted. Kay Warren's (1992) memorable evocation of Guatemalan Mayan intellectuals who are rescuing their past from anthropological studies in order to substantiate their claims to distinctiveness in the present political arena, is instructive to those who would trash these Chiapas studies prematurely.

10 In her review of the republication of Gary Gossen's *Los Chamulas en el Mundo del Sol* in 1989, Ana Bella Perez Castro recognized the wealth of ethnographic material (1993). When the book was first published in Spanish in 1974, it was categorized along with other community studies of the "Harvard School" as yet another functionalist study. Yet by comparing cultural "wholes" as described in the many community studies in the Mesoamerican area, we now have the basis for reconstructing larger preconquest formations that diffused intellectual and cultural patterns throughout Mexico and Central America.

11 Florencia Mallon's (1995) comment on the local relationship of peasant villages to the development of capitalism contributes to the awareness of the value of community studies: "Because I examine the local process in the Yanamarca Valley using concrete empirical data, it is possible to put flesh on the bones that historians call 'the development of capitalism.'"

12 Lee Whiting (1994) indicates that in western Chiapas, sites such as Santa Elena, Poco Unic, Chinkultic, Tenam Puente, Tenam Rosario, Lagartero, Ojo de Agua, Guajilar, and Piedra Labrada had strong relations with classic Mayan centers of the rain forest, with ball courts, civil ceremonial centers, and writing characteristic of the classic Mayan. One can certainly add Toniná to that list as ongoing excavations reveal the history of the connection with Palenque.

13 Blanton and Feinman's (1984) use of the term "world system" in the context of Mesoamerica prior to the conquest may seem incongruous to scholars with a worldview cultivated in the European axis. It does serve their purpose in rendering intelligible the scope of activities in the competing sphere of influence of these early civilizations that shared pervasive themes in common and acted in terms of these universalizing premises.

14 The practice of allocating communal lands followed Spanish as well as preconquest patterns. The Aztec term *calpulli* which Zurita defined as "a barrio inhabited by a family, known as of very ancient origins, which for a long time owns a territory of well-defined boundaries, and all the members are of the same lineage," was found in use in Oxchuc (Villa Rojas 1946:366, 376) and in Chenalhó (Giiteras Holmes 1961), as well as Amatenango. While the usage implies preconquest roots for the divisions in contemporary indigenous towns, the Spaniards may have imposed the term they had learned in the central plateau. The use of the Nahuatl term in Chiapas suggests the strong contacts with Aztecs and Toltecs prior to the Spanish invasion (Calnek 1962).

15 See the discussion below of the Tzeltal communities and their attempts to ensure the balance of Tatik K'al, Father Sun, and Me'tik U, Grandmother Moon, p. 66–76.

16 There were mitigating circumstances in the decrees concerning the dispensation of communal properties, as Mallon (1994:73–74) points out. The June 1856 land laws during the "Liberal Revolution" did not charge poorer peasants court fees when they attempted to purchase lands in competition with speculators.

17 *Cientificos* refers to the intellectuals influenced by the positivist principles of August Compte, who fostered liberal government policies countering corporatist interests of the Church and state that sheltered indigenous communal holdings.

18 In the north of Mexico, Nugent and Alonso found that the people of Namiquipa, Chihuahua, conceived of the land grants as their right, due to their winning the territory from "barbarians." As descendants of *ladinos,* they assumed the rights of conquerors.

19 *Ejido* is derived from the Latin term *exitus,* or exit, derived from Roman Law that set aside lands near the town exits to recreation and rest that were not to be cultivated. It was introduced by Spain during the colonial empire, but acquired a new meaning after the Revolution of 1910–1917.

20 In towns with dispersed hamlets, patrilocal residence often cuts women off from their families of orien-

tation. Amatenango's nucleated center ensures close residence of daughters after marriage, ensuring a lasting cooperation in pottery production. This daily interaction with their own kin promotes a bilateral kin network, and, along with the important contribution of women's pottery to household income, is a factor in the more equitable gender relations prevailing in Amatenango in comparison with Chamula or Oxchuc.

21   Typically the *ladinos* of Chiapas refer to indigenous languages as *lengua*, "tongues," or dialects, reserving the term *idioma* (language) for Spanish or other European languages.

22   Vogt (1994:107) recounts Roberta Montagu's "insightful" comment that Oxchuc might have been susceptible to Protestant conversion because there were not enough offices to be distributed throughout the population since they were controlled by a clique that passed them around among themselves. This limitation exists in all indigenous communities without in itself causing system breakdown. It is not sufficient to explain the breakdown of an institution that was central to the reproduction of culture. Villa Rojas (1990) has a more comprehensive analysis of the massive conversion of 5,000 converts during Mariana Slocum's stay in Oxchuc. He records how many Oxchuqueños were turning against the harsh social sanctioning system exercised by curer diviners and lineage patriarchs. Protestants offered a relief from arbitrary use of force by traditional practitioners.

23   I was disappointed to learn not long after hearing this story, in which I interpreted Don Klabil to be the Lord of the Underworld, that Don Klabil referred to a *ladino* moneylender in Teopisca who had died not many years before. He may, of course, have been an historical personification of the underlying power of the Lord of the Underworld, just as I discovered the Shuntón brothers, who in local legends were the intermediaries for the community of Amatenango in Antigua, capital of the Province of Guatemala during the colonial period, carried out exploits identical to those of the twin brothers in the Popul Vuh.

24   Amatenango officials once allowed a wide range of entrepreneurs to run contraband stills during the period when the federal government prohibited the distillation of alcoholic beverages. The beer concession was controlled by leading PRI officials in the 1980s and is now joined by a competing beer monopoly held by the leading PRD officials. San Juan Chamula allowed ritual officeholders to control distilled beverages until the substitution of soft drinks became accepted as tradition during fiestas. Commercial opportunities in Chamula are all controlled by officeholders who occupy large elaborate houses in the town centers.

25   Prior to 1937, all records were destroyed when the town hall was burned in a conflict between *colonos*, or foreign Indians, and Amatenangueros.

26   The special identification of indigenous people with these three fiestas—Carnival, Easter, and the Day of the Cross—that Hermitte discovered in the bicultural community of Pinola (1992) is echoed in communities where *ladinos* are absent. In Chamula, the festival of games during Carnival, or "Crazy February," evokes the indigenous rebellion of 1867–1869 (Bricker 1981) and shows parallels with the celebration of the end of the 52-year Mesoamerican calendar cycle. It is a time of chaos and terror that is expressed in the releasing of ordinary controls. Zoques celebrate it with dances of the ancestors during the five-day period equated with the ritual calendar (Cruz Ramirez 1998). May 3rd is a time to honor the *me'iltatil*—literally, the mothers and fathers of the pueblo—in Amatenango del Valle, with civil and religious officials marking the crosses at the major entrances to the town center with sacred plants and flowers. The Cora of El Nayar celebrate the Crucifixion with the dance of the turtle before the shrine housing the crucified Christ, clearly attempting to fertilize the area as they simulate copulation and masturbate until their seed is ejected on the sword each carries (José María Castro, investigator quoted in *La Jornada* April 3, 1999:19). In Amatenango the ritual killing of Judas, identified as a *ladino*, symbolizes the indigenous recapture of their sacred spaces (Nash 1968), a ritual that has been reformulated as a contest with specific targeting of *ladino* alterity (Nash 1994a). In some Guatemalan municipalities, local officials carried the box containing deeds to the common lands around the perimeter of the town on May 3rd, decorating the crosses marking the entryway to the pueblo, as Bunzel (1952) noted in Chichicastenango. The cycle of regeneration and death dramatized in Christ's Crucifixion is clearly related to Mayan conceptions of the flowering of the dead and the cycle of death and rebirth enacted in the rituals of Santiago Atitlán, Guatemala (Carlsen 1997:47 *et seq.*). It is not surprising, then, that these ritual efforts to reactivate the cycle of life and death at the time that the Christians celebrate the Crucifixion invoke the collective life of the community as participants in the ritual striving to regain the balance of their habitus.

27   This deference was a calculated ploy, shared among the few truck drivers. I attended the funeral of two children of two drivers that occurred simultaneously in 1966. I expected to hear the fathers discuss the probability of witchcraft-caused illness in the kind of kangaroo court that such funerals always provided.

Instead the fathers shared their experience with state highway patrol police, noting that when they were blamed for their violations of highway rules, each of them explained, "I am a poor ignorant Indian who doesn't know how to read." Both claimed that they did not have to pay a fine.

28 Although there is depletion of the forest cover in the vicinity of Amatenango, the greatest cutting occurs in the new settlement areas of expelled Protestant indigenes in the neighboring town of Teopisca. There, the people who lack land for cultivation make charcoal that is sold in regional markets. It convinced me that there is as little loss in the forty-year period that I have been in the area, because the people are concerned with renewal of the forest and do not engage in the clear-cutting of trees that takes place in the Lacandón rain forest.

Chapter 3
Exodus from Communities

1 I discovered that the teenage girl whom I employed to help with my two-year-old son had tuberculosis, and when I went with her to the clinic I learned of the pervasiveness of this disease of poverty in the migrant settlement.

2 Another measure of the decline in social spending is the ratio of public spending, which declined from 31.2 percent of GDP to 23 percent in the period from 1981 to 1983 (Lustig 1992:79).

3 Assessing the effects of the reforms carried out with liberalization of trade and privatization of industry, Nora Lustig reports that the debt crisis resulted in severe stagnation and even in decline in most Latin American countries, and particularly in those areas where reforms were most strongly instituted. The percentage below the poverty level increased from 33 percent in 1980 to 39 percent in 1985, with an absolute increase in the number of the poor from 120 to 160 million (Lustig 1995:62).

4 Warman's book *Venimos para Contradecir* (1980) extols the behavior of *campesinos* in defense of their lands that the Solicitors Office was designed to subvert.

5 With data from Economic Commission on Latin American Society, Ramirez (1997) analyzes income distribution by quintile from 1963 to 1992 as a percentage of total national income, showing that between 1984 and 1989 the concentration in the distribution of income became increasingly skewed. The share of the top 20 percent of Mexican families rose from 49.5 percent in 1984 to 53.5 percent in 1989.

6 On March 25, 2000, decisions were being made on Mexico's index rating. The tension resulted in precipitous daily fluctuations as Mexicans tried to contain the ongoing conflict in Chiapas to look good to the analysts. As global analysts are very aware, Moody's Investor's Service or Standard and Poor's downgrading its bonds in its index ratings could threaten the entire economy of lesser players in the global freeway (T. Friedman 1999:32). A year later Moody's Investor's Service gave Mexico a coveted sovereign investment-grade rating paving the way for large-scale investment (ET online March 9, 2001).

7 Eduardo Santos of ECLAS in Chile (1989:121) suggests that vested interests deliberately delay publishing such data during periods of crisis, when they are most urgent and necessary in order to minimize the impact they might have in stimulating social protest. This may not be the reason, but it is clear that there are difficulties in finding data on social indicators for Latin America. The Interamerican Development ment Bank (1997) has a "Latest Available Estimate" on social indicators that is post-1985 but prior to 1992, representing a 7-year delay on reporting when I looked for data in June 1999.

8 Conroy and West (1999:45).

9 After the Zapatista uprising, Salinas admitted that he neglected the issue of poverty and government redistribution policies, a comment that is now well substantiated. Conroy and West (1999:46) show that federal expenditures per capita in the southern states were lower than in states with lower levels of impoverishment. They conclude that: "The southern states of Mexico are not just the poorest in the Mexican federation; they are also states that have been singularly disadvantaged by the national fiscal reforms and structural adjustment of 1992." They show that the percentage of change in federal expenditures declined in the southern states by 88 percent in Chiapas, and 74 percent in all southern states of Mexico, compared to 44 percent declines in all of Mexico in per capita outlays from 1988 to 1992.

10 Given the collective orientation to land, this strategy of collective purchases of land to form a new community was not unproblematic, as I discovered in 1988. While waiting for a bus to Venustiano Carranzo, I saw a tent village of about fifty Amatenangueros on the roadside near San Caralampio. One of the men recognized me from my earlier field trips to the town, when I used to visit his uncle's house in Alannantic. He said that the ten families in the group had been evicted on the charge that they were Protestants,

although they had been living together peacefully for the past fifteen years. He explained that families with older sons now of an age to make a claim on the common property voted to divide up the plots among all adult males. That left younger men, whose children had not reached maturity, with only a single claim to the lots. He rejected the claim of his adversaries that the decision to evict them was because they were Protestants, asserting that it was because the younger families (who were indeed Protestant but who had been so since the formation of the hamlet) were objecting to the decision made by the majority.

11 Jan Rus (1995:77) summarizes the available statistics for landholding, showing that 79 percent of Amatenangueros had less than two hectares of land in 1983, compared with 87 percent in Chamula and 90 percent in Zinacantán. In my census of landholding in Amatenango in 1987, that figure dipped down to less than half an acre of *ejido* land for 60 percent of households in the *cabecera*, and less than 1 hectare for half those householders.

12 What Cancian (1992) saw as a decline of community could also be interpreted as a resurgence of community from the perspective of the hamlets. Many hamlets were gaining representation with officials in charge of the *ejido* lands and important civil and religious offices. Protestant conversion seemed to spread in the hamlets, as shown in Tenejapa, Nash census in Amatenango, and Sullivan (1998) in Chamula. The breaking away of hamlets from the center reflects the opposition to PRI centralization at national, state, and municipal levels.

13 It should be noted, however, that it was not until after the uprising and the process of militarization that roads were constructed connecting villages within the Lacandón with the outside world.

14 Because the *ladino* truck drivers hired by the truck cooperative would not teach any of the Indians to drive for fear of losing their jobs, I taught one of the members to drive.

15 Salinas demonstrated his favor of González Garrido's repressive tactics by naming him to the post of minister of the interior in his cabinet. He served in this office until the EZLN uprising in 1994, after which he went into exile.

16 I worked with Christine Kovic, a graduate student at the Graduate Center of the City University of New York, who was one of the National Science Foundation scholars funded for research training. Our co-authored paper (Nash and Kovic 1996) includes some of this analysis.

17 Salinas wrote his doctoral thesis at Harvard on the correlation between public spending and political support for the system, concluding that there was none (Wood 1993:12). Yet he was a master in using national and international funding to reinforce the flagging position of the PRI.

18 In Oaxaca the government-instigated Municipal Funds Program promoted more equitable distribution, since it earmarked 85 percent of funds for the outlying localities. As Fox and Aranda (1999:190) point out, the program worked as long as there were democratically elected local officials, a condition that scarcely exists in Chiapas. Shortsighted projects were encouraged by the limited planning scope, and as a result, basketball courts proliferated instead of potable water and drainage systems.

19 Another conflict was avoided in 2000 when presumed Lacandón Indians threatened to invade the settlements in the biosphere reserve of the Tzeltales who vowed not to leave their communities. A total of 32 hamlets with 311 families were affected. A tentative agreement for the relocation of 50 percent of the settlers in the twelve communities was negotiated between ARIC–Independiente Democratica and members of the Interinstitutional Commission who arrived at the conflict area aboard three helicopters of the Federal Preventive Police on April 5, 2000. ARIC-ID (Independent Democratic) noted that their conciliatory behavior was prompted by a desire to avoid conflict with "their brothers," the Lacandón Indians (*Cuarto Poder* April 5, 2000:9).

20 Leyva Solano and Franco (1995) suggest that these contrasts in government patronage exacerbated the sense of disenfranchisement that contributed to the recent uprising by the settlers of Las Margaritas and Ocosingo, when their population was outstripping a limited land base. Periodically, the conflict breaks out in aggression, as happened most recently in the threatened eviction of the Tzeltal colonizers within the biosphere reserve, recounted in note 19.

21 As discussed in chapter 5, ARIC became the mediator in many of the conflicts that broke out after the Zapatista uprising. Following the invasion of the Lacandón rain forest in February, 1995, the ARIC split into an "official" and an "independent" wing over differences in relating to the army barracks in their communities, with the "officials" supporting the allocation of lands for army barracks, and ARIC independent dissenting. Both wings of the ARIC agreed that the *campesinos* are the primary guardians of the forest, following the rhetoric of NGOs and United Nations covenants (*Cuarto Poder* 16 March 2000:21).

22 Arizpe, Fernanda, and Velásquez (1993:123), who carried out a study of the area in 1991, reported that, despite the fact that colonizers have experienced increasing aridity and heat accompanied by high winds

and torrential rains as the jungle disappeared, some expressed resentment at the government's urging them to save the forest. The protestors were quite clear that they objected to the fact that the government seized the wood they had cut to clear land without paying for it, as it had agreed.

23 OCEZ evolved out of the Coalition of Independent Revolutionary Campesinos (CCRI), formed in 1975, and the National Coalition of the Plan of Ayala Campesinos (Coordinadora Nacional Plan de Ayala Campesinos), formed in 1977.

24 Amatenango's homicide rate, which averaged from six to seven a year in the period from 1963 to 1967, or 198 per 100,000, exceeded that of the Morelos village studied by Romanucci-Ross (1976)—178 per 100,000—where there was greater ethnic and wealth diversity. The increase in the 1960s seemed related to the perceived breakdown of local boundaries. James B. Greenberg (1989), who found a similar rise in homicide among members of the rural Mexican community where he worked twenty years after what I recorded in Chiapas, attributes the increase to the breakdown of reciprocal relations in the moral economy of peasants. His use of Toennies's Gemeinschaft-Gesellschaft dichotomy fails to consider the structural changes attendant upon the shift in moral climate noted in other communities: e.g., the substitution of young literate leaders for the gerontocracy that legitimized authority on the basis of age in Amatenango del Valle, or the increased commodification that led to wealth differences and new means of validating such distinctions in Zinacantán. Paul Friedrich (1977 and 1986) relates homicide to a deep cultural historical analysis that enables us to perceive how the Revolution and its aftermath promoted this behavior.

25 Neil Harvey quotes Amnesty reports of 841 *campesinos* killed between 1982 and December 1987 throughout Mexico (1990:192).

Chapter 4
Radical Democratic Mobilization, 1994—1996

1 Kay Warren expresses a similar discomfort with anthropological contextualizing of the Pan-Mayanism movement in Guatemala. She finds the "revitalization movements," "invented traditions," "ethnic nationalism," "new social movements," "minority," and "ethnic nationalist" models inadequate attempts to comprehend the multifaceted complexity represented by the Pan-Mayanist movement she studied. I sympathize with her sentiment (Warren 1998:210) that such movements as the Guatemalan Pan-Mayanist "will offer lessons about nonviolent options for rethinking political marginalization in multiethnic states that seek democratic futures," but I see the lesson as going beyond marginalization to rethinking societies as multicentric, nonhierarchical, and potentially alternative models for organization that will change mainstream practices.

2 Daniel Nugent (1995) contests the use of "postmodern" applied by Roger Burback and others to the Zapatista revolution. I first heard the term postmodern in reference to the Zapatista when Roger Bartra was quoted in Mexican newspapers soon after the uprising as stating that the EZLN was "the first postmodern movement" because they wanted to introduce democratic processes, not to overthrow an elected government and take power, marking a break with "modern" guerrilla operations that advocate taking power by force. In this chapter I use the term "postmodern" to address the singularity of their uprising and its continuity with culturally distinctive patterns that include the multivocalic and pluralistic emphasis identified with the term postmodern.

3 Arturo Warman (1988) shows the centrality of land redistribution to the reorganization of society around agrarian communities. This was the major objective of *campesino* action taken in Morelos in the decades preceeding and leading up to the 1910 Revolution. Warman's praise of the democratic actions inspiring their struggles throughout the nineteenth century, when the corporate lands of indigenes were seized by large landholders, stands in marked contrast to his position as director of the Procuraduría Agraria and later of the Secretaría de la Reforma Agraria under Salinas. His position, more than that of almost any other PRI functionary, embodies the contradictory currents in which the PRI government was caught when it began to undo its own institutional structures. Roger Bartra, who perceived a dim future for the semi-subsistence agrarian sector, was enthusiastic about the EZLN, in contrast to Warman who, as President Salinas' Secretary of Agrarian Reform, played a revisionist role.

4 The formation of Civil Society in Chiapas is discussed in chapter 5.

5 I attended the elections in Patihuitz and San Miguel in the Lacandón rain forest on August 21, 1994. Long lines of people waited for over two hours after the scheduled opening hour for the government

trucks to arrive with the ballots. Many of the towns in the Lacandón territory lacked sufficient ballots, and people were beginning to give up in the late afternoon since their return home took two hours. The people I interviewed in the line at San Miguel said that this was the first election ever held in their towns, and for the women it was the first time they had voted anywhere.

6 I was accompanied by students from the Graduate School and University Center of the City University of New York who had been chosen as recipients of the National Science Foundation training grants. They included Molly Doane, Kelley Ready, Pauline Herriman, and Susan Scheld.

7 Avendaño's supporters assert that the accident was planned by the PRI state machine. While Avendaño was campaigning in Tapachula with his campaign managers, he received a call to attend an "urgent" meeting of the candidates by the acting governor of the state, who was also the PRI candidate, Robles. On his return, at a high curve of the one road connecting Tapachula with Tuxtla Gutierriez over the Sierra Madre, a truck without identifying license plates forced his small car off the highway, where it fell over the steep *barranca*. Two of his companions were killed, but his son, who was thrown out of the car, survived to tell the tale. Avendaño was unconscious from a severe concussion that nearly caused his death.

8 Planning for the autonomy movement came from the National Plural Indigenous Assembly for Autonomy (ANIPA), Chamber of Representatives, Parlamentary Group PRD, LVI Legislatura 1996, cited in Díaz-Polanco 1997:191.

9 In a recent review of the "ethnic revival" in Mesoamerica, Scott Cook (1995) divided the field into "primordialist" and "situational-circumstantial" views, siding with the latter in his empiricist approach to studying Oaxacan cultural revivalism. Categorization of contemporary movements of ethnic revitalization fails to capture the fluid political process in which Mayans are constantly transforming the identities they project and the premises they share.

10 The prosecutors seized without a warrant Gloria Benavides Guevara, who was designated as *La Subcomandante* "Elisa." According to her deposition after she was released, her captors beat her and threatened to kill her daughter in order to force her to sign a statements implicating herself and four others in the "conspiracy", that is, the EZLN uprising. Other people designated as terrorists were picked up, among them Jorge Santiago Santiago, who had worked with a nongovernmental organization on development projects, and a filmmaker activist, Javier Elorreaga Berdegue they were bold held without charges for months in the Tuxtla Gutierrez prison.

11 *"El precio de la cabeza de los zapatistas es el único que se mantiene al alza en el sube y baja de la especulacíon financiera. El señor Zedillo inició el pago del prestamo. Su mensaje es claro: o hablar con sumisión y de rodillas frente al supremo gobierno, o, con el aval de mis complices en el congreso, te aniquilo" (La Jornada* February 13, 1995).

12 *"Los que le ensenaron a los actuales gobernantes lo que no aprendieron en los posgrados en el extranjero y que ya no aparece en los libros de texto con los que deseducan a los niños mexicanos; lo que es la verguenza, la dignidad de seres humanos, el amor a la patria y la historia."*

13 Peace camps were houses, often those abandoned by colonizers, that were designated as habitations for visiting NGOs who acted as witnesses to report human rights violations in the Lacandón rain forest.

14 Larrainzar was the surname of a former large landowner who was driven out in the 1970s by indigenous people of the town. Since it was identified with the serflike relations in which the Indians were held, they opted for the previous indigenous place term, Sacam Ch'en, or White Cave, and added the phrase, "de los Pobres" (of the Poor).

15 The game of basketball played by the contemporary Mayans is considered to be a U.S sport initiated in Springfield, Massachusetts, by James Naismith, a YMCA community worker. Folk historians of Plainfield, Massachusetts, claim that he learned the game from a woman missionary who was inspired by her visit to Mayan ceremonial ball courts in Chichén Itzá. Based on her vision of the ball court and the basrelief of players, she invented the game that she taught to the children of Plainfield for their winter recreation. At first the baskets were placed on a vertical plane such as that which she had seen in the Yucatan, but since she used stiff baskets of the type employed by the people of Plainfield to store potatoes and peaches, the hoop was converted from a vertical plane as the Mayans had placed their stone hoop, to a flat plane, so the ball would fall through rather than having it become suspended on the rim of the basket. During a summer field session in Plainfield, Joseph Naismith learned the game and formulated some of the rules that now characterize this national sport. Drawing from the *Popol Vuh*, the Quiché Maya bible, the ball game played by the twin heroes of the upper world with the lords of the underworld was a contest to keep the motion of the sun and the moon in their cycles, allowing the grandmother moon to bring the refreshing rains and rest of the night, following the heat of the sun that would otherwise burn the crops if the night did not follow the day. The game had political implications

affecting the status of the victors and the conquered in the wider political arena of competing Mayan city-states. It was, therefore, fitting that the basketball court in San Andrés was the location for the dialogues, in more ways than the participants imagined.

16 AEDPCH was formed in July, 1994, bringing together several of the citizens' support groups that had worked in Chiapas in the organization of the National Democratic Convention. The coalition included numerous support groups of the EZLN and the peace movement within the state, as well as NGOs (see following chapter; N. Harvey 1998:204–205).

17 When questionnaires from without the country and the world were tallied, there were more than a million and a half registering a positive assessment for the EZLN proposals.

18 Stephen (1997b) points out that popular organization in Chiapas has been more peasant than Indian in their structure and demands because of the Marxist leaning of CIOAC. Hence the RAP differed from the communal model of autonomy inspired by indigenous examples in Oaxaca.

19 Alfonso Villa Rojas (1990), one of the first indigenous anthropologists in Mexico, documented the many violations of human rights within the municipality of Oxchuc, where the rule by elders prejudicing women and young men led to abuses of public beatings and extreme exploitation economically and politically in the 1940s, when he was doing fieldwork. I have suggested in chapter 3 that this provoked the large-scale conversion when Protestant missionaries arrived. I have experienced the arbitrary rule of elders and curers in Amatenango, when a witch-hunt led to the murder of curers who had abused their power as well as young literate leaders who challenged the arbitrary rule of traditionalists. Rosenbaum (1993) and Eber (1995) document the many abuses of women in the daily life of Chamula and Chenalhó.

20 Stephen points out that a lot of the input by women was dropped out in the final version of the San Andrés Accords, although more of those specific to Chiapas were included (personal communication).

21 My students who spoke to the ARIC guards in the security lines said that Marcos wanted to join the plenary session in the assembly hall of the Casa de Cultura, but that the other members of the high command detained him in his room because of fear for his safety. His absence allowed the participants to focus on the commanders of the EZLN, including Ramona, Ana María, David, and Tacho, who appeared at all the plenaries and work sessions.

22 In my early field study, when I asked what the duties of the officials were, I was told "to sit and watch."

23 Because the Huichol use peyote in their rituals, they have been subject to legal censure and arrests.

24 The discussion papers were presented prior to meetings in the Lacandón, at sessions of "Chiapas en la Nación" held in San Cristóbal in the Universidad Autónoma de Chiapas, Table 2, "Autonomía y Transición Democrática," Moderator: Antonio Mosquera and Relatora Lic. Ma. Eugenia Santana E. in July 1996, which I attended with six students of the City University of New York who were chosen for National Science Foundation ethnographic training.

25 Eleanor Leacock and I (Leacock and Nash 1977) objected to the opposition of male to female as culture to nature in the propositions about the universal versus the particular status of women. We contested these Cartesian oppositions that were prevalent in early anthropological premises about masculinity and femininity using ethnographic and ethnohistorical sources showing very different cultural constructions about the nature of gender and of the world.

26 *Ahora se trata de pasar del socialismo revolucionario a algo que no tiene nombre todavía, pero que vincula la democracia con la defensa de los derechos culturales, la capacidad de comunicación y la defensa de la diversidad. La unión de lo identitatario, lo específico, con lo universal. . . . Creo que la opinión internacional siente mucho que estas comunidades indias de Chiapas (ubicadas en un lugar, un tiempo, una cultura) hablan una lenguaje universal. De cierta manera, el pasamontaña significa "somos ustedes," el universalismo. Yo soy al tiempo miembro de mi comunidad pero con la voz de mi montaña habla con la palabra yo soy ustedes, que con la palabra mandar obedeciendo lo de las mejores definiciones que hay de democracia.*

Chapter 5
Civil Society in Crisis

1 In his *Two Treatises of Government*, Locke (1690) proposed that the one right that the individual surrenders when he enters civil society is the right to judge and punish his fellow man. By arming PRI supporters, as is alleged in the white paper on Acteal, Zedillo threatened the very role that civil society plays in contested political arenas.

2 See especially IUCN Intercommission Task Force 1997.

3   Sassen (1998) qualifies her argument regarding denationalization, showing the important roles performed by nations in the interest of promoting globalization. For nationals within the country, these concessions to the global financial and industrial institutions are precisely the proof of denationalization. Karl Marx (1964:134) recognized that nations came into being with international trade, as manufacturers in alliance with shippers sought to regulate trade through custom duties and protection in the trade wars between nations. These same needs can be met only by nations, which often run the risk of dismantling their welfare systems and protection of jobs through tariffs in order to respond to the priorities of international capitalists.

4   Gupta and Ferguson (1997) suggest some of the dimensions of global communities that are emergent in the "pulverized space" coincident with the loss of spatially localized communities. Space is not lost but reterritorialized.

5   Lowe and Lloyd (1997) address the cultural formation of these new constituencies in their book, *The Politics of Culture in the Shadow of Capital*.

6   This continuing conflict became very apparent in the 1990s when Bishop Samuel Ruíz challenged the PRI government to address the needs of the rebellious Zapatistas at the same time that the *nuncio* Prigione was doing his utmost to remove the bishop while he cultivated elites of the dominant PRI government in Mexico City and Chiapas. When the new bishop, Raul Vera, was assigned to the San Cristóbal diocese in the spring of 1997, most parishioners assumed that he would replace Don Samuel upon his retirement. Yet when Bishop Raul Vera arrived, he seconded all that Don Samuel had said about the conditions of indigenous people. He joined Bishop Ruíz to endorse a major pilgrimage with over 20,000 participants who walked to the northern region during Easter week in April 1997 to show the support of the diocese for their efforts to gain peace with justice. Many believe that his active support for social change led to the Church's decision to transfer him rather than to have him consecrated as Don Samuel's successor.

7   Samuel Ruíz Garcia, "The Church in the Present-Day Transformation of Latin America in the Light of the Council," Second General Conference of Latin American Bishops, 2 vols, Bogota: General Secretariat of CELAM 1970, I Medellín, Colombia, pp. 155–177, cited in Womack (1999:119–127).

8   I interviewed Pablo Romo in 1991 when I became aware of the outreach of the center for human rights in Venustiano Carranza and the impact it was having in the indigenous communities.

9   Kay Warren (1998) advises us that fear of rebellion is a classic rhetorical move that justifies preemptive repressive tactics in Guatemala.

10 See "Estamos Buscando la Libertad: Los Tzeltales de la Selva Anuncian la Buena Nueva," Misión de Ocosingo, Altamirano, 1972–74, pp. 43–52, Jan Rus translator, included in Womack 1999:142.

11 Jorge Ramón González-Ponciano (1995) attributes this to the social isolation of a population: "Ignorant of the national situation, [they] seek in ritual and religion the daily orientation that neither political parties nor *campesino* organizations offered." He ignores the fact that political activists and religious proselytizers were circulating throughout the area, and religious missionaries were often highly political.

12 I owe this insight to Kay Warren.

13 When reporters were restricted from entering the war zone, many relied on press releases from the Pastors for Peace and the Human Rights Center, "Fray Bartolomé de Las Casas." The government-controlled radio and television stations succeeded in suppressing news of federal troops' attacks on the jungle communities, emphasizing only their attempts to reestablish order. TV and radio were less successful in controlling the press because of the outstanding journalism in *La Jornada, El Financiero*, and the weekly journal, *Proceso*, that reported extensively on the invasion and its aftermath (Nash 1997c). *El Tiempo*, the San Cristóbal newspaper that was published daily prior to the uprising, continued to appear sporadically with news of the EZLN and indigenous engagement in the ongoing struggle.

14 This remarkable surge of civil action negates the platitudes regarding indigenous peoples' inability to organize. Kay Warren comments that the often-repeated refrain, "They will never generate a unified, natural organization with a single agenda," was a common condemnation of Pan-Mayan organizers in Guatemala by *ladinos*, gringos, and international donors (personal communication).

15 I am grateful to Christine Kovic for providing me with this citation.

16 I was accompanied on this trip by four of my students from the National Science Foundation Research Experience for Undergraduates project—Christine Kovic, Liliana Fasanella, Courtney Gutherie, and Melissa Castillo.

17 Information on the organization of CIOAC is from "Exodus in Chiapas: The Tzeltal Catechism of Liberation, Ocosingo 1972," in Womack (1999:128–142).

18 Nancy Modiano (personal communication) said that Chamulan parents sometimes did not register their

daughters' births since they did not want to be forced to send them to school. As Jan Rus (personal communication) indicates, this negative attitude toward daughters' and wives' education is changing in Chamula as well as other indigenous communities as women have engaged in income-generating activities in artisan production and other outlets. Amatenango exercised less patriarchal control over daughters' schooling even when I lived there in the 1960s. Sex ratios were about equal in the primary schools up to the sixth grade, but further education was exclusively for boys.

19 Interview, April 6, 2000.

20 Womack (1999:252) states that the "Women's Revolutionary Law for women's rights actually guarantees (on paper) no more than existing law does (on paper) . . . ," with the exception of their call for the right to bear arms.

21 *Así también estamos convencidas de que las relaciones de nuestras vidas también están determinadas, como dice Marcela Lagarde, por las relaciones que establecemos con los hombres (los de nuestras étnias y los no indígenas); que estas relaciones tienen componentes opresivos para nosotras y que deben de ser transformadas. Por eso, un espacio que valoremos y que buscamos construir son las organizaciones de mujeres, en donde construímos nuestra propia identidad que marca y define la condición genérica, y permite el flujo y la interacción con los "otros" y las "otras" y nos ha permitido establecer un diálogo de reencuentro con nuestro propio pueblo, con nuestras costumbres y hacer alianzas y acciones con las mujeres en general para demandar un reconocimiento como mujeres indígenas.*

22 I attended the meeting with one of our National Science Foundation training grantees, Molly Doane.

23 Zinacantán, Chalchihuitán, Huixtán, Chenalhó and Pantelhó had voted for the opposition party PRD in 1994, but as a result of the abstentions, PRI took over these and other offices (Henríquez 1999:17).

24 According to Juan Balboa, a reporter for *La Jornada* who spoke at a meeting at El Puente in San Cristóbal on April 14, 1997, the Tuxtla Gutierrez press came of age after the uprising, moving from a press that was accustomed to being paid for reporting events by interested parties to a more independent corps of reporters sent out to the scene of action. Reporters began to take opposition to the official press releases based on their interviews with participants in the events recorded.

25 Government funding had never reached the northern region prior to the uprising and the declaration of their autonomy, as the Abuxu declared in their 1993 march to Oxchuc to attend the meeting with Salinas.

26 Soon after the Acteal massacre, Father Michel Henri Jean Chanteau, for over 34 years the parish priest of Chenalhó, where the massacre took place on December 22, 1997, was exiled to France. Although he sympathized with the Zapatista movement, Father Chanteau not only did not advocate taking up arms, but even prohibited Catholics from holding positions in the Church if they chose to take up arms with the Zapatistas. His crime was that he gave shelter and food to members of the parish who were forced out of their homes by the paramilitary forces. *New York Times* reporter Julia Preston quotes him (February 27, 1998: International section) as saying, "We now have two gospels here: the Gospel according to Saint Mark and the Gospel according to Subcommander Marcos; I prefer Saint Mark."

27 CEOIC came into being shortly after the uprising and self-destructed when the land titles it drafted were assigned to partisans of PRI rather than to those *campesino* organizations that initiated the takeovers. The AEDPCH picked up the action the following year.

28 *Motivos* no. 8, February 1994, Mexico, cited in Díaz-Polanco 1997.

29 Stephen (1999) notes the many parallels in the government's reaction to the autonomy movement in Oaxaca and Guerrero, with what is happening in Chiapas, with the same types of controls and coordinated actions by *Judiciales*, state security police, army and immigration officers.

30 As Kay Warren comments, the "cultural" level to which they refer is the trait listing divorced from dynamic exchanges among and between ethnic groups.

31 I have never witnessed a firemaking ceremony in Chiapas indigenous ceremonies, nor the blowing of a conch in the four directions. On the last day of the *consulta*, the young man who led this prelude, was "arrested" by national guards, and released upon the arrival of two American tourists who were attracted to the "demonstration" for the "release" of the purported "Zapatista." The tourists were then escorted to the National Immigration Service office, where they were accused of meddling in the political affairs of the country.

32 Karel Vasak announced these objectives at the July 1979 Tenth Study Session of the International Institute of Human Rights.

33 The United Nations Commission on Human Rights has since vindicated the position of the group and censured the Mexican government for human rights violation.

Chapter 6
Pluricultural Survival in the Global Ecumene

1   Franz Boas and his students thought of the American Indian populations they studied and worked with as a vanishing society, and their priorities were to investigate those expected to become extinct for museums and archives.

2   The Inter-American Commission on Human Rights specified the results of the war in its 1983 report: 250,000 to one million people displaced; killing and torture of hundreds of thousands by the Guatemalan army, decimating 10 percent to 25 percent of the population in Indian townships of the central zone, and leaving over 50,000 orphans in the Department of El Quiche and San Marcos alone (Davis 1988; Jonas 2000; Klare 1988; C. Smith 1990). Linda Green (1999) counts among the victims the widows and children orphaned: in addition to the more than 100,000 people killed and 40,000 who disappeared during the thirty-year insurgency in Guatemala, more than 80,000 women were widowed and over 250,000 children orphaned. The Truth Commission, empowered in the peace negotiations to investigate and publicize the crimes committed during the war, presented its report in February, 1999. It confirmed the numbers of those killed, tortured, and raped, adding details that are leading to court cases (Jonas 2000:154 *et seq.*). Indigenous people of Guatemala are in the forefront of efforts to denounce the criminal acts of the military leaders between 1962 and 1996, marked by the denunciation introduced by Rigoberta Menchú in the National Court of Spain on March 27, 2000.

3   Kay Warren (1998) demonstrates the importance of Mayan intellectuals in forging a vision of pluricultural coexistence in Guatemala.

4   Holistic inquiry is simply a shortcut to framing more than the immediate action of people in a particular space. It has always conveyed the unattainable hope of embracing all the phenomena that have an impact on a community, a region, a nation, or even an individual. Now, when all of the above are threatened by being engulfed in the global ecumene, it is even more unattainable but is ever more desirable.

5   Among the contributions of Margery Wolf's illuminating book is her tracing of the many innovations attributed to the postmodern cultural critique to earlier feminist scholarship that succeeded in advancing multivocal, multiple-centered discourses in ethnographies while at the same time retaining a structural analysis that transcended identity.

6   I use the deep structures of Chomsky's linguistic analysis as the underlying grammar that enables people to produce new and ever variant sentences that will be understood by an audience.

7   The opening lines of the Gospel According to John, "In the beginning was the Word, and the Word was with God, and the Word was God," is a reminder from Christian culture of the spell cast by words in human destiny. Don Antonio, the Lacandón sage often quoted in Zapatista communiqués, refers to yet another mythic world in which words reflected against the polished stones of the ancestors defined the central principles for living. In Tzeltal villages, the repetition of the words of the ancestors is central to the role of ritual mediators. Called the *pat'otan* (behind the heart), the ritual speech is believed to have the power to maintain the world intact (Nash 1996; see also chapter 2).

8   I have analyzed the press reports and television coverage of the uprising not only as a technological breakthrough, with the use of email and the Internet carrying instantaneous news of the Zapatista movement around the world, but also as a social movement that evoked sympathetic responses on the part of many sectors that suffered the impact of globalization. The media agents acted as a "third army," as they were called, transmitting the communications and reports on conditions of the Zapatista communities in the low-intensity counterinsurgency warfare carried on from 1995 to the present. The search for a locus in which to act on the shared consciousness of their plight led Zapatistas and their supporters to innovative approaches to communicating in the global ecumene (Nash 1997c; see also chapter 5).

9   In an article that I wrote on "The Reassertion of Ethnic Identity" (Nash 1995) just before the 1994 uprising, and that I revised before publication to take into account the significance of this dramatic reassertion of their ethnic claims to full citizenship, I emphasized the nationalist character of their movement. With each succeeding national and international convention and congress called by the Zapatistas, the widening integration of their alliances led to a broadening of their horizons, as I tried to capture in a later article written during and following the 1996 National Forum of Indigenous Peoples in January 1996 and the negotiations with COCOPA that followed in February (Nash 1997b). It is important to remind oneself in analyzing or reading discourse that the words are part of a social process that is ever-changing, yet the tendency is that once words have been spoken or published to gain a life of their

own, they can be used to refute the truthfulness of a speaker who is responding to this proccess.

10 *Cajitas* are possibly a reference to the boxes in which images of a saint were carried. These images spoke, advising Indians of their fate in the rebellions of Chamula in 1867–1869 and a century and a half earlier, in Cancuc in 1712 (see chapter 3).

11 Mexican intellectuals, such as Carlos Fuentes (1994:82), retain the stereotyped belief that "the first loss of the religious world, of the cosmovision irreparably damaged by the Spanish conquest," required *indios* to create an identity that had to be imported: "the new religious attachment moved by the appearance of a Christian culture reinforced by the syncretic assimilation of the ancient Mexican world." However, anthropologists are more likely to recognize, as does Bonfil Batalla (1987:94), "the vast reserves of alternative cultural resources, the value of which, negated until today, would be absurd to ignore."

12 Le Bot (1997:154) notes that the Votan is one of the mythical Mayan figures. It is the name of a Mayan lineage that left the Yucatán during the Postclassic period to settle in the northern region of Chiapas. The name is still invoked in Chol stories (Alejos Garcia, 1994; Pérez Chacón 1993). The opposite of the *ik'al* is the *cha'uk*, the lightning bolt, and there are some in Amatenango who speculated that this powerful force might be *subcomandante* Marcos.

13 Casteñeda's novelistic ethnography, *The Teachings of Don Juan*, was repudiated by his own professors at the University of California in Los Angeles, where he had earned his Ph.D., for its lack of authenticity and questionable ethnography. It is somewhat ironical to have that body of work reinserted in the discourse of the Zapatistas by their *subcomandante* Marcos some twenty years after its publication.

14 According to reports on the identity of Marcos, Rafael Guillén was a student at the Universidad Nacional Autónoma de México, and may have also studied at the Sorbonne. He claims to have traveled in other Central American countries and lived with rebels.

15 *A la hora en que se da el contacto con las comunidades, el elemento indígena es ya mayoritario en la organización politico-militar, aunque esto no se refleje en la estructura de mando. Pero en su vida interna si, se refleja, porque ya hubo un primer choque cultural que fue necesario asimilar, resolver: aprendar el dialecto, pero también aprender algo mas que el dialecto: el manejo del lenguaje, de los símbolos, lo que representan unas cosas y otras, lo que representaba el sentido del simbolo en la comunicación y todo eso.*

16 *La idea de un mundo mas justo, enriquecido con elementos humanitarios, éticos, moral, mas que estrictamente indígena. De pronto, la revolución se transforma en algo esencialmente moral. Ético. Mas que el reparto de la riqueza o la expropiación de los medios de producción, la revolución comienza a ser la posibilidad de que el ser humano tenga un espacio de dignidad (Le Bot 1997:146).*

17 See especially chapter 2, p. 34–39.

18 A similar rupture between indigenes and their environment occurred in the Peten in Guatemala in May 2000, when squatters who had settled in the jungle engaged in traditional slash-and-burn practices but did not exercise the judgment or control typical of resident indigenes (*NewYork Times* May 21, 2000).

19 Analyzing the "mess of Foucauldian discourse," Sahlins (1998) abhors the trend toward turning from culture to discourse. He cites as an example of this "mess" Escobar's (1995:40–41) definition of discourse as "the process through which social reality comes into being, determining what can be said, perceived or even imagined." The power of discourse is presented as even more determinant than class position, even though proponents of the discourse model attack Marxian models for their overdetermination. The paradigm also fails to take into account the perceptions of the audience, ignored by most post-Foucauldians.

20 I put the adjective "new" in quotation marks to indicate that the movements are in themselves not so much new as they are newly recognized currents that have always been related to class movements or whatever is categorized as "old."

21 There are many parallels to Zapatista insights in Guatemala, as Kay Warren amply documents (1998).

22 See chapter 2 on the Shuntón brothers' trip to Guatemala and its parallel in the twin gods' visit to the underworld.

23 *Pues son indios los que se refugian en las fiestas, ritos curativos, costumbres y tradiciones que les fueron heredados de sus antepasados; son indios lo que en su búsqueda de seguirle dando sentido a su existencia han vuelto los ojos a las enseñanzas evangélicas; no son mas indios los priístas ni menos indios los que se apoyan en las plataformas ideologicas de los partidos de oposición; el maestro o profesionista que se viste al estilo mestizo no es más indio que aquél que gusta ataviarse con la indumentaria que conserva parte de los diseños y motivos precolombinos; el que reacciona violentamente ante lo que considera injusticia no es menos batz'il vinik que el que se comporta con resignación ante ella; es tan indio el que vuelve los ojos al pasado como el que se arma de valor y quiere trascenderse buscando respuestas a sus incognitas penetrando en las marañ del mundo moderno, sin renegar de sus raíces (Árias 1994:398).*

24 Rumors in San Cristóbal had it that Salinas ignored early warnings in 1993 of the presence of guerrillas

in the jungle so that he could have a ready excuse to invade the rain forest because of the discovery of "an ocean of oil" there, as journalists for *El Financiero* expressed it.

25 I was mystified as to why oil exploration was carried out in Chamula at altitudes of 7,000 feet and above until my neighbor, a retired PEMEX engineer, said that the extent of an oil vein could be assessed by the degree to which it rose in the montains surrounding any discovery of oil. It was then, in 1988, that I first gained a sense of what was happening in the rain forest.

26 Molly Doane described how this format of drawing the world of bureaucrats and technicians into the *selva*, which was so successful in Chiapas, was adapted by NGOs and indigenous groups in Chimalapas, Oaxaca, to launch a campaign for a natural reserve (Doane n.d.).

27 Kay Warren argues that in the Guatemalan pan-Mayan movement there is a dynamic interplay and mutual influence among the different critical movements—blacks, ethnics, feminists, and classes—that create stimulating tensions.

28 Inoue Nobutaka (1997) sees globalism as a greater threat to national integrity than internationalization, a process, he points out, that recognizes the mutual existence and independence of others. For Japanese businessmen and intellectuals, the characteristic of being "borderless" spells anarchy in a "stateless condition where cultures are mixed on a global scale." Japanese society and culture were often remarked upon as being able to enter the international era of exchanges after World War II without losing their identity as people (Dore 1973). With globalization, the Japanese are now expressing a fundamental challenge to national identity (Nobutaka 1997:12), whereas internationalization promotes mutual understanding among nation states and ethnic groups since the nations's border remained intact.

29 Eric Wolf (1982) defined the outlines of national and colonial dependencies in his magisterial work, *Europe and the People without History*. Mayans are writing a supplement to that work as they create their own history at the end of the millennium dominated by the colonizers.

30 Among the open, or nonhierarchical, societies that retained a high degree of equality were the Bari of eastern Colombia and northwestern Venezuela. Elisa Buenaventura-Poso and Susan Brown (1980:115) quote a letter written in 1772 by Guillen, a Spanish envoy, who commented that: "They do not live subject to anyone's domination, and as I observed, they live in fraternal union, making decisions by unanimous agreement." Even children were consulted when decisions are made. Yet in most aboriginal indigenous societies, even in those that still have traces of gender complementarity, the women often experience subordination in public and private spaces (Bourque and Warren 1981).

31 For indigenous denunciations of the army and paramilitary, see Rojas (1995) and Marcos (1997). Rosa Luxemburg (1971) foresaw the growing militarization contingent on the taking over of indigenous territories over seventy years ago.

32 *Cf.* citations in di Leonardo (1985).

33 Although abuse of women is prevalent in many indigenous communities, some retain practices to restrain the abusers. In Amatenango, indigenous judges heard cases of abuse, and although women had to prove they had a right to be where they were when it happened, the case was often settled in their favor. The relatives of the women were then allowed to publicly beat the accused in the town hall. Bourque and Warren (1981) record Andean village practices in which an old woman ritually beat the abuser in public to express village outrage.

34 Rudolfo Stavenhagen (1996) summarizes the progress in focusing on indigenous rights in the international arena, from the 1953 International Labor Organization's first definition of *Pueblos Indigenas* to the 1957 Convention 107 calling for the protection of indigenous populations and tribal groups. This convention asserted the right of indigenous peoples to define what and who is indigenous and to determine how "to preserve, develop and transmit to future generations their ancestral territories and their ethnic identity as a base for continued existence as a people in accord with cultural practices." The United Nations constituted a Subcommittee for the Prevention of Discrimination and Protection of Minorities in 1970, and a decade later, in 1981, the Working Group on Indigenous Populations prepared the Universal Declaration on Indigenous Rights.

35 The quintessential feature of modernity, as Giddens points out (1990:20 *et seq.*), is the disembedding of social relations from local contexts of interaction and the restructuring across indefinite spans of time-space. The bridges that connect populations traumatized by modernization with civil society are often structured in the relations between transnational and local NGOs.

36 The "intergalactic" conventions that I have attended attract people from the Americas and Europe, but I have never spoken to participants from China, Southeast Asia, India, or the former Soviet Union.

REFERENCES CITED

Adams, Robert M. 1961 "Changing Patterns of Territorial Organization in the Central Highlands of Chiapas, Mexico," *American Antiquities*, 26:2331–60.

Aglietta, Michael. 1979 *A Theory of Capitalist Revolution: The United States Experience*. London: Verso.

Albo, Xavier. 1995 "Our Identity Starting from Pluralism in the Base," in John Beverley, Michael Aronna, Michael and José Oviedo, eds. *The Postmodernism Debate in Latin America*, 18–34. Durham: Duke University Press.

Alderete, Wara. 1998 "Healthy Communities, Healthy Women, Sociey and Gender in the Andes," in Diana Vinding, ed. *Indigenous Women: The Right to a Voice*, 52–74. Copenhagen: International Work Group on Indigenous Affairs.

Alejos García, José. 1994 *Mosoj'antel: Etnografía del discurso agrarista entre los ch'oles de Chiapas*, Mexico, D.F.: Universidad Nacional Autónoma de Mexico.

Alvarez Gadara, Miguel. 1998 "Sociedad civil y construcción de la paz en América atina" paper given in the Latin American Conference on the Construction of Peace, 30 de Noviembre, 1998.

Amin, Samir. 1970. *L'accumulation a l'echele mondiale. Critique de la theorie du sous-developpement*. Paris: Editions Anthropos.

Annis, Sheldon, and Peter Hakim, eds. 1988 *Direct to the Poor: Grassroots Development in Latin America*. Boulder, CO: Lynne Rienner.

Appadurai, Arjun. 1996 *Modernity at Large: Cultural Dimensions of Modernity*. Minneapolis: University of Minnesota Press.

Arhem, Kaj. 1984 *From Subsistence to Poverty: The Demise of a Pastoral Economy in Tanzania*. Working Papers in African Studies #5, Sweden: University of Uppsala, Department of Cultural Anthropology, African Studies.

Arias Perez, Jacinto. 1991 "Expulsiones religiosas en San Juan Chamula," pp. 103–106 in *Memoria de la audiencia pública sobre las expulsiones indígenas y el respeto a las culturas, costumbres, y tradiciones de esos pueblos*, 22 and 23 Abril, 1992 Tuxtla Gutiérrez, H. Congreso del Estado de Chiapas.

———. 1994 "Movimientos indígenas contemporaneos del estado de Chiapas," in J. Arias Perez, coordinator, *El arreglo de los pueblos indios: La incansable tarea de reconstitución*. Tuxtla Gutiérrez: SEP, Instituto Chiapaneco de Cultura, pp. 379–399.

Arizpe, Lourdes. 1994 "Chiapas: Los Problemas de fondo," pp. 19–31 in David MM. Navarro, coordinador. *Chiapas: Los problemas de fondo*. Cuernavaca: UNAM.

Arizpe, Lourdes, María Fernanda, and Margarita Velásquez. 1993 *Cultura y cambio global: percepciones sociales sobre la deforestación en la selva lacandona*. México: CRIM UNAM y Grupo Editorial Miguel Ángel Porrúa.

Arrighi, Giovanni, ed. 1985 *Semiperipheral Development: The Politics of Southern Europe in the Twentieth Century*. Beverly Hills, CA: Sage.

Arrighi, Giovanni, and Beverly J. Silver. 1999 *Chaos and Governance in the Modern World System*. Vol. 10 in *Contradictions of Modernity*, Minneapolis: University of Minnesota Press.

Asad, Talal. 1973. *Anthropology and the Colonial Encounter*. New York: Humanities Press.

Aubry, Andrés, and Angélica Inda. 1998 "Who Are the Paramilitaries in Chiapas," *NACLA Report on the Americas*, Vol. 31, No. 5 (March April): 8–9.

Barkin, David. 1987 "The End to Food Self-Sufficiency in Mexico," *Latin American Perspectives*, 54, Vol. 14, No. 3 (Summer): 271–97.

———. 1990 *Distorted Development: Mexico in the World Economy*. Boulder: Westview.

Barnes, J. A. 1967 "Some Ethical Problems in Modern Field Work." In *Anthropologists in the Field*, eds. D. C. Jongmans and P. Gutkind. Assen, The Netherlands: Van Gorcum, pp. 193–213.

Barrig, Maruja. 1990 "Quejas y contentamiento: historia de una politica social, los municipios y la organizacion femenina en Lima," in *Movimientos sociales: Elementos para una relectura*, Lima: DESCO.

Bartolomé, Miguel Alberto. 1994 "La represión de la pluralidad: Los derechos indígenas en Oaxaca," pp. 73–99 in *Derechos indígenas la actualidad*. Mexico: UNAM Instituto de Investiaciones Jurídicas.

———. 1995. "Movimientos etnopolíticos y autonomías indígenas en México," *América Indígena* 1-2: 361–382.

Bartra, Roger. 1982 "Capitalism and the Peasantry in Mexico." *Latin American Perspectives*, 32, Vol. 9:3.

Bebbington, Anthony, and Graham Thiele with Penelope Davies. 1993. *Nongovernmental Organizations and the State in Latin America: Rethinking Roles in Sustainable Agricultural Development*. London: Routledge.

Bell, Daniel. 1973 *The Coming of Post-Industrial Society: A Venture in Social Forecasting*. New York: Basic Books.

Beneria, Lourdes. 1989 "The Mexican Debt Crisis: Restructuring the Economy and the Household," Paper presented at the workshop on Labor Market Policies and Structural Adjustment, International Labor Organization Geneva, November 29–December 1, 1989.

————. 1992 "Women's Struggle for Survival in the Debt Crisis," Keynote address, Conference on Learning from Latin America, University of California, Latin Amereican Studies, Women's Studies, and Urban Planning, Feb 26–29.

Bennholdt-Thomsen, Veronika. 1981 "Subsistence Production and Extended Reproduction," in Kate Young et al., eds. *Of Marriage and the Market:Women's Subordination in International Perspective*, 41–54. London: CSE Books.

Bernstein, R. 1983 *Beyond Objectivism and Relativism*. Philadelphia: University of Pennsylvania Press.

Berryman, Phillip. 1984 *The Religious Roots of Rebellion: Christians in Central American Revolutions*. Maryknoll, NY: Orbis Books.

Blanton, Richard, and Gary Feinman. 1984 "The Mesoamerican World System." *American Anthropologist* 86:673–82.

Blim, George. 1992 "Introduction: The Emerging Global Factory and Anthropology," in Frances A Rothstein and Richard Blyn, eds. *Anthropology and the Global Factory: Studies of the New Industrialization in the Late Twentieth Century*. New York: Bergen and Garvey.

Blondet, Cecilia M. 1991 *Las mujeres y el poder: una historia de villa El Salvador*. Lima: Instituto de Estudios Peruanos.

————. 1992 "Organizaciones femeninas y violencia en las barriadas de Lima," paper prepared for the conference Learning from Latin America: Women's Struggles for Livelihood, University of California at Los Angeles, February 27–29.

Bodley, John. 1988 *Tribal Peoples and Development Issues: A Global Overview*. Mountainview, CA: Mayfield Press.

Bolles, Lynn. 1986 "Economic Crisis and Female-Headed Households in Urban Jamaica," in June Nash and Helen Safa, eds. *Women and Change in Latin America*. South Hadley, MA: Bergin and Garvey.

Bonfil Batalla, Guillermo. 1970 "Del indigenismo de la revolución a la antropología crítica," in *De eso wue llaman antropología Mexicana*, 89–97. México, D.F.: Editorial Nuestro Tiempo.

————. 1996 *México Profundo: Reclaiming a Civilization*. Austin: University of Texas Press. First published in 1987 as *México profundo: Una civilización negada*. México: Secretaría de Educación Pública.

Bose, Christine, and Edna Acosta-Belen. 1995 *Women in the Latin American Development Process*. Philadelphia: Temple University Press.

Boserup, Esther. 1970 *Women's Role in Economic Development*. London: Allen and Unwin.

Bowulding, Elise. 1992 "The Concept of Peace Culture." in *Peace and Conflict Issues After the Cold War*, pp. 107–33. UNESCO Studies on Peace and Conflict. Paris: UNESCO.

Bourdieu, Pierre. 1977 *Outline of a Theory of Practice*. Cambridge: University of Cambridge Press.

Bourdieu, Pierre, and Loïc J.D. Wacquant. 1992 *An Invitation to Reflexive Sociology*. Chicago: The University of Chicago Press.

Bourque, Susan, and Kay Warren. 1981 *Women of the Andes: Patriarchy and Social Change in Two Andean Towns*. Ann Arbor: University of Michigan Press.

Bowie, Katherine A. 1992 "Unraveling the Myth of the Subsistence Economy: Textile Production in Nineteenth-Century Northern Thailand," *Journal of Asian Studies* 51, no. 4 (November):797–823.

Bowles, Samuel, David M. Gordon, and Thomas E. Weisskopf. 1990 *After the Wasteland: A Democratic Economics for the Year 2000*. Armonk, NY: A.E. Sharpe.

Bretón, Alain. 1984 *Bachajón: Organización socioterritorial de una comunidad Tzeltal*. México, D.F.: INI.

Bricker, Victoria Reifler. 1981 *The Indian Christ, the Indian King: The Historical Substrate of Maya Myth and Ritual*. Austin: University of Texas Press.

Buechler, Hans, and Judith-Maria Buechler. 1992 *Against the Odds: Small-Scale Industry in Bolivia*. Boulder: Westview Press.

Buenaventura-Pozo, Elisa, and Susan E. Brown. 1980 "Forced Transition from Egalitarianism to Male Dominance: The Bari of Colombia," in Mona Etiene and Eleanor Leacock, *Women and Colonization: Anthropological Perspectives*, 109–13. New York: J. F. Bergin Publishers.

Bunzel, Ruth. 1952 *Chichicastenango*. Publications of the American Ethnological Society 22. New York: J. J. Augustin.

Burguete Cal, and Mayor, Araceli. n.d. "En Venustiano Carranza la historia la ven asi: Pobres contra ricos," San Cristóbal de Las Casas: INAREMAC archive.

————. 1999 *Coordinadora, México: Experiencias de autonomía indígena*. Copenhagen: IWGIA No. 28.

Cabrera Vargas, María del Refugio. 1995 "El indio en las relaciones geográficas del siglo xvi: La construcción de un significado," in R. Barcelo, M. A. Portal, M. J. Sánchez, eds. pp. 13–46.

Calderon, Fernando. 1995 "Latin American Identity and Mixed Temporalities: or, How to be Postmodern and Indian at the Same Time." In John Beverley, Michael Aronna, and Jose Oviedo pp. 55–64.

Calnek, Edward E. 1962 "Highland Chiapas before the Spanish Conquest." Unpublished Ph.D. dissertation. University of Chicago, Department of Anthropology.

Camacho, Daniel. 1993 "Latin America: A Society in Motion," in Ponna Wignaraja, ed., *New Social Movements in the South: Empowering People*. London: Zed, 36–58.

Cancian, Frank. 1965 *Economics and Prestige in a Maya Community: The Religious Cargo System in Zinacantan*. Stanford: Stanford University Press.

———. 1987 "Proletarianization in Zinacantan, 1960 to 1983," in *Household Economies and their Transformations*, ed. Morgan D. Maclachlan. Lanham, MD: University Press of America.

———. 1992 *The Decline of Community in Zinacantan*. Stanford: Stanford University Press.

Cardoso, F. H., and E. Faletto. 1971 *Dependencia y desarrollo en América Latina*. México, D.F.: Siglo XXI.

Carlsen, Robert S. 1997 *The War for the Heart and Soul of a Highland Maya Town*. Austin: University of Texas Press.

Casanova, José. 1997 "Globalizing Catholicism and the Return to a 'Universal' Church," in S. H. Rudolph, ed. *Transnational Religion and Fading States*. Boulder: Westview, 1–26.

Casillas, Rodolfo. 1995 "La participante social de los creyentes: ¿Quien fija las fronteras?" in Jane-Dale Lloyd and Laura Perez Rosales, coordinadoras, *Paisajes rebeldes: Una larga noche de rebelión indígena*, 271–91. México, D.F.: Universidad Iberoamericana.

Castañeda, Jorge. *The Mexican Shock: Its Meaning for the U.S*. New York: The New Press.

Ce-Acatl: *Revista de cultura de Anahuac*. 1995 No. 74–75 (December 17):6.

———. 1996 "Diálogo de Sacam Ch'en," pp. 74–75, December 17.

Censo General de La Población. 1991 México D.F.

Centro de Derechos Humanos Fray Bartolome de Las Casas. 1993 *En la ausencia de justicia: Informe semestral Julio A Diciembre del 1993*. San Cristóbal de Las Casas.

———. 1996 Archivos.

———. 1997 Archivos.

———. 1998 *Camino a la masacre. Informe especial sobre Chenalhó*. San Cristobal de Las Casas: Centro de Derechos Humanos Fray Bartolomé de Las Casas.

Centro de Información y Análisis de Chiapas. February 16 1996, Acuerdos de San Andrés. Special bulletin.

Chant, Sylvia. 1991 *Women and Survival in Mexican Cities: Perspectives on Gender, Labour, Markets and Low-Income Households*. Manchester: Manchester University Press.

Chayanov, A. V. 1966 *The Theory of Peasant Economy*, Daniel Thorner, Basile Kerblay, and R. E. F. Smith eds. Homewood, IL: Richard D. Irwin, Inc.

Clark, John E., and Michael Blake. 1993 "Los Mokayas," in Victor Manuel Esponda Jimeno, ed. *La población indígena de Chiapas*. p. 25–48. Tuxtla Gutiérrez: Instituto Chiapaneco de Cultura, Gobierno del Estado de Chiapas. Soconusco de Chiapas, Méxic."

Clifford, James, and George Marcus, eds. 1986 *Writing Culture*. Berkeley: University of California Press.

Cohen, Jean L., and Andrew Arato. 1992 *Civil Society and Political Theory*. Cambridge: Massachusetts Institute of Technology Press.

Collier, George. 1990 "Seeking Food and Seeking Money: Changing Productive Relations in a Highland Mexican Community." Discussion Paper 11. Geneva: United Nations Research Institute for Social Development.

———. 1997 "Reaction and Retrenchment in the Highlands of Chiapas," *Journal of Latin American Anthropology*, 3, 1:14–31.

Collier, George A., with Elizabeth Lowery Quaratiello. 1994 *Basta! Land and the Zapatista Rebellion in Chiapas*. Oakland, CA: The Institute for Food and Development Policy.

Collins, Carole. February 24, 1995 "Ending Abject Poverty Is U.N. Summit Goal," *National Catholic Reporter* 31, 17: 6.

Collins, Jane and Marta Gimenez. 1990 *Work without Wages: Comparative Studies of Domestic Labor and Self Employment*. Albany: SUNY Press.

Comaroff, Jean, and John Comaroff. 1992 *Ethnography and the Historical Imagination*. Boulder: Westview Press.

Comunicación Popular Alternativa, Grupo de Trabajo, San Cristóbal de Las Casas. December 32, 1997 "Cronología de una Masacre Denunciada, Acteal, Chenalhó, 22 de Diciembre de 1997." Photocopy.

Conable, Barber B. 1990 "Commentary: Africa's Development Crisis," *Columbia Journal of World Business*, 255, 1 & 2:7–9.

Conde, Raul, Robert Boyer, Hugue Bertrand, Bruno Theret. 1984 *La crisis actual y los modos de regulación del capitalismo*. Mexico, D.F.: Cuadernos Universitarios 8, División de Ciencias Sociales y Humanidades, Universidad Autónoma Metropolitano.

Conroy, Michael E., and Sarah Elizabeth West. 1999 "The Impact of NAFTA and the World Trade Organization on Chiapas and South Mexico, Hypotheses and Preliminary Evidence," pp. 41–58 in R. Tardanico and B. Rosenberg, eds. *Poverty or Development: Global Restructuring and Regional Transformation in the U.S. South and Mexican South*. New York: Routledge.

Cook, Scott. 1984 *Peasant Capitalist Industry*. Lanham, MD: University Press of America.

Cook, Scott and Jong Taick Joo. 1996 "Ethnicity and Economy in Rural Mexico: A Critique of the Indigenista Approach," *Latin American Research Review* 30, 2:33–59.

Corea, Gamani. 1975 *The Instability of an Export Economy*. Sri Lanka: The Marga Institute.

Coutinho Ferrera, Arturo. 1987 *Forestales, Conflictos, Agrarios, Colonizacíon sin Freno y Absigamiento de PEMEX*, PERFIL Nov.-Dec. 5:22–23.

Cox, Robert W. 1996 "A Perspective on Globalization," in J. Mittelman, ed. *Globalization: Critical Reflections*, pp. 21–32. Boulder: Lynne Rienner Publications.

Cronicas Intergalacticas. 1996 Borrador de los Procedimientos en Aguascalientes. Photocopy flyer.

Cruz Ramirez, Nelson. 1998 "Traducción de leyes en lengua zoque," pp. 249–251 in Dolores Aramoni, Thomas A. Lee, Miguel Lisbona, eds. *Cultura y Etnicidad Zoque Universidad Autónoma de Chiapas*, Tuxtla Gutiérrez.

Dalla Costa, Mariarosa. 1972 "Women and the Subversion of Community," in M. Dalla Costa and Selma James eds. *The Power of Women and the Subversion of the Community*. Bristol: Falling Wall Press.

Davis, Shelton. 1977 *Victims of the Miracle: Development and the Indians of Brazil*. New York: Cambridge University Press.

————. 1988 *Land Rights and Indigenous People: The Role of the Inter-American Commission on Human Rights*. Cambridge MA: Cultural Survival.

Deere, Carmen Diana. 1990 *Household and Class Relations: Peasants and Landlords in Northern Peru*. Berkeley: University of California Press.

di Leonardo, Micaela. 1985 "Review Essay: Morals, Mothers and Militarism: Antimilitarism and Feminist Theory" *Feminist Studies* 11, 3 (Fall):599–615.

Díaz-Polanco, Héctor. 1987 "Lo nacional y lo étnico en Mexico. El misterio de los proyectos," *Revista de Cuadernos Politicós*, No. 52 (October-December):36.

————. 1991 *Étnia y Nación en América Latina*. México, D.F.: Consejo de Cultura y Arte.

————. 1992 "Indian Communities and the Quincentenary," *Latin American Perspectives*, 74, Vol. 19, no. 3 (Summer):6–24.

————. 1995 "Etnia, clase y cuestión nacional," in Días-Polanco, ed. *Etnia y nación en América Latina*, pp. 53–57. México, D.F.: Consejo de Cultura y Arte.

————. 1997 *La rebelión Zapatista y la autonomía*. México D.F.l: Siglo XXI.

Direct Investment Yearbook. 1998 New York.

Doane, Molly. "Nature, Autonomy, and Power: Local Environmental Plans and Hemispheric Regulation in Mexico," Paper read at 98th American Anthropological Association Meetings in Chicago Nov. 17–19.

Dore, Ronald. 1973 *British Factory—Japanese Factory: The Origins of National Diversity in Industrial Relations*. Berkeley: University of California Press.

Dover, Robert V. H., and Joanne Rappaport. 1996 "Introduction," in Joanne Rappaport, special ed., "Ethnicity Reconfigured: Indigenous Legislators and the Colombian Constitution of 1991." *Journal of Latin American Anthropology*, Vol. 1, no. 2:2–18.

Drinan, Robert F. 1993 "World Conference on Human Rights June 14–25, 1993," America June 5.

Drucker, Peter F. 1986 "The Changed World Economy." *Foreign Affairs*.

Durand Alcántara, Carlos. 1994 *Derechos indios en México . . . derechos pendientes*. México: Universidad Autónoma Chapingo.

Eagleton, Terry. 1996 *The Illusion of Postmodernism*. Oxford: Oxford University Press.

Eber, Christine. 1995 *Women and Alcohol in a Highland Maya Township*. Austin: University of Texas Press.

————. 1998 "Las mujeres y el movimiento por la democracia en San Pedro Chenalhó," pp. 85–113 in Rosalva Aída Hernández Castillo, coordinadora, *La otra palabra: Mujeres y violencia en Chiapas, antes y después de Acteal, San Cristóbal de Las Casas*. Chiapas: CIESAS.

Eber, Christine, and Brenda Rosenbaum. 1993 "'That We May Serve beneath Your Hands and Feet': Women Weavers in Highland Chiapas, Mexico," in June Nash, ed., *Crafts in the World Market: The Impact of Global Exchange on Middle American Artisans*, 155–182. Albany: SUNY Press.

(ECLAS) Economic Commission for Latin American States. 1989 Editorial CEPAL Review.

————. 1991 *The Latin American and Caribbean Economies in 1989. Economic Survey of Latin America and the Caribbean*. Santiago, Chile: United Nations.

Edelman, Mark. 1998 "Transnational Peasant Politics in Central America," *Latin American Research Review*, Vol. 33, no. 3:49–86.

Edsforth, 1987 *Class Conflict, Cultural Consensus: The Making of a Mass Consumer Society in Flint, Michigan*. New Brunswick, NJ: Rutgers Press.

Ehrenreich, Jeffrey David. 1989 "Lifting the Burden of Secrecy: The Emergence of the Awa Biosphere Reserve," *Latin American Anthropology Review* 2, No. 2 (Winter):49–54.

Enge, Kpell I., and Scott Whiteford. 1989 *The Keepers of Water and Earth: Mexican Rural Social Organization and Irrigation*. Austin: University of Texas Press.

Enloe, Cynthia. 1983 *Does Khaki Become You? The Militarization of Women's Lives*. South End Press.

Escobar, Arturo. 1995 *Encountering Development: The Making, Strategy, and Unmaking of the Third World*. Princeton: Princeton University Press.

Escobar, Arturo, and Sonia E. Alvarez. 1992 *The Making of Social Movements in Latin America: Identity, Strategy, and Democracy*. Boulder: Westview Press

Etienne, Mona, and Leacock, eds. 1980 *Women and Colonization: Anthropological Perspectives*. New York: Praeger Scientific Studies.

EZLN. 1998 *Documentos y comunicados*. México D.F.: Ediciones ERA.

Farias, Pedro. 1991 Field Notes, National Science Foundation, Research Experience for Undergraduates.

Farrington, John, and David L. Lewis with S. Satish and Aurea Miclat Leve. 1993 *NGOs and the State in Asia: Rethinking Roles in Sustainable Agricultural Development*. London: Routledge.

Favre, Henri. 1983 *Cambio y continuidad entre los Mayas de Mexico: Contribución al estudio de la situación colonial en America Latina*. México, D.F.: INI.

Ferguson, J., and A. Gupta, eds. 1992 "Space, Identity, and the Politics of Difference," *Cultural Anthropology*, 7, 2.

Fernandez-Kelly, M. Patricia. 1983. *For We Are Sold, I and My People*. Albany: SUNY Press.

Fiagoy, Geraldine L. 1990 "The Indigenous Women of the Cordillera Region, Northern Philippines: A Situationer," in Mary Ellen Turpel, ed. *The Women of Many Nations in Canada*, pp. 21–35. Copenhagen: IWGIA.

Field, Les W. 1999 "Complicities and Collaborations: Anthropologists and the 'Unacknowledged' Tribes of California," *Current Anthropology*, 40, 2:193–209.

Findji, María Teresa. 1992 "From Resistance to Social Movements: The Indigenist Authorities Movement in Colombia," in A. Escobar and S. Alvarez, *The Making of Social Movements in Latin America: Identity, Strategy, and Democracy*. 112–153. Berkeley: University of California Press.

Forsythe, David P. 1992 *Human Rights and Peace: International and National Dimensions*. Lincoln: University of Nebraska.

Foster, George. 1965 "Peasant Society and the Notion of the Limited Good," *American Anthropologist* 67(2):293–315.

Foucault, Michel. 1980 *Power/Knowledge*. New York: Pantheon Books.

Fox, Jonathan, and Josefina Aranda. 1999 "Politics of Decentralized Rural Poverty Programs: Local Government and Community Participation in Oaxaca," pp. 179–196 in Richard Tardanico and Mark B. Rosenberg, eds. *Poverty or Development: Global Restructuring or Regional Transformation in the U.S. South and Mexican South*. New York: Routledge.

Frank, Andre Gunder. 1967 *Capitalism and Underdevelopment in Latin America*. New York: Monthly Review Press.

———. 1980 *Crisis in the World Economy*. New York: Holmes and Meier.

Friedman, Jonathan. 1994 *Cultural Identity and Global Process*. London: Sage.

Friedman, Thomas. 1999 *The Lexus and the Olive Tree: Understanding Globalization*. New York: Farrar, Straus, Giroux.

Friedrich, Paul. 1977 *Agrarian Revolt in a Mexican Village*. Chicago: University of Chicago Press.

Fröbel, Folker, Jurgen Heinrichs, and Otto Kreye. 1980 *The New International Division of Labour*. New York: Cambridge University Press.

Fuentes, Carlos. 1994 *Nuevo tiempo mexicano*. Mexico City: Nuevo Siglo Aguilar.

Gamio, Manuel. 1960 *Forjando patria*. Mexico City: Editorial Porrua. First published 1916.

García García, Lucina. 1995 "Lenguas, Ordenes Religiosas e Identidad. Siglos XVI-XVII en Nueva España," in Raquel Barceló, Mario Ana Portal, Martha Judith Sanchez, coord. *Diversidad Etnica y Conflicto en América Latina: El indio como metáforo en la identidad nacional*, Vol. II, 47–79. Mexico D.F.: Plaza y Valdés Editorial.

García de León, Antonio. 1984 *Resistencia y utopia: Memorial de agrarios crónicas de revuelto y profecías caecidas en la provincia de Chiapas durante los últimos quinientos años de su historia*. México D.F.: Ediciones Era.

Garza Caligaris, Ana María, and Rosalva Aída Hernández Castillo. 1998 "Encuentros y enfrentamientos de los Tzotziles Pedranos con el estado mexicano: Una perspectiva histórica antropológica para entender la violencia en Chenalhó," in Rosalva Aída Hernández Castillo, coordinora, *La otra palabra: Mujeres y violencia en Chiapas antes y después de Acteal, 1998 Marzo*, 39–60. San Cristobal de Las Casas: Centro de Investigaciones y Estudios Superiores en Antropología Social. Grupo de Mujeres Colectivos de Encuentro dentro Mujeres (COLEM) y Centro de Investigaciones y Acción para la Mujer (CIAM). Mexico.

Gelles, Paul H. 1998 *Water, Ethnicity, and Power: The Cultural Politics of Irrigation, Community, and Development in Highland Peru*. Ms.

Gibson, Charles. 1964 *The Aztecs Under Spanish Rule: A History of the Valley of Mexico, 1519–1810*. Stanford: Stanford University Press.

Giddens, Anthony. 1990 *The Consequences of Modernity*. Stanford: Stanford University Press.

Gilly, Adolfo. 1994 "Chiapas and the Rebellion of the Enchanted World," in Daniel Nugent, ed. *Rural Revolt in Mexico: U.S. Intervention and the Domain of Subaltern Politics*, pp. 261–333. Durham and London: Duke University Press.

Global Exchange 1995 Press conference.

Gluckman, Max. 1947 "Malinowski's 'Functional Analysis' of Social Change," *Africa* 42 (Reprinted 1963 in *Order and Rebellion in African Society*).

Gomez Cruz, Patricia and Christina Maria Kovic. 1995 *Con un pueblo vivo, en tierra negada: un ensayo sobre los derechos humanos y el conflict agrario en Chiapas 1989–1993*. San Cristóbal de las Casas: Centro de Derechos Humanos Fray Bartolomé de las Casas.

Gomezcésar Hernandez, Ivan. 1995 "Los liberales méxicanos frente al problema indígena: la comunidad y la integración nacional" in R. Barceló, M.A.Portal, M.J. Sánchez, pp. 13–46.

González Casanova, Pablo. 1970 *Sociología de la explotación*. Mexico City: Siglo Veintiuno.

———. 1993 "Prologue: Some Reflections on Liberation Struggles in Latin America." In Ponna Wignaraja, ed. *New Social Movements in the South: Empowering the People*. London: Zed.

———. 1995 "Repensar la Revolución," *América Indígena* (1–2):341–364.

Gonzalez-Ponciano, Jorgé Ramón. 1995 "Frontera Ecología y Soberanía Nacional: La Colonización de la Franja Fronteriza Sur de Marqués de Comillas," *América Indígena* 1–2:169–199. Instituto Indigenista Interamericano.

Gossen, Gary H. 1974 *Chamulas in the World of the Sun*. Cambridge: Harvard University Press.

———. 1986 "Mesoamerican Ideas as a Foundation for Regional Synthesis," in G. Gossen, ed. *Symbol and Meaning Beyond the Closed Community: Essays in Mesoamerican Ideas*. Albany: Studies on Culture and Society Vol. 1, Institute for Mesoamerican Studies, The University at Albany, SUNY, pp. 1–8.

———. 1989 Los Chamulas en el mundo del sol. México: Instituto Nacional Indígena.

———. 1996 "Maya Zapatistas Move to the Ancient Future," *American Anthropologist* 98(3):528–538.

———. 1999 *Telling Maya Tales*. New York: Routledge.

Gossen, Gary, and Richard Leventhal. 1989, "The Topography of Ancient Maya Religious Pluralism: A Dialogue with the Present," in *Lowland Maya Civilization in the Eighth Century AD: A Symposium*, Jeremy A Sabloff and John S. Henderson, eds. Washington, D.C.: Dumbarton Oaks.

Graburn, Nelson. 1976 *Ethnic and Tourist Arts: Cultural Expressions from the Fourth World*. Los Angeles: University of California.

Gramont, Hubert C. de. 1996 "Introducción: La organización gremial de los agricultures frente a los procesos de globalización en la agrícultura," in H.C. Grammont, coordinador, *Neoliberalismo y Organización social en el Campo Mexicano*, pp. 9–68. Mexico, D.F.: Plaza y Valdés.

Grasmuck, Sherri, and Patricia R. Pessar. 1991 *Between Two Islands: Dominican International Migration*. Berkeley: University of California Press.

Green, Linda. 1999 *Fear as a Way of Life: Mayan Widows in Rural Guatemala*. New York: Columbia University Press.

Greenberg, James B. 1989 *Blood Ties: Life and Violence in Rural Mexico*. Tucson: University of Arizona Press.

Grimes, Kimberly. n.d. *To Market, To Market: Crafts, Trade and Anthropologists*.

Groupe d'Etude des Relaciones Economiques Internationales, Instituto Nacional de la Researche Agronomique, San Cristóbal de Las Casas, Chiapas, México. February 1978 Economie et Sociologie Rurales. INAREMAC.

Guiteras Holmes, Calixta. 1961 *Perils of the Soul: The World View of a Tzotzil Indian*. Glencoe, IL: The Free Press.

Gupta, Akhil, and James Ferguson. 1997 "Beyond 'Culture,' Space, Identity, and the Politics of Difference," pp. 6–23 in *Culture, Power, Place: Ethnography at the End of an Era*. Durham: Duke University Press.

Gutiérrez, Margarita and Nellys Palomo. 1999 "Autonomía con mirada de mujer," pp. 54–86 in Aracely Burguete Cal y Mayor, coordinador. *México: Experiencias de autonomía indígena*. Copenhagen: Documento IWGIA No. 28.

Hall, Stuart. 1991 "The Local and the Global: Globalization and Ethnicity," in Anthony D. King, ed. *Culture, Globalization and the World System: Current Debates in Art History* 3, pp. 19. Minneapolis: University of Minnesota Press.

Hannerz, Ulf. 1991 "Scenarios for Peripheral Cultures," in Arthur D. King, ed. *Culture, Globalization and the World System: Current Debates in Art History* 3, 107–128. Minneapolis: University of Minnesota Press.

———. 1996 *Transnational Connections: Culture, People, Place*. London: Routledge.

Harbottle, Brigadier Michael N. 1984 "Introduction," in *Generals for Peace and Dsarmament: A Challenge to US/NATO Strategy*. New York: Universe Books.

Harris, Marvin. 1964 *Patterns of Race in the Americas*. New York: Walker.

Harvey, David. 1989 *The Condition of Postmodernity: An Enquiry into the Origins of Cultural Change*. Cambridge, MA and Oxford: Blackwell.

———. 2000 *Spaces of Hope*. Berkeley: University of California Press.

Harvey, Neil. 1990 "Peasant Strategies and Corporatism in Chiapas," in Joe Foweraker and Ann L. Craig, eds., *Popular Movements and Political Change in Mexico*, pp. 183–198. Boulder and London: Lynne Rienner Publisher.

———. 1991 "Estrategías corporativistas y respuestas populares en México rural: Estado y organizaciones campesinas en Chiapas desde 1970," *CIHMECH* Vol. 2:51–66.

————. 1994 *Rebellion in Chiapas: Rural Reforms, Campesino Radicalism, and the Limits to Salinismo.* Transformation of Rural Mexico Series, No. 5. La Jolla, CA: Center for U.S.-Mexican Studies, University of California at San Diego.

————. 1998 *The Chiapas Rebellion: The Struggle for Land and Democracy.* Durham, N.C.: Duke University Press.

Henríquez Arellano, Edmundo. 1999 "Usos, costumbres y pluralismo en Los Altos de Chiapas," pp. 7–22 in *Los indígenas y las elecciones en Los Altos de Chiapas,* Edmundo Henríquez Arellano coordinador. San Cristóbal de Las Casas: Instituto Federal Electoral and CIESAS.

Henríquez, Elio. 1996 "Exigen freno a la violencia miles de campesinos del norte de Chiapas," *Proceso,* June, 1996, no. 4234.

Hermitte, M. Esther. 1992 "Poder Sobrenatural y Control Social en un Pueblo Maya Contemporaneo," Tuxtla Gutiérrez: Instituto Chiapaneco de Cultura. Thesis presented in 1964, University of Chicago.

Hernández Castillo, Rosalva Aída. 1997 "Between Hope and Adversity: The Struggle of Organized Women in Chiapas Since the Zapatista Rebellion," *Journal of Latin American Anthropology,* Vol. 3, no. 1, 102–120.

————. 1998 "Introducción," and "Antes y después de Acteal: Voces, memorias y experiencias desde las mujeres de San Pedro Chenalhó," pp. 1–37 in R.A. Hernandez, coordinadora, *La otra palabra.* San Cristobal: Grupo de Mujeres de San Cristobal, Centro de Investigaciones y Estudios Superiores en Antropología Social, CIESAS, and Centro de Investigación y Acción para la Mujer.

Hernández Castillo, R. Aída, and Ronald Nigh. 1998 "Globalization Processes and Local Identity among Mayan Coffee Growers in Chiapas, Mexico," *American Anthropologist,* Vol. 99, no. 1: 36–49.

Hernández Navarro, Luis. 1998 "The Escalation of the War in Chiapas," *NACLA Report on the Americas,* Vol. 31, no. 5 (March/April): 6–14.

Hewitt de Alcántara, Cynthia. 1984 *Anthropological Perspectives on Rural Mexico.* London: Routledge and Kegan Paul.

Hill, Jonathan D. 1989 "Demystifying Structural Violence," *Latin American Anthropology Review* 1, 2(Winter): 42–48.

Hollis, Martin and Steven Lukes, eds. 1982 "Introduction," *Rationality and Relativism.* Cambridge: MIT.

Hunt, Eva. 1977 *The Transformation of the Hummingbird: Cultural Roots of a Zinacantecan Mythical Poem.* Ithaca: Cornell University Press.

Hunt, Eva, and June Nash. 1967 "Local and Territorial Unity," in Manning Nash, ed. *Social Anthropology,* Vol. 6 of *History of Middle American Indians,* Robert Wauchope general editor, pp. 253–282. Austin: University of Texas Press.

Hymes, Dell, ed. 1972 *Reinventing Anthropology.* New York: Random House.

Inter-American Development Bank. Annual Report 1987, 1993, 1997.

————. 1987 *Economic and Social Progress Report.* Washington, DC.

IUCN Inter-Commission Task Force on Indigenous Peoples. 1997 Indigenous Peoples and Sustainability: Cases and Actions. Utrecht: International Books. Instituto Nacional Estadistica General I (INEGI). 1991 *Censos Generales de la Población.* México, D.F.

Jameson, Fredric. 1982 *The Political Unconscious: Narrative as Socially Symbolic Act.* Ithaca: Cornell University Press.

Jelin, Elizabeth. 1987 *Movimientos sociales y democracia emergente.* Buenos Aires: Centro Editor de América Latina.

————. 1990 *Women and Social Change in Latin America.* London: United Nations Research Institute for Social Development and Zed Books.

Jonas, Susanne. 2000 *Of Centaurs and Doves: Guatemala's Peace Process.* Boulder, CO: Westview Press.

Joseph, Gilbert M., and Daniel Nugent, eds. 1994 *Everyday Forms of State Formation: Revolution and the Negotiation of Rule in Modern Mexico.* Durham and London: Duke University Press.

Kajese, Kingston. 1987 "An Agenda of Future Tasks for International and Indigenous NGOs: Views from the South," *World Development,* Vol. 15 Supp: 79–85.

Katz, Friedrich. 1988 "Rural Uprisings in Preconquest and Colonial Mexico," in Friedrich Katz, ed., *Riot, Rebellion, and Revolution: Rural Social Conflict in Mexico,* 65–94. Princeton: University of Princeton Press.

Kearney, Michael. 1988 "Mixtec Political Consciousness: From Passive to Active Resistance," in Daniel Nugent, ed. *Rural Revolt in Mexico and U.S. Intervention.* San Diego: Center for U.S.-Mexican Studies, University of California.

————. 1995 "The Local and the Global: The Anthropology of Globalization and Transnationalism," *Annual Review of Anthropology* 24: 547–565.

————. 1996 *Reconceptualizing the Peasantry: Anthropology in Global Perspective.* Boulder: Westview.

Klare, Michael T. 1988 "The Interventionist Impulse: U.S. Military Doctrine for Low-Intensity Warfare," in Michael T. Klare and Peter Kornbluh, eds. *Low-Intensity Warfare,* pp. 49–79. New York: Pantheon Books.

Knauft, Bruce M. 1994 "Pushing Anthropology Past the Posts," *Critique of Anthropology: Critical Note on Cultural Anthropology and Cultural Studies as Influenced by Postmodernism and Existentialism,* vol. 14 (2): 117–152.

Kovic, Christine. 1995 "Con un solo corazón": La iglesia católica, la identidad indígena y los derechos humanos en Chiapas," en J. Nash et al., *La explosión de comunidades en Chiapas.* Copenhagen: IWGIA No. 16.

————. 1997 "'Walking with One Heart': Human Relations and the Catholic Church among the Maya of Highland Chiapas." Ph.D. Dissertation, CUNY Graduate School, Department of Anthropology.

Laclau, Ernesto and Chantal Mouffe. 1985 *Hegemony and Socialist Strategy: Towards a Radical Democratic Politics*. London: Verso.

Lafaye, Jacques. 1992 *Quetzalcoatl and Guadalupe: The Formation of Mexican National Consciousness, 1531–1813*. Chicago: University of Chicago Press.

Lamphere, Louise. 1987 *From Working Daughters to Working Mothers: Immigrant Women in a New England Industrial Community*. Ithaca, NY: Cornell University Press.

Landim, Leilah. 1987 "NGOs in Latin America," *World Development* 15, Supp.: 29–38.

Lara Resende, André, moderator. 1995 "Policies for Growth in Latin American Experience," Proceedings of a Conference in Mangaratiba, Rio de Janeiro, Brazil, March 16, 1994. Washington, D.C.: IMF.

Le Bot, Yvon. 1997 *Subcomandante Marcos: El sueño Zapatista*. Barcelona: Plaza and Janes, Editores.

Leacock, Eleanor Burke. 1976 "Montagnais Marriage and the Jesuits in the Seventeenth Century: Incidents from the Relations of Paul Le Jeune," *Western Canadian Journal of Anthropology* 6, 3:77–91.

————. 1978 "Woman's Status in Egalitarian Society: Implications for Social Evolution." *Current Anthropology* 29, 2:247–75.

Leacock, Eleanor Burke, and Jacqueline Goodman. 1975 "Class, Commodity, and the Status of Women," in R. Rohrlich-Leavitt, ed. *Women Cross-Culturally: Change and Challenge*. The Hague: Mouton.

Leacock, Eleanor, and June Nash. 1977 "The Ideology of Sex: Archetypes and Stereotypes," *Annals of the New York Academy of Science*, 285; reprinted in L. Adler, ed. *Cross Cultural Research at Issue*. New York: Academic Press 1982.

Lee, Richard B. 1992 "Art, Science, or Politics? The Crisis in Hunter-Gatherer Studies," *American Anthropologist* 94, l:31–54.

Lee Whiting, Thomas A. 1994 "La perspectiva diacrónica y resistencia étnica en Chiapas," in Jacinto Arias Perez, *El arreglo de los pueblos indios: La incansable tarea de reconstitución*. Tuxtla Gutiérrez: Secretaría de Educación Pública, Gobierno del Estado de Chiapas, Instituto de Cultura.

León de Leal, Magdalena and Carmen Diana Deere. 1980 *Mujer y capitalismo agrario: Estudio de cuatro regiones Colombianas*. Bogota: Asociación Colombiana para el Estudio de la Población (ACEP).

León Portillo. 1963 *Aztec Thought and Culture: A Study of the Ancient Nahuatl Mind*. Norman: University of Oklahoma Press.

Levine, Daniel H., and David Stoll. 1997 "Bridging the Gap Between Empowerment and Power in Latin America," in Susanne Hoeber Rudolph and James Piscatori, *Transnational Religion and Fading State*, pp. 1–26. Boulder: Westview 1997.

Lewis, Oscar. 1963 *Life in a Mexican Village: Tepoztlán Restudied*. Urbana: University of Illinois.

Leyva Solano, Xochitl, and Gabriel Ascencio Franco. 1995 "Del Común al Leviatán: Síntesis de un proceso sociopolitico en el medio rural mexicano," *América Indígena* 1–2, (January to June):201–34.

————. 1996 *Lacandonia al Filo del Agua*. Mexico, D.F.: Fondo de Cultura Economica.

Li, Tania. 1991 *Culture, Ecology and Livelihood in the Tinombo Region of Central Sulawesi*. Halifax, Canada: Environmental Development in Indonesia Project.

Lipietz, Alai. 1987 *Mirages and Miracles: The Crisis of Global Fordism*. Trans. David Macey. London: Verso.

Lipschutz, Ronnie D. 1992 "Reconstructing World Politics: The Emergence of Global Civil Society." *Millennium: Journal of International Studies* 21, 3:389–420.

Lipton, Michael. 1983 *Poverty, Undernutrition and Hunger*. Washington, D.C.: World Bank Staff Working Papers, 597.

Locke, John. 1690 *Two Treatises of Government*. London.

Lomnitz-Adler, Claudio. 1992 *Exits from the Labyrinth: Culture and Ideology in the Mexican National Space*. Berkeley: University of California Press.

Long, Norman. 1984 *Family and Work in Rural Societies: Perspectives on Non-wage Labour*. London: Tavistock.

Lopez, Julio Cesar, and Guillermo Correa. 1995 "Podemos ceder en todo, menos en nuestra dignidad, planteo el EZLN," *Proceso*, 967, 15 May 1995, 32–3.

Lovera, Sara and Nellys Palomo, Coordinadoras. 1999 *Comunicación e información de la mujer convergencia socialista*, 2nd ed. México, D.F.: Las Alzadas.

Lowe, Lisa, and David Lloyd. 1997 *The Politics of Culture in the Shadow of Capital*. Durham, NC: Duke University Press.

Lumsdaine, Peter. 1995 "Global Exchange." Communication given at press conference, Centro de Derechos Humanos "Fray Bartolomé de Las Casas, San Cristobal de Las Casas," Chiapas, Mexico.

Lustig, Nora. 1990 "Economic Crisis, Adjustment and Living Standards in Mexico, 1982–1985." *World Development* 189 (July):1325–42.

————. 1992 *The Remaking of an Economy*. Washington, D.C.: The Brookings Institute.

————. 1995 "Equity and Development," in James L. Dietz, ed. *Latin America's Economic: Confronting Crisis*, 2nd ed., pp. 55–68. Boulder: Westport.

Luxemburg, Rosa. 1951 *The Accumulation of Capital*. New York, London: Routledge and Keegan Paul and Monthly Review Republication. Translated by Agnes Schwarzschild and Introduction by Joan Robinson. See also 1971 edition with introduction by Tarbuck, Monthly Review Press. First edition *Die Akkumulation des Kapitals* 1913.

MacEwan, Arthur, and William K. Tabb, eds. 1989 *Instability and Change in the World Economy*. New York: Monthly Review Press.

MacLeod, Murdo. 1973 *Spanish Central America: A Socioeconomic History, 1520–1720*. Berkeley and Los Angeles: University of California Press.

McQuown, Norman A., and Julian A. Pitt-Rivers, eds. 1970 *Ensayos de antropología en la zona central de Chiapas*. México D.F.: Instituto Nacional Indígena.

MacShane, Dennis. 1993 "The New Age of the Internationals," *New Statesman and Society* 6 (April 30):23–6.

Magdoff, Harry. 1992 *Globalization to What End?* New York: A Monthly Review Press Pamphlet.

Mahane, Riahine. 1987 "From Fordism to ?: Technology, Labour Markets, and Unions," *Economic and Industrial Democracy*, 8, 1 (Feb.):5–60.

Mallon, Florencia E. 1989 *The Defense of Community in Peru's Central Highlands: Peasant Struggle and Capitalist Transition, 1860–1940*. Princeton: Princeton University Press.

————. 1994 "Reflections on the Ruins: Everyday Forms of State Formation in Nineteenth Century Mexico," in Gilbert M. Joseph and Daniel Nugent, eds. *Everyday Forms of State Formation: Revolution and the Negotiation of Rule in Modern Mexico*, pp. 69–106. Durham and London: Duke University Press.

————. 1995 *Peasant and Nation: The Making of Postcolonial Mexico and Peru*. Berkeley: University of California Press.

Mandel, Ernest. 1975 *Late Capitalism*. London: NLB.

Maquet, Jacques. 1964 "Objectivity in Anthropology," *Current Anthropology* 5:47–55.

Marcus, George. 1998 *Ethnography through Thick and Thin*. Princeton: University of Chicago Press.

Marcos, Sylvia. 1997 "Mujeres indígenas: notas sobre un feminismo naciente," *Cuadernos Femininas*, 1, 2:13–17.

Marriott, McKim. 1952 "Technological Change in Overdeveloped Rural Areas," *Economic Development and Cultural Change* I (4):261–72.

Marx, Karl. 1964 *Pre-Capitalist Economic Formations*, translated by Jack Cohen, edited and introduction E. J. Hobsbawm. New York: International Publishers.

Marx, Karl, and Friedrich Engels. 1959 *The Communist Manifesto and Other Writings*. New York: The Modern Library.

Massey, Garth. 1987 *Subsistence and Change: Lessons of Agropastoralism*. Boulder: Westview Press.

Mattiace, Shannon. 1997 "!Zapata Vive! The EZLN, Indian Politics and the Autonomy Movement in Mexico," *Journal of Latin American Anthropology*, 3, 1:32–71.

Maurer, Eugenio. 1984 *Los Tzeltales: Paganos o Cristianos? Su religión: Sincretismo o sintesis?* Mexico D.F.: Centro de Estudios Educativos, A.C.

Meggid, Amos. 1996 *Exporting the Catholic Reformation: Local Religion in Early-Colonial Mexico*. Leiden and New York: E. J. Brill.

Mencher, Joan. 1978 "Why Grow More Food? An Analysis of Some of the Contradictions in the Green Revolution in Kerala." *Economic and Political Weekly*, Bombay. 23–30: A98–A282104.

————. 1985 "The Forgotten Ones: Female Landless Labourers in Southern India." In *Women Creating Wealth: Transforming Economic Development*. Washington, D.C.: J. T. and A. for the Association of Women in Development.

Mexican Notebook: The Newsletter of the Consulate General of Mexico in New York. 1999 "On Chiapas: Mexico's Attorney General Presents 'White Paper' on Chiapas Massacre." Vol. 8, no. 1, February: 5.

————. 1999 Editorial, Vol. 8, no. 1, March: 1.

Mintz, Sidney. 1977 "The So-Called World Systems: Local Initiatives and Local Responses," *Dialectical Anthropology* 2:253–70.

Mittelman, James H. 1996 "The Dynamics of Globalization," in J. Mittleman, ed., *Globalization: Critical Reflections*, pp. 1–20. Boulder: Lynne Rienner.

Moncada, María. 1983 "Movimiento campesino y estructura de poder: Venustiano Carranza, Chiapas." *Textual* Vol. 4, no. 13:69–79.

Montes Ruíz, Fernando. 1986 *La mascara de piedra: Simbolismo y personalidad aymaras en la historia*. La Paz: Quipus.

Montgomery, David. 1979 *Workers' Control in America: Studies in the History of Work, Technology and Labor Struggles*. New York: Cambridge University Press.

————. 1993 *Citizen Worker*. Cambridge: University of Cambridge Press.

Mullings, Leith. 1989 "Gender and the Application of Anthropological Knowledge to Public Policy in the United States," in Sandra Morgan, ed., *Gender and Anthropology: Critical Reviews for Research and Teaching*. Washington, D.C.: American Anthropological Association.

NACLA Report on the Americas. "The Wars Within: Counterinsurgency in Chiapas and Colombia," Vol. 31, March/April:6–21.

Nader, Laura. 1990 *Harmony Ideology: Justice and Control in a Zapotec Mountain Village*. Stanford University.

———. 1996 ed. *Naked Science: Anthropological Inquiry into Boundaries, Power, and Knowledge*. London and New York: Routledge and Co.

Nagengast, Carole. 1994 "Violence, Terror, and the Crisis of the State," Annual Reviews of Anthropology 23:109–136.

Nagengast, Carole, and Michael Kearney. 1990 "Mixtec Ethnicity: Social Identity, Political Consciousness and Political Activism," *Latin American Perspectives*, 25, 2:61–92.

Nash, June. 1966 "Social Resources of a Latin American Peasantry," *Social and Economic Studies*, 15, 4:353–67.

———. 1967 "Death as a Way of Life: The Increasing Recourse to Homicide in a Maya Community," *American Anthropologist* 69, 5:435–77.

———. 1968 "The Passion Play in Maya Indian Communities," *Comparative Studies in Society and History* 20 (3):318–27.

———. 1970 *In the Eyes of the Ancestors: Belief and Behavior in a Maya Community*. New Haven: Yale University.

———. 1975 "Nationalism and Fieldwork," *Annual Review of Anthropology*, 4:225–46. Palo Alto: University of Stanford Press.

———. 1979 *We Eat the Mines and the Mines Eat Us: Dependency and Exploitation in Bolivia's Tin Mines*. New York: Columbia University Press.

———. 1980 "Aztec Women: The Transition from Status to Class in Empire and Colony," in Mona Etienne and Eleanor Leacock, eds., *Women and Colonization: Anthropological Perspectives, Annals of the New York Academy of Science* 134–148. New York: J. F. Bergin.

———. 1981 "Ethnographic Aspects of the World Capitalist System," *Annual Review of Anthropology* 20:393–423. Palo Alto: University of Stanford Press.

———. 1982 "Implications of Technological Change for Household Level and Rural Development," pp. 75–128 in P.M. Weil and J. Elterich, eds. *Technological Change and Rural Development*. Newark, DE: University of Delaware Press.

———. 1988 "Cultural Resistance and Class Consciousness in Bolivian Tin-Mining Communities," in Susan Eckstein, ed. *Power and Popular Protest: Latin American Experience*, pp. 182–202. Berkeley: University of California Press.

———. 1989 *From Tank Town to High Tech: The Clash of Community and Corporate Cycles*. New York: Columbia University Press.

———. 1990 "Latin American Women in the World Capitalist Crisis." *Gender and Society* 4, 3:338–53.

———. 1992a "Interpreting Social Movements: Bolivian Resistance to the Economic Conditions Imposed by the International Monetary Fund," *American Ethnologist* 19, 2:275–93.

———. 1992b *I Spent My Life in the Mines: The Story of Juan Rojas, Bolivian Tin Miner*. New York: Columbia University Press.

———. 1993 *Crafts in the World Market: The Impact of Global Exchange on Middle American Artisans*. Albany: SUNY Press.

———. 1994a "Judas Transformed," *Natural History* Vol. 10–3, No. 3 (March):47–53.

———. 1994b "The Reassertion of Indigenous Identity: Mayan Responses to State Intervention in Chiapas," *Latin American Research Review*, Vol. 30, no. 3:7–41.

———. 1994c "The Challenge of Trade Liberalization to Cultural Survival on the Southern Frontier of Mexico," *Indiana Journal of Global Legal Studies*, Vol. 1, 2:367–395.

———. 1994d "Global Integration and Subsistence Insecurity," *American Anthropologist* 96(2):1–31.

———. 1995a "The Power of the Powerless: Update from Chiapas," *Cultural Survival* 19, 1, Spring:14–18.

———. 1995b "The Reassertion of Indigenous Identity: Mayan Responses to State Intervention in Chiapas, Mexico," *Latin American Research Review* 30, 4:7–42.

———. 1997a "Gendered Deities and the Survival of Culture," *Journal of the History of Religion* 36, 4:333–356.

———. 1997b "The Fiesta of the Word: The Zapatista Uprising and Radical Democracy in Mexico," *American Anthropologist* 99(2):261–74.

———. 1997c "Press Reports on the Chiapas Uprising: Towards a Transnationalized Communication," *Journal of Latin American Anthropology* 2(2):42–75.

———. 1997d "When Isms become Wasms: Structuralism, Functionalism, Marxism, Feminism, and Postmodernisms," *Cultural Critique* 17(1):11–22.

———. n.d. "The War of the Peace in Chiapas, Mexico: Indigenous Women's Struggle for Peace and Justice," in Susan Eckstein and Timothy P. Wickham-Crowley, eds. *The Politics of Injustice in Latin America*. Berkeley: University of California Press.

Nash, June, and Eleanor Burke Leacock. 1977 "The Ideology of Sex: Archetypes and Stereotypes." *Annals of the New York Academy of Science*, New York, no. 285.

Nash, June and M. Patricia Fernandez-Kelly. 1983 *Women, Men, and the International Division of Labor*. Albany: SUNY Press.

Nash, June, and Kathleen Sullivan. 1992 "The Return to Porfirismo," *Cultural Survival* 16(2) (May):13–16.

Nash, June, with George A. Collier, Rosalva Aída Hernández Castillo, Kathleen Sullivan, Maria Eugenia Santana E., Christine Marie Kovic, Marie-Odile Marion Singer, Hermann Bellinghausen. 1995 *La explosión de comunidades en Chiapas*. Copenhagen: IWGIA.

Nash, June, and Christine Kovic. 1996 "The Reconstitution of Hegemony: The Free Trade Act and the Transformation of Rural Mexico," in James Mittelman, ed. *Globalization: Critical Reflections*, 165–186. Boulder: Lynne Reiner.

National Catholic Reporter. Feb. 24, 1995 Carole Collins, "Ending Abject Poverty is U.N. Summit Goal," 31, 17:6.

National Science Foundatation Research Experience for Undergraduates. 1990 Field Reports. Robert Martinez, Field Notes on Venustiano Carranza.

———. 1991 Field Reports. Pedro Farias, Field Notes on the Unión de Uniones.

Newman, Katherine S. 1988 *Falling from Grace: The Meaning of Downward Mobility in American Culture*. New York: Free Press.

Nigh, Ronald. 1992 "La agricultura organica y el nuevo movimiento campesino en Mexico," *Anthropologica*.

———. 1994 "Zapata Rose in 1994: The Indian Rebellion in Chiapas," *Cultural Survival Quarterly*, Spring 18(l):9–12).

Nobutaka, Inoue, ed. 1997 *Globalization and Indigenous Culture*. Tokyo: Institute for Japanese Culture and Clasics, Kokugokuin University.

Nolasco Armas, M. 1970 "La antropología aplicada en México," In *De eso lo que se llaman antropología*. México D.F.: Nuestro Tiempo.

Nordstrom, Carolyn, and Antonious C.B.M. Robben, eds. 1995 *Fieldwork under Fire: Contemporary Studies of Violence and Survival*. Berkeley: University of California Press.

Nugent, Daniel. 1989 "'Are We Not [Civilized] Men?': The Formation and Devolution of Community in Northern Mexico," *Journal of Historical Sociology* 2, 3 (September):208–239.

———. 1995 "Northern Intellectuals and the EZLN," *Monthly Review*, July/August:224–133.

Nugent, Daniel, and Ana María Alonso. 1994 "Multiple Selective Traditions in Agrarian Struggle: Popular Culture and State Formation in the Ejido of Namiquipa, Chihuahua," in Gilbert M. Joseph and Daniel Nugent, eds., *Everyday Forms of State Formation: Revolution and the Negotiation of Rule in Modern Mexico*, pp. 209–246. Durham and London: Duke University Press.

Nyoni, Sithembiso. 1987 "Indigenous NGOs: Liberation, Self-Reliance, and Development," *World Development* 15 (Suppl):51–56.

O'Connor, James. 1984 *Accumulation Crisis*. London: Basil Blackwell.

Okoko, Kumse A.B. 1987 *Socialism and Self-Reliance in Tanzania*. London: Routledge and Kegan Paul.

Ong, Aiwa. 1982. *Spirits of Resistance*. Albany: SUNY Press.

Organization for Economic Cooperation and Development. 1998 "Direct Investment Flows in Organization for Economic Cooperation and Development Countries." *Direct Investment Yearbook*. Washington, D.C.: OECD

Page-Reeves, Janet. 1998 "Alpaca Sweater Designs and Marketing: Problems and Prospects for Cooperative Knitting Organization in Bolivia," *Human Organization* Vol. 57, No. 1 (Spring):83–94.

Parra Vásquez, Manuel, and Reyna Moguel Viveros. 1994 "El estado nacional y los indígenas: Los limites de la iteragración" *La Jornada del Campo*, no. 29.

Pastore, Manuel, and Carol Wise. 1997 "State Policy, Distribution and Neoliberal Reform in Mexico," *Journal of Latin American Studies* 29:419–56.

Pecchioli, R.M. 1983 *The Internationalization of Banking*: The Policy Issues. Washington, D.C.

Perez Castro, Ana Bella. 1993 Revista de los Chamulas en el mundo del sol, CIHMECH, San Cristobal Centro de Investigaciones Humanisticas de Mesoamérica y el Estado de Chiapas, Vol. 3, no. 1:231–239.

Pérez Chacón, José. 1993 *Los choles de tila y su mundo: Tradición oral*. Tuxtla Gutiérrez, Chiapas: Gobierno del Estado de Chiapas, Instituto Chiapaneco de Cultura.

Pessar, Patricia. 1982 "The Role of Gender in International Migration and the Case of United States–Bound Migration from the Dominican Republic," *International Migration Review* 16(2):342–64.

———. 1986 "The Role of Gender in Dominican Settlement in the United States," in June Nash and Helen Safa, eds., *Women and Change in Latin America*, pp. 273–294. Hadley, MA: Bergin and Garvey.

Petras, James. 1997 "Latin America: The Resurgence of the Left," *New Left Review* 223:17–47.

Pohlentz, C. 1987 "La Selva Lacandona," *Perfil* l; 5:22–23.

Polanyi, Karl. 1957 "The Economy as Instituted Process," in Karl Polanyi, Conrad Arensberg, and Harry Pierson, *Trade and Market in the Early Empires*. Chicago: Henry Regnery.

Polanyi, Karl, Conrad Arensberg, and Harry Pearson. 1957 *Trade and Market in the Early Empires*. Chicago: Henry Regnery.

Posey, Darrell A. 1983 "Indigenous Ecolocal Knowledge and Development of the Amazon," in Emilio F. Moran, ed. *The Dilemma of Amazonian Development*. 225–57. Boulder: Westview Press.

————. 1998 "Biodiversity Conservation, Traditional Resource Rights, and Indigenous Peoples," in S. Büchi, C. Erni, L. Jurt, and C. Rüegg, eds. *Indigenous Peoples, Environment and Development*, Proceedings of the conference, Zurich, May 15–18, 1995. Copenhagen International Work Group for Indigenous Affairs and Department of Social Anthropology, University of Zurich. Copenhagen: IWGIA.

Pozas Arciniega, Ricardo. 1944 "Chamula 1943–1944." Ph.D. Thesis, Instituto Nacional de Antropología e Historia, México, D.F.

————. 1952 *Juan Pérez Jolote: Biografía de un Tzotzil*. México: Fondo de Cultura Económica.

Pozas Arciniega, Ricardo, and Isabel H. de Pozas. 1971 *Los indios en las clases sociales de México*. México: Siglo Veintiuno.

Prager, Martin, and Hernando Riveros. 1993 *Non-Governmental Organizations and the State in Latin America: Rethinking Roles in Sustainable Agricultural Development*. London: Routledge.

Prebisch, Raul. 1985 *Revista*. CEPAL. Chile: ECLAS.

Procuraduría Agraria, Tuxtla Gutiérrez, Chiapas. 1992 *La nueva ley agraria*. México, D.F.: Procuradería Agraria.

————. 1993 Archivos 8:13.

Pryor, Frederic L. 1990 *Malawi and Madagascar: The Political Economy of Poverty, Equity and Growth*. Washington, D.C.: World Bank.

Quijano, Aníbal. 1988, "Imagines desconocidas: la modernidad en la incrucijada postmoderna," in Fernando Calderon G., coordinadora, *Identidad Latinoamericana premodernidad, modernidad, y postmodernidad*. Buenos Aires, Argentina.

Rabasa, Emilio, and Gloria Caballero. 1996 *Mexicano, ésta es tu constitución*. Texto vigente 1996. México, D.F.: Miguel Angel Porrúa Grupo Editorial.

Ramirez, Miguel. 1997 "Mexico," in Laura Randall, ed., *The Political Economy of Latin America in the Post-War Period*, 111–148. Austin: University of Texas Press.

Ramos de Castro, Edna Maria. 1992 "Genero e classe: O fazer politico de mulheres camponesas na Amazonia." Paper prepared for the conference "Learning from Latin America: Women's Struggles for Livelihood," University of California at Los Angeles, February 27–29.

Rappaport, Joanne, and Robert V.H. Dover 1996 "The Construction of Difference by Native Legislators," *Journal of Latin American Anthropology* Vol. 1, no. 2 (spring):22–45.

Ready, Carol A. 1999 "Between Transnational Feminism, Political Parties and Popular Movements: Mujeres por la Dignidad y la Vida en Postwar El Salvador." Ph.D. Thesis, Graduate School and University Center, City University of New York.

Redfield, Robert. 1930 *Tepoztlan: A Mexican Village*. Chicago: University of Chicago Press.

————. 1941 *The Folk Culture of Yucatan*. Chicago: University of Chicago Press.

Reyes Ramos, María Eugenia. 1991 "Legislación agraria en Chiapas 1914–21," *Revista CIHMECH*, UNAM, Tomo 2:95–111.

————. 1992 "El reparto de tierras y la política agraria en Chiapas, 1914–1988," *CIHMECH*, UNAM, Tomo 3 México, D.F.

————. 1994 "Colonización de tierras en Chiapas," *Revista CIHMECH* Tomo 4, 1 and 2:53–71, UNACH.

Ricard, Robert. 1966 *The Spiritual Conquest of Mexico: An Essay on the Apostolate and the Evangelizing Methods of the Mendicant Orders in New Spain, 1523–1572*. Translated by Lesley Byrd. Berkeley: University of California Press.

Rojas, Juan, and June Nash. 1976 *He agotado mi vida en la mina: Autobiografía de un minero boliviano*. Buenos Aires: Nueva Visión. New edition, *I Spent My Life in the Mines*, New York: Columbia University.

Rojas, Rosa. 1995 *Chiapas: Y las mujeres que? Colección del dicho al hecho, Tomo II*. México, D.F.: Editorial La Correa Feminista, Centro de Investigación y Capacitación de la Mujber.

Romanucci-Ross, Lola. 1976 (reprinted 1983) *Conflict, Violence and Morality in a Mexican Village*. Chicago: University of Chicago Press.

Romany, Celina. 1993 "Women as Aliens: A Feminist Critique of the Public and Private Distinction," *Harvard Human Rights Journal* 87.

Roseberry, William. 1989 *Anthropologies and Histories: Essays in Culture, History, and Political Economy*. New Brunswick. Rutgers University Press.

Rosenbaum, Brenda. 1993 *With Our Heads Bowed: The Dynamics of Gender in a Maya Community*. Austin: University of Texas Press.

Rothstein, Frances A., and Michael Blim, eds. 1992 *Anthropology and the Global Factory: Studies of the New Industrialization in the Late Twentieth Century*. New York: Bergen and Garvey.

Rubín Bamaca, Homero. 1999 "El abstencionismo en Los Altos de Chiapas: La otra cara de las elecciones," in *Los indígenas y las elecciones en Los Altos de Chiapas*. San Cristóbal de as Casas, CIESAS and Instituto Federal Electoral.

Ruccio, David F.

————. 1991 "Legislación agraria en Chiapas 1914–21," *Revista CIHMECH* 2:95–111.

Rudolph, Susanne Hoeber. 1997 "Introduction: Religion, States, and Transnational Civil Society," in Rudolf, Susanne Hoeber and James Piscatori, eds., pp. 1–26. *Transnational Religion and Fading States*. Denver: Westview Press.

Ruíz Hernández, Margarito. 1999 "México: Experiencias de Autonomía Indígena," pp. 21–53 in Aracely Burguete Cal y Mayor, Coord. *México experiencias de autonomía indígena*. Copenhagen: Documento IWGIA No. 28.

Rus, Diane. 1997 *Mujeres de tierra fría: Conversaciones con las coletas*. San Cristóbal de Las Casas, Chiapas: Universidad de Ciencias y Artes del Estado de Chiapas.

Rus, Jan. 1994 "The Comunidad Revolucionaria Institucional: The Subversion of Native Government in Highland Chiapas 1936–1968," in Gilbert Joseph and Daniel Nugent, eds., *Everyday Forms of State Formation: Revolution and the Negotiation of Rule in Modern Mexico*, pp. 265–300. Duke University Press.

————. 1995 "Local Adaptation to Global Change: The Reordering of Native Society in Highland Chiapas, Mexico, 1974–1994," *European Review of Latin American and Caribbean Studies* 58, June 1995:71–89.

Rus, Jan, and Robert Wasserstrom. 1980 "Civil-Religious Hierarchies in Central Chiapas: A Critical Perspective" *American Ethnology* 7:466–78.

Ruz, Mario Humberto. 1994 "Maya Resistance to Colonial Rule in Everyday Life," *Latin American Anthropology Review* 6(l):33–4.

————. 1981 *Los legítimos hombres: Aproximación antropologica al grupo Tojolaba*. México, D.F.: INI.

Safa, Helen Icken. 1981 "Runaway Shops and Female Employment: The Search for Cheap Labor." *Signs* 7, 2:418–433.

————. 1996 *The Myth of the Male Breadwinner*. Boulder, CO: Westview Press.

Sahlins, Marshall. 1998 "Two or Three Things That I Know about Culture," Huxley Lectures, UCLA, November 18.

Salomon, Nahmod, and Alvaro González. 1988 "Medio ambiente y technologías entre los Mayas de Quintana Roo," in Rodolfo Uribe Iniesta, ed., *Conferencia Medio Ambiente y Communidades Indígenas del Sureste: Practicas Tradicionales de Producción, Rituales, y Manejo de Reservas*.

Sangren, Steven. 1988 "Rhetoric and the Authority of Ethnography: 'Postmodernism' and the Social Reproduction of Texts," *Current Anthropology* 29(3):405–35.

Santana Echeagaray, Maria Eugenia. 1996 "Mujeres indígenas y derechos reproductivos: el caso de las mujeres de San Juan Chamula," *Anuario de Estudios Indigenas* 6:193–222. San Cristóbal de Las Casas: Universidad Autonoma de Chiapas, Instituto de Estudios Indígenas.

Santos, Eduardo. 1989 "Poverty in Ecuador." *CEPAL Review* 38:121–32. Santiago, Chile.

Sarmiento, Sergio. 1992 "La lucha de los pueblos indios en la decada de los ochenta," en Enrique de la Garza Toledo, coordinadora, *Crises y sujetos sociales en Mexico*, Vol. II:447–79. Toledo: Centro de Investigaciones Interdisciplinarias en Humanidades. México: Miguel Angel Porrua.

Sassen, Saskia. 1983 "Labor Migrations and the New International Division of Labor," in Nash and Fernandez-Kelly, eds. *Women, Men, and the International Division of Labor*, pp. 175–204. Albany: State University of New York Press.

————. 1996a *Losing Control: Sovereignty in an Age of Globalization*. New York: Columbia University Press.

————. 1996b "The Spatial Organization of Information Industries: Implications for the Role of the State," pp. 33–52 in James H. Mittleman, ed., *Globalization: Critical Reflections*. Boulder, CO: Westview.

————. 1998 *Globalization and Its Discontents*. New York: The New Press.

Schiller, Nina Glick, Linda Basch, and Christine Blanc-Szanton. 1992 "Toward a Transnational Perspective on Migration: Race, Class, Ethnicity, and Nationalism Reconsidered," *Annals of the New York Academy of Sciences*, Vol. 645. New York.

Schneider, Jane. 1977 "Was there a Pre-Capitalist World-System?" *Journal of Peasant Studies* 6:20–28.

Schneider, Jane, and Peter Schneider. 1976 *Culture and Political Economy in Western Sicily*. New York: Academic Press.

Scott, James. 1976 *The Moral Economy of a Backward Society*. New Haven: Yale University Press.

————. 1985 *Weapons of the Weak: Everyday Forms of Peasant Resistance*. New Haven: Yale University Press.

Selverston, Melina. 1992 "Politicized Ethnicity and the Nation-State in Ecuador," Paper presented to the Latin American Studies Association, September 24–27, Los Angeles.

Serron, Luis A. 1980. *Scarcity, Exploitation and Poverty: Malthus and Marx in Mexico*. Norman: University of Oklahoma Press.

Sinclair, Minor, ed. 1995 *The New Politics of Survival: Grassroots Movements in Central America*. New York: Monthly Review Press.

Singer, Marion Odilon. 1988 "La Dominación de la Naturaleza," in Rodolfo Uribe Iniesta, ed., *Conferencia medio ambiente y comunidades indígenas del sureste: Practicas tradicionales de producción, rituales, y manejo de reservas*. México, D.F.

SIPAZ Report. 1998 Members of Las Abejas, cited in Vol. 3, No. 2, April.

Sivert, Henning. 1973 *Oxchuc: Un pueblo indígena de los Altos*. Mexico City: Instituto Nacional Indígena.

Smith, Brian. 1987 "An Agenda of Future Tasks for International and Indigenous NGOs: Views from the North," *World Development* 15, Suppl:87–93.

Smith, Carol A. 1984 "Local History in Global Context: Social and Economic Transitions in Western Guatemala." *Comparative Studies in Society and History* 26, no. 2:193–229.

————. 1990 "The Militarization of Civil Society in Guatemala: Economic Reorganization as a Continuation of War," *Latin American Perspectives* 67, 4:8–41.

Soros, George. 1998 *The Crisis of Global Capitalism: Open Society Endangered*. New York: BBS Public Affairs.

Starn, Orin. 1992 "'I Dreamed of Foxes and Hawks': Reflections on Peasant Protest, New Social Movements, and the Rondas Campesinas of Northern Peru," in A. Escobar and S. Alvarez, eds. *The Making of Social Movements in Latin America: Identity, Strategy, and Democracy*, pp. 89–111. Berkeley, University of California Press.

Stavenhagen, Rudolpho. 1965 "Classes, Colonialism, and Acculturation," *Studies in Comparative International Development* 1, no. 6:53–77.

————. 1978 "Capitalism and Peasantry in Mexico," *Latin American Perspectives* 3(3):27–37.

————. 1996 *Ethnic Conflicts and the Nation State*. New York: St. Marks Press 1996.

Stephen, Lynn. 1991 *Zapotec Women*. Austin: University of Texas Press.

————. 1994 "Viva Zapata!: Generation, Gender, and Historical Consciousness in the Reception of Ejido Reform in Oaxaca." *Transformation of Rural Mexico*, no. 6, Ejido Reform Research Project. San Diego: Center for US.-Mexican Studies.

————. 1997a *Women and Social Movements in Latin America: Power from Below*. Austin University of Texas Press.

————. 1997b "Redefined Nationalism in Building a Movement for Indigenous Autonomy in Southern Mexico," *Journal of Latin American Anthropology* 3, 1:72–101.

Stern, Steve J. 1995 *The Secret History of Gender: Women, Men and Power in Late Colonial Mexico*. Chapel Hill: University of North Carolina.

Steward, Julian. 1951 "Levels of Sociocultural Integration: An Operational Concept." *American Anthropologist*, Vol. 53.

Stoudemire, Sterling A. trans. and ed. 1970 *Pedro de Cordoba, Christian Doctrine for the Instruction of the Indians*. Coral Gables: University of Miami Press.

Sullivan, Kathleen. 1992 "Protagonists of Change," *Cultural Survival* 16, 4:38.

————. 1995 "Reestructuración rural-urbana entre los indigenas chamula en los Altos de Chiapas, Mexico," in J. Nash, ed. *La explosión de comunidades en Chiapas*, 69–96. Copenhagen: IWGIA.

————. 1998 "Religious Change and the Recreation of Community in an Urban Setting among the Tzotzil Maya of Highland Chiapas, Mexico." Ph.D. dissertation submitted to the Graduate Faculty in Anthropology, City University of New York.

Susser, Ida. 1997 "Introduction, Critiquing the New World Order." *Critique of Anthropology* 17(4):349–62.

Tanksi, Janet M. and Christine E. Eber. n.d. Confronting Globalization in Mexico."

Tarn, Nathaniel, ed. 1991 *Views from the Weaving Mountain: Selected Essays in Poetics and Anthropology*. Albuquerque: An American Poetry Book/University of New Mexico Press.

————. 1997 (with Martin Prechtel) *Scandals in the House of Birds: Shamans and Priests on Lake Atitlán*. New York: Marsillo.

Tax, Sol. 1937 "The Municipios of the Midwestern Highlands of Guatemala," *American Anthropologist* 39, no. 3:423–44.

————. 1941 "World View and Social Relations in Guatemala," *American Anthropologist* 43:27–43.

————. 1952 "Penny Capitalism," Smithsonian Institution: Institute of Social Anthropology.

Tedlock, Barbara. 1982 *Time and the Highland Maya*. Albuquerque: University of New Mexico Press.

Tedlock, Dennis. 1984 *Popol Vuh: The Mayan Book of the Dawn of Life*. New York: Simon and Schuster.

————. 1993 *Breath on the Mirror: Mythic Voices and Visions of the Living Maya*. San Francisco: Harper.

Tejada Gaona, Hector. 1995 "La comunidad indígena en México: La utopía irrealizada," in Raquel Barceló, Mario Ana Portal, Martha Judith Sanchez, coord. *Diversidad etnica y conflicto en América Latina: El indio como metáforo en la identidad nacional*, Vol. II. Mexico D.F.: Plaza y Valdés Editorial.

Tickell, Oliver. 1991 "Indigenous Expulsions in the Highlands of Chiapas." Copenhagen: *International Work Group on Indigenous Affairs Newsletter* 2:9–14.

Touraine, Alaine. 1971 *The Post-Industrial Society: Tomorrow's Social History: Classes, Conflicts and Culture in the Programmed Society*. New York: Random House.

————. 1988 *Return of the Actor*. Minneapolis: University of Minnesota Press.

Tristan, Flora. 1983 *Workers' Union*. Translation of *L'Union ouvrier*, published in Paris 1837. Carbondale: University of Illinois Press.

Turok, Marta. 1988 *Como acercarse a la artesanía?* Mexico, D.F.: Plaza y Valdez.

Turpel, Mary Ellen. 1998 "The Women of Many Nations in Canada," in *Indigenous Women on the Move.*, 93–104.Copenhagen: IWGIA Document No. 66.

Tylor, E. B. 1889 "On a Method of Investigating the Development of Institution: Applied to Laws of Marriage and Descent," *Journal of the Royal Anthropological Institute of Great Britain and Ireland* 18:245–73.

United Nations Development Program. 1991 *Measuring Human Development and Freedom.* Human Development Report. New York: Oxford University Press.

———. 1994 and 1996 Statistical Yearbook.

Viqueira, Juan Pedro. 2000 "Presentación," in *Los indígenas y las elecciones en Los Altos de Chiapas.* San Cristóbal de Las Casas: Ciesas and IFE.

Vilakazi;, H.W. 1972 "Social Science as Anthropology." Paper presented at the Ninth International Congress of Anthropological Sciences, Chicago.

Villa Rojas, Alfonso. 1946 *Etnología de Oxchuc.* University of Chicago, Microfilm Studies in Middle American Ethnology.

———. 1990 *Etnografía Tzeltal de Chiapas: Modalidades de una cosmovisión prehispanica.* Tuxtla: Gobierno del Estado para el Fomento a la Investigación y Difusión de la Cultura.

Villafuerte Solis, Daniel, Salvador Meza Díaz, Gabriel Ascencio Franco, Maria del Carmen García Aguilar Carolina Rivera Farfán, Miguel Lisbona Guillén, Jesús Morales Ramirez. 1999 *La tierra en Chiapas, viejas problemas, nuevos.* México, D.F.: Universidad de Ciencias y Artes de Chiapas.

Vincent, Joan. 1991 "Framing the Underclass," *Critical Anthropology* 13; 3:215–231.

Vinding, Diana. 1998 "Tribal Women in Uttar Pradesh," in Diana Vinding, ed., *Indigenous Women: The Right to a Voice.* Copenhagen: IWGIA Document No. 88.

Viqueira, Juan Pedro. 1999 "Presentación," pp. 3–5 in *Los indígenas y las elecciones en Los Altos de Chiapas,* E.H.J. Arellano, coordinador. San Cristóbal de Las Casas: Instituto Electoral Federal del Estado de Chiapas and CIESAS-Sureste.

Vogt, Evon Z. 1969 *Zinacantan: A Maya Community in the Highlands of Chiapas.* Cambridge: Harvard University Press.

———. 1976a "Some Aspects of the Sacred Geography of Highland Chiapas," in Elizabeth P. Benson, ed., *Meso-American Sites and World View,* 229–42. Washington, D.C.: Dumbarton Oaks.

———. 1976b *Tortillas for the Gods: A Symbolic Analysis of Zinacanteco Rituals.* Cambridge, MA: Harvard University Press.

———. 1994 *Fieldwork Among the Maya: Reflections on the Harvard Chiapas Project.* Albuquerque: University of New Mexico Press.

Vos, Jan de. 1991 Lecture: "The Struggle for Land in Chiapas," National Science Foundation, Research Experience for Undergraduates.

Wachtel, Howard M. 1986 *The Money Mandarins: The Making of a New Supranational Economic Order.* New York: Pantheon Books.

Walker, Anthony R. ed. 1985 "Studies of Resource Utilization." *Contributions to Southeast Asian Ethnography,* 4.

Wallerstein, Emmanuel. 1974 *The Modern World System: Capitalist Agriculture and the Origins of the European World Economy in the Fifteenth Century.* New York: Academic Press.

———. 1983 "Crisis: The World-Economy, the Movements, and the Ideologies," in *Crisis in the World System.* Albert Bergesen, ed. Beverly Hills: Sage Publication.

Warman, Arturo, Bonfil Batalla, and Nolasco Armas, coordinadores. 1970 *De eso lo que se llaman antropología mexicana .* México D.F.: Editorial Nuestro Tiempo.

———. 1980 *Ensayos sobre el Campesinado en México.* México, D.F.: Editorial Nueva Imagen.

———. 1988 "The Political Project of Zapatismo," in Friedrich Katz, ed., *Riot, Rebellion and Revolution: Rural Social Conflict in Mexico.* Princeton: Princeton University Press.

———. 1990 *Venimos para Contradecir.* México D.F.

Warman, Arturo, and Arturo Argiel. 1980 "Presentación," *Movimientos indígenas contemporaneos en Mexico.* México: Centro de Investigaciones en Humanidades, UNAM: Miguel Angel Poruta.

Warren, Kay B. 1985 "Creation Narratives and the Moral Order: Implications of Multiple Models in Highland Guatemala," pp. 251–278 in Robin W. Lovin and Frank E. Reynolds, eds. *Cosmogony and Ethical Order: New Studies in Comparative Ethics.* Chicago: University of Chicago Press.

———. 1989 *The Symbolism of Subordination: Indian Identity in a Guatemalan Town.* Austin: University of Texas Press (originally published 1978).

———. 1992 "Transforming Memories and Histories: Meanings of Ethnic Resurgence for Maya Indians," in Alfred Stepan, ed. *Americans: New Interpretive Essays,* 189–219. Oxford: Oxford University Press.

———. 1993 "Interpreting La Violencia in Guatemala: Shapes of Mayan Silence and Resistance," in Kay B. Warren, ed. *The Violence Within: Cultural and Political Opposition in Divided Nations,* pp. 25–86. Boulder: Westview.

————. 1998 *Indigenous Movements and Their Critics: Pan-Maya Activism in Guatemala*. Princeton: Princeton University Press.

Wasserstrom, Robert. 1983a *Class and Society in Central Chiapas*. Berkeley: University of California Press.

————. 1983b "Spaniards and Indians in Colonial Chiapas, 1528–1790," in Murdo J. Macleod and Robert Wasserstrom, *Spaniards and Indians in Southeast Mesoamerica: Essays on the History of Ethnic Relations*, pp. 92–125. Lincoln: University of Nebraska.

Watanabe, John M. 1990 "From Saints to Shibboleths: Image, Structure, and Identity in Maya Religious Syncretism," *American Ethnologist*, Vol. 17(l):131–150.

————. 1992 *Maya Saints and Souls in a Changing World*. Austin: University of Texas Press.

Willis, W. S., Jr. 1972 "Skeletons in the Anthropological Closets," in Del Hymnes ed., *Reinventing Anthropology*. New York: Pantheon.

Wolf, Eric. 1957 "Closed Corporate Peasant Communities in Mesoamerica and Central Java," *Southwestern Journal of Anthropology* 13 (Spring):1–18.

————. 1982 *Europe and the People without History*. Berkeley: University of California Press.

————. 1987 "The Peasant War in Germany: Friedrich Engels as Social Historian." *Science and Society*, 51(Spring).

Wolf, Margery. 1992 *A Thrice-Told Tale: Feminism and the Ethnographic Responsibility*. Stanford University Press. World Bank

Womack, John Jr. 1999 *Rebellion in Chiapas: An Historical Reader*. New York: The New Press.

World Bank. 1987, 1988, 1989, 1990, 1991, 1994 Annual Report.

————. 1990a *Indonesia: Strategy for a Sustained Reduction in Poverty*. Washington, D.C.: World Bank.

————. 1990b *Social Programs for the Alleviation of Poverty*. Washington, D.C.: World Bank.

Zengotite, Thomas de. 1989 "Speakers of Being: Romantic Refusion and Cultural Anthropology." In George Stocking, ed., *Romantic Motives: Essays on Anthropological Sensibility*. History of Anthropology 67. Madison: University of Wisconsin Press.

Zucher, H. G. 1977 "More Solutions to Galton's Problem," *Current Anthropology* 13:117–9.

NEWSPAPER ARTICLES AND PERIODICALS

Bangkok Post
   1999 November 8, p. 8 "A New Theory."
Cuarto Poder Tuxtla Gutiérrez, Chiapas
   December 28, 1994 James Brooke, "La decada perdida," *New York Times* exclusive for *Cuarto Poder*, Tuxtla Gutiérrez, Section C, p. 24.
   June 29, 1996, Rodolfo Sol, "Marcha en Chilón realizaran indígenas," p. 1.
   April 2, 1998, p. 8.
   March 16, 2000, p. 21.
   March 24, 2000 "Diputados de oposición reprueban desalojos," p. 10.
   March 24, 2000, Carlos Herrera, "Embajador britanico visita Zinacantán," p. 15.
   March 24, 2000 Juan Carlos Pérez, "Inician plantón en alcaldía de Altamirano," p. 15, and "Prevén mobilizationes en Ocosingo," p. 15.
   March 24, 2000, "Diputados de oposición repruebandesalojos," p. 10.
   March 24, 2000, Javier Sevilla, "Propinan policías golpiza a mujer desalojada en Ixtapa," p. 23.
   March 29, 2000, Rodolf Sol, "Crece hostigamiento contra cioacistas de Ixtapa," p. 18.
   April 1, 2000 Mesa de Redacción, "Atestigua Albores retorno de desplazados a Chenalho," p. 17.
   April 3, 2000 Rodolfo Sol, "Ariqueros, en asamblea permanente," p. 6.
   April 4, 2000 Universal, "División entre organizaciones campesinas," p. 48.
   April 5, 2000 Rodolfo Sol, "Rechaza comité estatal divisionismo en CIOAC," p. 13.
   April 5, 2000 Rudolfo Sol, "Reubicación del 50%: ARIC-ID," p. 9.
   April 6, 2000 Abel Bravo, "Edil de Ixtapa interpone queja ante Derechos Humanos," p. 10.
   August 4, 2000, Carlos Herrera, "No mas masacres esperan Las Abejas," p. 11.
   August 11, 2000, Carlos Herrera, "'La Abejas' exigen el retiro de paramiliatres," p. 23.
The Economist
   February 13, 1993 Christopher Wood, "Mexico's Respect Restored" 326 (7798), pp. 6–12.
Expreso, Tuxtla Gutiérrez, Chiapas
   December 31, 1994, p. 7.
   February 2, 1995 Gaspar Morquecho, "Municipios rebeldes, regiones autóbinas y parlamentos indígenas," p. 7.
   February 3, 1995 Gaspar Morquecho, "Municipios rebeldes, regiones autónomas y parlamentos indígenas," p. 7.
   February 10, 1995, p. 8.

February 20, 1995, "Despliegue militar provocó comoción en Chiapas," February 10:1, 10.

April 7, 1995 Fredy Martin, "Se suman a la solicitud de desaparicion de poderes en Las Margaritas," p. l.

May 7, 1995 Gaspar Morquecho, "60 Indias en la Convención Estatal de Mujeres," p. l.

June 21, 1996. "Inda."

El Financiero

December 30, 1994, reprint of interview with Josephine Jimenez, analyst of Montgomery Assets, published in *La Jornada*, Vol 11, no. 3703, pp. 128.

February 26, 1995, p. 57.

February 28, 1995.

March 15, 1995, Lourdes Edith Rudiño, "Perjudicará a los trabajadores del campo la liberación de precios," p. 25.

March 17, 1995.

April 2, 1995, Elvia Gutiérrez Financier, "Tres sexenios de programas de subdesarrollo," pp. 5–6.

April 13, 1995, Gustavo Sauri, "Salieron del pais 45 mil 832 mdd entre 1989 y 1994," p. 3A.

La Jornada Mexico City

April 11, 1991.

October 19, 1991.

November 3, 1991

November 21, 1991 Gustavo Gordilla.

November 23, 1991, "La iniciativa dereformas podria abrir siete vias al latifundismo."

December 3, 1991.

December 19, 1991, "Anuncian plan de insurgencia contra reformas al articulo 27."

January 6, 1992.

September 26, 1992, "Warman: en estudio, cambios a la LFT para protejer a los jornaleros."

February 27, 1994.

December 26, 1994 Afp, Xinhjua y Ansa, "La crisis de Mexico, fracaso de las políticas de organismos mundiales."

December 30, 1994 Interview in *New York Times*, reprinted.

February 12, 1995.

March 13, 1995.

March 31, 1995, "Aumentará la inestabilidad en México: Ifigenia Martínez."

April 22, 1995 M. Zuniga, Juan Antonio, and José Gil Olmos, 1995, "En San Andrés, tensión antes de retirarse 7 mil indígenas," p. 14.

April 24, 1995, pp. 1–2.

April 26, 1995, p. 12.

September 11, 1995 José Gil Olmos, Elio Henriquez, "La consulta nacional abrió los ojos del gobierno: Zapatistas," p. 5.

June 24, 1996.

July 6, 1996 Hermann Bellinghausen, "El foro, mezcla de obreros, campesinos e intelectuales," p. 11.

August 10, 1996, p. 11.

December 28, 1997, pp. 6, 8.

March 22, 1998 Emilio Krieger, "Maiosare," p. 12.

April 1, 1998 Kyra Nuñez, "Analizara la ONU designar un relator para Chiapas," p. 3.

April 2, 1998, "Nuevo llamada de la Cocopa al EZLN para una reunión," p. 15.

April 2, 1998, "Fin a la descalificación de la Conai: PAN, PRD, y PT."

April 3, 1998 Angeles Mariscal, "Detenidos, un general y un soldado raso por la massacre de Acteal," p. 3.

April 3, 1998 Carlos San Juan Victoria, "El Congreso ante la Ley Indígena," pp. 4–5.

April 4, 1998 Topiltzin Ochoa Rudolfo Villalba and Alma E Muñoz, "Pide Mullor dejar el diálogo político-ideológico en Chiapas," pp. 3, 5.

April 4, 1998 San Juan Victoria, Carlos, "El Congreso Ante La Ley Indígena," pp. 3–5 *La Jornada del Campo*.

April 5, 1998, pp. 5, 6.

April 6, 1998 Juan Balboa, "Cerrados, destruidos o profanados, 36 templos de la diocesis de San Cristobal," p. 6.

April 9, 1998, pp 1–3, 7.

April 10, 1998, "Inaugurara hoy el EZLN el municipio autónomo Flores Magon," p. 7.

April 11, 1998, p. 3.

April 13, 1998 María García, "Anuncia el CNI la creación de 20 municipios autónomos," p. 3.

April 3, 1999.

March 20, 1999 Fausto Martínez, "Encuentro Banquetero, de los indígenas con la sociedad civil," p. 6.

March 21, 1999, p. 14.

March 28, 1999 Xóchitl Leyva, Mercedes Olivera, and Aracely Burguete, Los Pasos Atras en la Ley Albores, "Masiosare."

April 3, 1999, p. 19.

March 16, 2000, Juan Sanchez, "Persiste amenaza de desalojo en limites con Montes Azules," p. 21.

March 12, 2000.

March 19, 2000 Miriam Posada Garcia, "Pemex reducido a ser apéndice de trasnacionales," p. 21, quoting from Angel de la Vega, "La evolución del componente petrolero en el desarrollo y la transicion en Mexico."

March 30, 2000 Elio Henríquez, "Legisladores europeos cuestionan a Albores."

Motivos

February 1999, no. 8, "Propuesta para la Creación de Reglamientos Autónomos Plurietnicos."

The New York Review of Books

July 14, 1994 Felix Rohatyn,"World Capital:The Need and the Risk," Vol. 41, (13):48–53.

The New York Times

January 18, 1994 Tim Golden, "Mexican Rebels Give Statement to Government," p. A10.

September 11, 1995. Reuters, "Chiapas Talks Going Well, Both Sides Say."

August 17, 1995, "Mexican Recession Worse; Output Off 10% in Quarter" Reuters.

February 15, 1996, Preston, Julia, "Mexico and Insurgent Group Reach Pact on Indian Rights," A12.

May 16, 1996 "Postmodern Gravity Deconstructed Slyly," pp. A1, 21.

November 3, 1997 p. A23, op ed. commentary by Jeffrey Sachs.

February 27, 1998 Julia Preston International Section.

March 6, 1998 Julia Preston, "Mexico's Overtures to the Zapatisas Bring Tensions in Chiapas to a New Boiling Point," p. A8.

October 5, 1998, Julia Preston, "Boycott Confuses Elections in Mexican State," p. A10.

October 2, 1998, pp. 1, 10.

October 16, 1998 Pope John Paul II Encyclical, pp. A1 and 10.

February 21, 1999 Serge Schmemann, "What's Wrong with this Picture of Nationalism," Section 4, pp. 1 and 4.

May 7, 1999.

May 24, 1999.

May 1999.

May 19, 2000 Julia Preston, p. A8.

May 21, 2000, David Gonzalez, "Guatemalan Squatters Torching Park Forests," A5.

Proceso

January 29, 1977 Rodolfo Guzman, "Chiapas 76: Soldados en Vehiculos de UNICEF al asalto de pueblos indígenas."

Feb. 20, 1995, No. 955, pp. 13–15.

May 15, 1995, Julio Cesar López and Guillermo Correa, "Podemos ceder en todo, menos en nuestra dignidad, planteo el EZLN," No. 967, pp. 15 *et seq.* 32–3.

August 17, 1995, "Mexican Recession Worse; Output Off 10% in Quarter" *New York Times* (Reuters).

September 11, 1995, No. 984, pp. 23–4.

June 1996 Elio Henríquez "Exigen freno a la violencia miles de campesinos del norte de Chiapas," June, 1996, No. 4234.

December 28, 1997 Guillermo Correo, "1,500 indigenas asesinados durante el gobierno de Ruiz Ferro; siete grupos paramilitares actuan como escuadrones de la muerte," No. 1104, pp. 6–17.

April 5, 1998, Julio Ceasar Lopez and Rodrigo Vera, "Expulsiones, crimenes, destrucción y apostasias, en la guerra santa 'satizada por el gobierno federal' en Chiapas," No. 1127, pp. 6–111.

June 14, 1998 Salvador Corro, "El Diálogo en Chiapas, liquido por una estrategía de Estado donde se puso la lógica militar contra la política," No. 1128.

June 14, 1998, Javier Saciliga, "Gobierno acorralado," No. 1128, pp. 22–30.

March 14, 1999, pp. 32–33, No. 1176.

El Tiempo San Cristóbal de Las Casas, Chiapas

May 4, 1993 Daniel Lievano, "Llegaran hasta México las 'Arrieras Nocturnas?'" No. 1937.

November 2, 1995, p. 21.

U.S. News and World Report

January 24, 1994 Steven D. Kaye, "Stock Shocks in Asia and Mexico," Vol. 116, No. 3, p. 72.

The Wall Street Journal

March 8, 1995, Judy Shelton, "End the Currency Poker Game," p. A20, col 4.

The Washington Post

February 15, 1996 Molly Moore, "Mexican Rebel Supporters Accept Rights Accord," p. A17.

INDEX